MW00762745

DEFENDING WHOSE COUNTRY?

NOAH RISEMAN

DEFENDING WHOSE COUNTRY?

Indigenous Soldiers
in the Pacific War

University of Nebraska Press   Lincoln & London

Library of Congress Cataloging-in-Publication Data

Riseman, Noah J.
Defending whose country?: indigenous soldiers in the Pacific war / Noah Riseman.
    p. cm.
Includes bibliographical references and index.
ISBN 978-0-8032-3793-3 (cloth: alk. paper)
1. World War, 1939–1945—Cryptography.
2. World War, 1939–1945—Participation, Indian.
3. World War, 1939–1945—Participation, Aboriginal Australian. 4. World War, 1939–1945—Personal narratives, Australian. 5. Australia—Armed Forces—Aboriginal Australians. 6. United States—Armed Forces—Indians. 7. Navajo code talkers.
8. Yolngu (Australian people)—Warfare. I. Title.
D810.C88R57 2012
940.54'04—dc23
2012015594

Set in Adobe Garamond.

CONTENTS

ILLUSTRATIONS

Maps

Photographs

Following page 66

Following page 134

PREFACE

It was by accident that I first encountered the Northern Territory Special Reconnaissance Unit (NTSRU). There in the library lay the abridged narrative of the force, tucked away in a tiny book next to a thick book about Aboriginal people in the Second World War. From that tiny book my investigation grew — first informally and then formally. The more I read, the more the same question kept emerging — why?

Why did Yolngu agree to fight for Australia? Why did white Australia seek Aboriginal help? Why did Donald Thomson propose the formation of the detachment? Why do most Australians know next to nothing about Aboriginal defense forces?

With these questions came more questions. Then came the need to provide a context: Aboriginal policy, Arnhem Land, the Second World War, settlement, colonial relations, assimilation, colonialism abroad. Then the project grew into a comparative study, asking similar questions of Papua New Guineans and the Navajo Code Talkers. But in the search for a context I sometimes lost sight of the fact that, at the time, indigenous understandings of the context were limited. What did a group of Aboriginal people in Arnhem Land or Papua New Guineans know about changes to policies and creeds that came from Canberra? And what did they care about structures of colonialism and international patterns? What concerned the Yolngu, the Papua New Guineans, and the Navajos was the protection of their country, their family, and their culture. They were human beings who made choices to support the Allies against Japan.

But again the question reemerged — why? I can speculate and argue and corroborate my discussion with evidence. I can contextualize and draw connections globally about colonial exploits. I can garner other examples of indigenous people fighting to defend colonial powers. But in the end no context or transnational links will account for the mindset of the participants. The Second World War derives from indigenous stories and forms part of indigenous histories as much as global history, and no research can lose sight of that truth.

Numerous people contributed to this book, derived from my PhD thesis. About two and a half years into my PhD a friend in the computer lab noticed that I had a file on my USB drive entitled "acknowledgments." She was shocked that I had already written my acknowledgments. I told her I had not actually written them. Rather, anytime someone helped me, I added her or his name to a running list to ensure that I did not accidentally forget. Needless to say, the list is quite extensive for work that commenced in 2004.

First and foremost I must thank my principal PhD supervisor, Professor Patricia Grimshaw. Pat's mentorship has been phenomenal, both in attending to career development and in steering me to completion of my PhD and this book. Her friendship, support, advice, and guidance went above and beyond what I ever expected from a supervisor. I thank Pat unequivocally for everything she has done for me.

I must also thank my associate supervisor, Dr. Richard Trembath. Richard has been there whenever I needed him, and he has also offered his friendship and attended to career development throughout his time as supervisor, for which I am incredibly grateful. I also want to express gratitude to Dr. Tracey Banivanua-Mar for her guidance in the initial stages of my research. Her advice sent me in directions I would never have considered, and her intellectual prowess continues to amaze me. Finally, I must thank my honors supervisor Professor Patty O'Brien of the Center for Australian and New Zealand Studies at Georgetown University. Patty piqued my interest in Australian history, so were it not for her I would never have gone on to do a PhD.

Two organizations provided financial assistance in the form of grants that assisted in the research for this book: the Australian Institute for Aboriginal and Torres Strait Islander Studies (AIATSIS) and the Northern Territory History Grant. At the Northern Territory Archives Service Francoise Barr provided immense support, suggesting records, arranging access, and providing general guidance about Darwin. AIATSIS funding contributed to research trips to Mata Mata outstation in Arnhem Land and one research trip to Canberra. I graciously acknowledge the immense support and friendship of the entire Mata Mata community. They took me in and welcomed me into their family. In particular thank you to Phyllis Batumbil, Doris Mambi, David Balawar, and Old Charlie. I also want to thank Will Stubbs of the Buku-Larrŋgay Mulka Centre for putting me in contact with Batumbil. Professor Marcia Langton also provided assistance as I prepared for my trips to Arnhem Land by explaining some protocols.

On my research trip to the United States Eunice Khan of the Navajo Nation Museum provided access and assistance with Navajo Code Talker records. I also thank her for her assistance in producing photos of the Navajo Code Talkers for this book. Funding for research at the Navajo Nation came from the assistance of the School of Historical Studies and the Faculty of Arts at the University of Melbourne.

Thank you to other colleagues who have provided support through the PhD and beyond: Amanda Barry, Catherine Bell, Roland Burke, Margot Hillel, Barbara Keys, Nell Musgrove, Shurlee Swain, and Naomi Wolfe. For their helpful comments on the first draft of the manuscript I am indebted to Professor Tom Holm and Professor Bruce Scates. Other friends of mine also deserve mention: for keeping photocopies of my notes as backup, Anna Madden, Matthew Swan, and Mikala Tai; for tolerating me as a housemate, my good friends Sarah Cooke and Magda Kvasnicka.

Acknowledgment is also made to those who assisted me in accessing research materials: Heather Gaunt and Rosemary Wrench of the Melbourne Museum for providing access to the Donald Thomson Collection; Natasha Lawrence of the Australian Broadcasting Corporation for providing me with a copy of *The Forgotten*; Henry Harper and Nick Brenner for providing me with the Northern Land Council DVD of Gordon Ritchie's visit to Milingimbi; and the nice librarian at the Northern Territory Library who secretly gave me a floppy disk when it was against the rules because the computers could not read my USB drive (and this was in 2005!). Thank you to Elisabeth Chretien and Matthew Bokovoy at the University of Nebraska Press for their editorial assistance and support in the production of this book.

The final people to thank are my family for supporting my decision (grudgingly at times) to move to Australia to pursue this research. I promised to refer to them individually: Mom and Marty, Dad and Ellen, and Deanna and Ari. Thank you also to my surrogate families in Australia who at different times provided the support only a family can: the Kvasnickas in Adelaide and the Smiths in Melbourne. And finally, thank you to my partner, Michael. You mean everything to me. I don't know where I'd be without you.

As a caution to indigenous readers: this book contains images of persons who are deceased. To be ethical in my selection of photographs, I have only included pictures of indigenous people in the following circumstances: when the subjects clearly knew they were being photographed or when the faces of the indigenous persons are obscured by the angle of the camera. I include photographs not to objectify persons but to present a better visual image of the historical content to the reader. Thank you to the Navajo Nation Museum, the Australian War Memorial, the National Archives and Records Administration in the United States, and the Thomson family and the Melbourne Museum for permission to reproduce the images.

A quick point about terminology: in this book I refer to the various Indigenous groups of present-day Papua New Guinea as Papuans and New Guineans before and during the Second World War because Papua and New Guinea were two separate colonies. References to the same peoples in the postwar era are to the contemporary terminology of Papua New Guineans. Finally, I capitalize *Indigenous* and *Native* when referring to a particular group's or nation's traditional owners; I use the lowercase *indigenous* and *native* when speaking generally about global First Nations.

ABBREVIATIONS

AIATSIS	Australian Institute for Aboriginal and Torres Strait Islander Studies
ANGAU	Australian New Guinea Administrative Unit
AWM	Australian War Memorial
BIA	Bureau of Indian Affairs
DORCA	Directorate of Research and Civil Affairs
NAA	National Archives of Australia
NAOU	North Australia Observer Unit
NARA	National Archives and Records Administration (United States)
NGIB	New Guinea Infantry Battalion
NGVR	New Guinea Volunteer Rifles
NORFORCE	North-West Mobile Force
NTAS	Northern Territory Archives Service
NTSRU	Northern Territory Special Reconnaissance Unit
PIB	Papuan Infantry Battalion
PIR	Pacific Islands Regiment
RAAF	Royal Australian Air Force
RPC	Royal Papuan Constabulary
RSL	Returned and Services League of Australia
TSLIB	Torres Strait Light Infantry Battalion

INTRODUCTION

Reading Colonialism and Indigenous Involvement in the Second World War

December 1941. Australian defense forces were engaged in the Middle East and North Africa as Germany and Italy continued their war in Europe, and Adolf Hitler's army advanced in the Soviet Union. Japan, still engaged in a bloody war with China, was organizing an assault on American and European allies at Pearl Harbor, the Pacific Islands, and Southeast Asia. The United States, whose neutrality in Europe was slowly waning, was still negotiating with Japan to arrive at a peaceful solution to the conflict in East Asia. Australian officials, recognizing the growing danger of Japan, built up defenses around the Northern Territory city of Darwin in case Japan declared war on Great Britain and, consequently, Australia. In the Australian colonies of Papua and New Guinea the navy accelerated the establishment of a network of coastwatching stations among local residents. Australia was at war, and very soon that conflict would hit home as Japan's plans for conquest in the Pacific came to fruition in December 1941.

Meanwhile, in Arnhem Land, east of Darwin, Yolngu continued life on their traditional lands, unaware of the imminent threat of invasion from thousands of miles away. Unlike white Australians, Yolngu had not only already witnessed foreign invasion but had coped with multiple incursions in their land. White intruders had reached Yolngu shores from Europe over 130 years earlier, but only in the last 50 years had white Australians entered the region in significant numbers. Many Japanese had arrived over the course of the last 20 years, when trepangers accelerated fishing off the coast. Even though Yolngu had resided for millennia before the new arrivals, Balanda (or white people's) law forbade the killing of foreigners, even if they violated Yolngu law. The area had been in a process of transformation since the Europeans' arrival, but life for the majority of Yolngu was neither dependent upon nor adhered to Balanda and their system. However, Balanda had already significantly affected Yolngu society. For instance, missionaries had held a permanent presence since 1908, the pastoral industry had emerged along the Roper River, and fishermen and trepangers employed Aboriginal labor as guides and divers. Other intruders initiated violent raids that resulted in brutal deaths of Yolngu people. The majority of Yolngu still lived in isolated country without the relative pressures of Balanda technology and law. Thus, despite centuries of change, daily life for Yolngu in the Balanda year of 1941 was not very different from that of 1939 or any other milestone leading up to the Balanda Second World War.

Papuans and New Guineans had also witnessed the arrival of white "mastas" almost sixty years prior. At first their numbers were small, but they slowly infiltrated the island of New Guinea and encountered its peoples. Some came to teach them about the gospel, but many others came to put the Papuans and New Guineans to work for them in unfair conditions on plantations and in mines. They introduced new ideas of "chiefs" and "laws" that benefited a few villagers while disadvantaging many others. The new chiefs and overseers told the Papuans and New Guineans that they must pay the mastas with their labor, whether on coconut plantations or in mines. Other Papuans and New Guineans eagerly volunteered their services as carriers on long journeys to the highlands, seeking to travel with the new arrivals. The mastas claimed they were helping the Papuans and New Guineans, but many only experienced physical abuse and degradation at the hands of the invaders and their local allies. In the span of sixty years much had changed. Clan had been turned against clan, and many locals had unwittingly become servants to a small number of white mastas. A return to the previous system may not have been possible, but certainly an alternative to the current mastas might not be such a bad thing.

The Navajos in the Southwest United States had withstood centuries of violence—at the hands of first the Spanish and then the United

States. In the 1850s and 1860s they fought and lost a series of wars against the American colonizers. They endured forced relocation, starvation, and crammed conditions before finally being granted limited dominion over their own land, which became known as the Navajo Reservation. The U.S. government rarely fulfilled the obligations laid down in its treaty, though. Whites came to Navajo land and encouraged Navajos to send their children away to boarding schools in the East. As the Great Depression struck, the supposedly enlightened leadership in the Department of the Interior forced Navajos to reduce their livestock—a staple of Navajo culture and economy. Health and living conditions on the reservation were bleak; opportunities for advancement off the reservation were limited by discrimination and inadequate understanding of the white ways. When the United States went to war, Navajos' status was precarious; the frontier wars and forced relocation may have ended, but life for most Navajos was not easy.

The above paragraphs depict the gaps between the historical contexts of the Second World War for settler governments and for their indigenous residents. Whereas one population was on full alert and bracing for potential Japanese attack, others had already felt the impact of several invasions and tried to maintain a sense of normality in their changing worlds. Despite the vast differences between whites and indigenous peoples, by 1942 various indigenous residents would be working with colonizers' militaries as servicemen and auxiliaries in the Pacific War. To the various participants the undertaking had different personal meanings, objectives, and interpretations. This book analyzes an assortment of accounts of Yolngu, Papua New Guinean, and Navajo participation in the Second World War. It frames their roles in the contexts of settler-indigenous relations and the common pasts of the then—and still—divided nations. The primary case studies are Yolngu units and "de facto" auxiliaries in Arnhem Land, Australia; laborers, police, coastwatchers, and the Pacific Islands Regiment in Papua and New Guinea; and Navajo Code Talkers in the U.S. Marine Corps. These three case studies are valuable both individually and collectively because they reveal remarkable stories from the war and also because they demonstrate ways in which colonial governments continued to exploit indigenous knowledge and labor during the war. Certainly these three case studies are not the only examples of indigenous participation in the Pacific War, but they have been selected because they represent examples of both *informal* employment of indigenous labor and *formal* indigenous units serving in the military.[1]

This book takes the parallel-dimensions approach to comparative history, meaning that it highlights "similarity among the cases — similarity, that is, in terms of the common applicability of the overall theoretical arguments."[2] The parallel-dimensions approach uses the differences in historical contexts to demonstrate the diverse manners in which common trends manifested. Indeed, the fact that Yolngu, Papua New Guineans, and Navajos all experienced different degrees of colonial contact and lived under varying conditions, but still confronted exploitative practices and policies in the Second World War, heightens the pertinence of the arguments set out in this book.

Although basic information about indigenous participation in the Pacific War effort is available in Australia, Papua New Guinea, and the United States, most Australians and Americans know only selected information about the existence of Aboriginal, Papua New Guinean, or Native American defenders during the Second World War. For those who do know about indigenous war histories, the general interpretation is that indigenous participation signifies an encouraging example of indigenous and non-indigenous people working together to protect their homelands. Consistent with this reading is the idea that forces such as the Northern Territory Special Reconnaissance Unit (NTSRU), the Royal Papuan Constabulary (RPC), the Pacific Islands Regiment (PIR), the Navajo Code Talkers, and the North Australia Observer Unit (NAOU) represented positive contrasts to the prejudiced government policies leading up to the Second World War. During an era when authorities overseeing indigenous affairs blatantly discriminated against native peoples, the Australian and American militaries looked to indigenous servicemen as a critical defense against Japanese invasion. Subsequent to this common interpretation, contemporary Australians and

Americans can look to Aboriginal, Pacific Islander, and Native ican defenders as exemplars of a common heritage that reflects ples of trust necessary for reconciliation.

Contrary to this "common-heritage" interpretation, this book the indigenous war effort within a wider context of colonialism. It contends that to white Australia and the United States—with some exceptions—the participation of indigenous servicemen in the war did *not* represent widespread appreciation of indigenous culture or fighting skills. Rather, given the general military guidelines on enlistment and the widening assimilation policies before and after the war, government officials discounted the need for, and effectiveness of, indigenous fighters. To government and military officials native defense was merely an undesirable response to Japanese aggression. Yolngu men served as adjunct defenses for Darwin with little regard for the war's impact on them or their families. Papuan and New Guinean coast-watchers and fighters represented a buffer to keep Japanese away from the mother country of Australia. Navajo Code Talkers' effectiveness merely strengthened government resolve to assimilate Native Americans. Furthermore, the participation of indigenous people in the war did not usher in widespread white support for civil rights. Certainly the postwar global conditions catalyzed movements for Native American, Pacific Islander, and Aboriginal rights in the 1960s, but their roles in the war were not pivotal factors in the fights for change or in governments' willingness to grant new rights.

This is not to say that Yolngu, Papua New Guinean, or Navajo fighters were inadequate in the defense of the Pacific. Indigenous scouts, servicemen, and guerillas were highly effective, because for the indigenous participants the war effort served a different purpose. Whereas the military utilized native peoples to defend the colonizers and their territories, for indigenous residents the war represented another period of guarding their own homelands against outside assailants. Essentially, indigenous people fought to secure their own soil. Ultimately, the motivations for and experiences of the war differ depending upon who tells the story—white or native participant.

The position of indigenous agency is complex in this study, just as it is in any history of indigenous-settler relations. Until recently, most non-indigenous histories have represented indigenous people as objects acted upon in a white drama. Historical debates in the United States since the 1970s and in Australia since the 1990s have questioned to what extent indigenous people were active agents under colonialism. Failing to acknowledge indigenous attitudes and motivations would be to succumb to Robert Berkhofer's assertion that "the historian [traditionally has] treated Indians as passive objects responding to white stimuli rather than as individuals coping creatively in a variety of ways with the different situations in which they found themselves."[3] In the Australian context some historians such as Bain Attwood have argued that while certainly Aboriginal people played some role in shaping their own identities and fates, the sheer power dominance of Europeans meant that whites "made Aboriginal people" more so than Aboriginal people made themselves. Contrarily, historians such as Peggy Brock, Jackie Huggins, and Ann McGrath argue that negotiation, accommodation, and adaptation were common in Aboriginal communities, thus positioning Aboriginal people as active agents determining their own destinies within the power structures of colonialism. Amid the historical debate, though, all authors agree that indigenous agency cannot be discarded, even if Attwood cautions that "the boundaries and structures within which Aborigines acted can be overlooked and their autonomy and independence—or agency—exaggerated."[4] As the next section will outline, the levels of autonomy and agency among the three indigenous groups examined in this book varied both individually and collectively at the time of the Second World War. But as the coming chapters will show, even in cases of extreme colonial control during war, indigenous people managed to exert their own agency to varying degrees.

This book places a high value on indigenous sources, both written and oral, because a reliance exclusively on non-indigenous sources would continue to devalue indigenous agency and disregard indigenous knowledge of the Second World War. Incorporating indigenous sources refutes what Wilbur Jacobs describes as a trend to dismiss any Native American history as either nonexistent or merely as a function of white culture and history.[5] Donald Fixico explains that one must consider all nonwritten indigenous sources including pottery, weapons, ceremonial objects, and art. In the American Indian context Fixico argues that the incorporation of any Native sources must respect Native American people, accept Indigenous epistemology, and attempt to avoid Amerocentrism.[6] Fixico's cautions apply transnationally to other indigenous peoples, including Papua New Guineans and Aboriginal people. Aboriginal historians Jackie Huggins and John Maynard, Torres Strait Islander scholar Martin Nakata, Maori researcher Linda Tuhiwai Smith, and the black Australian author Mudrooroo have similarly argued for the centrality of Indigenous voices, styles, and involvement in academic research. They argue that proper incorporation of Aboriginal sources entails prioritizing and preserving Aboriginal storytellers' voices—whether through oral history or other Indigenous forms of storytelling (i.e., art, dance, film)—and respecting Indigenous epistemologies when presenting Indigenous sources in an academic text.[7] Certainly, as oral historian Alistair Thomson cautions, using war narratives requires careful considerations of memory, interviewee agendas, national narratives, and the intended audience.[8] This book accounts for such concerns in conjunction with the respect warranted to indigenous testimonies; indeed, the themes of national narratives and wider historical contexts surrounding indigenous peoples and the Second World War are central to this book's premise.

Thus this study aims to juxtapose indigenous and non-indigenous accounts and to analyze the relationships among the multiple Pacific War stories. The book highlights the transnational continuities of colonialism during the war, while concurrently recentering native peoples in the history of the Pacific War through analysis of their responses to colonialism and to the war. Before proceeding, though, this introduction will provide historical context about the colonial situations in the respective nations leading up to the Second World War. It will also present some preliminary theoretical points about "ethnic soldiers" and the notion of the "martial race" applicable to the understanding of the three case studies.

"Undesirable in principle, but . . .": Australia and the Yolngu

By 1881 the whole of Arnhem Land was, according to British/South Australian law, under the jurisdiction of eleven pastoral leases. There was continuing frontier violence from the 1880s through 1910 that impeded cattle stations, but most of that Aboriginal violence was in response to the station owners poisoning meat or engaging in widespread massacres.[9] The new federal administration of the Northern Territory in 1911 implemented protection policy, which entailed isolating Aboriginal people on reserves and missions. Northern Territory Chief Protector of Aborigines (1911–1912) W. Baldwin Spencer announced that "it is of primary importance that the reserves should be retained for the use of the natives with the idea of isolating them and preventing them from coming into contact with other people."[10]

By 1927 local police and the Northern Territory chief medical officer, who doubled as the chief protector of Aborigines, were the main "enforcers" of protection. Historians Suzanne Parry and Tony Austin highlight that "only spasmodic attempts were made to enforce the provisions by police protectors, who had other priorities."[11] Arnhem Land continued to be a special case because of its relative isolation and its small non-Indigenous population. In April 1931 the Commonwealth formalized the Arnhem Land Reserve, of over 79,900 square kilometers, restricting non-Indigenous entrance into the region. While these actions superficially indicate a desire to preserve Yolngu vitality, in reality the government had determined that the terrain of Arnhem Land was unsuitable for pastoral purposes. By the 1930s missionaries made up the majority of non-Indigenous settlers in Arnhem Land.[12] The other non-Indigenous residents included the owner at Urapunga Station near the Roper River and the accompanying police station. Officially, it was the job of the Roper River police to investigate all crimes and perpetrators—Aboriginal and non-Indigenous. Due to the enormity of the region, but more significantly because of indifference toward violence against Yolngu, police rarely patrolled to protect Yolngu. The few times police investigated crimes against Yolngu were usually to benefit non-Indigenous residents.[13]

Popular Northern Territory opinion continuously depicted Yolngu as savages. Victor Hall, a Northern Territory police constable, described one Yolngu clan as "killers-raiders and rapers of the other tribes of Arnhem Land."[14] C. L. A. Abbott, the administrator of the Northern Territory, described the typical Aboriginal individual as "a childlike person."[15] Rev. Alfred Dyer wrote, "The coastal tribes of the Gulf [of Carpentaria] were still in a 'wild' condition at the time of this story [1933–34]."[16] One government report assessed Yolngu as "malicious by nature," in contrast to Aboriginal people of Queensland.[17] The common theme prevalent among Territorian attitudes toward Yolngu in the period preceding the Second World War is the denigration of Yolngu civilization, whose existence contravened the interests of white Australia.

Arnhem Land reached the national spotlight in 1932, when a group of Yolngu men murdered several Japanese fishermen at Caledon Bay. The Australian government sent a police expedition to investigate, ending when the Yolngu man Dhakiyarr speared a police constable, killing him. Amid fears of a full-scale war between Yolngu and whites, a missionary peace expedition traveled to Arnhem Land and convinced Dhakiyarr and the killers of the Japanese fishermen to stand trial in Darwin. All were convicted of murder, but humanitarian outcry in southern Australia culminated in the High Court overturning Dhakiyarr's conviction. Upon his release Dhakiyarr mysteriously disappeared, and there is still no conclusive evidence as to his fate.[18] In the context of the escalating tensions the anthropologist Dr. Donald Thomson traveled to Arnhem Land as a peace emissary on two expeditions between 1935 and 1937. Thomson met with Yolngu leaders and studied Yolngu culture while concomitantly advocating peaceful relations among whites, Yolngu, and Japanese. When assessing the relationship between Yolngu and the Commonwealth, Thomson noted: "These natives believe that they are still living under their own laws, and that they have no reason to recognise the fact that a new regime has taken over their affairs, except that they know vaguely that there is, somewhere, an individual or a power, called the 'Gub'ment' that sometimes visits vengeance upon them."[19] Thomson's expeditions curbed the brewing hostilities in Arnhem Land, but his remarks indicate that there was no resolution to conflicting perceptions of sovereignty, leaving a tenuous peace leading up to the Second World War.

Meanwhile, Australia's declaration of war on Germany in September 1939 did not represent an immediate threat to the nation's defense. There was no shortage of servicemen, and therefore the government had leeway when addressing the issue of who could enlist in the armed forces. One matter the military confronted was in what circumstances, if at all, to permit Aboriginal and Torres Strait Islander people to enroll. Indigenous people had served in the First World War, but in that conflict the question of participation did not arise to the same extent. By 1939 government policies had shifted to ideas of assimilating Aboriginal people into white Australian society as second-class citizens. The Defence Act had no restrictions against enlistment of Aboriginal people, but they were exempt from call-up and from compulsory training.[20] In 1940, though, the government explicitly *prohibited* the enlistment of all nonwhite persons into the army and navy. Prime Minister Robert G. Menzies wrote to the Departments of the Army and Navy "that the admission of aliens or of British subjects of non-European origin or descent to the Australian Defence Forces is undesirable in principle, but that a departure from this principle is justified in order to provide for the special needs of any of the Services during the war."[21] One document deemed Aboriginal people as unclean, inattentive, and full of bad habits.[22] In no other material did military or government agents rationalize their disapproval of persons of "non-European origin or descent." The direct implication is, as politics professor Hugh Smith writes, that it was "government's determination to preserve a White Australia and an even whiter army."[23]

Nonetheless, historian Robert Hall estimates that approximately 3,000 Aboriginal and 850 Torres Strait Islander personnel served during the Second World War.[24] The reasons Aboriginal people managed to enlist varied individually, but many circumvented regulations because of state or territory laws. It was the job of medical officers to determine whether an applicant was of substantial European descent. Instructions said to consider "the laws and practices in force in the State or Territory in which the enlistment is effected."[25] Every state and territory had different laws defining Aboriginality—some included persons of mixed descent, referred to as "half-castes," whereas in other states multiracial persons were classified as non-Aboriginal. The use of blood quantifications reveals that as an institution the military also subscribed to the constructs of race that were prevalent in Australia. Thus, prior to 1941 the desire to preserve white armed forces superseded military escalation.

Some persons saw the armed forces as the perfect means to implement the new policies of assimilation meant to address the so-called Aboriginal problem. A. P. A. Burdeu of the Australian Aborigines' League wrote to the minister for the interior that military service could "mould the life of the native away from his present condition in which he is placed."[26] G. A. Street, minister for defense, similarly wrote: "The Protector of Aborigines is of the opinion that the militia training to be received will prove of value to them [half-castes] in providing some occupation in hours when they are not otherwise employed."[27] The proposals for Aboriginal enlistment as a vehicle for assimilation called for segregated Aboriginal units under the command of white officers. Such proposals were mostly rejected, and there were strict conditions under which Aboriginal people could join the military during the period from 1939 to 1941. In order to circumvent the prejudicial directives, they must negate their Aboriginality or let the government do so. The military experience would only further assimilation and continue to disconnect Aboriginal people from their culture and heritage through defense of white Australia.

The potential looming Japanese threat to northern Australia forced a reassessment of the issue of Aboriginal participation in the military. By 1941 the Northern Territory remained a vastly undefended region due to sparse population and deficient infrastructure. A 1937 Commonwealth report declared, "In the latest Territory figures, the population is given as 5,454, of whom 3,800 are Europeans, the balance being Asiatics, other races and half-castes."[28] Concomitant with the lack of human capital was the shortage of materiel. Coupled with the extremes of the wet and dry seasons, the mere construction of the defense base in Darwin was very difficult.[29]

Part of the solution to the labor shortage came in 1933, when military officials in Darwin proposed the employment of Aboriginal persons for duties such as cleaning, clearing, sanitation, and working as servers and orderlies. The rationale for employing Aboriginal labor was that "the duties of such labourers are those which normally [are] carried out in all tropical countries by cheap labour, not being assigned to Europeans for climatic and racial reasons."[30] The racial reasoning behind employment of Aboriginal people for such unskilled work underscores the continuing dynamics of colonialism functioning in the military through the racialization of job tasks. Moreover, these employees would not be formal enlistees, thus skirting the provisions against enrolling persons of non-European origin or descent. Instead these Aboriginal laborers would be hired through the Department of Native Affairs under conditions demarcated in the Aboriginal Ordinance.

Both the military and the Department of Native Affairs sought the segregation of white troops from these Aboriginal laborers.[31] By 1940, as the demand for Aboriginal labor increased, the Department of Native Affairs was espousing policies of assimilation. Nonetheless, there were still calls to segregate the two races in the military. From the military side this was to preserve the whiteness of the armed forces. The Department of the Interior advocated segregation to limit the allegedly demoralizing influence of interracial contact. To accommodate assimilationist goals, Lieutenant Colonel Robertson wrote in January 1940 about "the desire of the Department of Native Affairs that all aboriginals shall not be used solely as unskilled labourers, but shall be given some training in something which will be of value later."[32] Assimilation did not equate with egalitarian integration of Aboriginal people into mainstream society, but rather with Aboriginal people serving as a second-class, cheap source of unskilled menial labor.

The Japanese threat to the north hastened the need for labor, and consequently, beginning in April 1942, the Australian military established Aboriginal labor camps throughout the Northern Territory. The camps manifested assimilationist aims because, as the secretary of the Aborigines' Friends' Association wrote, "the natives will come under discipline and training for future usefulness."[33] In some ways these camps were beneficial for Aboriginal people because they did provide more economic opportunities than most had received previously. Regular wages supplemented a sense of equality, as long as Aboriginal people adhered to the rules of the settlements. There were marked improvements in standards of hygiene, housing, and food when contrasted with previous living conditions in towns.[34] Nonetheless, the Aboriginal workforce received less pay than soldiers despite maintaining similar facilities, clothing, issuances, and lodging. In fact, army officials discouraged paying equal wages for fear that it "may lead to dissatisfaction amongst the local natives."[35] More likely, though, officials did not want to pay Aboriginal people the same as whites because they did not consider Aboriginal people as equals. Additionally, there were fears that doing so would disturb the power relations between Indigenous labor and settler employers on cattle stations both during and after the war.[36] Hence, even as the army grew to rely on unskilled Aboriginal labor, it persisted in using its position of power to protect the status quo of discrimination for the sake of the settlers in the Northern Territory.

The other issue arising from Japan's thrust south was that of defending regions without significant settlement. Some proposals for Aboriginal scouts had emerged even before 1939. In the early stage of the war, though, the armed forces rejected calls for Aboriginal scouts and coastwatchers in the north because "it would be difficult to make available for this purpose men with the necessary qualifications to deal with aboriginals."[37] The changing circumstances of the war in 1941 led to the reconsideration of the black tracker issue.

The main incentives to consider black scouts were threefold — to hinder any Japanese influence over Aboriginal people, to provide logistical support for non-Indigenous troops in the bush, and to engage in guerilla warfare against any Japanese invaders. The importance of breaking any Japanese influence stemmed from the heightened Japanese presence along the north in the 1930s. Although relations were

usually quite poor between Japanese and Aboriginal people, some incidents made white Australians question Aboriginal allegiances. For
instance, in the Cooktown district of north Queensland, A. Stanfield
Sampson wrote in a letter, "these aboriginals have openly stated that
the Japs told them that the country belonged to the blacks, had been
stolen from them by the whites and that 'bye and bye' they (the Japs)
would give it back to them (the blacks)."[38] Though these fears were
real among the white populace, there is no evidence of any Aboriginal or Torres Strait Islander support for the Japanese during the war.
Yet these sentiments highlighted the need for white Australia to enlist
the support of Aboriginal people. The army achieved one such means
of obstructing Aboriginal support for the Japanese by establishing the
aforementioned labor camps.

The other tactic in less populated regions would be to employ Indigenous assistance directly. This would have the double benefit of
helping non-Indigenous personnel in isolated regions to learn scouting
and bush survival skills. The anthropologist A. P. Elkin wrote: "If it
comes to infiltration and counter-infiltration, then that side which en-
joys the support of the natives will be able to walk slow rings round the
other."[39] Elkin's suggestions noted that any Aboriginal coastwatchers
must function "under the guidance and supervision of a white man."[40]
The essentiality of working under white men indicates several problematic elements of continuing colonial relationships. Clearly, the Australian government did not trust Aboriginal people to work efficiently or
properly without white regulation and command. In addition to distrust, white control suggests Aboriginal inability to meet the task without the oversight of non-Indigenous personnel. Most significantly, it
continues to demonstrate that any concerns were exclusively about the
impact of Japanese invasion on white Australia. There were no considerations for how Japanese invasion might impact Aboriginal societies. This is not to say that Aboriginal people did not willingly engage
in coastal patrols. However, Aboriginal motivations, experiences, and
histories of the period differ from those of white Australia.

The first formal Indigenous unit in the north came to fruition in the Torres Strait. On 14 May 1941 the military gave approval for the raising of a battalion composed entirely of Torres Strait Islander soldiers, under white leadership of course. Significantly, racial hierarchical ideas played a key role in the question of who could join the Torres Strait Light Infantry Battalion. Queensland's former chief protector J. W. Bleakley informed the army "that the mentality of the islanders recruited would be approximate [to] that of any man educated to the 7th Grade of a Primary School. It is pointed out that many white personnel in the Army are not above this educational standard."[41] Even in the process of accepting Torres Strait Islander enlistees, racial hierarchical ideas came into play to reject Aboriginal people. Instructions clearly stated that "under no circumstances are Australian Aboriginals to be enlisted."[42] When recruiters accidentally did enlist some Aboriginal soldiers, officers commanding the Torres Strait Light Infantry Battalion expressed disdain for the mishap. One major wrote, "These Aboriginals, I feel certain, would be nothing but an embarrassment to me in the event of any action, as they are not in the same fighting class as the Torres Strait Islanders."[43] Under intense pressure the army discharged these Aboriginal men in 1944. A memo detailing their discharge remarked that "the aboriginals were of a lower standard and less useful to the Army than the Islanders and that it was not desirable to continue to employ Australian aboriginals in competent units."[44] The dismissal underlines power dynamics where Aboriginal people were only wanted when it was considered necessary for the nation's survival. In this situation an allegedly higher race — the Torres Strait Islanders — could perform that task.

Thus the entire relationship between the Australian military and Aboriginal people was one of unequal power relations and control. Aboriginal participation in the dominant structure (the military) was only allowed under exceptional circumstances, and the criteria for those circumstances were that the Aboriginal labor or skills must fill a gap impracticable for white personnel. Whether this gap had formed around cheap labor, tracking skills, or the higher demand for soldier-bodies after Japan's entrance into the Second World War, the Aboriginal people were expected to conform to the conditions and regulations laid by the military. Cases of Aboriginal and Torres Strait Islander participation were not exceptions *to* the rules; more accurately, they were exceptions *consistent with* the rules. These examples circumvented—rather than challenged—prejudicial regulations and, as such, at a structural level did *not* break barriers and did *not* represent strides toward egalitarianism. Granted, sometimes conditions were an improvement over the prior experience of Australian Indigenous people, but they *never* placed Aboriginal or Torres Strait Islander people on an equal footing with white personnel. Military regulations relating to Indigenous people were rife with colonial goals of cheap colored labor, white control of Aboriginal knowledge, and assimilation. Inequality continued, and the preservation of white Australia continued to reign supreme.

Forced Labor: Colonizing Papua and New Guinea

European imperialism in the Pacific dates back to the time of explorers such as Captain James Cook, but in Papua New Guinea the period deserving attention commenced in the late nineteenth century. British and Australian colonialism in Papua began primarily in 1884, when the British government declared the southeastern portion of the island of New Guinea (hereafter called Papua) a protectorate. In 1888 the Crown formally affirmed possession of Papua. The main British interests in Papua were always strategic because of German "possession" of the northeast portion of the island (hereafter called New Guinea). Many of the strategic and commercial interests actually derived from Australia rather than Great Britain. Some scholars have even argued that Australia's interests in Papua reflected an Australian Monroe Doctrine, with objectives "to keep this territory and others adjacent to the mainland out of the grasp of competing powers."[45] But unlike Australia, Papua would be a franchise colony—premised on the extraction of labor and resources—instead of a settler colony. British law claimed acquisition of Papua not by discovery, occupation, conquest, or cession, and as such the possession of Papua recognized customary law and native title to the land. This meant that local inhabitants must consent to the expropriation of land, even if the agreement was not always on just terms.[46]

To govern the province, British administrator Sir William Mac-Gregor appointed a series of local village chiefs in 1892. He aimed to establish a system of indirect rule modeled on the British experiences in Fiji and Africa. The village chiefs were responsible as interpreters and guides and were expected to maintain census data on the population, including able-bodied men. The purpose of the village leaders was fundamentally "to enforce a system of native regulations designed to introduce Papuans to western legal concepts and to acceptance of European control by means of simply worded laws."[47] A significant flaw in the village system was the fact that it was an anathema to Papuan societies. As such administration of Papua did not always proceed peacefully because, as historian Edward Wolfers notes, "in practice, the administration had to subdue almost every district by force."[48] The ultimate underlying point that MacGregor himself noted was that "we went to New Guinea solely and simply to serve our own ends, and this fact should never be forgotten in dealing with the natives of that country."[49]

Australia's direct colonial role in Papua and New Guinea began when the British Colonial Office permitted Australia to fund an administration in Papua, so long as the organization accepted Colonial Office doctrine, including native title. In 1901 Australia accepted responsibility for Papua, and in 1906 British New Guinea officially became the Australian territory of Papua. During the First World War Australia occupied German New Guinea from August 1914 with a larger administration than in Papua. At the Paris Peace Conference Australia insisted that control of New Guinea was essential for continuing security, and the League of Nations granted Australia authority over the Mandated Territory of New Guinea.[50] The administrations of Papua and New Guinea never merged until after the Second World War, primarily due to legal, financial, and racial reasoning. Though governors pursued different policies in the separate territories, similar structures of colonialism manifested in practice. In fact, in 1939, when discussing the possibility of amalgamating Papua and New Guinea, Sir Frederic William Eggleston described the administrative policies of both territories as having "always been basically similar."[51]

The lieutenant-governor of Papua from 1906 to 1940 was John Hubert Plunkett Murray, whose policies had a dramatic impact on Papuan labor and land rights. Throughout his tenure Murray emphasized "protection" of Papuans and sought peaceful exploration and penetration of the interior. Historians critical of Murray criticize supposed concerns for Papuan rights as secondary to the primacy of settler interests in acquiring Papuan labor.[52] The extent to which policies were truly designed to "improve" the status of Papuans and New Guineans is questionable. Heather Radi points out that in New Guinea "the administration's paternalism shielded the native, but by denying him initiative it made it more difficult for him to come to terms with what lay beyond that shield."[53] Wolfers similarly argues that "the primary aim of all colonial administrations in Papua and New Guinea until the 1960s was neither 'development' nor 'preparation' for self-government, but control."[54] These critiques highlight the fact that Papua and New Guinea were consistently treated as franchise colonies; as such the purpose of colonialism was economic extraction—albeit rather unsuccessful—and relied on the exploitation of Papuan and New Guinean labor.

Technically there was a prohibition on forced labor. Some Papuans and New Guineans volunteered their services to earn wages, clothing, tools, or tobacco or for travel or social advancement.[55] Administrators also used legislation to coerce Papuans and New Guineans into the plantation labor force. For instance, the Native Taxation Ordinance (1918) taxed all Papuan adult males capable of working, with the proceeds meant to fund Papuan health and education. Whether coercing recruits through regulation or deception, or finding genuine volunteers, employers and recruiters had to comply with certain regulations about Pacific Islander labor. For instance, a magistrate or inspector had to witness contracts and had the right to cancel them if the terms were deemed unfair.[56] Administrators such as Murray maintained a paternalistic, assimilationist attitude similar to that of Northern Territory administrators, believing that overall it was in Papuans' best interests to work for settlers. He wrote, "Give them [Papuans] every opportunity of serving under European employers, and so acquiring habits of industry which later on they may, if they like, put to a use which will be more directly to their own benefit."[57]

The conditions of Papuan and New Guinean workers were often deficient despite supposed humanitarian efforts to ensure their fair treatment. Employers of contract workers were obliged to provide accommodation, food, and minimal clothing and to pay wages upon completion of contracts. Recruiters had to ensure that employees understood the purpose, duration, location, and conditions of their employment.[58] Administrators such as Murray argued that "the good treatment of the labourers may be regarded as assured, and I think, would not be seriously questioned by any one who had a knowledge of the labour conditions in the territory."[59] Historians have debunked the assertion that employers usually applied the minimum legal protections for Papuan and New Guinean workers. Abuse of labor was also widespread; examples range from the use of boss-boys as plantation overseers to roping recruits together on journeys from the highlands to the coast.[60] A mining boom in New Guinea in the late 1920s hastened the demand for labor, and further abuses occurred. Anthropologist Lucy Mair summarizes race relations in both colonies thus: "New Guinea residents, pinning their faith on 'bashing the coons' as the only sound basis of race relations, regarded the 'humanitarian' attitude of Papuans as pure hypocrisy."[61] Employers justified violence on the grounds that Indigenous people's childlike nature required beatings or because as members of "warrior cultures" Papuans and New Guineans would respect violent employers more. More likely, though, imposing the fear of harsh punishment served to protect settlers from potential Papuan or New Guinean uprisings.[62]

Enforcement of such a system came through the recruitment of Papuan and New Guinean police, who would become the foundation of Indigenous units during the war. As early as 1890 MacGregor established an armed Pacific Islander police constabulary to complement the village chiefs. At first the constabulary consisted entirely of Fijians and Solomon Islanders, but within a few years Papuans became the principal recruits. German New Guinea established a similar police force in 1896, and the development of the New Guinea force post-1914 paralleled that in Papua.[63] Police recruiting usually occurred in areas where the inhabitants had reputations for being tough, dependable, and controllable. The Royal Papuan Constabulary Ordinance as late as 1939 declared: "Every male aboriginal native of the Territory who is of sound bodily constitution and who so far as can be ascertained by the person appointed to enroll such native is between the ages of seventeen and forty both ages inclusive and unmarried shall be liable to be enrolled as a member of the Force."[64] Administrators such as Murray claimed that police constables joined as savages but that through the course of training their capacities and intelligence developed.[65] As the men on the frontlines of contact in unexplored regions, the constables were often the main agents of cultural exchange between villagers and Europeans. Historian August Kituai also asserts that "the Papua New Guinean policemen were convinced that they were on a civilizing mission. They firmly believed that they had been given a head start and now it was their turn to tell others of the new order."[66] Contrary to what Europeans believed, many police were motivated not by the "allure of civilization," but rather by the wealth and power of the position. Through the 1920s and 1930s about eight hundred police were recruited in Papua and fourteen hundred in New Guinea. In New Guinea at the outbreak of the Second World War there were thirty-six European police supervising 946 Native constables.[67] In a 1907–8 annual report, Murray noted that "they [Papuan police] have kept order among a savage population of very many thousands."[68]

There was a dark side to the constabulary system. Kituai summarizes the situation: "The colonial system in general required the police to be tough, dictatorial, and sometimes brutal."[69] Police rationalized the use of force to halt "primitive" practices such as cannibalism, infanticide, polygamy, sorcery, and intertribal fighting. They often indiscriminately abused villagers with canes or scared them with guns. In some instances police kidnapped young boys to indoctrinate them. They either returned the newly indoctrinated boys to their villages or made them into police interpreters.[70] Governments recognized that police abused their positions of power, but officials almost always overlooked such abuses to preserve the colonial administration. For instance, Murray acknowledged that "the worst faults of the Constabulary are a tendency to practice extortion upon village natives, and to misconduct themselves with women, especially prisoners, without troubling about their consent."[71] One way in which administrators attempted to limit police mistreatment was the practice of providing all constables with handcuffs but no keys. Thus police would have to bring suspects to a magistrate or administrator for processing. Prisoners still experienced horrible conditions and suffered severe physical and mental abuse.[72] The police constabulary system represented some of the most blatant examples of exploitation characteristic of colonialism. Using Indigenous knowledge, skills, and labor to "pacify" Indigenous people allowed others to do Europeans' dirty work while concurrently maintaining unequal power relations over the Native police. Similar dynamics would operate for Pacific Islander coastwatchers and the Royal Papuan Constabulary (RPC) during the Second World War, and the prewar Papuan and New Guinean police constabularies would also serve as primary recruitment grounds for the PIR.

Frontier Wars, External Wars: Navajos before the Second World War

The Native Americans who would eventually become the Navajo Nation confronted Spanish colonialism as early as the seventeenth century. It was not until after the Mexican-American War (1846–48) that the loose association of clans united as the Navajo Nation to face the new common enemy — U.S. expansionists. Unbeknownst to the Navajos at the time, the new invaders would eventually come to dominate the region and never leave. The first formal "war" between U.S. Army forces and Navajos was in 1857 and lasted only a few months, ending with little more than a stalemate.[73] The conflict was a precursor to further engagements with the Navajos over land and resources.

By 1863 the U.S. government resolved to deal with the Navajo "problem" like it had dealt with other Native people s — by relocating the Native American group to a reservation where they could "educate" the tribe and "assimilate" its members into white society. Navajos resisted the U.S. government's and military's attempts to relocate them. The army officer Kit Carson launched a brutal campaign against the Navajos in 1863. After starvation ensued in the winter of 1863–64, the majority of Navajos surrendered. What came next was the "Long Walk": a series of marches from August 1863 until 1866, varying in numbers and routes, three hundred miles south to Fort Sumner. The commonalities that characterized the Long Walk were poor traveling conditions, inadequate food, and army brutality. At Fort Sumner the U.S. government forced Navajos to share space with Apaches, continuing a disregard for the heterogeneity of Native America. The time at Fort Sumner was a horrific experience characterized by continuing food shortages and tensions with Apaches. The survivors of the Long Walk were the great-grandparents of the Second World War generation. They passed on this history of oppression through oral history, and it was (and still is) well known among the Navajo community.[74]

On 1 October 1868 a group of Navajo leaders traveled to Washington DC hoping to obtain permission from the settler government to return to their ancestral lands, culminating in a treaty that Navajos refer to as "Naaltsoos" or "Old Paper." The treaty recognized Navajos' limited sovereignty under the dominion of the United States and granted land that formed the nucleus of the present-day Navajo Reservation.[75] Over the years the U.S. government would add or take away land from the Navajo Reservation depending upon its economic and strategic value. Additionally, private enterprises such as oil prospectors would attempt to cheat Navajos out of their land through shady lease agreements. While the treaty allegedly guaranteed rights and protections for Navajos, including the right to a free English education, very rarely would the United States fulfill its treaty obligations.[76]

From the conception of the Navajo Reservation in 1868 through the commencement of the Second World War, the U.S. government and other settlers continued to interfere in Navajo affairs with little regard for Navajo sovereignty or culture. During the height of American assimilation policies toward Native Americans, from 1879 to 1917, many

Navajo parents resisted pressure to send their children away to "Indian schools." They recognized that these schools represented forms of cultural genocide where their children "learned" to act like white people and thereby to "assimilate" into mainstream U.S. society. The underside of assimilation, which many Navajos recognized, included the loss of Native heritage, language, traditions, and culture. Moreover, parents were aware that disease spread quite easily through boarding schools such as the Carlisle Indian School in Pennsylvania.[77] For those Navajos remaining on the reservation educational and other economic opportunities were scarce. While some missions established schools in the early twentieth century, obtaining a secondary education necessitated leaving the reservation. The 1868 treaty included compulsory education for children aged six to sixteen, but from a practical standpoint this rarely happened. The few schools available tended to be rigid boarding schools run by the Bureau of Indian Affairs (BIA). From the 1930s the BIA began enforcing a policy of requiring parents to send at least one child away to school. Code Talker Peter MacDonald attended one of these schools in the 1930s and describes the purpose of such schools as "unrelated to the needs of the Navajo children. The hostile attitude toward my people was emotionally devastating, of course. We were taught that we were superstitious savages. . . . We were made to feel that our parents, our grandparents, and everyone who had come before us was inferior."[78] Amid such pressure, Navajo resistance to assimilation policies contributed to the endurance of Navajo culture today. The significance of assimilation policies, however, lies in the U.S. government's continuing desires to eliminate Navajo as a separate identity and to continue the settler colonial project.

Navajo life around the Second World War was still bleak. During the 1920s there was an extensive increase in livestock, but the onset of the Great Depression in the 1930s created controversy between Navajos and the Department of Interior over livestock reduction.[79] When Secretary of the Interior John Collier advocated a "New Deal" for Native Americans in 1934, the Navajo Nation resisted many of the reforms because they included the imposition of livestock reduction. Collier's approach to Native America was in some ways more progressive than that of previous administrations. Collier advocated an end to assimilation and instead promoted pluralistic education and more rights to self-determination among Native American nations. Yet he still maintained the patronizing attitude that he knew what was best for Native Americans. Self-determination in reality entailed adoption of Collier's proposals — both beneficial and detrimental to American Indian communities. As Navajo veteran Peter MacDonald writes, "It was not until the 1930s that the position of chairman of the Navajo Nation originated, and even then it was created by white men who did not feel comfortable adapting to our culture."[80] For the Navajo the 1930s, leading up to the war, continued to entail poor health, poor infrastructure, and poor economic opportunities. Prospects for Navajos to advance within mainstream U.S. society were also limited because of structural inequalities plaguing the Navajo Reservation. At the onset of the Second World War most Navajos still lived in clay dwellings known as hogans without electricity, telephones, or automobiles. The reservation had a population of forty thousand but one of the lowest literacy rates (20 percent) among all Native American nations. Despite being U.S. citizens, Navajos still had no voting rights.[81] Despite Navajo resistance to colonialism, assimilation, and even Collier's reforms, the aims of the U.S. government constantly outweighed the desires of the Navajo people. While on some occasions Navajos successfully implemented their own policies, when Navajo and U.S. wishes conflicted, the U.S. government's concerns would triumph.

The continuing colonial relationship for all Native Americans led to some debate over conscription when the draft enactment of September 1940 applied to American Indians. Some Indigenous and non-Indigenous persons opposed conscription because of omnipresent discrimination. The Iroquois Confederacy, for instance, asserted autonomy through its treaty rights and thus deemed itself not under American draft jurisdiction.[82] To circumvent the question of citizenship or sovereignty, bureaucrats highlighted that resident aliens had to enroll for the draft anyway. Additionally, Circuit Court Judge Jerome Frank ruled against the Iroquois in *Ex Parte Green* that "where a domestic law conflicts with an earlier treaty, . . . [that] the statute must be honored by the domestic courts has been well established."[83] The North Carolina Cherokee Tribe used its draft eligibility as grounds to criticize other discriminatory practices. In particular the tribe issued a resolution denouncing its members' lack of suffrage.[84] These examples outline some Native Americans' resistance to the draft, but the majority of American Indian and non-Indigenous groups supported the Second World War. Collier reported in 1943 that American Indians had a Selective Service registration rate of 99 percent, highlighting their general support for the war effort. Some estimates suggest that up to half of all Native Americans left reservations to work in war-related services, either as servicemen or in war industries.[85]

The status of Native American servicemen was precarious given the racial discrimination that saturated the military. Despite strong opposition from black organizations the military segregated black and white soldiers in separate units. Native Americans, not fitting easily in the black-white dichotomy, served in the same units as white soldiers. Even so, American Indians were well aware of the racial tensions posed by the segregated military.[86] Estimates of the number of Native Americans who ultimately served in the Second World War vary. Historian Donald Fixico estimates that there were 25,000 by the end of the war, while Jeré Bishop Franco calculates the number at 44,500.[87] Admiration for Native American servicemen, while a boon of integration, sometimes concurrently reinforced ethnic stereotypes. Interactions were often the first white exposure to American Indian culture. Common practices included the exchange of food, customs, and other cultural belongings from care packages. Sometimes an endearment subtly underlined warrior stereotypes. For example, a common accolade was to call Native soldiers "chief." Some considered the term a mark of respect for their warrior heritage, while others found it condescending. Media also misconstrued Native American customs as propaganda for the war effort. Cultural chants and war dances were common among American Indian combatants before battles — including one performed by eight Navajo

Code Talkers before the Battle of Okinawa.[88] A July 1943 *New York Times* article referenced one such ritual performed before the invasion of Sicily as a "Redskin war ceremonial."[89] Certainly amid the stereotypes and colonial constructs Native Americans had their own motivations to serve and agency in their dealings with the armed forces. Historian Al Carroll emphasizes that "Native people used these [stereotyped] images, turning them against themselves and defining what Native traditions in the military became."[90] Hence for American Indians military participation promoted harmonious interracial relations with individual white servicemen, but on a macrostructural level officials and media merely typecast them to rally support for the war. These patterns for all Native American soldiers also applied to the Navajos.

When the War Came: Weaponizing Indigenous Peoples

In Australia, Papua and New Guinea, and the United States the status of indigenous people was precarious when Japan attacked Pearl Harbor. While degrees of collective autonomy, state control, and individual freedom varied among and within the different states, all indigenous peoples were under the dominion of colonizing powers. Navajos had some degree of self-government, but within the framework of U.S. sovereignty and laws. Papuans and New Guineans were subjected to rigid labor laws, as Australia exerted control over the movement and lives of the territories' native inhabitants. In Arnhem Land the Australian government considered the Yolngu people to be under similar rigid conditions, but the remoteness of the region left most Yolngu to their own devices. In all three societies discrimination was rife, at both the institutional and the individual levels. In Australia prejudicial regulations — with exceptions — excluded Aboriginal people from the military. This applied by extension in the colonies of Papua and New Guinea, though Papuans and New Guineans were sought for employment in local constabulary forces. In the United States there were no regulations against Native American enlistment; contrarily, the military was one institution in which Native Americans were treated the same as whites. Thus, as this introduction has shown, there certainly were significant

Introduction

differences in the treatment of indigenous peoples and their degrees of autonomy in the different colonial societies. These differences should not be trivialized. But fundamentally, unequal power structures, discriminatory legislation, and racist attitudes underpinned colonial processes across colonial societies. Despite these continuing backdrops of colonialism, indigenous soldiers and auxiliaries would make remarkable contributions to the Pacific War effort.

This book will look at a range of issues surrounding the three case studies of indigenous people in the Second World War, including opposition to indigenous soldiers, desired tasks for indigenous labor, manners of recruitment, motivations to serve, treatment during the war, status within the armed forces, compensation after the war, and links between military participation and postwar citizenship. The three case studies demonstrate, both separately and collectively, that the employment of indigenous soldiers as weapons in the Second World War was a process rife with colonial exploitation, where the colonizers' interests reigned supreme at the expense of indigenous agency and civil rights.

The idea of indigenous skills being weaponized was not a new concept circa 1941. Some of the early historical manifestations of indigenous people serving as weapons for colonizers emerged as part of the colonizing process. As postcolonial theorist Frantz Fanon summarizes: "In colonized countries, colonialism, after having made use of the natives on the battlefields, uses them as trained soldiers to put down the movements of independence."[91] Imperialism scholar J. A. Hobson also highlights that the use of indigenous people as soldiers achieves multiple goals of colonialism. The labor is cheaper and more numerous, and military service provides an excellent means of assimilation. He sarcastically writes, "Let these 'niggers' fight for the empire in return for the services we render them by annexing and governing them and teaching them 'the dignity of labour.'"[92] Hobson terms the use of indigenous soldiers for colonial defense "parasitism."[93] In addition to limiting the need for troops from the colonizer's homeland, indigenous soldiers were successful at repressing local insurrections because they did not adhere to the same rules of engagement as trained officers. Colonizers also used strategies such as forming ethnically homogenous units, posting them away from their home region (often in an enemy clan's territory), and using different ethnic units to keep one another in check from mutiny.[94]

One term that describes indigenous minorities who became soldiers and police employed by colonizers is "ethnic soldiers." The most comprehensive scholar of ethnic soldiers in a global context (rather than localized to specific countries) is Cynthia Enloe, who effectively demonstrates historical and contemporary constructs of ethnic soldiers and police. Although her analysis focuses primarily on franchise colonial states, much of her theory applies to ethnic soldiers in settler societies as well. Enloe outlines how elites have constructed the military and ethnic units based on what will protect the interests of the privileged. As she summarizes, "The historical evolutions of armies, navies, air forces and police forces in countries as different as Britain and Indonesia have been shaped by state élites' ethnic calculations."[95] The concept Enloe discusses that has the most relevance to this study is the role of the "martial race":

> The concept of a "martial race" is usually applied by outsiders to flag certain ethnic groups in a society as somehow inherently inclined towards military occupations, possessing some characteristic so embedded in its physical make-up — its "blood" — that it passes beyond simply a cultural — that is, an ethnic — predilection. In reality, martial vocational learning and availability remain eminently ethnic.[96]

Historian Heather Streets argues that one reason martial race ideologies were so powerful is because of the flexibility and adaptability of such discourses across different geographical and historical sites of colonialism.[97] In the context of this book colonizers constructed all indigenous societies examined — Yolngu, Papua New Guinean, and Navajo — as "martial races" innately prone to aggression. As such they were perfect candidates for colonial governments to employ as ethnic soldiers.

Enloe's definition of a "martial race" focuses on colonial constructions of indigenous peoples. Importantly, these colonial constructs need to be distinguished from genuine indigenous cultural practices, traditions, and adaptations that indigenous groups *themselves* acknowledge as representing warrior traditions. Anthropologist and historian William C. Meadows analyzes Native self-constructions of warrior traditions among Southern Plains Indians in the United States from precolonial times through the present. Meadows refers to societies such as the Kiowa, Comanche, and Apache as "military societies" because their kinship, group organization, and cultural practices revolve around warrior traditions and practices. Meadows clearly distinguishes between indigenous self-constructions of military societies and colonial constructs and stereotypes. Meadows also highlights how such military societies have adapted over time, such as incorporating military service within the U.S. armed forces as a contemporary manifestation of the warrior tradition.[98] These self-constructions and indigenous-initiated military traditions—in contrast to Enloe's analysis of colonial constructs of the "martial race" and "ethnic soldiers"—center around Native motivations to serve in settler societies' armed forces. Meadows's analysis aligns closely with Carroll's argument: "Natives are not foolish or being used by the nation-state; the choices Natives make to be in the military are perfectly rational and in line with longstanding cultural values."[99] Like this book Carroll effectively juxtaposes and contrasts Native American motivations to serve with the colonizers' aims when securing indigenous soldiers.

Enloe's analysis—focused primarily on colonial matters rather than indigenous agency—points to the relationship between colonial-constructed "martial races" and recruitment as one that encourages allegiance to the colonizing state. Recruitment of members of the "martial race" was often easy because they come from groups already defeated by colonizers. As such they had few other options for survival within the new regime, and additionally recruiters preferred them because there was less chance of mutiny. This aligned with the colonial strategies of "divide and conquer"; many joined colonizers' militaries for fear of being outnumbered by rival clans or to improve their position in the colonizers' hierarchy.[100] Additionally, as historian Tom Holm explains in the American Indian context, the accessibility of recruitment, the continuing success of indigenous fighters, and their small population proving "a 'safe' minority rather than a tangible threat to the Euroamerican status quo" have been strong motivations to recruit indigenous soldiers.[101] Historian Warren L. Young similarly asserts that colonial governments have often taken into account the ability to continue denying citizenship rights to minority groups before recruiting their constituents into the armed forces.[102] Enloe points out that "the consequence for the group targeted to be a 'martial race' is often an increased sense of ethnic cohesion bought at the price of growing vulnerability to state manipulation."[103] Participation in the military can bolster an ethnic group's internal and external status, which was definitely true in the case of Papua New Guineans and the Navajo Code Talkers. As this book will show, though, the status boost coincided with continuing stereotypes and occurred under obedience to and within the context of the power relations of the colonizer.

Yet the role of ethnic soldiers could still serve as a base from which to empower the ethnic group through raised self-consciousness and politicization. As was definitely the case for Navajo Code Talkers, participation in the military could lead to exposure to the outside world and new self-constructs of communal uniqueness. It was this new empowerment and raised consciousness that led groups of veteran Navajos, Papua New Guineans, and Aboriginal people to challenge their social positions in new civil rights movements of the 1960s and 1970s. Yet the veterans still had to fight for rights and recognition. As Enloe explains, "The long-range result was not full-fledged acceptance and legitimation for the group, and the ethnic community's veterans formed a vanguard in rejecting later offers of cooptation from the ruling ethnic groups."[104] Thus, discussion of indigenous soldiers in the Second World War returns to a fundamental question of whether ethnic soldiers represented ideas of resistance to or collaboration with colonizers. As this book will show, facets of both resistance and collaboration are clearly discernible through the oral testimonies of Yolngu, Papua New Guineans, and Navajo Code Talkers. But what was more significant was how governments coerced, constructed, and disregarded indigenous services before, during, and after the Second World War.

This book proceeds across the three case studies of indigenous peoples in the Pacific War. Chapters 1 and 2 focus on the Yolngu of Arnhem Land, in the Northern Territory of Australia. Chapter 1 describes the work of Yolngu as members of forces such as the Northern Territory Special Reconnaissance Unit (NTSRU) and the North Australia Observer Unit (NAOU). The NTSRU was a force composed of fifty-one Yolngu men who patrolled Arnhem Land from February 1942 to April 1943. Although the group never physically engaged the Japanese, they were trained and prepared to fight a guerilla war against potential Japanese landings using traditional weapons. The NAOU was a white force that operated across north Australia during the same period. As the NAOU was a non-Indigenous force that employed Aboriginal people as trackers, the comparisons and contrasts between the two units highlight the disparities in government attitudes toward Aboriginal people versus white soldiers. Chapter 2 examines the variety of ways in which other Yolngu partook in the war effort unofficially. Various Yolngu men and women worked as coastwatchers and manual laborers and were even involved in the rescue of crashed Australian and American pilots. Chapter 2 also engages Yolngu oral history, providing a window into their perspectives on the war and its impact on their society. Yolngu stories challenge dominant non-Indigenous narratives, introduce hidden histories from the war, and also highlight the need for further study about Yolngu in the Second World War.

Chapters 3 and 4 scrutinize the Papua New Guinea case study. Chapter 3 details the role of Papuan and New Guinean laborers working for both Japan and the Allies in Papua and New Guinea. The chapter first examines racial constructs of Papuans and New Guineans and how such constructs guided labor principles during the war. The chapter then segues to discuss the recruitment, training, and sometimes abuse of laborers by both Japan and Australia. While the idea of the "Fuzzy Wuzzy Angel" has been prevalent in Australia's and Papua New Guinea's national memories of the Second World War, this chapter examines the actual experiences of Papuan and New Guinean laborers working for the Australian armed forces. Chapter 4 focuses on the coastwatchers, the Royal Papuan Constabulary (RPC), and the Pacific Islands Regiment (PIR) of Papua and New Guinea. Like the NTSRU in the Northern Territory, the PIR was a group of Papuan and New Guinean soldiers trained to fight against Japanese invaders. Despite its members being officially enlisted, the PIR received wages and treatment unequal to those of white soldiers serving in Papua and New Guinea. Moreover, colonial concerns about postwar reconstruction of Papua New Guinea signified the disbandment of such soldiers when the war was over with inadequate compensation and recognition. Chapter 4 examines the experiences of the coastwatchers, RPC, and PIR — both positive and negative — and how their participation linked with colonial practices both before and after the war.

The Navajo Code Talkers are the subject of chapters 5 and 6. The story of the Navajo Code Talkers is well known in the United States: the U.S. Marine Corps used the Navajo language as a secret, unbreakable code in the Pacific War. Unlike previous works about the Code Talkers, though, chapter 5 analyzes military motivations to form the group. Questions of exploitation of Native knowledge are explored, along with the many officials opposed to creation of the Code Talkers. Chapter 5 also analyzes Code Talkers' oral history, discussing their motivations to serve, and contrasts such motivations with the realities of the government's motives. Chapter 6 explores how the end of the war and return to the Navajo Reservation marked a return to inequality. While some Navajos did benefit from their time in the war, many continued to face discrimination and difficulties accessing veterans' benefits. Moreover, government policy makers misinterpreted Native American war participation to promote termination and relocation. Despite such trends the Navajo Nation resisted termination and relocation. While the Navajo Code Talker story has become part of mainstream U.S. Second World War history, this chapter questions to what extent the narrative has been (mis)appropriated by white American history.

The concluding chapter reflects on the three case studies and relates them to wider issues of colonialism in global history. The conclusion emphasizes the explicit comparisons across the three case studies and outlines a theory of soldier-warrior colonialism to explain the transnational trends of exploitation of indigenous knowledge and labor in modern war. The conclusion uses the parallel-dimensions theory of comparative history to outline the key components of soldier-warrior colonialism and some of their various manifestations. Finally, the conclusion relates the theoretical underpinnings of these three case studies to wider global history, as the ideas and arguments contained within this book are not confined exclusively to the case studies chosen.

CHAPTER 1. An Exception in the Equation?

Donald Thomson and the NTSRU

The Arnhem Land coast is more readily accessible to the Eastern Asian peoples than to those Australians who live in the more populous areas south of the latitude of Brisbane. — J. C. JENNISON, 8 January 1940[1]

It is considered that such [Aboriginal] patrols will prove of great value for night reconnaissance, guerilla warfare and ambush at night on the flank or behind the lines of an enemy landing force. — DONALD THOMSON[2]

They [Yolngu] needed little encouragement to begin preparing for the reception of possible landing parties, by forging their own "shovel" spears from odds and ends of metal. — DONALD THOMSON[3]

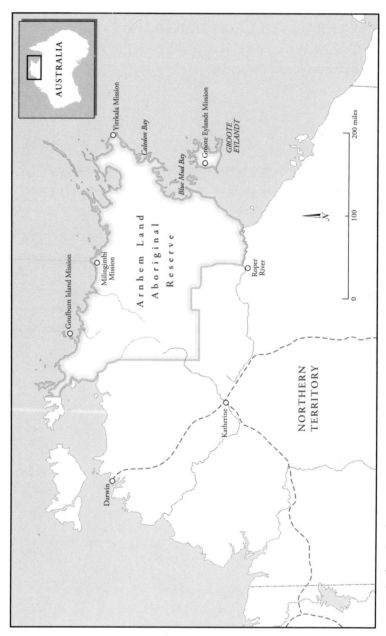

MAP 1. Arnhem Land

Arnhem Land, on the north coast to the east of Darwin, was one of the most vulnerable regions of the Northern Territory at the outbreak of the Pacific War. In addition to the usual non-Indigenous population woes, Arnhem Land also had a small Aboriginal presence. The anthropologist Donald Thomson in 1935 estimated an Aboriginal population of only fifteen hundred.[4] Thomson would also note the intensified Japanese coastal presence as late as December 1941, and he worried that Japanese attempts at friendship might "undermine the prestige of the white man."[5] The main susceptibility of Arnhem Land came from its vastness and the military's ignorance of its twenty-five thousand square miles. Thomson, and eventually his superiors, did not anticipate Japan would launch a full-scale invasion of the region. But he expressed concerns that the Japanese might use it as a staging area to invade Darwin or would occupy the aerodromes at Milingimbi or Groote Eylandt. It has been well documented by historians that in actuality Japan did not intend to invade Australia, but merely to neutralize the country through strategic bombings. Yet in early 1942 the fears of Japanese invasion were quite real among the Australian populace, and Arnhem Land was one potential hotspot.[6] Concerns consistently highlighted the relationship of Arnhem Land to white Australia's defense, and consequently the 1941 proposal for the Northern Territory Special Reconnaissance Unit (NTSRU) would relate to white Australia's protection.

Through all the discussion about government motives and the continuing exploitation of Aboriginal knowledge there was one steady exception—Donald Thomson. While for the majority of the Australian military and government personnel the NTSRU would represent a last resort, cheap colored labor, an auxiliary force, or flank protection for Darwin, for Thomson it was always a case of Yolngu people defending Yolngu land and society from invasion. Furthermore, Thomson saw the NTSRU as an opportunity both to prove the value of Yolngu civilization and to implement his recommendations for Aboriginal policy. Thomson accepted the notion of the "fatal impact" consequences of interracial contact, but he differed from the prevailing anthropologists in that he advocated complete segregation and preservation of an allegedly "pure" Yolngu civilization rather than assimilation. This chapter thus examines the NTSRU's orders, formation, training, and functioning and works through the lens of Thomson. The NTSRU functioned as an example of Thomson's ideology in practice, but the primary objective of defense precluded the execution of his anthropological designs in pure form.

This chapter also questions the accuracy of Thomson's self-perception. Thomson's narrative constantly suggests that the NTSRU was the only group capable of defending Arnhem Land and that it was the only force the military trusted with such a mission. To interrogate Thomson's continuing assertions of the exclusivity of the NTSRU, this chapter discusses the parallel development of the North Australia Observer Unit (NAOU) from March 1942 through to the end of the war. Juxtaposition of the NAOU with the NTSRU raises new issues that suggest that Thomson's praise of the NTSRU —while warranted—exaggerates the military's confidence in the unit. Moreover, the parallel relationship between the NAOU and Aboriginal people highlights the fact that the NTSRU was not atypical, as Thomson suggests, but rather fit with the dynamics of unequal power characteristic of white-Aboriginal relations continuing through the war.

Proposing Yolngu Guerillas

Thomson was not the first person to suggest the employment of Yolngu scouts in Arnhem Land. In his 1940 report "Eastern Arnhem Land: Australia's Open Door," J. C. Jennison wrote: "A valuable Coastguard

Service could be built up with aborigines as scouts. They are keen observers and could be taught to report any or all movements of seacraft along the coast."[7] Jennison's scheme, however, was never adopted. Instead, the eventual formation of the NTSRU culminated from a combination of Thomson's experience as an anthropologist in the 1930s, his work in 1940 organizing Pacific Islander coastwatchers in the Solomon Islands, and his being in the right place at the right time. In June 1941 Thomson, then serving in the Royal Australian Air Force (RAAF), delivered a speech to army staff entitled "Arnhem Land and the Native Tribes who inhabit that area." Attending the lecture was the army director of special operations, Lt. Col. W. J. R. Scott. Scott approached Thomson with the prospect of forming a guerilla unit in Arnhem Land composed of Yolngu, and the idea struck a chord with Thomson. He adopted the project as his own and within weeks suggested that "the natives of Arnhem Land could, if suitably organised, be employed not only to patrol the coastline of this territory, but that they might be organised into reconnaissance and fighting units which would be capable of locating, and of harrying, any Japanese forces or bases which might later be established in this territory."[8] The idea for the NTSRU was born.

Thomson's original proposal called for a "suitable white officer" to command Yolngu in systematic attacks directed against Japanese landing parties. The aim would be to disrupt Japanese campaigns and morale. Thomson stressed that Yolngu should not integrate with non-Indigenous troops. Rather than utilize contemporary military tactics or technology, they should retain "as far as practicable the tactics already perfected by and regularly employed among these fighting men."[9] Scott had a different vision of the potential Yolngu force. He proposed "that the natives shall erect, in selected areas, native huts which could house members of Independent Companies should it be considered desirable to station Independent Companies in the Areas."[10] By August Scott would expand his scheme to suggest that Yolngu provide training for Independent Companies—commandolike scouting forces—regarding bush survival over long periods of time. These proposals from Scott consistently appeared in minute papers related to the defense of Darwin.[11] Therefore, Scott constantly envisioned the NTSRU as a loose group of Yolngu recruits as auxiliaries to white personnel. He disregarded Yolngu bush skills unless applied under the proper direction of white forces. Scott also pictured the NTSRU as a cheap colored defense of white Australia with no consideration for how Japanese invasion might directly affect the Yolngu people.

Thomson disagreed with Scott's proposal, remarking, "It will be very difficult to maintain a body of men, already highly trained and eager for active service, in a contented state for any considerable period of time."[12] Thomson considered that Yolngu should be the primary soldiers rather than auxiliaries to whites. Thomson described fighting skills as embedded in the life experience of Yolngu men, "who had grown up in an area where tribal fueds [*sic*] were still carried on, and where guerilla fighting still plays an important part in their lives."[13] Scott accepted Thomson's calls for a more centralized Yolngu role as defenders of Arnhem Land. Perhaps Scott accepted Thomson's appraisal of Yolngu skills, but more likely Scott determined that Thomson, as organizer of the force, should direct the unit in the manner he saw fit.

Both Thomson and Scott received considerable opposition to the idea of an Aboriginal defense network. One such opposing memo summarized: "It is difficult to see how periodical recce. visits to the Western side of Cape York would be justified as this area would hardly be of significance in any attack on Australia by Japan."[14] The memo also worried that information obtained from Aboriginal people would travel too slowly and inefficiently. Instead, it would be more efficient to send paratroopers to counter invasion and to send planes, packhorses, or independent companies into the region. The communication declared that "organization of the local white stockmen would probably have more value than organization of the natives, for the stockmen would be more important as fighting men and for providing guides (either themselves or from their native stockmen) in the event of guerilla operations by our forces facing an invader."[15] These sentiments clearly represent colonial attitudes of white superiority and disregard for the abilities of Aboriginal people.

Scott responded to the criticism, first noting that, given the uncertainty of what would happen if Japan attacked, there was no way of knowing the strategic significance of Arnhem Land without scouting. More important, he endorsed organized Aboriginal people as the most efficient means of scouting or infiltrating an invasion force.[16] Despite some continued opposition to the NTSRU, the pressure from Thomson and Scott culminated in approval for the force's formation in September 1941. There is no clear indication of which of Scott's or Thomson's points convinced the military, but one detail that clearly helped their cause was the matter of compensation. Neither Thomson nor Scott envisioned a unit full of enlisted soldiers. There would be a small crew supervising and training the Yolngu fighters, but Yolngu would not be enrolled into the military. Scott told his superiors that they "would be repaid in trade tobacco (obtained in parcels of 26 sticks to the lb.), fish hooks, wire for fish spears, tomahawks and pipes."[17] Even if these items would benefit Yolngu practically, they would not represent sufficient compensation for the intensive nature of reconnaissance and guerilla warfare envisioned. Such inadequate payment reflected colonial sentiments and amounted to exploitation of Aboriginal labor, skills, and knowledge for the benefit of white Australia.

Planning and Preparation for the NTSRU: September 1941–February 1942

Scott granted Thomson autonomy over the creation of the NTSRU. Thomson had six months to prepare before traveling into Arnhem Land to recruit Yolngu fighters. The preliminary objectives laid out on 11 October 1941 summarized the mission purpose as twofold: "To assess the kind and degree of influence exerted upon the natives, especially in Arnhem Land, by Japanese. To take active steps to dispel any Japanese influence and undermine any prestige which may exist."[18] Thomson envisioned the formation of a nucleus of approximately fifty Yolngu fighters by March 1942. He would live and travel with them, and they would conduct training along the Roper River before embarking on detailed reconnaissance of Arnhem Land. Throughout their tour of duty they would also establish depots of emergency arms and supplies.[19] With this plan in mind Thomson went to work coordinating preliminary groundwork in Townsville.

The main issues of concern during the period from September 1941 to February 1942 were organization of the vessel *Aroetta* and an appropriate non-Yolngu crew. The crew would be responsible for the daily operations of the *Aroetta*, and additionally members would be responsible for training the Yolngu fighters. Thomson was very strict about his selection of personnel because "it would be worse than useless to place them [Yolngu] under charge of an officer whose attitude was unsympathetic or who regarded them with contempt."[20] Criterion number one, as far as Thomson was concerned, would be previous experience working with indigenous people. The other standards were that they "be temperamentally suited for life on a small boat, cramped and comfortless, and capable of standing up to long periods of service under conditions that were monotonous, always exacting, and sometimes severe."[21] Thomson settled on two sergeants—T. H. Elkington and A. E. Palmer—because he had prior experience working with them in the Solomon Islands. Scott spoke highly of both men's qualifications; both were "expert in their treatment of natives, are experts in the navigation and maintenance of luggers, and are highly trained in fieldcraft and bushcraft generally."[22] Thomson's insistence on men with prior experience with indigenous people would prove critical for the functioning of the NTSRU, particularly because Thomson did not want to interfere drastically with Yolngu cultural development.

Thomson determined that it would be difficult to find additional white crew for the *Aroetta*, so he looked for an alternative. Scott suggested, "Natives are particularly suitable for work of this nature in unchartered waters and under conditions which would be climatically severe and to most white men otherwise exacting and monotonous."[23] In response Thomson recruited six Solomon Islanders to serve on the *Aroetta* as engine driver, boatswain, general crew, and cook. On their enlistment records their existing occupations were given as plantation worker or boat worker, and their ages ranged from fifteen to thirty-

An Exception in the Equation?

one. Thomson obtained permission from the high commissioner for the Western Pacific at Suva for the crew to leave the Solomon Islands. After being declared fit, the six Solomon Islanders signed consent forms to join the army, which included pay conditions. The army determined that the engineer would be paid two pounds per month and the other five men 30 shillings per month. In order for them to enter Brisbane, Thomson had to obtain permission from the Department of the Interior.[24] The enlistment of the six Solomon Islanders finally occurred in Brisbane on 24 November 1941.

Analysis of the process of recruiting Solomon Islanders highlights the continuing racial and colonial dynamics that were being played out in the planning stages of the NTSRU. Although Scott was promoting indigenous capabilities when he proposed the employment of Solomon Islanders, he still subscribed to notions of different races being suited to different climates. The employment listings on the service records overlooked prior skilled jobs the various enlistees had performed and instead implied that they were merely untrained workers. For instance, Papai Lakapoli had already worked as a boatswain, Edwin Richardson had done engineer work at San Cristobal, and Gege was an air force cook prior to formal enlistment.[25] This lack of recognition conformed to colonial attitudes that placed indigenous people, in this case Pacific Islanders, in positions of menial labor and low value. The fact that Thomson required permission for the Pacific Islanders both to depart from the Solomons and to arrive in Australia highlights the continuing colonial administrations' enforcement of race regulations. Even though the individuals had to consent to enlistment, there was no recognition of freedom of movement for the colonial subjects.

The pay issue was one that would cause serious disruption later for the NTSRU because the rates were far lower than for white personnel enlisted in the Australian military. On 24 December 1942, while the *Aroetta* crew was in Townsville, interactions with other servicemen, including black Americans, would influence the Solomon Islanders to protest unanimously against their low wages. Thomson pointed out "(a) That it takes a great deal for these natives to submit a petition unanimously and that, when they do, they cannot be moved. (b) Their morale has suffered and they will not be dependable on active service unless their grievance is removed."[26] The army would grant a pay increase in January 1943, but even that still fell short of equaling the pay of white personnel, and payments would not be retroactive to the date of enlistment. The army's rationale for increasing their pay lay not in the Solomon Islanders' entitlement to higher wages; rather, it sought to quell opposition, which "has had an adverse effect on the efficiency of the unit."[27] The lower pay throughout the Solomon Islanders' tenure reflected the colonial attitude that indigenous labor was clearly not as valuable or as useful as that of as white persons.

Two other non-white crew members would officially enlist in the NTSRU — the Torres Strait Islander Kapiu and the western Arnhem Land Aboriginal man Raiwalla. Thomson described his interest in recruiting Kapiu thus: "He was not only a fine seaman, experienced in sail, but knew the waters off the Arnhem Land coast well. He was also on good terms with the natives of Arnhem Land, and knew their language."[28] One of the conditions of Kapiu's enlistment was that, since he was a Torres Strait Islander, it was the responsibility of the Queensland government, rather than the military, to set his wages.[29] Based on the Queensland government's treatment of other Torres Strait Islander soldiers, it is questionable how much of this money Kapiu actually received.

Raiwalla's enlistment in the NTSRU was also special because of his status as an Aboriginal person. Raiwalla had served Thomson as a guide during his expeditions into Arnhem Land in the 1930s, and they had formed a considerable friendship. Thomson wanted Raiwalla for the unit because he "was a fine hunter and was renowned throughout eastern Arnhem Land for his prowess as a spear fighter in single combat."[30] Raiwalla wound up being the only NTSRU member formally enlisted in the army, and as such he also was the only one to receive training in rifle and bayonet use. The influence of his involvement would prove enormous, and Thomson even stated that his "unfaltering loyalty and whole hearted devotion, more than any other single factor, contributed to the building up of the native unit and the maintenance of order and disci-

An Exception in the Equation?

pline within this."[31] Nowhere in the records is there mention of compensation paid to Raiwalla. With the enrollment of Raiwalla Thomson's non-Yolngu crew was ready to embark on the mission into Arnhem Land. The *Aroetta* left Darwin on 12 February 1942.[32] On 15 February Singapore fell to Japan, and on 19 February Darwin was bombed.

Recruitment and NTSRU Mission Objectives

The first Japanese bombing of Darwin, on 19 February 1942, confirmed northern Australia's status as a frontline in the Second World War. The Australian government and public believed that Japanese invasion was a real possibility. Thomson's plans for Yolngu defense of Arnhem Land, previously conceived of as a last resort, now became the only working plan to engage with potential Japanese entry into the region.

As the *Aroetta* travelled eastward, Thomson's objectives became twofold: to recruit members of the NTSRU and to secure local Yolngu support. Thomson wrote:

> Every effort was made to impress the natives with the armament and striking force of the ship, so that a greatly exaggerated idea of its size and armament would be spread among the people. The natives were shown the racks containing tiers of rifles in the main cabin, and whenever possible machine gun practice was carried out to impress them, particularly at night when the most effective use could be made of tracer ammunition. The object of these demonstrations was to impress upon the natives the fact that the vessel was very much better-equipped and more powerfully armed than the Japanese craft of a somewhat similar type.[33]

Thomson's decision essentially sought to scare Aboriginal people into supporting white Australia over Japan. This suggests that he, like other military officials, questioned Aboriginal loyalties. Thomson's willingness to use "fear" as a means of securing support also puts into question the extent to which Yolngu volunteered to assist versus being coerced to do so. Thomson used his position to create a climate of fear whereby Yolngu would feel compelled to support the NTSRU rather than volunteer without duress. Given the critical situation and strong threat posed by Japan, one may excuse Thomson, because total war necessitated extreme measures to secure Aboriginal support. However, Thomson's lingering suspicion and the somewhat dubious means he used to acquire Yolngu support still raise a question about the extent to which Yolngu volunteered out of goodwill.

Concurrently, Raiwalla journeyed overland from Derby Creek to the Goyder River to recruit other Yolngu. The *Aroetta* continued to travel around Arnhem Land, recruiting at Trial Bay, Caledon Bay, Roper River, and Groote Eylandt. Thomson's aim in recruitment was to select various people "representative of the dominant fighting men of the area" to form the nucleus of a force.[34] Historian Robert Hall attributes Thomson's decision to recruit a small core group thus: "It limited the number of Aboriginal warriors who would be exposed to the stress and cultural shock of military training adapted to white Australian needs."[35] While Hall's point has some merit, it is more likely that Thomson's decision to maintain a small force was a pragmatic one. A smaller force would be easier to train and deploy, and Thomson trusted that in the event of Japanese invasion the NTSRU members could garner the support of their local clans.

One significant issue Thomson confronted when recruiting members for the NTSRU was his need to reverse the government stance that he had promoted during his expeditions of the 1930s. He wrote, "It took some time to convince these people that they could really kill Japanese who landed in this territory, without incurring the ire of the Government, and being visited with yet another punitive expedition."[36] Yolngu hesitancy to kill Japanese was not a reflection of new attitudes toward Japanese, nor was it an indication that Yolngu suddenly supported the white Australian government. Rather, it highlights that Yolngu did not immediately see white Australia as an ally through a common enemy, because for decades their experience with the government had been punitive.

The main means by which Thomson enlisted Yolngu was to consult with regional leaders such as Wonggu and Bindjarpuma. Wonggu was a prominent warrior-leader whom Thomson befriended during the 1930s, and he promised Thomson whatever men and resources he might

An Exception in the Equation?

need. The other significant player whom Thomson approached was the Yolngu outlaw Bindjarpuma. Bindjarpuma had worked as a "freelance" tracker in Arnhem Land for explorers and missionaries since the mid-1920s, giving him a basic knowledge of English. After leaving a mission, Bindjarpuma united outcasts from other clans to form an outlaw gang that raided to steal women and children. Bindjarpuma had made peace with Wonggu after a series of killings in 1936, but in 1938 he broke that peace, killing four of Wonggu's clansmen on a hunting expedition.[37] Thomson described him thus: "Bindjarpuma, also known as 'Slippery' . . . was at this time the most powerful and aggressive man in this part of Arnhem Land, and . . . had for some years led the life of a predatory border chief, making periodical raids on his neighbours and then returning to the hills."[38] Bindjarpuma was suitable for Thomson's purposes for three reasons. First, he clearly had fighting experience and an ability to engage in guerilla warfare against potential Japanese invaders. Second, Bindjarpuma was the leader of a significant number of Yolngu, forming a rival clan to Wonggu's.

The third reason Thomson sought Bindjarpuma's participation in the NTSRU was to reconcile the hostilities in Arnhem Land. Thomson believed it essential that Yolngu unite in opposition to the Japanese not only for the sake of Australia's defense but also to end the ongoing interclan warfare plaguing Arnhem Land. Ending grievances and uniting warring members necessitated a Yolngu ceremony known as a *makaratta*. In order for a makaratta to happen, those who have been wronged must invite the perpetrators' participation. First there is a ceremonious dance; then the offenders must run a gauntlet of spears. Elders of both the runners and the spear throwers monitor the makaratta to ensure that emotions remain calm and to limit injury. If there is no injury during the gauntlet, the runner must offer his thigh for a spearing.[39] David Burrumurra describes his personal experience witnessing a makaratta in the 1930s: "It was a big gathering. I saw so many spears aimed against my brother that it made me feel sorry for him. They all threw their spears but none hit. He was too good; too quick. At the end of the *makarrata* [*sic*] a Marrakulu *Yolngu* put a spear through his thigh."[40] Making Bindjarpuma's men participate in a makaratta demonstrates Thomson working within a customary Yolngu framework in order to ensure a united force. Thomson's use of the makaratta also displayed his anthropological ideas in practice. Rather than urging or imposing a more "peaceful" means to rectify Yolngu grievances, Thomson preferred the established Yolngu system. For Thomson any other means would constitute assimilation, which he adamantly opposed for Yolngu.

Training the NTSRU

By 19 March 1942 Thomson and Raiwalla had recruited the fifty Yolngu men who would form the NTSRU. The group spotted a Japanese long-range reconnaissance flying boat overhead on 16 March, highlighting the continuing fears of invasion and the urgency to train the Yolngu recruits. Thomson remarked, "An appreciation of the situation in the Roper River at this time revealed the fact that it was wide open to any enemy party which might come upstream. No watching organization of any kind existed and there was not even a native camp for the first sixty or seventy miles from the north to give warning of an enemy landing or approach."[41] Thomson's anxieties about the openness of Arnhem Land imply that he stressed the importance of the force to all NTSRU members, giving them a sense of pride, direction, and honor to inspire them to protect their own territory from invasion.

Training the NTSRU was a tricky task because Thomson had only *studied* Yolngu warfare rather than *witnessing* or *partaking* in the experience. He wrote, "It was not intended to attempt, in training these nomadic people, . . . to turn them into orthodox soldiers or train them in parade ground tactics, although they were drilled with the [*Aroetta*] crew, but merely to instil [*sic*] into them the elements of discipline, so that they would be capable of carrying out scouting work in conjunction with regular formations."[42] Thomson only taught basic formal military movements of dress, turns, and attention. To infuse discipline, he instituted regular inspection of kits and weaponry. One of Thomson's drills entailed a long night swim through a mangrove-fringed river to practice silent approach, attack, dispersal, and rendezvous.[43] Historian

Kay Saunders argues that Thomson preferred Yolngu fighting rituals and maneuvers because they would be "the most effective method for guerilla tactics."[44] Thomson's espousal of Yolngu methods also attests to his using the NTSRU as a practical execution of his anthropological ideas. He wanted a Yolngu force to function strictly within a Yolngu framework to reflect the alleged advantages and necessity of preserving Yolngu civilization.

The other significant way in which Thomson adamantly ensured "traditional" Yolngu defense was in his selection of weaponry. Thomson insisted that rather than using conventional "modern" weapons such as rifles, Yolngu should use strictly "traditional" weapons such as spears and spear throwers. A full complement of weapons consisted of one spear thrower, three fighting spears, one wire fish spear, and—whenever possible for hunting—tomahawks, knives, fish lines, and hooks.[45] Hall argues that Thomson did not issue rifles and other modern weapons so that the Japanese would not recognize the group as an organized military force and retaliate against other Aboriginal people. Hall considers that Thomson "may also have been motivated by his desire to limit the impact of the war upon the Aborigines."[46] Hall's comments have merit, and clearly reservations about Japanese retaliation against Yolngu were a factor in Thomson's decision. Thomson's desire to "preserve" the "customary" Yolngu way of life, however, probably weighed more heavily on his decision not to incorporate modern technology. Thomson allowed some adaptations to traditional weaponry to improve the efficiency of Yolngu armaments and tools. For instance, just the introduction of fish lines and hooks would dramatically improve fishing and in that way change Yolngu cultural practices forever. Additionally, Thomson's one exception to his rule against modern technology was the training of Yolngu to make Molotov cocktails to attack targets such as parked aircraft.[47] The introduction of such devices hints at two important factors consistently at play throughout the NTSRU's existence. First, Thomson introduced outside goods solely to increase the efficiency of techniques and practices Yolngu already utilized. Therefore, Thomson would not introduce materials that might "taint" Yolngu civilization and lead, as he saw it, to degradation. Second, the interests of white Australia still came first. While Thomson clearly was concerned with Yolngu welfare and "protection" of Yolngu vitality and culture, he still understood that fundamentally the NTSRU must serve to protect white Australia by any means necessary.

The other issuances to the Yolngu members of the NTSRU and their daily routine also reflected Thomson's need to balance the interests of the nation and the military with Yolngu personal safety and "cultural preservation." Thomson issued to each NTSRU member two pieces of strong calico, a blanket, and brass discs for identification. He advised them to discard the discs and calico "uniforms" if the Japanese landed so as not to heighten knowledge of the force's existence or of white personnel in the area. Weekly, Thomson provided all members with three sticks of tobacco and tinned food, rice, and flour for when Yolngu were on the *Aroetta* or otherwise unable to hunt. He insisted that whenever possible Yolngu continue to hunt, and he even had Yolngu demonstrate strategies for capturing and preparing food to the Solomon Islander and non-Indigenous crew. Thomson wrote, "They hunted their food for in this way alone they do not become dependent and so lose their skill in hunting and stalking the qualities which are essential to the successful operation of such a force."[48] Daily routines included nightly guards, armament, cargo handling, fueling, swimming with fuel drums, filling freshwater drums, cutting firewood, cleaning the ship, and continuing martial drills. Thomson praised the behavior of the troops, writing, "Not one of the men obtained, or asked for, any leave or relief, there was no grumbling or discontent, but every man in this unit carried out willingly and cheerfully what should have been the work of two men."[49] Thomson's comments demonstrate his deep appreciation for Yolngu efforts and his belief that the NTSRU facilitated the preservation of Yolngu culture. He also underscored the intensive nature of the NTSRU's work.

Thomson participated in many, though not all, of the NTSRU's endeavors. He wrote: "The object of this training was to equip myself to lead the natives on night raids without leaving boot tracks to indicate the presence of a white leader with the natives."[50] Hall asserts that in addition to blending with the troops, Thomson's integration with the NTSRU was necessary for him to preserve his respected status as their leader.[51] Thomson constantly positioned himself as the central figure in the NTSRU — the only man capable of bringing together Yolngu because of his understanding of their culture. This position discounted other influential non-Indigenous persons in Arnhem Land. Nonetheless, this much seems clear: through the course of recruitment and training of NTSRU members, his personality, previous personal connections, respect for Yolngu culture, desire to preserve Yolngu vitality, and concerns for the welfare of Yolngu in the event of Japanese invasion placed him in a privileged position to direct the NTSRU.

Parallel Developments: The North Australia Observer Unit (NAOU)

From 5 to 8 April 1942 the *Aroetta* was in Darwin to accumulate supplies and undertake engine repairs and for Thomson to receive updated orders. Thomson also hoped to obtain some more formal commission for the NTSRU for the sake of boosting Yolngu morale. He wrote, "It was essential to have some permanent establishment for the organisation, and some basis to stimulate a feeling of pride and solidarity which would be provided by a separate colour patch."[52] Military commanders granted Thomson's wish; he received updated orders that officially granted his force the title "Northern Territory Special Reconnaissance Unit," placing it under Thomson's independent command. Thomson's sense of pride in both himself and the force increased tremendously in the wake of these updated orders. He also interpreted them as a sign that the military finally accepted that the NTSRU was more than a last resort, more than a source of cheap colored labor; it was an integral part of the Northern Territory's defense. He wrote:

> Hitherto we had heard nothing but disparagement of this native force. We knew now that our faith in the native force that we had been sent out to raise and which had been so laboriously built up and trained, was shared by the G.O.C. and his staff, and we returned with fresh heart to a task that had proved always exacting and difficult, and often disappointing.[53]

There was a significant line in the new orders that suggests Thomson misconstrued the extent to which the army now relied upon the NTSRU. The orders stated that the NTSRU's mission was "to pave the way for the Independent Companies and other flank forces, and to co-operate with these forces."[54] Therefore, as anthropologist and historian Geoffrey Gray points out, for the military the NTSRU "was seen only as a holding unit until the Independent Companies, and later the North Australia Observation Unit (NAOU), were trained to take over."[55] The role of the NAOU deserves more attention here for two reasons. First, its mission in many ways ran parallel to that of the NTSRU, but on a wider scale and utilizing white soldiers. Second, eventually the NAOU replaced the NTSRU as the primary defense force in Arnhem Land. Unlike the NTSRU the original proposals for the NAOU came in March 1942, *after* Japan's thrust through the Pacific. On 8 April 1942 the Department of the Navy declared the need for regular army listening posts, more wireless sets, more coded transmissions, guerilla training for local residents, and an expansive guerilla defense network across all of north Australia, from Western Australia to Queensland. On 11 May 1942 the Australian Army recruited the enlisted anthropologist W. E. H. Stanner to command the NAOU at a troop level of approximately four hundred. The continuing threat of invasion meant rapid recruitment and training of men for the NAOU. By 3 July 1942 the first company of NAOU men was ready and deployed at Katherine.[56] The quick raising of the NAOU is informative in relation to the NTSRU because military commanders considered the NAOU *the* solution to the allegedly open north coast. There was no discussion about an extant Aboriginal defense network. While it is possible that commanders such as Stanner did not know about the NTSRU's existence at this stage, there must have been someone in the chain of command who could have mentioned that a guerilla force already existed in Arnhem Land. Clearly the military preferred the white defense to the Aboriginal alternative, despite the Aboriginal group's prior experience with guerilla warfare.

While the NAOU parallels the NTSRU in many ways, there are some key differences. The obvious difference is that NAOU members were

An Exception in the Equation?

non-Indigenous, regularly enlisted soldiers, with corresponding pay rates. Although members received weapons training and conventional armaments, their primary purpose was scouting and enemy observation. Commanders specifically ordered NAOU members not to engage Japanese or any other enemy landings.[57] This is a stark contrast to the NTSRU, whose main purpose was to fight a guerilla campaign against Japanese invaders. The willingness to use Aboriginal troops in guerilla warfare implies an appreciation for their skills. It also might suggest that Aboriginal persons — rather than just soldiers — were expendable in the war effort. Another significant objective of the NAOU that differed from the aims of the NTSRU was its emphasis on working with locals — police, station owners, missionaries — to embark on counter-espionage campaigns and to remove local "enemy aliens." The counterespionage campaign specifically targeted local Aboriginal groups because Stanner called for "security control of all native and non-military European and Asiatic population."[58] Concomitantly, the Department of the Navy called for the NAOU to assist in the "rounding up of all uncontrolled aboriginals and half-castes — Detention of all those who are unruly or potentially dangerous — dispersal and segregation of remainder — confiscation of all weapons."[59] The detention of Aboriginal people highlights the continuing distrust white officials felt for Aboriginal people along the north coast. Moreover, the orders do not clarify what constituted an "unruly" or "potentially dangerous" individual, providing for vague interpretation at the discretion of NAOU members.

One might argue that Stanner's directives regarding disloyal Aboriginal people were vague because he personally considered the majority of Aboriginal people to be trustworthy. As Gray points out, "As far as can be determined Stanner took no active role in informing his troops about Aboriginal peoples and their ways of life."[60] One possibility is that Stanner relied on NAOU members' existing knowledge about local Aboriginal people. Stanner's requirements for NAOU recruits stated that "at least one man in each section must whenever possible have personal knowledge of the aboriginal tribes in that sector."[61] The need to understand local Aboriginal customs reflects several possibilities about the NAOU's relationship to Aboriginal people. One is that mentioned above—that knowledge of local Aboriginal people and their attitudes could distinguish "unruly" Aboriginal people from those who supported white Australia. A second possibility is that Stanner hoped that NAOU members could use their cross-cultural relations to hinder Aboriginal involvement in the war. In fact, as Saunders highlights, Stanner claimed: "I did not mean to involve the blacks in the war, though I had permission to do so."[62] The idea that Stanner did not wish to involve Aboriginal people in the war does not hold up under documentary and testimonial scrutiny. For instance, Stanner wrote that "provision must be made also for the employment of aborigines as trackers, interpreters, horse-trailers, agents, etc."[63] Moreover, Gray notes that Stanner's NAOU ultimately employed fifty-nine Aboriginal people, including women.[64] Therefore, Stanner clearly foresaw some role for Aboriginal people in the NAOU.

The third possible rationale for employing NAOU soldiers with knowledge of local Aboriginal people is the most probable. That is, Stanner conceived the involvement of Aboriginal people as "de facto" members to work as auxiliaries with the white enlisted soldiers. This policy was consistent with military regulations regarding Aboriginal enlistment and also continued to center the aims of all defense on the protection of white Australia. Thus, in the NAOU the non-Indigenous personnel were the main fighters and scouts, whereas the NTSRU reserved this fundamental position for Yolngu soldiers. Nonetheless, many of the employment conditions for Aboriginal auxiliaries to NAOU soldiers were almost the same as in the NTSRU. For instance, Aboriginal people taught NAOU soldiers about herbal remedies and techniques for hunting and fishing. Aboriginal people were responsible for seeking and finding fresh water for both the NAOU soldiers and their horses. Payment of Aboriginal employees was often merely a few sticks of tobacco or rations such as flour, rice, sugar, tea, and clothing.[65]

Not all Aboriginal employees were satisfied with these pittance "wages," particularly when they saw the provisions that NAOU members received. NAOU member Eric Wenban recalls what happened once when an Aboriginal worker challenged the disparity:

> I remember that we weren't very fair to Joshua. He was employed as a deckhand on the *Toorbul*, and one day we gave him his rations; six sticks of Nikki-Nikki [tobacco], a tin of condensed milk and some pay. Normally he would have gone away happy but on this day he threw his rations on the ground in disgust and said, "Me want white man tucker, same along you fellas." In those days the black man didn't say things like that, so one of us knocked him to the ground to make him be a good boy.[66]

Wenban admits this was a rare incident because most Aboriginal people did not challenge their unequal treatment so bluntly. The violent response of the non-Indigenous soldier highlights how essential it was for non-Indigenous personnel to preserve the unequal status quo. Just as in the NTSRU, for the NAOU Aboriginal people came to represent a cheap form of colored labor.

This is not to say that all NAOU members abused Aboriginal people. In fact, they often grew to rely on Aboriginal tracking and bush survival skills. As Des Harrison remarks, "You always felt safe when you had an Aborigine with you. You knew that you wouldn't starve."[67] Maurie Vane similarly recalls, "I don't think we travelled anywhere without at least one black tracker. And we'd have more than one, usually two or three. And on some patrols we ended up with a number because the black tracker would have a cousin who'd come along."[68] This begs the question of whether the NAOU soldiers' appreciation for Aboriginal people's skills translated to a wider admiration for the people's cultures and their civilizations' vitality. Personal recollections from various NAOU members provide diverging assessments about the level of respect white soldiers paid to Aboriginal trackers. "Tip" Carty recalls behaving respectfully "because they [Aboriginal people] were capable people in doing what they were doing and the way they lived up there."[69] Reg Oakley considers the extent of positive relations to be associated with maintaining authority: "But we respected them; they respected us too, but if you didn't keep just that little finger of authority there they could well be gone the next morning. If you let them get too familiar with you you was done."[70] Other NAOU members, such as Ron Rogers, found Aboriginal scouts to be undependable: "If they took them out on these places, they used to say, 'The debil-debil's there,' 'Moonlight Maggie lives here,' and if you camped there with them, in the morning you'd find that they'd be gone. So they found the black unreliable."[71] The dependability of Aboriginal scouts also came into question on a more institutional level because the Aboriginal view of distance and time did not conform to non-Indigenous constructs of mileage and hours. An incident when Aboriginal scouts falsely reported seeing a Japanese vessel near Nassua River also tainted superiors' opinions of Aboriginal reliability. Nevertheless, there are some signs that NAOU superiors wanted to end discriminatory practices if doing so would not upset power relations. One order in January 1944 stated: "It is the custom to refer to Male and Female Natives as ('Boong' and 'Gins') respectively. This practice is to cease. The former word in Aboriginal Language, is an opprobrious term corresponding to our 'Bastard' and its use is much resented by the Natives."[72]

The different perspectives from various NAOU members demonstrate that the treatment of Aboriginal people varied on an individual basis. Those who recall positive interactions with Aboriginal people also tended to be those more prone to fight for an end to discrimination and adequate compensation for Aboriginal assistants after the war. On an institutional level, with the exception of Thomson, employment of Aboriginal people continued to represent exploitation of their skills with little concern for preservation of their societies. Employment conditions were quite poor, particularly because their service was unofficial, as opposed to that of enlisted soldiers. Any orders recognizing Aboriginal people's right to respect paid only lip service without offering tangible benefits of egalitarianism or compensation. Most likely the lip service was more about keeping Aboriginal people happy so that they would continue to work for the NAOU without complaints.

As this section has outlined, despite differences of personnel and mission objectives, the NAOU very much paralleled the NTSRU. Both were scouting units in areas devoid of significant white settlement. Both employed Aboriginal people on unequal conditions as scouts. Both grew to rely on Aboriginal knowledge to accomplish the military's goals. Because the NAOU primarily consisted of non-Indigenous soldiers, the military considered it more important as a defense network in the north. By April 1943 the NAOU was maintaining all Northern Territory observer posts except at Daly River. Changing war matters in 1943 would also lead to the reduction and ultimate disbandment of the NAOU. In April 1943 the Northern Territory Force withdrew NAOU forces to the eastern boundary of the Northern Territory. By June 1944 the military had withdrawn all NAOU soldiers except those in Western Australia, and the final troops returned to headquarters by January 1945.[73] For the NAOU, decommission was a result of the reduced Japanese threat to Australia from 1943 to 1945. Although changing war conditions were one reason for the NTSRU's disbandment, the accessibility of white replacements was a more prominent cause.

NTSRU Tensions with Settlers

According to the *Aroetta* deck log, on 8 May 1942 Raiwalla reported that a group of Yolngu from the NTSRU had gone absent without leave. On 10 May 1942 Donald Thomson and Lt. A. E. Palmer traveled to the police depot at Roper River to investigate.[74] What ensued was a month-long drama highlighting the colonial tensions persisting in Arnhem Land. Jim Gibbs, the owner of Urapunga station, had reported a theft to the Roper Bar Police in May 1942. According to Thomson's narrative, "without any evidence other than the supposition of his own station boys he accused the Caledon Bay members of the native force of having entered his property."[75] The "supposition of the station boys" that Caledon Bay Yolngu were thieves reflected continuing negative constructs of "unassimilated" Yolngu as savages. There was no consideration of the fact that these Yolngu worked for the military, or that their mission was to protect Arnhem Land — including Urapunga Station — from Japanese attack. Constable Jack Mahony's police report worried about how the alleged crime would impact the work ethic of Aboriginal laborers in the region. Mahony alleged that the Caledon Bay

NTSRU members "went so far as to issue a challenge to all those who followed, and this seems to have had a demoralizing Psychological effect on the natives in this particular area."[76] Mahony proceeded to investigate the crime based on the flimsy testimony of station workers. There was no presumption of innocence because, as Mahony wrote, "they [Caledon Bay Yolngu] are a very tricky and murderous tribe to have dealings with."[77]

Mahony's investigation worsened the situation and simultaneously highlighted the enduring colonial tensions in Arnhem Land. The police did not treat the NTSRU with the same respect accorded a normal military force. Instead, Mahony intentionally or unintentionally intimidated the Yolngu fighters to the point that they fled for safety. Mahony visited the *Aroetta* unannounced while Thomson was not present. Thomson's narrative states: "When the Police took the unwarranted action of visiting the ship in my absence the natives whose previous experience of the Police was [of the times] when they came to their territory and shot up the area, became uneasy, and a few days later slipped away and set off overland for Caledon Bay."[78] The Yolngu fear of the police underscores the continuing colonial tensions in Arnhem Land. The incident also demonstrates that one cannot separate the Second World War from the wider history of settler-Yolngu relations in Arnhem Land because that prior history was still at play. The common Japanese enemy did not naturally make allies of the Arnhem Land settlers and the Yolngu.

Further investigation upon Thomson's return and intervention revealed that the true culprits were the Aboriginal station workers at Urapunga. They knew of the Caledon Bay Yolngu people's bad reputation and took advantage of their proximity to mastermind the theft and pin the blame on others. Thomson then found the Caledon Bay Yolngu and met with clan Elders to impart the seriousness of their desertion, and all Yolngu returned to the *Aroetta*. Upon their arrival they presented Thomson with a sacred object to ask forgiveness for their desertion.[79] The resolution to the episode continues to demonstrate the complex colonial dynamics at play in Arnhem Land. The culprits, as laborers working for a white employer, represented the theoretically ideal outcome of assimilation because of their subservient working status and "untraditional" mode of living. Arnhem Land resident Alec Boxall, in an oral history interview, described the inhabitants of Urapunga Station thus: "In a place like that [Urapunga] there would probably be a total of 100 population living on the station and round about. Lived together, after all their tribal and family people and Jimmy [Gibbs] was a big white boss. They'd do anything for him and Jimmy would do anything for them."[80] These men's adept manipulation of the situation signified their recognition of settlers' continuing disregard for "traditional" Yolngu—particularly those from Caledon Bay. Both Gibbs and Mahony believed the station hands without question and did not maintain a presumption of innocence. This also highlights their ongoing negative attitudes toward those Aboriginal people who did not mold to the assimilationist ideal. It was only because of Thomson that Mahony investigated further—otherwise the Caledon Bay Yolngu would have been blamed without recourse to defend themselves.

The NTSRU on Patrol

From April to September 1942 the NTSRU embarked on detailed reconnaissance of Arnhem Land both on foot and through coastal patrols aboard the *Aroetta*. Rather than describe at length the patrols and their findings, it is more important to highlight the key aspects of the NTSRU's work. On patrols the NTSRU created small dumps of reserves, such as ammunition, for later guerilla troops to access. The other significant work of the NTSRU was the construction of two small observation posts. Construction of the first base began in late March 1942 at Gulnare Bluff under the command of T. H. Elkington. Gulnare Bluff was approximately six miles from the mouth of the Roper River and therefore served as a good observation post for any vessels approaching the Roper River. Yolngu members of the NTSRU excavated the camp among the rocks and provided an iron roof, camouflaged with tree boughs. Once the works were completed at the end of April, the men installed a wireless set at Gulnare Bluff. Thomson was very proud of the base, particularly given the hardships associated with its location: "Conditions at the o.p. were severe and extremely monotonous. The surrounding country was flat and uninteresting, consisting merely of miles of salt pans and plains intersected with mangroves."[81]

The NTSRU maintained a detachment at Gulnare Bluff under Elkington through June 1942, while the *Aroetta* patrolled other areas of Arnhem Land. Upon Thomson's return he commented, "All the members of the detachment, were in good health, and spirits, but they were suffering severely with the mosquitos [*sic*] which were present in great numbers, and came out in hordes at night, and during the day were much troubled by flies."[82] Despite the hardships, as early as May 1942 Thomson's pride in Gulnare Bluff stimulated Major Walker's interest in acquiring the outpost. On 5 July 1942 Thomson handed over control of Gulnare Bluff, as well as the jurisdiction to patrol the Roper River, to Captain Thompson of No. 4 Independent Company.[83] One might argue that the handover was to relieve Thomson's men of the horrendous conditions at Gulnare Bluff and the concomitant arduous task of guarding so much territory. But the arrival of the independent company merely meant the redeployment of the NTSRU. NAOU members were not as adept as their Yolngu NTSRU counterparts at living in the region. For instance, missionaries had to teach NAOU soldiers how to get horses across the Roper River. The soldiers had to impress a dinghy from Jim Gibbs, the owner of nearby Urapunga station.[84] NAOU members experienced problems similar to those Thomson reported—extreme heat and humidity, a shortage of freshwater, extensive sand flies and mosquitoes. Albert Allen summarized Gulnare Bluff as "the greatest bastard of a place I've ever been in."[85] The conditions became so difficult that in March 1943 the NAOU abandoned the post until the onset of the dry season brought relief from the sand flies and mosquitoes.[86] Given the hardships NAOU members experienced, clearly they were not as suited to patrol the region as the local inhabitants. Nonetheless, the Australian Army preferred the NAOU over the NTSRU when planning for Arnhem Land defense.

An Exception in the Equation?

While the NTSRU continued its patrols through Arnhem Land, Thomson used the opportunity to provide assistance to local Yolngu residents. Thomson considered medical treatment an important means to promote goodwill and friendship without "tainting" Yolngu culture. The most common curable problem to beset Yolngu was yaws, which are skin lesions that disfigure and deform. Thomson wrote, "The people would bring their sick, especially the children who were suffering from yaws, for injections and other treatments."[87] As Thomson summarized, "Even the most difficult and otherwise unapproachable people are often won over by attentions to their children, and at length the natives learn to depend to trust the man who will always help them, and will bring all their troubles to him."[88] Despite his patronizing tone Thomson again demonstrated that he did genuinely care for the well-being of Yolngu, like a father cares for his children.

By July 1942 Thomson recognized that NTSRU members required some respite. He therefore decided to construct a second outpost to maintain a skeleton crew of Yolngu. Others would return to their home territories to "form the nucleus of an efficient coast watching system and . . . by making regular contacts with them on each subsequent patrol they would be available when called upon, to muster their own clansmen in the event of enemy action in the area."[89] On 4 August the *Aroetta* landed at Gray's Camp in Caledon Bay to begin construction of a new base and accompanying garden. The base home would double for storage, and as such the site would provide a sense of permanence for the unit and induce Yolngu to make regular visits. The garden was not meant for Yolngu, but rather for the one white officer who would remain in command at Gray's Camp.[90] Thomson left Gray's Camp under Kapiu's command, telling him, "You must remember that the reason why we have made this station is to make it possible for us to keep in touch with the fighting natives. . . . You must do everything you can to help these people, who have been serving with us, to remember the training we have given them during the last six months."[91] Significantly, Thomson also commanded, "While you are at the station no one but yourself must enter the house except for work. You must always lock the house when you are hunting and leave two natives as guard."[92]

Beginning on 20 September Thomson prepared the *Aroetta* to return to Townsville, and he left Elkington in command of Gray's Camp. He left Elkington with orders similar to those he had bestowed upon Kapiu a month before. He also emphasized the importance of Elkington maintaining close contact with Yolngu at Gray's Camp. He hoped that if war needs warranted it, between two hundred and three hundred fighters could mobilize on short notice.[93] Problems in October 1942 would eventually facilitate Thomson's return to Arnhem Land and a reconsideration of the NTSRU's fate.

Whites in the NTSRU: Divided Reactions to Yolngu

Thomson had been very particular in his selection of non-Indigenous troops for the NTSRU. It was his objective to select men with previous experience dealing with Aboriginal people, both to ensure a positive working relationship and to adhere to his anthropological belief that white men must not taint Yolngu civilization through excessive contact. For the most part Thomson was quite successful in this endeavor. By the end of the NTSRU's tenure Thomson would praise personnel such as Lt. A. E. Palmer as "exceptionally meritorious. . . . He proved such a loyal, efficient, and fearless officer under severe conditions and in many difficult situations, that he set an example to all members of the Unit."[94] Other hints at the positive relations emerge from white NTSRU veteran Gordon Ritchie, who fondly recalled the good work of the Yolngu soldiers: "If a Japanese had come ashore, and we'd told [Aboriginal people] to kill them, I don't think any Japs would've ever got back on the boat again because they'd killed them before."[95] Ritchie even traveled through Arnhem Land on a goodwill mission in the late 1990s to reconnect with families of other NTSRU soldiers and other Yolngu who helped in the war effort.[96] These positive relationships demonstrate that goodwill and mutual understanding were possible through the NTSRU's mission.

Another incident involving the NTSRU, however, demonstrates that

An Exception in the Equation?

not all white soldiers respected the work of the Yolngu fighters. In late November 1942 Landforces Melbourne received the following telegram from the North-West Mobile Force (NORFORCE) in Darwin:

ELKINGTON REPORTED THROUGH RAAF GROOTE NATIVES ENTERED HOUSE STOLE TOBACCO 22 NOV. RINGLEADER TURNED NASTY TOOK TO BUSH WITH GANG. . . . N A O U VESSEL FROM ROPER BEEN DES-PATCHED INVESTIGATE BUT DO NOT WISH PLACE UNTR(A)IN(E)D N A O U PERS THOMSON AREA. CONSIDER ONE THOMSONS PERS AT TOWNSVILLE SHOULD RETURN GROOTE BY FLYING BOAT.[97]

Several airmen from Groote Eylandt traveled to Caledon Bay and wound up staying until the end of November 1942. Thomson traveled to Gray's Camp at the end of December, and at that time he discovered some serious problems that had been occurring since at least October 1942.

Elkington had failed to padlock the storage shed while out hunting, so some Yolngu entered and stole small amounts of food and tobacco. The thefts escalated until Elkington threatened the Yolngu men with his gun. Thomson wrote, "Further troubles also occured [*sic*] between this N.C.O. and the natives with whom he adopted an aggressive over-bearing attitude."[98] Elkington's hostile reaction to the theft was not an isolated incident. Thomson's narrative reports two excerpts from Elk-ington's logs at Caledon Bay:

14 Oct 1942: "Slippery [Bindjarpuma] and his gang turned up today, and this afternoon had a 'makarat[t]a' at the beginning of which there was nearly a row, so had to put my foot down and use the .303 as umpire."

18 Oct 1942: "Slippery very peeved because some one wants to pinch his wife; bullets are the only things these people understand; they need a good swift kick in the crutch [*sic*]."[99]

Both of Elkington's remarks demonstrate general hostility toward Yolngu culture and its mores, such as the makaratta. Elkington's violent ap-proach via the .303 gun and his aggressive attitude demonstrate the con-tinuing racist attitudes of some white soldiers. Despite working with Yolngu for over six months, Elkington disrespected Yolngu and used force as a means of conflict resolution. He did not follow military protocol or Yolngu cultural norms, but rather reflected the colonial tensions of an era that clearly had not passed.

Thomson's response to the theft and his subsequent clash with Elkington represented a more enlightened approach to Aboriginal affairs. Thomson wrote, "It was essential for purposes of discipline and control, that once the natives knew that I was aware that they had stolen these things, some adequate form of punishment should be meted out."[100] When Thomson returned to Caledon Bay, he sent out the most reliable Yolngu to bring back the perpetrators of the crimes at Gray's Camp. They all returned and confessed their guilt to Thomson. He then administered punishments to three groups of Yolngu. The first he assigned to hard labor in the garden at Gray's Camp and assessed a "fine" of fish, and he restricted their hunting privileges. Thomson required the second group to hand over a large sea-going canoe as a token of apology. For the third group, led by Bindjarpuma, Thomson wrote:

> I talked to them, stressing the enormity of the betrayal of the trust I, as their leader, had placed in them, and the depth of my own humiliation. Then I told them that I was taking forty two of their finest spears in expiation of their offence. After this I sent them back to their own camp. For twenty four hours they remained. If they had left instantly, this would have portended trouble. As it was, within twenty four hours we were on our old footing except that my own prestige had been greatly increased throughout the whole area.[101]

Thomson dealt with the situation in a manner similar to the way he dealt with other matters. He used Yolngu customary norms regarding payback to make restitution for wrongs committed. Not only was Thomson's approach effective in contrast to Elkington's, but it also demonstrated that it was possible for whites and Yolngu to work together with mutual respect. As Elkington's attitude demonstrates, most white persons were not ready to take that extra step of adopting facets of Aboriginal customary law in their dealings. Rather, white personnel maintained attitudes of superiority that demonstrated settler colonial attitudes, and the changing circumstances relating to the war did not change their feelings or behavior. The contrast between Elkington's attitudes and those of Ritchie, Palmer, and Thomson demonstrates that perhaps there was hope for a change in white Australian attitudes, but not all of white Australia was ready to embrace Aboriginal soldiers.

The period from January to April 1943 saw the final stage of the NTSRU. Strained from his work over a sixteen-month period, Thomson requested to be relieved of command of the NTSRU. Because of the changing tide of the war and the new accessibility of the NAOU, commanders were keen to accept Thomson's recommendations. They still wanted the NTSRU members to serve as informal coastwatchers, but the official unit would terminate within months. Instead, the *Aroetta* would serve a new coastal reconnaissance unit with an exclusively white crew as replacements for Thomson's Pacific Islander recruits.[102] Between January and April 1943 the *Aroetta* embarked on its final patrols of Arnhem Land. The vessel then returned to Darwin, repatriating Yolngu soldiers along the way. In Darwin the Pacific Islander crew received repatriation benefits. Thomson soon went on a new mission to Dutch New Guinea.[103] The NTSRU officially no longer existed.

Anomalies and Consistencies

A persistent theme in this chapter has been the question of the extent (if any) to which the NTSRU represented an exception, examining the NTSRU through the eyes of Donald Thomson. As Thomson traveled through Arnhem Land, he consistently highlighted the need for Yolngu to take responsibility for their homeland's protection. Thomson was successful in garnering support from Yolngu because of his ability to work within the Yolngu customary framework. He knew which leaders to approach, and he even managed to join warring clans. When it came time to train troops, Thomson insisted that they use Yolngu customary weapons and fighting techniques. Thomson was wrong in his personal assessment that the NTSRU was unique. Although the missions of the NAOU and NTSRU varied slightly, their main tactics were similar in that they required long-term bush survival. Moreover, the NAOU witnessed similar exploitation of Aboriginal knowledge and skills through the inequitable "employment" of Aboriginal people as trackers and laborers to assist NAOU members. The Australian military would grow to favor the white NAOU, and eventually its presence would supersede the role of Aboriginal defense networks such as the NTSRU.

The matter of defense of the Australian north coast is still relevant, and in 1981 the Australian Army once again turned to Aboriginal knowledge for defense with the formation of North-West Mobile Force (NORFORCE). NORFORCE's mission is to scout and defend areas of northern Australia susceptible to potential invasion. A 1996 article in the *Australian Magazine* praised the success of NORFORCE: "Army recruitment officers, working closely with tribal elders on the settlements, find no shortage of suitable applicants."[104] Despite the successful deployment of NORFORCE since the mid-1980s, it was not until 1992 that the Australian government finally awarded medals and back pay to surviving NTSRU veterans and families.[105] Hence the stories of the NAOU and the NTSRU provide insight into the issue of exceptionalism in relation to military regulations against Aboriginal participation in the war. They demonstrate that despite the personal concerns of leaders such as Thomson and Stanner, the macroview of Aboriginal participation in the war still emphasized preservation of white Australia without concern for the impact on Aboriginal societies.

1. Flight lieutenant Dr. Donald Thomson,
commander and organizer of the Northern
Territory Special Reconnaissance Unit.
Courtesy Australian War Memorial,
Negative Number 000712.

2. The Northern Territory Special Reconnaissance
Unit unloading fuel at the base at Garthalala,
Northeastern Arnhem Land, Australia, 1942.
Rraywala [Raiwalla] at left. Photograph by D. F.
Thomson. Courtesy of the Thomson family and
Museum Victoria (TPH 2725).

3. (*Opposite top*) The Northern Territory Special
Reconnaissance Unit on parade, Caledon Bay,
Northeastern Arnhem Land, 1942. Photograph by
D. F. Thomson. Courtesy of the Thomson family
and Museum Victoria (TPH 2729).

4. (*Opposite bottom*) The Northern Territory
Special Reconnaissance Unit ashore in
Northeastern Arnhem Land, Australia, 1942.
Photograph by D. F. Thomson. Courtesy of the
Thomson family and Museum Victoria (TPH 2731).

5. (*Opposite top*) The Northern Territory Special Reconnaissance Unit setting out on reconnaissance, Northeastern Arnhem Land, Australia, 1942. Photograph by D. F. Thomson. Courtesy of the Thomson family and Museum Victoria (TPH 2736).

6. (*Opposite bottom*) The Northern Territory Special Reconnaissance Unit being given instruction against machine-gun fire by Sgt. Gordon Ritchie, Northeastern Arnhem Land, Australia. Photograph by D. F. Thomson. Courtesy of the Thomson family and Museum Victoria (TPH 2760).

7. (*Above*) The Northern Territory Special Reconnaissance Unit at base camp, Northeastern Arnhem Land, Australia, 1942. Rraywala {Raiwalla] and Wonggu in center. Photograph by D. F. Thomson. Courtesy of the Thomson family and Museum Victoria (TPH 2763).

8. Aboriginal men unloading petrol from a
barge at Milingimbi, 1943. The Aboriginal man
to the right of the bulldozer is Roy Wangirra of
Milingimbi. Photograph by William Donald
Martin. Courtesy Australian War Memorial,
Negative Number 060524.

CHAPTER 2. Allies at War

De Facto Yolngu Soldiers

To the best of my knowledge and belief there are no enemy Aliens resident in this District [Arnhem Land].—CONST. JAMES H. EDWARDS, 1 February 1942[1]

Learned Evac party at Roper + N.A. [Native Affairs] make no more arrangements—washed their hands of them [Aboriginal people]!
—MARGARET SOMERVILLE, 11 March 1942[2]

Something well we had to do that. Those things gonna go new Australia way. This is what happened. We really, you know, with the Yolngu, by killing them. The beginning the history was still there, the stories was still there, they still talk about the history, what happened in the past, they still talking about in the present. So when the peoples see this story, or read this story, in the library, or from the tape, giving them a picture to reflect it back and think back what happened in the beginning—in the past, with people, Yolngu people were follow walking side by side with the army people. And this is history for the people to think because this wasn't just happening here. It happens all over the world.—OLD CHARLIE[3]

In 1946 the Northern Territory administration proclaimed: "From enquiries made it appears that no Northern Territory aboriginals served with the Australian Defence Forces. A number of aboriginals actually worked for the Army in the Northern Territory, but they were employed under conditions prescribed by the Aboriginals Ordinance and were not enlisted in the Forces."[4] This statement highlights how, immediately after the war ended, national memory erased Aboriginal people from the Second World War. From the standpoint of formal enlistment just the case of Raiwalla and the NTSRU disproves the declaration. Additionally, white Australia procured the support of Aboriginal people in official and unofficial capacities as manual laborers, members of guerilla patrols, scouts, and servicemen.

The limited settler presence in Arnhem Land waned during the war, initially because many missionaries evacuated the coastal settlements following the bombing of Darwin. Not all missionaries left, and both the station at Urapunga and the Roper River police depot continued to operate. The war also brought an influx of white servicemen stationed at Groote Eylandt and Katherine, and later others who embarked on the construction of the Gove airstrip south of Yirrkala. One might speculate that the relations between settlers and Yolngu would be amicable, given their common Japanese enemy and desire to defend the region. One might also consider that they would unite against this enemy — as Donald Thomson envisioned — and usher in a new era of positive relations between the two races. Yet settlers in Arnhem Land persisted in their belittling and distrust of Yolngu, police maintained their hostile attitudes, and missionaries still insisted on assimilating Yolngu as second-class individuals. There were some positive signs — particularly when one examines the relationship between Yolngu and white servicemen working in Arnhem Land. Furthermore, Yolngu oral testimony of the war demonstrates ways in which Yolngu fondly recalled their war efforts acting as coastwatchers, rescuing crashed airmen, and actively firing upon Japanese bombers. But positive case studies coincide with negative occurrences of servicemen or missionaries abusing Yolngu while exploiting their cheap labor.

Servicemen-Yolngu Relations:
Advancement or Continued "Othering"?

Although the NTSRU was the key defense mechanism in Arnhem Land from 1942 to 1943, there were other servicemen in the vicinity. The NAOU eventually became the main patroller by 1943; there were troops in Katherine continually, and RAAF men occupied the aerodrome on Groote Eylandt throughout the war. As early as 1940 the rising number of military personnel in Arnhem Land paralleled a mounting demand for Yolngu assistance in coastwatching and performing tasks such as building huts or clearing runways.[5] Rev. G. R. Harris noted that by May 1942 the majority of persons traveling to Arnhem Land were RAAF servicemen. He wrote, "At this time — May, June, July 1942 — the R.A.A.F. personnel, and many others, were on 'tenterhooks' fully expecting a Japanese invasion of the Eylandt, reckoning the strategy of the Japs would be to take over the Eylandt and then to cut off the top of Australia by invading the country through the Roper River Valley westwards."[6] By August 1942 the permanent presence of the RAAF on Groote Eylandt had elicited labor from the majority of men from the mission station. At the RAAF base Aboriginal people worked in the gardens, guarded the aerodrome, and prepared to ambush potential Japanese invaders. Some men performed tasks with the boats and Catalinas, such as painting, and RAAF men occasionally rewarded them with a glass of beer. By July 1945 Groote Eylandt Aboriginal men were working to clear a new airstrip on the north side of the island.[7]

The integral role Aboriginal people played in the maintenance of the RAAF base at Groote Eylandt demonstrates the continuing need for Aboriginal support, labor, and skills in managing the frontline of north Australia. Mission records, government papers, and oral testimony provide similar examples of the significant role Aboriginal people played across Arnhem Land and complementary cross-cultural relations. In western Arnhem Land an RAAF unit constructed a forty-five-hundred-yard aerodrome three kilometers from the Milingimbi Mission.[8] Some of the most significant dealings between Yolngu and RAAF soldiers occurred near Yirrkala. In 1940 RAAF Squadron No. 13 began construction of an air base at Melville Bay — present-day Gove — seven kilometers from Yirrkala. According to the Yolngu Elder Wandjuk Marika, it was he who showed the site to RAAF servicemen:

> A long time after that, later, maybe around about 1943, a boat arrived at Yirrkala. It was still during the War. The Balanda tried to find a man like me or somebody else to guide them and show them about the place. They were looking for a good place, flat country or gravel, so they could make an airstrip. *I* did that work because I was the only one who spoke English to translate to show them.[9]

The massive task of constructing airbases such as Gove and Milingimbi required significant Aboriginal labor. Aboriginal Elder Gerry Blitner recollects the construction of Milingimbi:

> This is the type of strip that we built because the air force asked the mission. I had about 86 men altogether, and the strip that we built was 1700 yards long by 200 yards wide and was all done with hand work — shovel, hoe, pick, crowbar — and the only machinery they gave us was a forest cable. So there'd be about six men on this forest cable, and if the cable broke you'd get the whole forest cable on top of you, about 700 pound in weight. And it was hard yacker. We started in 1939, and by 1942 we had it completely finished.[10]

RAAF personnel recall positive relations between the two cultures. Kevin Graham states, "They [Yolngu] were happy to see it [Gove airstrip] I think. Happy to see the bulk of the RAAF people. They had a good time there. They had a good time with us too because later on when the liberty ships came in we got a jeep to run around and whenever you moved you were crowded with piccaninnies, they were all over you."[11]

The increasing interactions between Aboriginal and white servicemen at Groote Eylandt, Milingimbi, and Gove—similar to what was occurring across the north—provided some tangible benefits for Aboriginal people. Aboriginal people at Groote Eylandt had access to the RAAF doctor and dentist. When an American intelligence officer visited in June and July 1943, he brought flour as a gift for the Aboriginal residents. H. C. Evans reported that the work at Gove advanced skills in industry, construction, and English for those Yolngu in the Yirrkala area. Some Aboriginal women learned new skills through their work in wireless telegraphy stations.[12] Overall the interracial relationships brought a sense of appreciation to the non-Indigenous soldiers stationed in Arnhem Land. Gough Whitlam, prime minister of Australia from 1972 to 1975, was one such member of the RAAF stationed at Gove in 1944, and he summarized the situation in 1997: "The inhabitants and the intruders went their own ways but their contacts were friendly and healthy."[13] A 1943 article in the newspaper *Argus* expressed appreciation: "In the acid test of war they have proved themselves steadfast, resourceful, and possessed of a high degree of intelligence. They have played a magnificent, though unspectacular, part in holding this country against enemy attack."[14] The positive reception of white servicemen and journalists demonstrated the *potential* for a newfound relationship between white and Aboriginal Australia based on successful war workings. That gratitude, however, would prove to be little more than superficial rhetoric.

While war work brought new skills to Yolngu in Arnhem Land, it did little to provide social or economic opportunities because of the continuing colonial restrictions imposed on Aboriginal labor. One example is the ongoing matter of wages and compensation. Rev. G. R. Harris wrote, "Most of the able bodied men were now 'pressed' into service with the R.A.A.F. [on Groote]. They were employed in making bomb dumps, clearing roads, off loading supplies from ships, to accompany guards on duty, and in the kitchen. Initially these men worked for their keep, that is food and tobacco."[15] Nonetheless, Aboriginal people often suffered food and clothing shortages for months without complaint. Those Aboriginal people who helped in the creation of the airfields at Milingimbi received only tobacco as payment.[16] For those lucky enough to receive wages, there was difficulty accessing the money because of the manner in which the military administered funds. The RAAF billed the majority of laborers on Groote Eylandt simply as handling drums of fuel, which did not account for the wide array of work noted above. Even the task of handling drums took a harsh toll on laborers. Blitner describes such work at Milingimbi: "Had to roll them over the beaches. And we lost toenails, fingernails, toe joints, you know, from the bombs rolling on it."[17] The RAAF only paid the limited wages to missionary societies, which in turn placed the money into trust rather than dispensing the funds to Aboriginal laborers. Even though the Yolngu did not see the wages directly, missionaries still complained about the inadequate level of compensation. Rev. Len Harris wrote, "Some 12 single natives have been employed by the R.A.A.F. of late but I trust even less natives will be required soon. I do not consider the sum of 5/- per week plus food as adequate payment for their work."[18] That the military was not providing sufficient recompense to Aboriginal people highlights the continuing colonial attitudes adopted by the military in its relationship with Aboriginal auxiliary labor.

Thus overall the interactions between white servicemen and Indigenous laborers proved to be symptomatic of "appreciative colonialism." The white servicemen recognized the assistance of Aboriginal people, and they were more than happy to acknowledge it in reports. Yet they never saw the Aboriginal people as equals. The lack of adequate compensation for Indigenous laborers continued to highlight their inequitable situation despite their performing vital tasks necessary both for the military's defense of Arnhem Land and for the survival of non-Indigenous troops in the region. With the exception of the NTSRU none of the Aboriginal residents were actually formally commissioned by the Australian military, propagating the idea that Aboriginal men were only acceptable as a cheap source of colored labor.

An Inconvenient Interruption: Missionaries and Yolngu

The presence of servicemen and the new relationships also had an impact on the extant relationships between Yolngu and missionaries because the war interrupted the assimilationist work of missionaries. By the onset of the Second World War the various missionary denominations were well and truly embedded in Arnhem Land. Religious denominations and individual missionaries took different approaches to the promotion of assimilation. For instance, the Methodist Gordon Sweeney remarked that "our policy, given out by the chairman, was to interfere as little as possible with Aboriginal culture, but learn as much as we could of it and work with it."[19] A document entitled "Report on Goulburn Island Mission. 1933" similarly stated, "*Tribal Organization*. This apparently survives more or less completely amongst the natives who come in contact with the Mission. The Mission policy aims at avoiding interference in this matter."[20] The Anglican Church Missionary Society policy espoused a similar blend of the two cultures to "advance" Yolngu civilization. Its 1944 "Constitution and Policy" declared "that the natives shall not be cut off from their own tribal life, but rather that the Mission shall aim at the far more difficult task of helping those natives to build up the Kingdom of God on the basis of their old tribal organisation and customs, where those are not opposed to Christianity."[21] On Groote Eylandt the proposed aim was normative assimilation instead of the blending of two cultures. Donald Fowler observed, "The ultimate objective in this aboriginal work [on Groote Eylandt] is to have all the aborigines housed in small huts made by themselves and for all the aborigines to be able to work in the Mission gardens and not only be paid for this work but to receive a portion of the production."[22] The Methodist reverend T. T. Webb summarized all missionaries' aims succinctly: "We believe that by the time white settlement reaches this district, as no doubt ultimately [it] will do, these aborigines will in a measure at least be prepared for its impact, and will be able to take some worth-while place in it."[23]

The missionaries at Croker Island, Goulburn Island, Milingimbi, Yirrkala, and Groote Eylandt had been more than happy to work as coastwatchers for Naval Intelligence since late 1940. Often the Aboriginal residents at the missions assisted in coastwatching duties in the missions' surrounding areas. Prior to the Japanese bombings in early 1943 most missionaries did not express sentiments of fear or danger. The defensive needs of the region became more pronounced when the Japanese bombed Milingimbi and Goulburn Island in early 1943.[24]

While missionaries recognized that war matters necessitated military employment of Aboriginal people, they were not wholly pleased with servicemen's "interference" with missionary assimilationist work. Subtle disapproval emerged in statements such as the Groote Eylandt report: "All native men available working for R.A.A.F. Three only on Mission work."[25] Taken in isolation this entry might be read as a neutral statement of fact, but other log entries imply a pattern of displeasure. For instance, another record from June 1943 states: "Chapel services begin [at] sunrise in order to get attendance from increased number of natives working for R.A.A.F."[26] The pattern emerging through such records suggests that missionaries perceived Aboriginal work with the RAAF as an inconvenience. One might think that Aboriginal work with white servicemen would be compatible with the missionaries' ultimate aim of assimilation. Working with non-Indigenous personnel would expose Aboriginal people to the work ethic of white society, while concurrently providing skills and "detribalizing" Indigenous people. But missionaries considered that Aboriginal people were not ready for contact with white persons. Rev. Len Harris of Groote Eylandt, for instance, worried "that their contact with white people is not in their best interests."[27] Missionaries believed that exposure to white military personnel would corrupt and demoralize Aboriginal people. Thus even during the war missionaries continued to exhibit historian Pam Oliver's observation that "mission success hinged in part on controlling contact between Aboriginals and outsiders in order that the Christian influence could become the dominant external influence on Aboriginal people."[28]

To limit interracial contact, Rupert Kentish of Yirrkala required Yolngu laborers to return at night to camps that were off-limits to servicemen. Kentish still found it difficult to enforce this regulation. One incident validates to an extent missionary desires to inhibit interracial contact. Rev. Canon G. R. Harris wrote:

> Rupert [Kentish] told us of the difficulty he experienced in keeping the [Yirrkala] Mission area free of Army personnel: of one instance of a soldier who came into the grounds shooting with a .303 rifle — of how he knocked the fellow down, threw him into the back of a utility, drove him to Army Headquarters and said to the c.o., "Keep your men at home." Thereafter he had much less bother in keeping the Army off the Mission![29]

Clearly in this situation the intervention of the missionary protected Yolngu residents from potential violence. This is the only violent episode mentioned in documents from Arnhem Land during the war; as such it is unclear whether or not it was an isolated incident. Certainly, if the military acted aggressively, then missionary mediation was in the best interests of Yolngu. As mentioned earlier, documents and oral testimony suggest that generally the relations among Yolngu and the armed forces were constructive. While in this case missionary intervention seems justified, in other cases interference may have been unwarranted or excessive.

Missionaries also worried that after the war Yolngu would not be content to return to their mission jobs and conditions. Even before the war missionaries such as Webb worried that Aboriginal men who could find work would move to Darwin. This would lead to a "brain drain" as the most skilled and intelligent Aboriginal people left behind a deteriorating populace. Leonard Kentish similarly wrote in 1937, "One wonders what chances tribal groups will have of surviving for long when some of their best youths are allowed to detribalise in the town and lose all vital contact with their own people."[30] The fears of Yolngu displeasure eventually did come to fruition at Yirrkala. In 1951 H. C. Evans wrote that Yolngu who returned to the mission after working with the RAAF at Gove were disgruntled because they could not use the skills they had learned or earn wages for mission work.[31] The missionary attitude suggests that concern for Yolngu welfare was a consideration secondary to the assimilationist work of the individual missions. Rather than support

Allies at War

Yolngu enterprise and opportunities for Yolngu to advance themselves through work with white servicemen, missionaries preferred that they stay at the missions. Thus the assimilation(ism) advocated by missionaries entailed their vision of Aboriginal Christian workers remaining subservient to missionaries in Arnhem Land. The war did not change missionaries' colonial attitudes, nor did it usher in any sense of self-determination for those Aboriginal people still associated with missions.

Overall the war did not change the perspective of missionaries toward Aboriginal people. They continued their assimilationist efforts even when confronting the possibility of Japanese invasion. Missionaries allowed the military to use the missions' Indigenous residents as labor, but they were not happy about this because they believed it interfered with the delicate assimilationist work of the missions. Furthermore, similar to the situation with settlers in Arnhem Land, the hard work of Aboriginal people did not change missionaries' determination or their colonial relationship with Aboriginal people. They continued to pursue their interests without consideration for Indigenous agency or self-determination. Thus for a brief period the war disrupted missionary work in the region, but it led to neither a cessation nor a drastic modification of the missionaries' approach in their determination to assimilate Aboriginal people.

Yolngu Motivations to Serve

Until this point the focus of this chapter has been the way that white Australia constructed Aboriginal people and maintained an unequal relationship with them leading up to and during the Second World War. The government, missionaries, anthropologists, settlers, military commanders, and individual servicemen all had their own motives and attitudes toward Aboriginal people during the war. Clearly they all to some degree shaped the behavior of Aboriginal people. Yet the perspective of one group of actors remains that requires consideration—the Yolngu themselves. Yolngu histories—like all Indigenous histories—exist in numerous forms, the most accessible in oral tradition because they are oral societies. There are a variety of questions and issues to consider when analyzing oral traditions and oral history. First is the issue of memory and its reliability; this is a predicament to consider with written history as well, but the difficulty is more complex with oral history. Whereas in written history it is only important to regard how memory has transformed an author until the point of writing, with oral tradition it is essential to bear in mind the memories of multiple storytellers leading up to the contemporary teller. As with any written historical record the period of its telling influences oral tradition. It is even more significant for oral history, however, because the time that has passed since the recollected events also has a bearing on the narrators' accounts. Oral historians deem the amalgamation of storytellers in oral societies to be a boon instead of a drawback because the oral tradition relates to something greater than just the narrator's life experience, including the knowledge and existence of his or her predecessors as well. When using oral testimonies, one must also consider the problems associated with footage, tapes, or transcripts edited for format and content. This is a problem analogous to the altering of written sources, but it is more significant because oral history requires a combination of senses to comprehend meaning—visual and auditory.[32]

The Aboriginal stories contained in the rest of this chapter by no means represent a complete account of Yolngu Second World War history, nor do they present a unanimous Yolngu version of events. Rather, the stories contained are a starting point from which to extrapolate wider understandings of Yolngu perceptions of the war and its impact on Yolngu-Balanda relations. As oral historian Heather Goodall advocated in 2002: "The most constructive outcome of such [oral history] collaborations, whether community or academic and whatever the technical form of their products, would be to have created opportunities for further conversations and exchange."[33]

The seemingly simple question of why Yolngu chose to participate in the war effort engenders other queries. Whose war was this anyway? Whose land was being defended? Was there really a choice about whether or not to help? The first reason Yolngu supported the war was that Yolngu were not *members* of the general Australian war effort so

Allies at War

much as they were *allies*. They were allies because of their common hatred for the Japanese and their desire to protect their own homeland—Arnhem Land. Phyllis Batumbil, an Elder now residing at Mata Mata outstation in Arnhem Land, hints that Yolngu assistance in the war was an alliance between Yolngu fighters and servicemen, rather than Yolngu working as employees of white Australia: "And they knew that they'll help the Army—Balanda [white persons] army, Australian, and Americans, and New Zealand because they knew that Japanese were the enemy."[34] The concept of Yolngu as allies during the war challenges the colonial relationship conceived by white Australia; Yolngu as allies rather than as adjuncts or conscripts repositions Yolngu as significant actors in Arnhem Land. This contradicts the colonial perception of Yolngu as subjects who would be expected to serve white Australia's military unquestionably. Yolngu did not see their relationship with Balanda as based on the colonial footing that white Australia assumed. To return to a quote from Donald Thomson in 1937: "These natives believe that they are still living under their own laws, and that they have no reason to recognise the fact that a new regime has taken over their affairs."[35]

Under the paradigm of Yolngu custodianship over Arnhem Land, the threat of Japanese attack would amount to an act of war against Yolngu. NTSRU veteran Mowarra Gamanbarr recollects, "Thomson said, 'If they win, this will be Japanese country, and our children won't have the chance to learn our culture.' Thomson said we had to combine with the white people. This was never done before. We all went to war, fighting for this country of ours."[36] Mowarra's assertion places a common goal for both white Australia and Yolngu, but it does so in a framework of defense of Yolngu land. Gerry Blitner also describes the Japanese in Arnhem Land as a threat to Aboriginal people:

> The Japs used to tell the [Torres Strait] Islanders, and the Aboriginals, that we are not coming back to fight Aboriginals, Torres Strait Islanders; we are coming back to fight the white man. I don't know whether they were trying to gain favor with them or not. But not one Aboriginal or Islander took their side. Everybody was ready to fight the Japs, and we knew that they were our enemies.[37]

Comments that further allude to Aboriginal defense of their own land come from George Djalming, who recalls the Japanese attack on Milingimbi: "We see 'em ground come up; bing bing bing bing bing bing bing [demonstrating machine-gun fire]. I'll get up. Run tree. We come up. Ah, miss 'em. Ah miss 'em. Japan fight. Aboriginal people fight. European people fight. Aboriginal people, me fight. I'll get up. What? Me now, I kill them. Fight Japan. [Throws spear]."[38] Djalming frames Japan's raid on Milingimbi as a direct assault on Aboriginal people. Mata Mata Elder Old Charlie similarly remarks, "Because the air force, army, they were all there, Yolngu people, and they were just, you know, giving them the bullet. Bombing, bombing Milingimbi. So people has to scattered everywhere because of the bombing."[39] Consequently, both Old Charlie and Djalming posit Yolngu decisions to fight Japan alongside Europeans as self-defense of Yolngu and their land. Batumbil actually refers to the Second World War not as one conflict, but as two parallel struggles: "Yeah, that was during the war, Balanda—same time, Balanda war ga Yolngu war. So, you know, Balanda ga Yolngu lived together, sleep with together, to fight against Japanese."[40]

The common Japanese enemy also had a profound impact on the internal affairs of Yolngu. Yolngu themselves used the war as an opportunity to halt the cycles of violence that Batumbil refers to as the Yolngu war: "They used to go from place to place moving around. And, you know, like, they used to have the war because of, like, other men—other clans stolen another clan's woman. And it comes to Yolngu justice, to get the payback."[41] Old Charlie describes how Raiwalla and Thomson convinced Yolngu that fighting with Balanda could end the Yolngu war:

> So they were fighting—so the people were still enemy to each other, so when the Balanda came around they bring them together. And the person by the name of Raiwalla said, "Please, you're not going to cause any trouble for yourself because we are heading to fight with the Balanda." We'll help them to sneak it in because we know more than they know how to kill people in the night [Batumbil chuckles]. . . . "Don't have to fight Yolngu to Yolngu again." So we'll help the Balanda. So we'll join the force. Yolngu will join the force, with the Balanda.[42]

Like the alliance between Australian soldiers and Yolngu the war proved an effective means of uniting warring factions of Yolngu society. Nonetheless, as Batumbil remarks, "that, that was only temporary. To going in with them. Just to get, you know, get rid of the Japanese. And then, you know, they got back again."[43] Although Yolngu unity was ephemeral, the mutual Japanese adversary clearly proved an effective motivation to mobilize major segments of Yolngu society.

Not all participation was voluntary. Yolngu oral history brings to light the possibility that Thomson's narrative was not entirely forthcoming and that there were elements of compulsion in the NTSRU. This is not to say that Yolngu oral history dismisses Thomson's account of events, as some testimonies align well with Thomson's account. But Batumbil hints at obligatory Yolngu work for Balanda: "This what happened. Because, you know, they were follower only, with the Balanda. Yolngu. And they had only one choice, they had only choice, which is to fight to withstand the Japanese only the night, during the night. And, that was the different."[44] For the NTSRU Batumbil and Old Charlie both describe an intermediary's role in coercing Yolngu participation. That individual was not Donald Thomson — it was Raiwalla. Batumbil states:

> PHYLLIS BATUMBIL: That time [pause]. They were only forced; that was made by forced.
>
> NOAH RISEMAN: Made by force?
>
> PB: Yeah. Forced. Because, the someone was, I forgot his name. One of Yolngu, he was in Darwin. And, he made bosses.
>
> NR: Raiwalla?
>
> PB: Yo, Raiwalla. Now you thinking [chuckle]. Raiwalla. He's the one, he's the Yolngu that . . . told the other Yolngu about the war. So what he got the message from those two, I think it's from the military or corporal people, in Darwin, from the boss. And he went back to Ramingining and to Milingimbi. And, you know, he spread the news around, news around to the other Yolngu. And, that way he made it decision to gather up the men only to join in the war.[45]

Batumbil rationalizes Raiwalla's allegedly forceful role in securing Yolngu assistance because of the critical situation and the common

Japanese threat. Old Charlie elaborates on Raiwalla's significance as liaison:

OLD CHARLIE: Because the Army Air Force forced them to join them.

NOAH RISEMAN: They forced them?

PHYLLIS BATUMBIL: They forced them to come and join with us.

OC: So, when they choose that Yolngu people, because they wanted to have them — to put them as their guide people. Because people can, you know, like, watch out, seen over day and night. So the Balanda they were following them. [PB and OC discussing.] So they were chosen for reason. Because they had that Yolngu to Yolngu killing and they picked up from each clan all their leaders to involve them [in] the war with Balanda. And also they had to explain to them first where they taking them, why they collecting them for. To explain to them, to the person; who was the person name? Raiwalla, eh? So he was the only person that he understands the English. So like, you know, like interpreter person when they, the force talk to him, telling him what's going on. So he explain to the Yolngu people, and that's why Yolngu people they come to agreement and join in to the force.

NOAH: So they trusted Raiwalla?

OLD CHARLIE: Yes, they trusted. So he explained to those people who are people, the boss people. Told them about the people that they no one really knows about their technique.[46]

Old Charlie's and Batumbil's accounts dispute portions of Thomson's narrative, but the versions are not irreconcilable. The narratives only differ over the extent to which Raiwalla, rather than Thomson, was the key figure in securing NTSRU members. Thomson probably saw Raiwalla as an agent only, not an independent player, as most Yolngu would see him. Although both Old Charlie and Batumbil use the word *force* in the context of their family members' decisions to join the NTSRU, the rest of their comments do not suggest any resentment about Yolngu enlistment. Quite the contrary — their stories imply genuine support for Raiwalla's recruitment efforts. To merge the two positions, it would seem most likely that Raiwalla expressed the gravity of the wartime situation. His account may have made Yolngu *feel* as though they had no

Allies at War

choice but to sign up for the war effort. Thus, a better word to illustrate the conditions of Yolngu participation in the NTSRU would be *coercion* rather than force or compulsion. The idea of Raiwalla coercing Yolngu support still problematizes Thomson's portrayal of Yolngu participating enthusiastically, but it does not adversely contradict his narrative. If anything, the conflicting oral testimony promotes the role of Raiwalla as more significant to the war effort than Thomson suggests.

Yolngu Rescuing Crashed Airmen

Aboriginal people on the north coast had a profound impact on the war effort. One benefit of local Aboriginal assistance and knowledge was the capture of Japanese who were shot down. Tiwi Islanders provided many of the stories regarding capture of Japanese soldiers because their proximity to Darwin made the islands the likely site of crashed Japanese planes. The first Japanese prisoner ever captured on Australian soil—a pilot shot down during the first raid on Darwin, on 19 February 1942—crashed on Melville Island, off the coast of Darwin.[47] The stories end with Aboriginal pride in their heroic actions capturing Japanese prisoners. This satisfaction and dignity were common across north Australia because of the Aboriginal people's valiant work. James Gaykamangu of Milingimbi states:

> Yeah, actually, when the Japanese was hit, and somewhere landed either this plane, or the other plane, and the Japanese was captured by non-Aboriginal air force, and army, who were there also combined services were done during the war—both Aboriginal, and non-Aboriginal. Our people joined air force and army because, as we can tell, that northern Aboriginal coastline was the frontline during the Second World War. And, the result of that—Japanese never ever taken Australian, northern part of Australia.[48]

Gaykamangu's assessment of the Yolngu people's integral role in defending the north may exaggerate the degree to which their work saved Australia. Yet his reflections demonstrate how Yolngu perceive their fundamental position as defenders of the north and protectors of Aboriginal and white Australia.

While Tiwi Islanders successfully captured Japanese prisoners, Yolngu patrols in Arnhem Land successfully rescued crashed American and Australian pilots. The missionaries were very significant prior to such patrols because, as Wandjuk Marika explains, they taught Yolngu: "Japan red circle, British blue and white, and America stars. We were all taught to look for the planes."[49] Missionary Harold Thornell of Yirrkala describes a Yolngu patrol known as the Black Watch rescuing American lieutenant Clarence Sanford. Thornell describes how at Sanford's pre-mission briefing his commanding officer indicated that the Aboriginal residents of Caledon Bay were all hostile. After crashing in Caledon Bay, Sanford saw two Aboriginal men approaching and feared they would murder him. Instead, upon seeing a crucifix around Sanford's neck, they made friendly overtures and escorted him to safety at Yirrkala Mission.[50]

Sanford's rescue also receives considerable attention in Yolngu oral tradition. Roy Marika summarizes:

> He was came into the church, and of the church, and the community. Rather [pause], killem him. If he could have hand the Japanese here, they could've killed him easy. But they found the two friend, our friends, an American. Because they know problem, was Japanese problem in Caledon Bay before and been killem the problem to all Aboriginal people.[51]

Wandjuk Marika relays the story in more detail:

> When we looked up again a second time we saw the man jump out by parachute and then Roy's brother held my hand tightly and dragged me into the bush. But I said, "No, no, that's the Balanda (white man) jumped from the plane by parachute, we go to look and try to find him." . . .
>
> And then we walk along the beach until we find this man lying on the beach, on the edge of the water. He only have a singlet and shorts. . . .
>
> And then I asked him, "Hey, can you tell us who you is? Australian or British or somebody else?" And he answer us right back, "I am Japanese." So! I was ready to spear him with my fish spear, then he said, "No, no, no, no, I am an American." . . .

Then I said, "OK, come towards me." And then he said, "I lose my plane. It drown right on the sea and I just been swim, maybe one mile or two." He was very lucky he landed on the shore safely, otherwise he would have died right there in the middle of the sea. . . .

Half way there, at Mount Dundas, or Djawulpa, I sent one of Roy's brothers to go and get shoes for him and also water and food because by this time he was very sick. I thought we were going to keep on going but he said to me, "OK Wandjuk—I'm so tired. You tricked me, you're going to take me to the Japanese camp."

And I said, "No, no, no we're not going to take you to the Japanese camp, we're taking you to the mission." . . .

And he said to me, "I won't believe you." Sounds like he called me a "black bastard." But I didn't take any notice of what he was saying because he was so tired.[52]

Marika's story is enlightening for its portrayal of non-Indigenous persons as well as Yolngu during the war. It is highly instructive that the American did not know whether or not Yolngu were allies in the war. His mistrust underscores the denigrating colonial attitudes plaguing both the settlers and in this situation American allies of the settlers. From the Yolngu side the story demonstrates great courage and perseverance in supporting the war effort. Despite the hardships and despite the American pilot's crude comments and resistance, Marika and his friends stayed with the man to ensure he received help. They were also willing to kill him when they thought he was Japanese. Thus their loyalty to local missionaries translated to unquestioning hostility toward Japanese and to support for Australia's ally—the United States.

Analysis of a non-Indigenous account of another Yolngu rescue raises similar issues. George Booth's book describes how he and two other RAAF servicemen survived a plane crash near Caledon Bay on 19 May 1942. Their initial reaction was fear of the local Aboriginal people because of one pilot's knowledge of the Caledon Bay killings of 1932. There are also some suggestions that Booth and his men feared cannibalism. They determined that their best chance for survival would be to make their way to the mission at Elcho Island, "because official policy has been to encourage them [Aboriginal people at missions] to rescue people like ourselves."[53] After twenty-five days traveling on their own, enduring hardship and injury, the three men reached a Yolngu camp on Elcho Island. On day twenty-six an Aboriginal man with the mission name Paddy and the Yolngu name Matui came to their rescue. To convince Matui to take them to Milingimbi, Booth and his men offered him trade goods upon arrival at Milingimbi. Booth writes:

> "Paddy! You take us longa Milingimbi, we get you plenty good tucker, plenty good baccy! Look!" Frank showed Paddy a handful of coins.
>
> Paddy's grin grew even wider. "Me takem, me got plenty canoe. Me catchem Milingimbi, plenty baccy!"[54]

Booth's narrative thus implies that Matui was helping the survivors grudgingly until they bribed him. He furthers this suggestion when he describes how the journey went slowly until Frank asked Matui what goods he wanted. Matui listed a number of materials, including sugar, rice, blankets, tomahawks, silk, razors, flour, tobacco, axes, matches, beads, calico, wire, and even mirrors.[55] Booth's incorporation of Matui's alleged greediness suggests self-interest in providing assistance to the surviving servicemen. It is likely that Booth misjudged Matui's motives for providing assistance because many other Yolngu offered rescue support without seeking recompense. Given Matui's knowledge of the war, it is probable he was ready to assist Booth and his men regardless of reimbursement. Booth's descriptions of Matui's strenuous efforts during the canoe journey — "to paddle a heavy canoe, single handed, for most of that stifling day must have taken him to the limits of his endurance" — demonstrate that Matui went above and beyond the call of duty.[56] Unfortunately, despite press coverage in June 1942, there was little mention of the role Aboriginal people played in Booth's rescue. Even as a remarkable story of survival against the odds emerged during the war, the media reports essentially erased the integral Aboriginal role.

Another story of rescue comes from western Arnhem Land. Lazarus Lamilami describes the rescue of American pilots near Croker Island Mission:

> In the afternoon we saw a big bomber circling the Mission. It wasn't very long before we could see something white in the sky up to the north. People were bailing out with their parachutes. We counted them—one, two, three, four, five, six. Then the plane came down. It couldn't let its wheels down. It landed on its belly and caught fire. . . .
>
> . . . When we got out in the clear, we could see the plane—it was still in flames and smoke was coming out. We went up close and we could see a man just lying there, moaning to himself. We could see his brains working. He must have jumped out just before the plane caught on fire. There were four inside—two pilots in front got burnt, and one beside his machine gun and one beside the wireless. . . .
>
> Then we went looking for the other men who had come down in their parachutes. One man had come down in the creek and the tide had swept him right out. He managed to get back to the beach, and we picked him up. We swam over the creek and we could hear someone calling. We found another man just around the point. Another man we found walking along the beach, and one landed just beside a cliff and managed to get back.[57]

Lamilami's story, like Marika's and other similar testimonies, demonstrates the pivotal role of Aboriginal people in the north. Their intimate knowledge of the land and survival skills were critical, and it was difficult for non-Indigenous personnel to mimic such feats.

These stories of Aboriginal people rescuing Americans and Australians highlight Yolngu and other Aboriginal goodwill toward Balanda amid the continuing backdrop of settler colonialism. On an interpersonal level the rescue of Allied servicemen broke down negative attitudes and stereotypes for those men who were fortunate enough to receive Yolngu assistance. The incidents themselves forced Balanda to confront their prejudices when they reacted aggressively or grudgingly toward Yolngu. In the end they appreciated the Yolngu war effort in a way most other Balanda would never understand. These individuals were neither influential nor numerous enough to change macrostructures of settler colonialism. While Yolngu valiantly served their allies in a common struggle against Japan, their partners could see Aboriginal people only as their subordinates.

Yolngu as Victims of Japanese Assaults

As the custodians and primary inhabitants of Arnhem Land, Yolngu were also the principal victims of Japanese assaults on the region. They may not have been the chief target, but their civilian status mattered little to Japanese bombers. Given that two Yolngu died and at least three were injured in the three 1943 raids on Milingimbi, it seems reasonable for Yolngu to have considered the attacks as acts of aggression against Yolngu.[58] Eva Number One, Djambarrpuyngu, describes the Japanese bombing of Milingimbi:

> INTERVIEWER: What were you doing when they came?
>
> EVA: Nearly walk, yeah. Some people they bin walk, behind one. "They bin coming now, plane, yeah. Oh yeah, Japanese coming now, comin'." Yeah, they bin reckon: "Oh Japanese coming now. Come on, all you mob. Come on, run away from mango tree now, yeah. They bin coming, shooting me." Yeah.
>
> INTERVIEWER: Where did you go? Did you climb a tree, or into a hole, or into the truck, or what?
>
> EVA: In the middle. In the tree, yeah, big one mango tree same like this, see. They bin going inside, and sit here, taking up baby and little girl and little boy: "Come on, sit here," mother and father, like, talk, for children, yeah, "Mummy, mummy!" "Oh, don't cry, don't cry." Mummy and father, like that. They bin bombing now. . . . They bin coming more planes again, coming back and bombing, large one, like, yeah. Oh, everything they bin burn, houses, petrol. They bin no good place here, yeah. But one week more they, Milingimbi now, in the bush, one week wait, they bin call. . . . Air Force, yeah, like captain, eh, yeah. They bin call, tell missionary. Oh, all people coming back now, because Japanese, all finish now. They bin fighting long way now.[59]

Old Charlie describes how Yolngu learned from the experience at Milingimbi to protect other areas such as the Wessel Islands:

> Those people that they were in the boat, they didn't . . . get killed in the boat. But people were killed in Milingimbi and in Darwin by bombing. Think about Milingimbi and all those little islands they dropped the bombs, to each islands. . . . Wessel Island no one's got killed because of the, lot of planes came and guns, they only drops the bombs . . . along the coast. So the same boat . . . took the people around from each clan, when it crossed to Wessel, and there's a place called Arakala[?]. That boat—they put that boat into a small creek to hide it in, hide away, so they won't see it. That's where the people got saved and the boat. So every, like, midnight, people are—they sneaking out from the creek, not the daylight, but every night, every like . . . after twelve or one, they sail back here to the same spot, Ramingining. They doing the same thing. Every night they have to move from place to place, not during the day. They not day, only night time they said that's the lucky one. . . . So wherever the boats are like getting their break, they have to stop there, have to get the leaves of the trees and put the leaves to cover the boat with, because, you know, Japanese used to fly over them and the Japanese could [see] that it wasn't a boat, look that's a rock. Because, you know, the leaves covers all the shapes of the boats and the people. Now, like, the Japanese they won't recognize or realize that that was a boat because, you know, they chopped the big trees and they put over it, covered the boats in.[60]

Old Charlie's story demonstrates how the Japanese attack on Milingimbi represented a threat to all Yolngu. The camouflage tactics at the Wessel Islands reveal Yolngu ingenuity in the wake of a sense of urgency. Yolngu saw the pressing need to defend themselves from assault and took necessary precautions. They knew they were in harm's way and, unlike white Australia's indifference toward Aboriginal survival, sought the preservation of their families and society.

Learning Hidden Histories: Yolngu with Guns!

"Hidden histories" are rich oral stories that, while well known in certain Aboriginal communities, have received little dissemination in the wider Australian community. One could consider many of the stories already presented in this chapter as hidden histories because of their lack of prominence in mainstream narratives of Australian, Northern Territory, Aboriginal, or Pacific War history. The following stories are even more profound because they challenge readers' knowledge, confront non-Indigenous sources, and reveal remarkable situations from the Second World War in Arnhem Land.

The first significant story is from Phyllis Batumbil, who describes defense measures at the Wessel Islands:

PHYLLIS BATUMBIL: Yeah. So, he was the first Yolngu throughout Arnhem Land knows how to handle a big machine because, you know, he was tall, solid, that's why the Balanda taught him that old man. His name's Dhapa. They want him to be in charge. So, he was the Yolngu military to overseeing that the force. So, there were about four or five Yolngu going in with Balanda in Wessel. And he was the person . . . that he was handling the machine gun firing at the Japanese [planes].

NOAH RISEMAN: . . . Why did the Balanda have him fire at Japanese instead of them firing at the Japanese?

PB: Well because, like, you know, Japanese can easily saw Balanda. Down there, from above, because you know they put the spotlight headlights in the plane to see clear below. And Balanda they hide themselves away and they put Yolngu outside because it's, you know, something that they won't see who's firing. Our skin, our color, is too hard to see in the dark [chuckles]. And that was surprise for them, for the Japanese, to see just only the firing of the gun and not the person [chuckles].

NR: So it was mostly at night?

PB: Yeah, mostly at night. Because during the day Balanda turn to the firing at them. But during the night it's Yolngu turn. Instead of, you know, spearing them, he used the machine gun to fire the planes.

NR: Did they ever shoot any planes down?

PB: He did. He did about two or three planes. . . . Yeah. So that's why they put him as a military person in charge. And no one ever brought that story out. No one ever brought the history about him, or that history about him.

Allies at War

NR: Did he ever get a medal or anything?

PB: No. Because of his name wasn't brought out, challenged.[61]

Batumbil's testimony presents a new picture of Yolngu work during the war. White accounts focus on Aboriginal people performing unskilled tasks or engaging in patrols through inhospitable regions. There is no mention in any non-Indigenous records of Aboriginal people receiving weapons training or of them firing on Japanese planes overhead. Batumbil's story presents Yolngu as natural candidates for night defense because their black skins served as concealment. She also implies discontent that those Yolngu who performed the defense at Wessel never received recognition or compensation. Batumbil's story thus presents Yolngu not as unskilled adjuncts, but rather as soldiers on par with their white allies. They performed the same tasks yet received no credit.

The idea of Balanda giving Aboriginal people guns is not isolated to Batumbil's story. Keith Willey makes a desultory reference to a group of Aboriginal men armed with .303 rifles who patrolled from Darwin to Arnhem Land.[62] A dance on Bathurst Island that commemorates the Second World War reenacts Japanese planes overhead through arm movements. Then the dancers take long sticks and aim them at the sky. As they point at the sky, they motion as if the sticks were machine guns. Some singers mimic the sound of gunfire while others sing, "The planes are coming! The planes are coming! Shoot them! Shoot them!"[63] More definitive descriptions of guns also emerge in the oral testimony of Old Charlie:

OLD CHARLIE: No. But they [Balanda] teach them [Yolngu] how to use the gun. It's bit hard for them to, you know, to throw spear at Japanese. Bit difficult for them, for Balanda. So, Balanda they teach Yolngu how to handle the gun, and how to fire with the gun. . . . So people then they learned, the young generations from the, because they learned first how to handle the gun.

NOAH RISEMAN: What happened to the guns when the war was over?

OC: They took it back. . . . When the war's over they took everything back.[64]

The recurring references to Balanda arming Yolngu raise the question of why these and similar stories have not reached the public domain. One possible reason is that north Australian Second World War history—Aboriginal and non-Indigenous alike—has often disappeared from the collective memory of Pacific War history. The more likely reason is that the idea of arming Yolngu contravened general military and colonial policies of the Second World War epoch. Given the contemporaneous constructs of Yolngu as savages, it seems unlikely that white Australia would welcome news that servicemen were arming Yolngu. Moreover, despite some persons of mixed descent circumventing regulations and serving in normal units, just the idea of Aboriginal servicemen contravened regulations against enlistment of persons not of substantial European origin or descent. The structural distrust of Aboriginal people and the ongoing colonial project meant not only that white servicemen had to disarm Yolngu after the war but also that after the war the idea of Yolngu with guns would disappear.

More Hidden Histories: Yolngu
Omissions from the Written Records

Discussions with Batumbil also exposed the participation of persons in the NTSRU that Thomson overlooks. Batumbil asserts:

> Yeah. Um, I think he [Thomson] . . . had only ideas to speak with the Caledon people. Because they were, they all mixture people, mix the clan. And, something important real thing like the people that he missed us to be included. So, people can see, then you know this is something that we want to identify ourselves, because of this. So that's between you know like the big gap. Some names they show, and some not. Like, you, what you just heard, that my father and who was one who was handling the machine gun in Wessel.[65]

At first it seemed as though Batumbil was talking about non-NTSRU Yolngu. Further discussion, however, revealed that she was referring both to non-NTSRU Yolngu and to members of the force omitted from Thomson's narrative. She and Old Charlie later listed at least three members of the force, named Birrikitji, Buwatpuy, and Ḻiyakarany. Why Thomson did not list these people is unclear. Perhaps they were not primary trainees of Thomson and Raiwalla. Maybe Thomson did not know their names. Possibly Batumbil and Old Charlie confused the NTSRU with different forces such as the NAOU or the RAAF. Regardless, the testimony reveals that Thomson's narrative is not the complete story of Yolngu in the war, and as such further work remains to uncover hidden histories from the war. Although such a conclusion may seem self-evident, historiographically Thomson's narrative has been the focal point of histories of the Second World War in Arnhem Land and the role of Yolngu.

Another factor that deserves more considerable attention is the role of Yolngu women in the Second World War. The majority of Yolngu patrols, soldiers, and laborers were men. Accordingly, much of the material from the period leading up to the war primarily considers men as the main actors. Women's role in this book has been primarily acting in the background or, as in the case of Batumbil, as storyteller. Old Charlie and Batumbil also did not provide very detailed or forthcoming information about women in the Second World War:

OLD CHARLIE: On this coast, on this like inland, they left the wives and the kids behind. Only men joined in. But in Wessel Island, they join in.

NOAH RISEMAN: And what did they do? [Phyllis Batumbil and OC discussing.]

OC: Only ladies, only ladies. Talking about the—still talking about this area. They're only kids like the boys, little ones, and their moms. All their dads are disappeared to war.

NR: But the women knew how to survive on their own?

OC: Only the young ones, young kids looked after them. Some kind of like Jonathan here [indicating a Yolngu boy of about twenty-one]. And all the adults they joined in with the army.

NR: Does he know what the women on Wessel Island did? [PB chuckles.]

NR: What's so funny?

PB: The first that I'm telling you about the ladies from Wessel. Because they come as a problem to him. So, I just, you know, I missed him. So what he saying, that he said that the woman's did on Wessel, they stopped in the cave, in the jungle, no one going out, and let them during the night they allow.[66]

The interactions between Batumbil and Old Charlie reveal that even today Yolngu men may not display much knowledge about Yolngu women during the war. It may also reflect cultural practices where women, as bearers of the knowledge, are the only ones allowed to tell the stories. Even so, the limited information indicates that women were capable of surviving long periods in the bush. They did not need men to provide for them, and they felt quite safe from Japanese attack on their own.

Some further information about Yolngu women in the war is available through Thomson's photographs of the NTSRU and from the testimony of NAOU members. Thomson's photographs show women and children—the families of NTSRU soldiers—accompanying the troops. (see illustration 4 in this volume) NAOU veteran Maurie Vane testifies that women and babies often followed NAOU patrols in order not to lose contact with their men serving as trackers. Sometimes the women were so determined that soldiers could not convince them to remain behind. If there were not too many women, then the patrols tolerated their presence.[67] Interactions between Aboriginal women and non-Indigenous servicemen were more serious than Vane suggests. Orders in 1944 clarified that civilian and military penalties for miscegenation and cohabitation under Aboriginal Ordinance 1918–1933 applied to NAOU soldiers.[68] Len Taylor recognized the importance of not fraternizing with women because "that was the first way to get into an argument with the Aborigines."[69] Despite these warnings there is significant evidence that there were sexual relations between white servicemen and Aboriginal women. An anonymous NAOU member writes, "There was some interaction between the troops and the gins. A nineteen-year-old boy in our Company caught gonorrhea and without telling anyone, tried to cure himself with tablets."[70] A military report claimed that 48 percent of the 120 troops in an independent company stationed at the Roper River in 1942 contracted venereal disease.[71] These references to Aboriginal women are brief and, in the case of non-Indigenous primary sources, often degrading. They reveal that Aboriginal women were present on patrols, and their stories must surface to complement the current discourse about the war in the north.

When the War Was Over:
Continuing Colonialism in Arnhem Land

The end of the war entailed the disengagement of non-Indigenous servicemen from Arnhem Land. There was little if any compensation paid to Yolngu for their work; the appreciation servicemen left behind was tokenistic at best. There is evidence that Aboriginal people begrudged the lack of compensation and recognition. Jack Gordon of Katherine commented in 1962: "We fix up camps, dig trenches, carry supplies, build huts and concrete slabs and help find lost soldiers. . . . The Army pay us nothing—just tucker and a bit of tobacco."[72]

Government records also reveal colonial opposition to recognizing the work of NTSRU members. In 1949 the Commonwealth minister for the interior requested that Raiwalla attend the Darwin Anzac Day March "as a mark of respect for the work that Australian aboriginals did for Australia during the difficult period of administration in the Northern Territory during the war."[73] The director of native affairs opposed Raiwalla's participation on the grounds that "Raiwalla is just recovering from two Broken Ribs and is run down in health."[74] It is true that Raiwalla was recovering from injuries sustained from Aboriginal clan violence. Nonetheless, the government made a decision without consulting Raiwalla and instead assumed paternalistic control over his movements. A likely factor in the government's decision was the continuing public opinion that a *Melbourne Herald* article summarized in strident tones: "Anyone who suggested that a full-blooded Northern Territory aboriginal should be taken to a southern capital for any reason was probably signing the native's death warrant."[75] As late as 1963 Raiwalla still had unclaimed pay for his work while he was formally enlisted in the NTSRU. Thus despite Raiwalla's valiant work during the war, the government continued white domination by speaking on Rai-walla's behalf, rather than letting him act for himself in official matters.

Raiwalla's situation is just one example of how the end of the war represented the continuity of settler colonialism. The government policies on paper translated in Arnhem Land to the acceleration of assimilation, enduring harassment from police, and continuing subservience to the interests of settlers. Assimilation policies accelerated especially after Minister for the Territories Paul Hasluck convened a Native Welfare Conference in 1951. Hasluck writes that his goals were "a change towards positive attempts to make life better for them [Aboriginal people and] . . . [a cessation of] treating them as sub-normal people . . . [to] regard[ing] them in the same way as all other Australians."[76] Hasluck addressed Parliament after the Native Welfare Conference: "Assimilation means, in practical terms, that, in the course of time, it is expected that all persons of aboriginal blood or mixed blood in Australia will live like white Australians do."[77] While Hasluck's goals seem noble, the reality of assimilation policy was detrimental to Aboriginal communities. Historian John Murphy argues, "The promise of equality was experienced as a form of cultural genocide."[78] Assimilation in the 1950s and 1960s entailed increasing control of Aboriginal lives under the auspices of "welfare" and intensified child removals.

The sentiments of Aboriginal ex-servicemen in the wake of continuing government prejudice amounted to a combination of pride in their achievements and simultaneous resentment at discrimination. As Gerry Blitner summarizes, "I didn't come out with no bars on my shoulder, no ribbons on my chest, no money in my pocket, no deserved pay, no land to go back to and say this is my land."[79] Aboriginal veteran Cec Fisher summarizes such mixed feelings best in excerpts from two of his poems:

> Granny was treated like a Queen Anzac Day
> See the shiny medals flashing from far away
> Next day they crossed the street racism was back
> Didn't treat her equal just because she was black.
>
> . . . .

His medals he keeps hidden away from prying eyes
No one knows no one sees the tears in his old black eyes
He's been outcast just left by himself to die
Recognition at last black Anzac hold your head high.[80]

Conclusion

As this chapter has demonstrated, any changes to the relationships between Yolngu and whites in Arnhem Land occurred on the individual
level rather than on a macrostructural level. For many Yolngu the presence of the military and consequent employment brought new skills.
Obviously not everyone in Arnhem Land disregarded the Aboriginal
contribution to the war effort. Interactions between Aboriginal people
and servicemen often broke down stereotypes and led to appreciation
of Indigenous services on behalf of individual white servicemen. These
encounters and experiences were significant to change individual view-
points about Aboriginal rights, but they were not considerable enough
to rupture the macrostructures of settler colonialism. On a broader level
labor relations were still rife with exploitative characteristics such as
cheap colored labor and inadequate resources. For missionaries as well
the war did not mark a change in attitudes toward Aboriginal people.
Any appreciation missionaries felt for Aboriginal contributions toward
their defense was overshadowed by their dissatisfaction with servicemen's interference in their assimilationist efforts. The end of the war
continued to be business as usual in Arnhem Land because the structures of settler colonialism remained intact.

There is an eclectic array of Yolngu histories of the Second World
War. The different accounts reveal a variety of motives for Yolngu participation, including defense of Yolngu land, genuine support for Balanda, and possible elements of coercion. The collective sentiment contained within the Yolngu stories points to Yolngu self-perception as
allies of white Australia, rather than as subjects working for the armed
forces. Yolngu accounts of the war describe their participation as cru-
cial in the white Australian and American victory over Japan. This
position seems exaggerated when confronted with the wider events of

the Second World War, but one can also say that white Australia's fear of invasion in 1942 was also exaggerated. Nonetheless, for those men who survived the Second World War because of their Aboriginal saviors, it is quite clear that Yolngu were important allies in the war. Hidden histories—those previously unknown to non-Indigenous Australians—point to omissions from non-Indigenous accounts of the war. The oral testimony in this chapter also contains gaps that deserve further attention, such as the position of Yolngu women during the conflict. The Aboriginal testimonies taken in total reveal a need for white Australia to reexamine existing histories of the Second World War and to find ways to incorporate, juxtapose, and reconcile Aboriginal and non-Indigenous narratives.

One fundamental question still deserves attention: why are the stories in this chapter—even those previously published—still on the periphery of white Australia's history of the Second World War? The Northern Territory in general has received minimal attention in mainstream Australian history, but there is ample documentation of and increasing interest in the history of the Japanese assaults on Darwin. Texts aimed at redressing the neglect of the Northern Territory effectively portray the war's impact on Darwin and its administration south to Alice Springs. Yet they merely gloss over regions devoid of significant non-Indigenous settlement. Even the Australian War Memorial downplays the extensive Aboriginal participation in the war—only a single glass case in the Second World War gallery addresses it. The exhibit reads, "Indigenous Australians used their knowledge of the bush to help observer units and to rescue crashed airmen. Their service went mostly unnoticed."[81] Although the display acknowledges the underappreciation of Aboriginal participation, the exhibit continues to downplay the integral responsibility of Aboriginal people, casting them as mere auxiliaries to non-Indigenous soldiers. It also continues to neglect the rich diversity of experiences of Aboriginal people in the war. This chapter presents only some pieces of the story, but clearly there is a great deal more work to be done to continue sharing Aboriginal histories of war.

Allies at War

CHAPTER 3. Black Skins, Black Work

Papuan and New Guinean Labor

We saw the masta soldiers dying and the Japanese dying and [we] were very frightened. Blood was like water and we were completely soaked in it. Where were we to hide? We just laid on the ground and moved along on our stomachs. If we raised our heads bullets would have got us in no time. — ABRAHAM PAP[1]

The Japanese caught village men and forced them to make gardens. They used men at the airfield at Tobera and at other places there, and one more place in the town. It was hard work. It was hard work indeed. We were surprised to see the Japanese way of working. After work started at 8 o'clock, the men just repeated actions of bending their backs and standing up straight. The Japanese said in Japanese, "Cut! Cut!" They formed us into a long line and gave us knives. When the boss said, "Kakare!", we bent our backs, then worked, worked, worked. Nobody could rest. — JACOB TIMELE[2]

They put this man in my care and I led him down the track. The photograph was taken near Siremi bridge. We went on walking until the Japanese started fighting and we hid beside the track. Shells were bursting all around us. When it was safe to go on walking he asked for water and I found some. He said he was hungry so I found a biscuit for him. He insisted that I have half and so we shared it. When we reached the hospital at Dobuduru they couldn't help him so they flew him to Port Moresby but there George Whittington died. After the war I went to Port Moresby and I met his widow. She asked me about my children. She said, when your son marries and has a son name him after my husband, George Whittington. And so my son's first child was named George Whittington. Then my daughter named her first child after the widow and my other daughter named her son after me. So the whole story now lives on in my grandchildren. — RAPHAEL OMIBARI[3]

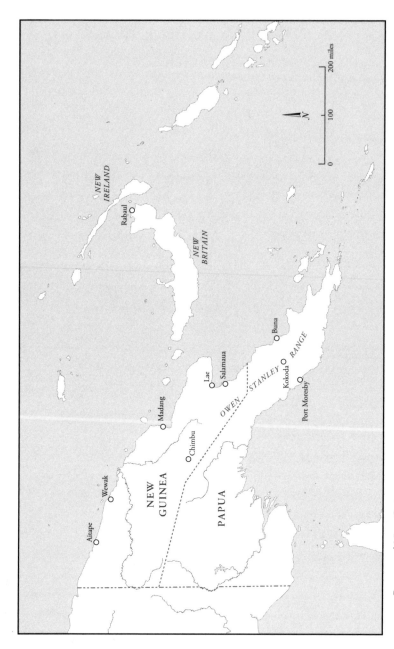

MAP 2. Papua and New Guinea

P apua and New Guinea were the only buffers that stood between Japanese expansion and Australia. The colonies were fragmented; white settlement was sparse; and despite strict regulations regarding labor and movement, Australian administration was minimal. There were only about 4,400 white residents of New Guinea and 1,500 in Papua; approximately 2,000 Chinese resided in New Guinea as well.[4] But the impending Japanese attacks from December 1941 plunged Papua and New Guinea into crisis mode that required significant militarization and labor. Japanese quickly overwhelmed Australian forces to occupy the port of Rabaul on the island of New Britain from 23 January 1942. For the duration of the war the Japanese used Rabaul as a significant base for operations in Papua and New Guinea. Soon thereafter the Japanese also took Lae, the capital of New Guinea, in preparation for an assault on Port Moresby and Tulagi in the nearby British Solomon Islands. Capturing Port Moresby and Tulagi would allow significant raids along Australia's east coast and disrupt the United States' communication with Australia.

A series of events between March and May 1942 changed Japan's tactical approach to Papua and New Guinea. A surprise American bombing raid on 10 March 1942 at Lae sank four Japanese transports and severely damaged a number of other Japanese vessels. The Japanese Navy determined that taking Port Moresby and Tulagi would require aircraft-carrier support. Two months later, in early May 1942, Japan was dealt a serious blow. While Japanese forces successfully invaded Tulagi on 3 and 4 May 1942, from 4–8 May U.S. and Japanese naval aircraft fought the critical Battle of the Coral Sea. Though there was no clear victor, the battle successfully averted Japanese efforts to take Port Moresby by sea. But Papua was not out of the woods yet; Japan still wanted Port Moresby, and its new strategy would entail an overland assault through the Owen Stanley Range of Papua.

Throughout this period and beyond, Papuans and New Guineans were thrust into the thick of action by virtue of Japanese occupation and Allied defense. New Guineans in Japanese-occupied territory were forced to bear the burdens and blessings of Japanese occupation. Papuans and New Guineans in unoccupied territories had to protect both their own livelihoods and the interests of their white Australian mastas. Loyalties throughout the island were divided, and the extent of hardship varied. Local knowledge of terrain and guerilla fighting suddenly became valuable commodities, as both Japanese and Australians sought Papuan and New Guinean support. The manner of recruitment, and means of assistance, varied from hard labor to scouting to actual fighting. Treatment ranged from goodwill and friendship to harsh intimidation and brute force. The duration of this chapter focuses on two significant themes pervading Allied and Japanese employment of Papuan and New Guinean labor. First is the racial construction of Papuans and New Guineans as members of an inferior race naturally inclined toward militarism. Following is the way in which racial constructs of Papuans and New Guineans as primitives played out through the organization and treatment of informal Papuan and New Guinean laborers—working for both Japan and Australia—during the Pacific War. The following chapter examines formal Papuan and New Guinean units, including the Royal Papuan Constabulary, coastwatchers, and the Pacific Islands Regiment.

Racial Constructs of Papuans and New Guineans

Racial discourse about Pacific Islanders contributed considerably to the portrayal of many Pacific Islander cultures as militaristic. Europeans often regarded Melanesians as primitive and thus unsuitable for indirect rule, unlike Polynesians. Historian Amirah Inglis points out that

Black Skins, Black Work

when the Australian Commonwealth debated the Papua Bill in 1903, the administrators consistently referred to Papuans as both childlike and savage. A Royal Commission on Papua in 1906 determined that Papuans were lazy and needed to learn work habits.[5] The discourse about Papuans and New Guineans changed over the course of Australia's colonial project in Papua and New Guinea to suit the goals of the administration. Brenda Johnson Clay argues that discourse about inhabitants of New Ireland shifted over three phases: as warlike and savage at the end of the nineteenth century, as lazy but with good bodies during the early period of Australian colonial control, and as weak-bodied victims of nonhumanitarian colonialism in the late 1920s to 1930s.[6] Clay's argument is applicable to both Papua and New Guinea because it demonstrates how racial discourses of the savage or of childlike indigenes reflected the labor needs of the franchise colonies. Racial constructs also rationalized Europeans' control of Papuan and New Guinean labor and laws regulating interracial contact.

The evolution of the racial discourse from one of savagery to one of inferior workers mirrored the growth of the colonial economy and white expansion into the interior. For instance, in the early years of colonization Papuan and New Guinean acts of resistance were often construed as continuing "signs" of alleged savagery. In the 1930s white explorers encountered new groups in the highlands; despite some explorers' and missionaries' praise for highlands cultures, the "savage" discourse continued. As anthropologist Jeffrey Clark summarizes, "The more remote and unknown the natives are, the further from civilization, the blacker, shorter, uglier, and even more violent they become [in discourse]."[7] Clark also observes that constructs of highlanders changed from primitive savages to productive colonial subjects as more entered the labor force. Stella points out that Europeans often rationalized coerced plantation labor "by framing it as 'rescuing' them [laborers] from savagery and the brutal life of their own communities."[8] For instance, Papuan administrator Sir John Hubert Plunkett Murray commented that "an uncivilised people who come into contact with Europeans will inevitably be led, sooner or later, to abandon their old customs and beliefs."[9]

These assimilationist ideas also reflected the ongoing discourse about Australian Indigenous people. As in Australia ideas of assimilation(ism) did not entail promoting indigenous peoples to equal status with whites. Inglis emphasizes that "no amount of giving up dancing and other foolishness, no amount of embracing Christianity, no amount of going to work, or learning English could make the Papuan an equal."[10] Murray himself argued in his 1937-38 annual report that "it would be unwise to give the Papuan a first class education unless the way to advancement is to be fully opened to him. . . . And to give them the same opportunities as we give to Europeans would, under present conditions, be out of the question."[11] Instead what a Papuan could best achieve, in European eyes, was to emulate and mimic Europeans.

Racial constructs of Papuans and New Guineans circa 1940 justified white superiority, segregation of the two races, and the racialization of labor. As Woke Kilasi of the Walingai people on the Huon Peninsula recalls: "Today you mix around with white men. Previously this was not so; the whites and blacks were separated. Today you sit down together, tell stories, and eat together. This was not so in the past."[12] Ideas of the "white man's burden" combined with images of Papuans and New Guineans as primitive, from the Stone Age, childlike, and lacking compassion or gratitude. There were some individuals who did not necessarily mark Papuans and New Guineans as inferior. For instance, a number of anthropologists condemned Australia's treatment of the colonies, alleging that its rac(ial)ist policies perpetuated hardship. But these persons were certainly in the minority, and most were foreigners from the United States or the United Kingdom.[13] Murray acknowledged that not all Papuans were innately inferior but still upheld white supremacy when he stated that "the best Papuans are superior to the worst Europeans, but that Europeans as a whole have an innate superiority over Papuans."[14] These prevalent denigrating attitudes justified abuse of Papuan and New Guinean laborers, which was common practice leading up to and even during the Pacific War. Local settlers took painstaking cautions to ensure that interracial relations did not become too friendly because of notions that "familiarity breeds con-

Black Skins, Black Work

tempt."[15] In contrast to indigenes' role in society, white men's purpose, according to the 1937 *Official Handbook of the Territory of New Guinea*, was "not to labour with his hands, but to direct and control a plentiful and efficient supply of native labour and assist in the government of the country, or to engage in opportunities for trade and commerce from an office desk in a bank or mercantile firm."[16] The preservation of separate spheres was thus central to the continuity of the colonial projects in Papua and New Guinea. The Second World War would rapidly disrupt the separation of indigenes and whites in the public sphere, but as this chapter and the following one reveal, this transformation of black-white roles still preserved the dichotomy of racialized spaces.

The significance of the racial discourse about Papuans and New Guineans relates to the Second World War period in a manner similar to the racial constructs of Yolngu. With exceptions popular white opinion persistently portrayed Pacific Islanders, like Yolngu, as savage, childlike, and inferior to whites. Therefore, leading up to the Second World War colonialism entailed consistent disenfranchisement, disregard, abuse, and disparagement of Pacific Islanders. As for the Yolngu the Second World War would not constitute a rupture of the structures of colonialism for Pacific Islanders; rather, familiar patterns would continue through the progressive exploitation of Papuan and New Guinean skills, labor, and knowledge.

Papuan and New Guinean Uncertainties in War

Across the South Pacific, Pacific Islanders played pivotal roles as coast-watchers, stretcher bearers, hunters, and in many instances soldiers. Like Yolngu in Arnhem Land they worked as *allies* in the war effort, while the Australian and other colonial governments continued to treat them as *subjects* obliged to work for the colonizers. Often the intersection between ally and subject is the point where exploitation of knowledge and labor emerged. Continuing racist constructs of the "primitive other" played a role here, and as in northern Australia there were concerns that Papuan and New Guinean inhabitants would support Japanese invaders. Granted, in some regions that was the reality—but worrying about such an outcome indicates that colonial powers and residents recognized their own position as invaders and agonized about local response to a new imperial presence. Fundamentally, the Papuan and New Guinean contributions to the war effort proved extremely significant, but that effort continued to exhibit unequal power relations. As Stella succinctly summarizes, "The war taught the two races friendship, but this friendship was on the white soldiers' terms."[17]

The Second World War had a dramatic impact across the Pacific, but the focus here is primarily on Papua and New Guinea. By the time of Japan's attack on Pearl Harbor in December 1941 one battalion and one company had arrived in Port Moresby. In January 1942 two more battalions arrived. On 23 January 1942 Japan conquered the New Britain capital of Rabaul and rapidly occupied the islands of New Britain and New Ireland before occupying the northern portion of New Guinea. Australia evacuated white women and children from Papua and New Guinea, as well as all white men in Port Moresby who could not be placed in the military. Japan began bombing Port Moresby on 3 February 1942. On 14 February the civilian administration of Papua ended, and the commanding officer of the eighth military district assumed control.[18] The rest of the war in Papua and New Guinea is the stuff of legend—the Battle of the Coral Sea; the heroism of Australian soldiers on the Kokoda Trail; and Papuans' and New Guineans' assistance as carriers, coastwatchers, and members of the Pacific Islands Regiment.

Papuans and New Guineans did not ask for the war, and many were disillusioned because it was not their conflict. The 1943 pamphlet *You and the Native,* issued to Australian soldiers stationed in Papua and New Guinea, stated: "They [natives] are now in an unfortunate position. This fight is not theirs, and they might well be excused for wanting to keep out of it."[19] Oral testimony from Papua New Guinean John Paliau confirms this: "We didn't understand what the reason was behind this war. The Japanese and Americans knew about it, because this fight was theirs not ours. But for us we were afraid of the bombs and machine guns and other weapons used which affected many of our people."[20] Historian Neville K. Robinson similarly summarizes: "Some villagers were reluctant to help in the war effort because they felt it was none of their business, it was a 'white man's war' and they did not understand how or why it took place."[21] While in hindsight it seems as though Japanese overexpansion made an Allied victory inevitable, at the time this was not so clear. And if Australians living in Papua and New Guinea were uncertain of victory, then for Papuan and New Guinean residents—who did not have access to outside news—the question of who would prevail was even more unclear. As Australian Peter Ryan observed, "Circumstances had made shrewd politicians of these natives, for they were caught between two opposing forces and were determined to side with the ultimate winners."[22] Mwahliye Mungulpe, who resided at Ngahmbole village when the Japanese Army occupied the north coast, recalls:

> We walked back to our villages and called all the people together. We told them what had happened. I did not tell them Australia is finished, because I did not know. Instead, I said, "They say Australia is finished, but when we were at Yakamul we saw some planes flying along the coast and we could see the pilots had white skins." We were very concerned. What would happen to us if we sided with the Japanese and the Australians were not really gone?[23]

In some regions, particularly in northern New Guinea and New Britain, villagers believed even to the very end of the war that the Japanese were stronger than the Allies. In other parts of Japanese-occupied territory loyalties split among villages. In the Sepik district, for instance, some New Guinean police withdrew into villages, some evacuated to Allied areas, and others killed white residents and assumed control of the Sepik region.[24]

Australians were well aware of the strong possibility of Papuans and New Guineans siding with the Japanese against them in war. Alan Hooper, an Australian soldier who later worked with the Papuan Infantry Battalion, remarked, "For them [Orokaivians], treachery and aggression went hand in hand, and sorcery still exerted a more malign influence here than elsewhere."[25] An assessment by R. M. Melrose in August 1941 stated:

A native is not capable of distinguishing between the nationalities of the white races. With him they are just white men — in which definition he includes the Chinese and Japanese. Therefore they are all the same to him and it simply means that the white man in possession for the moment is his overlord. A change of white man simply means a change of overlord.[26]

To ensure Papuan and New Guinean loyalty, the Australian military embarked on a two-pronged campaign to win over the hearts and minds of locals. First, white coastwatchers and patrol officers aimed to garner support by convincing village heads of Australia's capacity to regain control of all New Guinea. Coastwatcher Malcolm Wright reasoned "that it would take the Japanese longer than the seven months that they had been in occupation of New Britain to convert the natives to their ideas."[27] Peter Ryan similarly deduced, "As long as we kept contact with the kanakas they would protect us from the Japanese. Once we lose touch, however, . . . one would hardly be able to blame them if they concluded that the Japanese had won the war."[28]

The other component of the strategy to ensure Papuan and New Guinean loyalty was through propaganda. As one appraisal of the situation in March 1942 stated, "It seems important (if it is not too late) that the natives should be convinced by propaganda methods that the Japanese are their enemies."[29] The propaganda machine shows some interesting parallels and contrasts with the Yolngu example. As the previous chapters reveal, there were certainly concerns about Aboriginal disloyalty and expressions of the need for propaganda. Yet in the Yolngu context it was Donald Thomson who spread propaganda through his Aboriginal intermediaries in Arnhem Land. Although other Aboriginal groups were sent to labor camps, the Yolngu people were never removed from Arnhem Land. In Papua and New Guinea, though, the Australian military flew representatives to Australia to visit army camps, cities, airfields, and shopping centers. The goal was to impress the Papuans and New Guineans with knowledge of new developments in weaponry, ammunition, and factories.[30] The contrasting propaganda methods suggest a stronger sense of urgency and a more pressing need for Papuan and New Guinean labor than for their Yolngu counterparts. The notion of Japanese invading Arnhem Land and Yolngu allying with them was speculative; Japanese were actually attacking Papua and New Guinea and drafting laborers in New Guinea. In regions of Papua and New Guinea where Australia maintained ostensible control throughout the war, loyalty was, for all intents and purposes, ensured. But it would be New Guinea—under Japanese occupation for part, if not all, of the war—that proved the most likely place for Indigenous people to support Japan instead of Australia.

New Guineans Working for the Japanese

The Japanese easily conquered the island of New Britain, establishing the port of Rabaul as Japan's headquarters for operations in Papua and New Guinea. Indigenous people who resided in Rabaul recall the conquest; Joseph Takankan remarks: "The Australians died everywhere like dogs and it was very sad. The fighting was almost over when the Japanese were doing this. They wiped out the Australians and only a few got away. A few fought back until eventually all their bullets were finished and then they threw down their guns and ran away."[31] Roughly 100,000 Japanese (including Koreans and Taiwanese) would live among the 20,000 Indigenous residents in Rabaul and its surroundings. By the end of the war approximately 150,000 Japanese, including captive and civilian labor, would be living in New Guinea. Most of these Japanese were prohibited from mingling with local New Guineans, except when assigned to oversee labor or civilian affairs. The Japanese presence brought a new government and new order to life in occupied New Guinea. Japanese propaganda promoted the Japanese as liberators on a crusade to free colonized peoples throughout Asia and the Pacific.[32] To what extent life was better than under Australia is questionable; indeed, as anthropologists Marty Zelenietz and Hisafumi Saito discovered while conducting fieldwork interviews, recollections of Japanese occupation vary not only among groups but also depending upon the racial background of the interviewer. Kilenge people from New Britain gave neutral or favorable assessments to a Japanese interviewer while providing harsh reflections on Japanese occupation to white researchers.[33] Zelenietz's and Saito's experience is important to take into account when analyzing oral recollections of the war in Papua New Guinea. Yet the congruence of multiple oral testimonies about the war suggests an incredibly complex situation and varied experiences in relation to the Japanese–New Guinean experience. Belying the complex relationships, as historian Hiromitsu Iwamoto summarizes, "the Japanese never planned to be 'liberators' but only to be better 'masters' than their white counter-parts because they thought that the economic gains were more important than ruling New Guineans."[34]

Japanese racial constructs of New Guineans were, in many ways, not much different from white Australian constructs. The Japanese considered villagers to be inferior savages, sometimes subhuman. Flt. Sgt. Yamaguchi Keizo commented, "The village showed no sign of civilization. . . . How on earth does such a miserable life exist in the 20th century?"[35] Japanese impressions of New Guineans changed somewhat once individuals began to intermingle. In some instances Japanese attitudes toward New Guinean civilization improved. Pvt. Yoshikazu Tamura wrote in his diary in 1943: "Everybody says the natives look very vicious at first, but are pleased to find out that they are really gentle and innocent. The way they live seems to be primitive."[36] The messages of primitiveness combined with the Japanese party line about Japan's mission to improve the lot of the colonized across the Pacific. Kikuo Kajizuka, a captain in the Japanese Army, recalls: "We were also told that the Papua New Guinea native people were blacks and were very primitive people. The official case of our invasion was to liberate these people from the whites."[37] Japanese propaganda at home also pushed the line of liberation and improvement of Papuans' and New Guineans' lives. A Japanese propaganda film from the war stated: "The people of New Guinea are learning to grow rice with brilliant results under the guidance of our soldiers. Their sweat and toil contribute much to the growth of our Greater Co-Prosperity Sphere."[38] Thus while the Japanese considered themselves so-called rescuers of the Pacific Islanders, they still had to maintain a racial hierarchy to justify their own subordination of the New Guinean race.

Japanese immediately went to work spreading their propaganda throughout Rabaul and occupied territory in New Guinea. First, they excessively abused captured white prisoners to impress upon the local villagers esteem for Japanese authority. They made promises to teach villagers how to make rice, guns, and knives and how to read and write. They offered rewards of beautiful clothes and sweet rice in exchange for assistance rendered. They promised clothes; shoes; and future industrial factories to manufacture automobiles, ships, and planes. Historian Janice Newton writes about the New Guinean figure Embogi, who supported Japan because of promises to liberate Pacific Islanders from white control.[39] Japanese also used New Guinean superstitions about sorcery to their advantage, claiming that the spirits of Papuan and New Guinean dead went to Japan and that they would be punished if New Guineans did not assist in the war effort. Propaganda also entailed downplaying the strength of Allied forces. Australian Peter Ryan remembers, "The Japanese were spreading stories among the natives that there was scarcely a white man left in New Guinea."[40] Japanese messages to the people of Amele said:

> We Japanese have been sorry for you natives of New Guinea for a long time. We have thought about you a great deal and now have come to help you. Before the Americans [Australians] in this country made laws and restrictions which were wrong. We have come to remedy the injustices that are inflicted on you and to make life good for you. We are your brothers. Your skins and ours are the same. Will you help us with our cargo and show us roads and tracks? Will all your headmen help us pray to God to help us in our work?[41]

In many instances the Japanese bribery and propaganda worked. Villagers accepted Japanese rations, medallions, trousers, coats, and other goods. Villages assumed that when they worked for the Japanese, their previous obligations to Australians officially ceased. In some regions certain villages sided with Japan because rival villages continued to support Australia.[42]

In many other instances New Guinean assistance to Japanese was coerced or forced, rather than voluntary. As coastwatcher Eric Feldt summarizes, "This [Mandated Territory of New Guinea] was now part of the Empire of Nippon, religious and other teachings were to cease, and the natives were to supply labour and food when called upon. There would be no neutrality."[43] In the Sepik Hills coastal men appointed by the Japanese told villagers that they must travel down to the coast, accept Japanese rule, and contribute to the construction of Japanese airstrips. Japanese threatened to destroy villages if their inhabitants helped the Allies. They established a special military police unit of New Guineans called the *kempei-tai*. It was the job of the kempei-tai to travel to villages on behalf of the Japanese command, persecuting the local populations into supporting Japanese rule. Former kempei-tai James Tumat summarizes: "My work was to keep law and order and make sure that people abide by the laws that were set up during the war. I brought people to court."[44]

Although the Australian government was unhappy about local collaboration with Japanese, some settlers did at least understand it. As one anonymous letter in 1945 commented: "I'll grant you that these natives had been working with the Japs, but who can blame them, for it was a case of co-operate or be killed. And besides, what did the white population of New Guinea do for them when the Japs invaded? — nothing but clear out and leave the natives to fend for themselves!"[45] New Guinea Volunteer Rifle member Ian Downs similarly remarked: "In Japanese-occupied areas their [New Guinean] loyalty of course was extremely limited. You can't blame them. . . . If you were confronted with someone about to stick a bayonet up your backside it's extraordinary how co-operative you become."[46] By the time of Japanese surrender there were officially 2,617 Indigenous people under Japanese employment in Rabaul and several thousand in other regions.[47]

Despite the often-coercive nature of employment, many New Guineans and Japanese look favorably upon their work together. Historian Alan Powell comments, "The natives were quick to observe that Japanese soldiers were prone to eat with their native helpers, to share quarters on the track and to display generally much less racial separatism than their previous masters."[48] There are oral recollections of Japanese opening hospitals, providing medical treatment in villages, starting schools for villagers, and giving gifts of caps and armbands. Some Kaliai people from New Britain recall Japanese labor supervisors aiming to protect workers from American bombing raids.[49] Former Papua New Guinean prime minister Michael Somare recalls Japanese schooling as a youngster. He learned mathematics, studied the Japanese language, and performed basic chores for Japanese. Significantly, Somare recalls: "But on the whole we had very good relationships with the Japanese. We often danced for them, and they performed their sword dances for us."[50] Other oral testimony corroborates Somare's recollections about Japanese schooling being a positive experience. Joe Leleng describes children happily learning literacy and numeracy, though he also suggests that for older students schooling served as a means to indoctrinate Indigenous boys as soldiers. Leleng states, "Yes, the kids were very happy to go to the school. . . . [The teacher] treated us well. If we did anything wrong he would only tell us not to do that thing and did not do anything physically. He was a very nice guy."[51] Other testimony suggests that as with adult laborers, children who stepped out of line were severely punished. Eliab Kaplimut's memories of school are mostly positive, but he recollects, "On one occasion while we were doing marching practice a boy and a girl made a mistake and the teacher punished them with fifty strokes of the cane each. In the evening the boy and the girl could not walk properly."[52] W. ToKilala similarly summarizes the mixed treatment villagers received from Japanese: "The Japanese were on the whole quite friendly, providing everything went well."[53]

Japanese soldiers also recall positive interpersonal relations with New Guinean residents. Second Lt. Yanagiba Yutaka stated that "they [New Guineans in Rabaul] said, 'We like Japanese better than Australians.' Officers and men of the South Seas Force worked with them shoulder to shoulder, shook hands and ate together. For those who had been discriminated against [by Australians], those small things pleased them so deeply."[54] Mizuki Shigeru developed a friendship with the inhabitants of one village that endured even after the war: "Then I started visiting her village more often, and I became like a member of the family. They looked after me well. . . . When the war finished, they told me to run away from the army and come to live in their village."[55] Other Japanese reports talk about how ongoing cooperation led to growing trustful relations between Japanese and villagers. Kazuo Hoshino recalls:

> One night we stayed at a village [between Maprik and Wingei]. It was like a paradise. We ate *udon* noodles made from sago starch supplied by villagers and pork given to us by another unit. . . . In the evening, we gathered together with them and sang Umi Yukaba, a Japanese military song, and bowed towards the Imperial Palace in Tokyo. After this we all sat around the fire and smoked and chatted.[56]

The reasons for Japanese goodwill seem based more on pragmatism than on anything else. Japanese often relied on villagers for food or for help escaping Allied advances, so friendship was a good means to ensure loyalty. Anthropologist Carl E. Thune argues that the relationships between Japanese and Normanby Islanders, though peaceful and friendly, represented a form of paternalism where Japanese substituted for previous white overseers.[57] But benevolent paternalism was not the only way that Japanese sought to guarantee New Guinean allegiance.

Other New Guinean oral testimony distinguishes between what they consider "good Japanese" and "bad Japanese." Remi remarks: "Some Japanese good to us, but some weren't. Some of them killed us—cut us up and ate us! But men like this one were good."[58] Misiaiyai from the Musendai Village similarly states: "Our Japanese were good people. But another sort of Japanese, they called them Kempeitai, they killed people and ate them. Our Japanese were called Army."[59] Reports of solely bad Japanese are also quite common in various Papua New Guinean oral traditions. Many of these testimonies refer to brutal punishments strictly for disobedience, while others describe arbitrary atrocities. For instance, stealing from Japanese could be punished by one month's hard labor or torture. Historian Peter Brune describes retributive Japanese atrocities at Milne Bay on 25–26 August 1942:

Black Skins, Black Work

A Papuan who had been forced to accompany the invasion force as a guide was executed for supposedly directing the fleet to the wrong venue; numerous others were tied to trees and used for bayonet practice; a young boy was executed by the use of a flamethrower, his only crime being that he happened to live near the enemy landing site; Papuan women were sexually assaulted and mutilitated.[60]

Tutal Kaminiel witnessed brutalities: "Other people were put into a hole with sticks and leaves, which were then burnt; they were nearly smoked to death. Sometimes people were made to drink water and were then jumped on; they were hung upside down and bashed about the face and buttocks."[61]

Torture was a common tactic Japanese utilized to secure information. Many villagers already had knowledge about Japanese torturing whites and New Guineans to death in Rabaul and thus knew this outcome was possible. Danks Tomila recalls one instance:

> They tied our legs to pieces of logs and made us sit with the logs on top of our legs. This was a very painful experience. We were told not to move any part of our body but to sit still. The Japanese watched us closely, and when anyone moved they stepped on him and kicked him with their boots. Finally, one of the men, unable to stand the pain any longer, declared himself to be the man responsible for the theft and so was taken away from us. We did not know what they did with him. The rest of us were set free.[62]

Japanese also used fear of torture to ensure loyalty and to force laborers to work harder, a tactic that had limited success. Australian war correspondent George Johnston reported in 1942:

> It appears, also that the Japanese force which occupied Salamaua lined up more than 100 natives against the wall of a hangar at Salamaua airfield and shot them as a terrorist lesson to the rest of the native population. Other natives were branded with a red mark on the forehead and put to work unloading Japanese storeships. They were given one army biscuit as the day's ration. That night all the natives went bush.[63]

Often it was not the Japanese themselves who embarked upon torture campaigns, but rather New Guineans working as kempei-tai. Pamoi, a New Guinean policeman from Aitape, reported:

> The two Japanese instructed us police boys to tie the hands of all the natives and suspend them by their hands from a beam so that their toes barely touched the ground. The Japanese then asked them again about the natives they were supposed to be hiding in the village. They made denial again and the Japanese ordered us police boys to thrash them. They were beaten with canes, sticks and pieces of wood by us.[64]

Sasa Goreg, another policeman working for Japanese, similarly recalls that "during the whole of the war period I killed or shot men under orders."[65] John Kapelis states: "I was taken and put into the military police—the Kempeitai. I helped the Kempeitai with their work. I used to go and arrest people and when they were sentenced I beat them. If I hadn't beaten them, I would've been beaten myself. I did it out of fear."[66] The common trend among Goreg's, Pamoi's, and Kapelis's testimony is the idea that kempei-tai police were following Japanese orders. While there is little doubt that Japanese probably ordered such brutality, the issue of merely "following orders" is one that requires a bit more scrutiny. Certainly there were some benefits for New Guineans in becoming Japanese police. Kempei-tai received food as payment, but this was not necessarily different from other New Guinean laborers.[67] Many New Guineans who joined the kempei-tai did so for the prestige of the position and to take revenge on rival villagers. But Kesbuk claims that he became a Japanese *kapitan* solely because this meant the Japanese left him alone.[68] Generally, as historian August Kituai effectively argues, "some of them may have hoped for favors from the Japanese for being enthusiastic bashers, but more frequently they attempted to soften or divert the savagery of the Japanese."[69]

When the war was over, some crimes Japanese committed against New Guineans were prosecuted as war crimes. For instance, one allegation stated that a Japanese commander had ordered a sergeant to behead a New Guinean deserter at Salate. A war crimes investigation determined that "the two natives were taken to the head of a small stream close to BALIF village, and a shallow hole was dug. One at a time, WARI and USASIM, their hands bound behind their backs, were fastened to a stake at the side of the hole and beheaded."[70] Another incident in which Japanese massacred sixteen New Guineans—including women and children—for allegedly receiving meat and rice from Australian troops was also prosecuted as a war crime. A survivor named Longin later declared: "I heard the Japanese sergeant speak to Luluai SAPAU and then draw his revolver and shoot SAPAU and KAMBAIAMA. The machine gun then opened fire from behind us, and many of the natives in the line fell to the ground dead. I, with four others, managed to escape. Luluai SAPAU did not make any movement, threatening or otherwise, before he was shot."[71] That these crimes were even reported and prosecuted is itself a remarkable feat; they suggest a wider pattern of Japanese abusing Indigenous residents during the occupation of New Guinea.

Overall, despite some favorable recollections of Japanese–New Guinean relations, the majority of oral testimonies indicate antipathy for Japanese occupation. Even those New Guineans who express favorable opinions about Japanese occupation provide examples of Japanese brutality and executions. For other New Guineans Japanese atrocities such as gang rape and murder deterred groups initially welcoming of their presence. Horrible working conditions and insufficient rations—particularly for those twelve hundred men sent from New Ireland to Papua and New Guinea as carriers during the Kokoda Campaign—led to many desertions.[72] Johnston reported, "There are the bodies, too, of native carriers, tossed aside by the Japs to die, discarded callously and left unburied in the jungle."[73] Japanese plundered local villagers' food supplies and abused villagers who protested. Benggo Aikeng testifies: "They finished the food in the gardens. They finished all our cattle. Excreted, urinated—they spoiled the church, they killed and ate pigs. They said, *buta, buta* and ate the pigs."[74] Thus the Japanese occupation of New Guinea holds a prominent but contentious place in the nation's history. Memories of atrocity, violence, and coerced labor coincide with feelings of empathy, support, and tolerance. The heterogeneity of experiences makes it difficult to generalize about Japanese–New Guinean relations, and indeed Powell uses the word "unpredictable" to characterize Japanese rule.[75] But one thing is certain: Japanese survival in the region, as for their Allied counterparts, depended heavily on New Guinean labor, wherewithal, and support.

Working for Australia: Papuan and New Guinean Laborers and ANGAU

Before examining the official capacities of Papuan and New Guinean soldiers working for the Allies, one must consider the thousands who participated in the war effort in unofficial capacities. As in the Aboriginal labor camps in the Northern Territory, a great number of Papuans and New Guineans provided logistical support although they never enlisted or received adequate compensation. In fact, military commanders discouraged enlistment of Indigenous labor on the grounds that "enlistment under the Defence Act is not understood by the natives and in any event it is difficult to administer. It offers no advantage over the present system of indenture under local native Labour Ordinances other than giving the CO of units power to deal with disciplinary cases."[76] Because actual warfare occurred in Papua and New Guinea, necessitating the mass mobilization of all sectors of society, the number of workers under labor ordinances was high, and their roles were pronounced, in both combat and noncombat positions.

The recruitment of Papuan and New Guinean labor proceeded aggressively, without consideration for the desires or needs of the locals themselves. The Australian New Guinea Administrative Unit (ANGAU) assumed government powers over areas of Papua and New Guinea not under Japanese occupation on 10 April 1942. Its main tasks were to recruit and manage Indigenous labor, maintain law and order, and gather limited military intelligence behind enemy lines when possible. ANGAU was also responsible for maintaining the prewar civil administration and for providing "native rehabilitation" in areas recaptured from Japanese.[77] Summarizing the multitudinous tasks under ANGAU direction, historian Alan Powell writes:

ANGAU's carrier lines fed and armed Australian and American soldiers fighting in the rainforests, the swamps, and the mountains—and they carried away the wounded; ANGAU's labour forces built the airstrips and manned their bases; ANGAU's scouts and networks of informants in operational areas were their eyes, ears, and often the spearhead of their clashes with the Japanese enemy; and ANGAU's patrols brought rehabilitation from the war in reconquered areas. . . . All this is added to the multifarious tasks of civil government and labour recruitment in the Highlands and southern regions which the Japanese did not reach.[78]

Although ANGAU was the civilian administrative body for Papua and New Guinea during the war, really the army was in command, and ANGAU was subservient to military needs and policies formulated by the Directorate of Research and Civil Affairs (DORCA).[79] Nonetheless, ANGAU wielded significant influence and control over the daily lives of Papuan and New Guinean laborers. The size of ANGAU grew from a white staff of 452 at the end of 1942 to one of 2,026 in July 1945.[80] Initially there was a six-week training school for the ANGAU Native Labour Section, but it was rapidly disbanded because commanders determined that personnel could not be spared for six weeks.[81] When seeking non-Indigenous employees to oversee labor, qualifications included bush experience; time spent, ideally, in Papua, New Guinea, or the Solomon Islands; and a "desire to understand the peculiarities of the native and the manner in which he must be treated to obtain better results."[82] Thus, like Donald Thomson in his search for non-Indigenous commanders of the NTSRU, ANGAU wished for candidates with interracial experience. Yet there is a significant difference between Thomson's motives and ANGAU's: whereas Thomson sought to preserve the integrity of Yolngu culture and civilization, ANGAU sought to maintain white supremacy over Papuans and New Guineans. As in the NTSRU, though, a number of racist non-Indigenous personnel did wind up supervising Papuan and New Guinean labor with brutal tactics. In 1943 the ratio of overseer to laborer in New Guinea was estimated at one to one hundred.[83]

At first recruitment of Papuans and New Guineans was voluntary. The pay rate throughout the war for unskilled labor was between six and fifteen shillings per month, while skilled laborers could earn up to one hundred shillings. There was also a scale of rewards depending on the task performed, with achievements such as rescuing pilots and capturing enemies more valuable than salvaging aircraft or reporting on enemy movements.[84] The pay rate depended upon the location of the contract; prewar New Guinea had a minimum wage of six shillings per month, while Papua's minimum wage was ten shillings. These minimums continued to operate throughout the course of the war — another signifier of the continuing colonial labor regime in operation. Like in the Northern Territory Aboriginal labor camps the army justified Papuan and New Guinean wages on the grounds of "particularly having in mind the future labour market in the Territory under peacetime commercial conditions."[85]

Rarua Tau, a volunteer who worked for ANGAU during the war, recalls being recruited:

> Next morning Labour in charge rang the bell and blew the whistle and told us to stand in line so we did stand in line. An ANGAU officer came around and asked the people could they tell them the names of the places — i.e. departments they worked. After that some men were sent to labour work. . . . After some days I was sent to work at the ANGAU Quartermaster store with Mr B. Wyatt.[86]

But the lack of sufficient volunteers in early 1942 led to conscription, separating families and villages. The National Security (Emergency) Control Regulations Act and subsequent regulations gave ANGAU loose powers to draft Papuan and New Guinean laborers, "subject to such conditions not inconsistent with the order as he may see fit."[87] District officers and their assistants were the principal administrators of conscription. Often they would summon village leaders and demand that they provide ANGAU with able-bodied men. Despite standing orders against recruiting more than 25 percent of able-bodied men from villages, in some regions excessive enrollment led to labor that was insufficient for local villages to function properly.[88] As the war progressed

Black Skins, Black Work

and the Allies made advances, the demands for labor actually increased because manual workers were needed to fill the gaps when machinery moved north with the frontlines and to work for Americans. In some instances the new laborers recruited were those who had previously been working for Japanese under harsh conditions.[89] When not enough men volunteered, ANGAU officers and police sometimes seized valuables, ate household food, threatened to rape women, and recruited young boys. These tactics represented an extension of previous colonial ploys and did not occur in either the Yolngu or the Navajo contexts. The significant continuity in recruitment methods stems primarily from the fact that Papua and New Guinea were battlefronts in the war, whereas Australia and the United States remained, with exceptions, home fronts. Consequently, soldiers in Papua and New Guinea's "chaotic warzone" could depart from the niceties of law and order maintained in Australia and the United States. The fact that Papuan and New Guinean villagers had little recourse against such tactics left them in vulnerable situations.

By the end of the war quotas allowed army patrols to recruit up to 40 percent of all adult males in Papua and New Guinea. One ANGAU report from New Britain in late 1945 declared:

> Practically the only villages under-recruited were the inland ones and the people thereof showed a marked reluctance to leave home. In one case recruits who had been ordered to work deserted, and when recovered had to be placed under police guards. On word of termination of hostilities recruiting ceased and those obtained were sent home, and I carried on with a much clearer conscience with the ending of a distasteful task.[90]

In another 1945 report on ANGAU labour, Brig. Gen. J. E. Lloyd acknowledged, "Recruitment since the inception [of ANGAU] has *not* been voluntary, but on close observation it is found that the natives in general once signed on have carried out the tasks allotted in good spirit."[91] The numbers of laborers under ANGAU control were 25,500 by June 1943; 32,600 by March 1944; 37,900 in May 1944; and 31,170 at war's end. Official ANGAU estimates from February 1942 to November 1945 place the number of Papuan indentured laborers at 24,500 and

New Guineans at 25,500, for a total of 50,000 out of the estimated population of 2 million.[92] Laborers were contracted for three years, but one ANGAU report indicates:

> We have been unable [to] release [Indigenous labor] owing inability recruit new labourers due over recruitment coastal areas. . . . Most [of] these natives recruited three years ago by methods that could not be regarded fully voluntary on grounds operational necessity that time. These methods can no longer be countenanced under present conditions in base areas.[93]

To rationalize the increasingly conscriptive nature of recruitment, a military document stated:

> Despite the popular belief that the native is out to help us to the limit (there is a danger of too great sentimentality towards the native) at the present time it is doubtful whether more than 5% of the eligible males would recruit. So the fact must be faced that it will be impossible to provide the labor estimated, by the voluntary systems.[94]

While clearly the war necessitated increasing numbers of Papuan and New Guinean laborers, the military and ANGAU's position negated the agency of participants. Papuan and New Guinean support equated solely to Indigenous labor under the control of white authorities. Captain Gloucester even declared in July 1944: "Their patriotism was referred (i.e. appealed) to with nil result, until finally they were informed of the main and customary reason for going—they had to. . . . I personally have recruited over 2,000 natives for work in forward areas. . . . Of these about 20 were not forcibly recruited."[95] A popular carrier song from the war demonstrates the sorrow villagers felt when their husbands left to become laborers:

> On the canoe bank all were standing.
> When the husbands looked back they saw their wives and
>   children were waving to them
> The husbands saw that they were waving to them with
>   colourful grass skirts.[96]

Black Skins, Black Work

The most common contribution of Papuan and New Guinean indentured labor came less from their intelligence or knowledge and more from their physical prowess. Like the work of Aboriginal people in the Northern Territory, Papuans' and New Guineans' tasks included serving as stewards and laundrymen; unloading ships and aircraft; stacking equipment; digging ditches; carrying supplies to the frontlines; constructing airstrips, bridges, wharfs, barracks, and drains; growing vegetables; fumigating mosquitoes; cutting grass; and working in repair yards. Some Papuans and New Guineans also continued to operate prewar industries such as rubber tapping.[97] Military officers considered Papuans and New Guineans more valuable for menial manual labor because "whites can do cooking, cleaning, shelter erection as they were trained."[98] The racialization of labor was prevalent because military officials believed this was the most efficient means to provide "suitable" work for Pacific Islanders. Lieutenant Colonel Sharpe remarked, "In MORESBY and PAPUA it was found far more satisfactory to use native labor on the basis to which it was accustomed and under which it had been working efficiently rather than set up a native force within the Army."[99] Gen. Iven Mackay similarly declared, "The general policy has been to employ natives on those tasks to which they are naturally adapted."[100] *You and the Native* stated: "The native does not expect the white man to do manual labour. He is ready to do the hard work or the dirty work himself under the white man's supervision."[101] The racialization of labor based on "natural" affinity also entailed segregation of the white and Pacific Islander races for fear of undermining the "superiority" of whites. *You and the Native* instructed Australian soldiers: "Always, without overdoing it, be the master. The time may come when you will want a native to obey you. He won't obey you if you have been in the habit of treating him as an equal."[102] Military records reinforced this message:

The native is overawed by the white man's powers and regards him as a superior being, adopts a submissive attitude and accepts the European as a superior. It is worth a lot of trouble to maintain this state of affairs.

Some members of the forces have, by fraternising with the natives, tended to lower the prestige of the European. Drastic action should be taken to warn troops of this danger—you cannot fraternise with natives then expect their obediance [*sic*].[103]

The racialization of labor—similar to in northern Australia—points to the continuing colonial mindset and racist ideas playing out in Papua and New Guinea, even as Australians grew to depend on the support and participation of Papuans and New Guineans.

For Papuan and New Guinean workers life under the military and ANGAU was not easy. There are some signs that laborers' diets and medical conditions improved over prewar conditions. In some areas, such as Hisui Point, testimony indicates that ANGAU rations were ample and handed out methodically. Mr. Mea testifies: "The Angau soldiers had all our names written down and twice a week we were called out to collect our ration. There was plenty of tinned meat and rice but we were told to build gardens in case the supplies ran out."[104] In addition to teaching hygiene, ANGAU provided treatment for common prewar conditions such as malaria, hookworm, tropical ulcers, tuberculosis, gonorrhea, leprosy, dysentery, pneumonia, scabies, and beri beri.[105] The army alone had a good medical budget, treating approximately eighty-five thousand Papuans and New Guineans—including women and children—between February 1942 and September 1944. Anthropologist W. E. H. Stanner estimates that ANGAU oversaw one million medical treatments to Papuans and New Guineans by April 1946.[106] ANGAU even occasionally screened motion pictures and presented radio shows in Motu and Pidgin English.

But there are other indications that living conditions were less than desirable. Historian Paul Ham writes that "natives were rounded up and 'held' for service—they were corralled into pens. Many were pushed to the limits of physical endurance."[107] Accommodation was always segregated from that for white troops, although sometimes this merely served "as a malaria control measure."[108] While sanitation and water supply were generally good, housing was not weatherproofed, and clothing issuances were unsatisfactory.[109] In many camps there were problems of poor food, poor hygiene, overwork, and lack of adequate medical attention. Nora Vagi Brash recalls:

> Be carriers, laborers, that sort of thing. And when they were sick—if they fell ill—they wouldn't take them back to their village but they'd take them to Wakemo hospital and some of the young men died outside. And the families didn't know about the deaths of the husbands and later, you know, when they found out they just cried their eyes out. All of the young men in the village went, only these, the old and what the army saw useless. Any young man who was able, you know, from the age of 14, 15, 16, 17.[110]

Some officers, such as Capt. Geoffrey H. Vernon, recognized these poor conditions, describing camp life as "a meal that consisted only of rice and none too much of that, and a night of shivering discomfort for most as there were only enough blankets to issue one to every two men."[111] Whenever possible officers such as Vernon tried to improve Indigenous laborers' diets, rations, and rest. This was not across the board, because it was the job of ANGAU—not the military—to administer, feed, house, pay, repatriate, and hospitalize Papuan and New Guinean labor. Indeed, historian Paul Ham uses the phrase "unusual devotion" to describe Vernon's support for Papuans and New Guineans during the war.[112] One official report from 1944 declared, "Every native who worked for the Army [in Mambare District] was issued with sufficient rations, but enough was not available up to that time, for distribution to refugee natives."[113] Thus it was often the strain of wartime resources, rather than malicious intent, that prevented ANGAU from supplying adequate rations to Papuans and New Guineans. Yet even if there were not sufficient supplies for Indigenous laborers, it did not lessen their work burdens.

Poor conditions extended from the living environment to the actual work of Papuan and New Guinean laborers as well. Carriers in particular had a rough time given the nature of their task, carrying large quantities of weaponry or injured soldiers over rough terrain. Sometimes Australian soldiers would even throw their own packs or weapons on top of the overloaded carriers.[114] One description of carriers' loads stated:

"Mortar bombs had to be carried into an attack. Each bomb carried 10 pounds. . . . They were in strong cardboard containers—packed four to a box—two slung on a pole. You can see we needed carriers . . . to supply the mortars and of course the ammunition for the Vickers guns. It was a problem."[115] War correspondent George Johnston described the conditions: "On the track back to Moresby there are long lines of loyal Papuans, slipping and stumbling back with crude stretchers on their shoulders."[116] Somu Sigob recollects: "They [Australian soldiers] worked hard to fight the Japanese as well as look after us, and we also toiled to carry the wounded, many of whom had broken arms, had lost their eyes or had intestines hanging out. We carried many of them, and some died on the way, while others managed to reach the hospital."[117] William Metpi testifies:

> The carriers each had a load of fifty pounds weight. Their daily ration was one meal of boiled rice, which they cooked for themselves each night. They had each a packet of army biscuits in the mornings, usually eaten on the march and they set out from Bulldog with a small tin of meat, a piece which they ate the first day so as not to have to carry it. Apart from his loin-cloth or "rami," each carrier had one trade basket.[118]

An ANGAU report succinctly summarizes the significance of the carriers in the Kokoda Campaign of 1942: "They in fact formed a living supply line without which the [Kokoda] campaign could never have been brought to a successful conclusion as expeditiously was the case."[119]

Despite the critical nature of carriers' jobs, their experience and treatment were less than ideal. Often carriers' wakeup call was at 5:00 a.m., breakfast was at 5:45 a.m., and the carrying began at 7:00 a.m. There were problems with overloading, overwork, exposure, and bruised and battered feet covered with blisters, contradicting instructions to white soldiers: "Do not demand the impossible, whether in working hours or weight of loads."[120] Many carriers were not accustomed to the highlands climate, as they were coastal Papuans. Malnourishment often forced carriers to rely on local villagers' charity for sustenance.[121] Asi Arere testifies: "Many of the carriers got sick and died in the bush. There was very

Black Skins, Black Work

little food. I was lucky to get home."[122] Carrier veteran Ovivi Arai recalls the horrific experience: "It was so terrible as a labourer that we had to sleep in our own shit. Australia has treated us like that—like shit! I had to sleep on the corpses of the Japanese. I drank water full of their rotting flesh. But for enduring all this we have got nothing."[123] When they finished the terms of their employment, most carriers were not repatriated but instead were diverted to other tasks.[124] Thus even as Papuans and New Guineans grew to occupy a critical position in the Allied war effort, they continued to receive poor treatment and little relief.

The poor conditions led a number of Indigenous laborers to desert ANGAU or their carrier positions. The high desertion rate—estimated as high as 30 percent after the Battle of Isurava—was attributed primarily to sickness, exhaustion, demoralization at the sight of the wounded, lack of blankets, visiting wives, or a shortage of tobacco and other commodities. Somu Sigob recalls: "When they [deserters] ran away they didn't head for Moresby but went through the bush until they reached their villages. Later the *kiaps* caught them, gave them some punishments and then sent them back."[125] In some instances—despite the ANGAU prohibition of physical abuse—these punishments were severe, including being thrashed, stretched across a drum, caned, hung from a tree in a bag, or cuffed or being assigned to dig drains or cut grass.[126] ANGAU considered the fundamental causes of desertion to be as follows:

1. They are not volunteers; 2. In the heat of the moment, many promises were made that when the Japs were driven away, the labour would be returned to their homes—circumstances have prevented these promises being kept; 3. Villages have been so heavily recruited that labourers are worrying about their gardens, womenfolk, etc. 4. Unsuitability of some of the natives for the work on which they are employed, and 5. Lack of experienced control.[127]

You and the Native recognized that "if a man treats his labourers too badly they will desert, and when they have fled into the New Guinea bush he will not get them back in a hurry."[128] Despite recognizing the causal relationship between poor conditions and carrier desertion, the armed forces and ANGAU chose to punish the symptom instead of addressing its causes. According to government documents the motivation behind punishing desertion was fear that Papuan and New Guinean deserters might collude with Japanese. Given the collaboration described already, in some areas collusion was indeed a legitimate concern.

But documents and oral testimony point to abuse of Papuan and New Guinean laborers as more than just a matter of isolated incidents or as grounded strictly in fears of conspiracy. Asi Arere recalls: "Some Angau soldiers were looking after us and organising the labour line. They did not treat us properly. They were always hitting people and knocking us over. One man from Porebada who was making copra was kicked in the stomach by an Angau soldier with boots on, and was badly hurt. He died the next day."[129] Though condemning the practice, *You and the Native* acknowledged that "punching natives grows into a habit with some people. They even boast of their victories."[130] Anthropologist L. P. Mair suggests that ANGAU officers also flogged into submission Papuans and New Guineans who did not wish to re-engage with ANGAU upon completion of their contracts.[131] Oral testimonies in regions of Papua and New Guinea that had significant contact with Americans demonstrate disapproval of ANGAU methods by contrasting benevolent Americans with abusive ANGAU members. For instance, Auwepo of Kegebwai hamlet, Loboda, remarks:

> They [Americans] would call, they said, "Hey, boys, you come and let's eat." We thought about it and we went up and ate with the American soldiers. But we were afraid of the ANGAU soldiers. We said, "If we go up and eat with the Americans, they [the ANGAU soldiers] will see us and they will scold us."[132]

Anthropologists Zelenietz and Saito similarly describe situations when ANGAU agents confiscated and destroyed food and clothing provided to Kilenge by Americans.[133]

One anonymous white resident of Papua wrote a complaint to the minister for the army in 1945, condemning the abuse of Papuan labor. The letter alleged, "When these poor illiterate natives did not supply satisfactory answers to his [WOII Healy's] questions, *he had two of them unmercifully flogged and later one was forced to dig his own grave and then callously murdered in cold blood.*"[134] An investigation into the behavior of Healy uncovered testimony from both Papuans and white soldiers indicating incidents when Healy beat Indigenous laborers, but Healy was acquitted of any wrongdoing. Maj. John Steward Milligan summarized his views in his ruling: "Summary punishment promptly inflicted for disobedience was a means that justified the ends in the circumstances."[135] The term *disobedience* could have a loose interpretation, though. Soldier Eddie Allan Stanton wrote in his diary:

> Today, a native was hit with a paling by the A.D.O. because he persisted in smiling while being spoken to. This action cannot be tolerated in any form. The native cannot hit back, and the white man knows it. If he could return the blow, the white man would not have the courage to hit him. Thus, we see a good example of the uplifting nature of a certain type of Government Officer.[136]

Stanton on another occasion similarly wrote: "The Australian native Labour Overseers seem to take delight in hitting the natives."[137] Stanton's comments suggest that abuse of Papuan and New Guinean labor was not about merely punishment for crimes and misdemeanors. Rather, violence and brutality were means to reinforce the unequal power relationships characteristic of white men in control of Indigenous labor.

Sexual relations also became an arena of violence in two ways. Despite explicit warnings that "if the woman is not consenting, then intercourse is rape—whether the victim be white or brown,"[138] there are some stories of white Americans and black Americans sexually assaulting Papuan or New Guinean women.[139] Stanton wrote: "In New Guinea, the [Australian] troops had much pleasure in offering native girls sticks of tobacco for sexual satisfaction. When tobacco is short, might exerts itself. In Port Moresby, one girl died from such an attack."[140] Stanton excused sexual abuse on the grounds that "in New Guinea, the native woman is the only cure for oversexed gents. Consequently, one must not blame the soldier too much."[141] The abuse of Papuan and New Guinean women suggests continuing dehumanizing attitudes toward the Indigenous "other," playing out in a violent arena. But there was also disconcertion among white Australians about Papuan and New Guinean men and white women. Stanton records that when a group of Indigenous men saw a USO show and expressed interest in the white female performers, they received a flogging.[142] Indigenous overseer Arthur Dunas's oral testimony describes a similar incident (if not the same one):

> DUNAS: Two laborers on my team asked an Australian soldier if he could find some white nurses to sleep with them. They were arrested straight away and then they came to arrest me as well.
>
> INTERVIEWER: You hadn't done anything!
>
> DUNAS: They said I was leader of the labor line and I was responsible for what my men did. I was beaten first with a cane this long [motions arms spread out].
>
> INTERVIEWER: How many times?
>
> DUNAS: I lost count.
>
> INTERVIEWER: Did you bleed?
>
> DUNAS: Yes.
>
> INTERVIEWER: And the other two?
>
> DUNAS: They were beaten so hard their piss and shit ran out. They had to be taken to hospital so that they could be looked after.[143]

Dunas's testimony highlights the severity of the supposed crime of miscegenation between Papuan or New Guinean males and white females. Even the *hint* of breaking down longstanding barriers warranted severe punishment. The group beating sent a message to all Papuan and New Guinean men: do not lust after white women. While this was nothing new per se in Papua and New Guinea, it certainly demonstrates the continuity of colonialism and the abuses associated with it as the Second World War impacted the region.

Compensation and Recognition for Papua New Guinean Laborers

The question of compensation is one that continues to attract attention among segments of present-day Papua New Guinean society because of the nature of Papuans' and New Guineans' war work and the inad-

Black Skins, Black Work

equate recompense given during the war. Payment under ANGAU was at a rate of ten shillings per month as of August 1943, and most slept in compounds and were trucked to work near the military bases daily. Enemy action killed an estimated 46 indentured laborers, and between 1,962 and 2,024 workers died of other causes. Despite some camaraderie with Australian soldiers, the poor living and working conditions translated to general Papuan and New Guinean resentment and dissatisfaction with the ANGAU.[144] As early as September 1945 reports were coming out of places such as Wewak declaring, "Dissatisfaction is being expressed . . . on the failure to fulfil the promise of payments of prewar wage claims, and natives are feeling it is unwise to make further labour contracts when they remain unpaid for work previously done."[145]

The main reason that most laborers did not receive significant compensation postwar is that, as civilians, they were deemed ineligible for war gratuities. The outcome of deliberations over gratuities in 1946 determined: "It is intended to pay War Gratuities only to such natives who were actually members of the Australian Forces and not to those employed in a civilian capacity."[146] As historian Liz Reed highlights, even years later segments of the Papua New Guinean population do not accept the rhetoric of appreciation common from white Australia because it lacks accompanying compensation.[147] Veteran carrier Wamanari remarks:

The Australian government said, you work and later you'll be like us. But it hasn't happened. They said you work for us then we'll all sit down at the same table — same spoon, same food. But it hasn't happened. I heard their promises and I worked day and night so that things would change. I thought of nothing else. When the war finished in 1945 the Australian soldiers went home and got pensions. They're well off now, but I worked hard for nothing. Now Papua New Guinea is independent — young men wear shoes and trousers and look smart. But me, I'm just rubbish. Old men like me are dying without getting anything.[148]

Asina Papau similarly claims: "Since the war nothing has been done for the labourers. Young people don't know how hard things were for us. People are forgetting that we carried the wounded on one shoulder and bombs on the other. We were not afraid of the Japanese. We worked hard despite all the danger. We were promised compensation and I ask now for what we were promised."[149] Stella notes that "the job the natives perform is, by implication, not comparable to soldiering; they are merely carriers of the wounded."[150] As recently as 2004 Ham described veteran Papua New Guinean laborers living "much as they did then, in villages without sanitation, proper medical care or running water, dependent on their market gardens for food. In fact, their circumstances have regressed; little Australian aid finds its way to their mountain villages, which no longer receive weekly air deliveries of supplies and mail—a distant echo of the shortages faced in very different circumstances."[151] Fundamentally, this lack of compensation and inadequate recognition parallels the Yolngu case.

Most white coastwatchers and officers recognized the valuable role Papuans and New Guineans played in their security. For instance, one major general wrote in 1943: "During and subsequent to the recent operations over the Owen Stanley Range and in the Kokoda-Buna Area the work of the Native Carriers received general approbation. The devotion to duty of the natives, their care of the wounded and their general helpfulness were probably the more appreciated as they were unexpected by officers and men."[152] Gen. Thomas Blamey declared:

> These natives can't be given too much praise. . . . They've carried stretchers through feet-deep mud with the Australian wounded, down slimy defiles, through terrible jungles. They were almost at the point of exhaustion, but they always kept two men awake at night to take care of the patients, to wash their muddy limbs, to attend to their bandages and to give them their meals. The work of these natives has been astounding. We owe them a lasting debt.[153]

Yet similar to the situation for Yolngu, many white assessments meant to praise Pacific Islanders were tainted with racial constructs of inferiority or inherent militarism. Newton argues that constructs of the "Melanesian Big Man" included "capable of independent action, of attracting loyal followers, of carrying out a brutal guerilla warfare,

Black Skins, Black Work

and of making astute alliances with those in power."[154] American constructs of Papuans and New Guineans also adhered to the racialized notions of primitiveness prevalent among Australians. Interestingly, a Navajo non–Code Talker serviceman named Luke Romero similarly subscribed to such ideas:

> In New Guinea there's lots of natives. Got bushy hair. No clothes, nothing. Just piece of cloth around waist. These natives worked for Australians building a shack. They paid them thirty-six cents a month. Those people were funny. They don't know any English. The women they just wore grass skirts.[155]

Romero's comment links to the most ubiquitous archetype from the war, which still endures in Australian cultural memory — the idea of the "Fuzzy Wuzzy Angel." The term emerged from a poem by Sapper Bert Beros, which describes Papuan carriers:

> Only holes slashed in their ears,
> And their faces worked by tattoos . . .
> With their fuzzy wuzzy hair.[156]

Papua New Guineans have received the expression "Fuzzy Wuzzy Angel" with a mixture of intrigue and misgiving. Morea Mea states:

> Australian people are laughing at to our country people, Papuan people because they call them Fuzzy Wuzzy Angels. They don't know what the meaning of what Fuzzy Wuzzy Angel is. What are they laughing about to them. That's why, they say, "we help them, we carried them from front line because they are wounded people. We brought them to the hospital and after they when they get all right, after the war, they call us Fuzzy Wuzzy Angels." You know, during the time, when we looked in the dictionary we found there was no word, no meaning in the dictionary for Fuzzy Wuzzy Angels. So that's something they call us, slang word or something, from Australia.[157]

Liz Reed argues persuasively that the enduring construct of the Fuzzy Wuzzy Angel constructs Papua New Guineans "as a homogeneous 'other' and suggests a desire to maintain control over what had remained the preferred image of the colonised subject."[158] One significant appraisal that departs from the homogenous Fuzzy Wuzzy Angel pattern is coast-watcher Eric Feldt's statement: "The sum of individual experience was general opinion, so that there was trust and friendship between native and European. On the other hand, the European did not glamorize the native; he was no 'Fuzzy Wuzzy Angel'; he was a human being who had his rights and was expected to concede the accepted rights of others."[159] Despite his passionate insistence on the humanity of Pacific Islanders, Feldt in other instances constructs notions of primitiveness through his description of Islanders' animal instincts. He writes, "As with an animal, some sixth sense tells a native if a stranger is hostile or not."[160] In another instance he states, "The native is slow to assimilate a new idea—slower still to reason out its implications."[161] M. Murray likewise constructs Pacific Islanders on a racial hierarchy of mental capacity. He contrasts the allegedly superior intellect of Baski to other Islanders: "a mature adult living among a mob of easily led children, possessing an intellect far beyond that of the usual primitive native living in an isolated village."[162] A British soldier touring Australia after the war encapsulates constructs of the Papua New Guinean "other": "How could one fail to be fascinated at meeting the fierce looking dark skinned and sparsely clad little men who crowded around one at a remote jungle post . . . ?"[163] Overall, as Feldt summarizes, "only the Coast Watchers knew how essential was native good-will, how much success was due to native assistance and what risks were run by natives. And only those who had worked with natives would go to real trouble to protect them. To many, natives were just 'expendable,' and not even human expendables."[164] Though white commanders may have considered Papuans and New Guineans to be "childlike," they still clearly relied on them to ensure victory in the Pacific. They had no qualms about exploiting and relying upon the support and knowledge of the "primitive."

Black Skins, Black Work

9. Waiwai, New Guinea, 1942. Papua New
Guineans unloading communications equipment
from a canoe. Photograph by Thomas Fisher.
Courtesy Australian War Memorial, Negative
Number 127574.

10. (*Opposite top*) Lae, New Guinea, 1944. Papua
New Guineans supplied by the Australian New
Guinea Administrative Unit lift a crate of filled
bottles from a conveyor belt during manufacture
at an army canteens service soft-drink factory
within the Lae base subarea. Courtesy Australian
War Memorial, Negative Number 083931.

11. (*Opposite bottom*) Buna, Papua, 25 December
1942. Pvt. George C. "Dick" Whittington being
helped along a track through the kunai grass
by Papuan Raphael Oimbari. Photograph by
George Silk. Courtesy Australian War Memorial,
Negative Number 014028.

12. (*Above*) Bearers (popularly known as Fuzzy
Wuzzy Angels) walked long distances carrying
heavy loads of supplies and equipment for
Australian troops. Photograph by Damien Peter
Parer. Courtesy Australian War Memorial,
Negative Number 013002.

13. New Guinea, 1944. Members of the Royal Papuan Constabulary on the march. Courtesy Australian War Memorial, Negative Number 016928.

14. (*Opposite top*) Song River area, New Guinea, 1944. Members of C Company, Papuan Infantry Battalion, with rifles "at the slope" in their camp. Photograph by Keith Carr Rainsford. Courtesy Australian War Memorial, Negative Number 071964.

15. (*Opposite bottom*) A section from A Company, First Papuan Infantry Battalion, at the start of a patrol. Identified personnel are (*front to back of line*) 473 Corporal Akwi, Sgt. Stone, 422 Loklok, 625 Tiadu, 626 Tambukta, 491 Lance Corporal Tommi, Tomalin, 553 Nugea, remaining two unidentified. Courtesy Australian War Memorial, Negative Number 070752.

16. Singorkai, New Guinea, 1944. Four Japanese prisoners being interrogated by a patrol of the Papuan Infantry Battalion. Photograph by Keith Carr Rainsford. Courtesy Australian War Memorial, Negative Number 071539.

CHAPTER 4. Guerillas for the White Men

Formal Papuan and New Guinean Fighters

"Your European way of fighting should be thrown out, and you must follow the native way. If you want to attack a certain place, you don't send them a message so that they can kill you." I explained my ideas to them: "Put black paint on the face, or cover it up with mud. Surround the place to be attacked at five o'clock in the morning, then at six o'clock, attack." They said this was a better way to fight. — PALILI[1]

We were camped in very rough country. A big force of Japanese and village people came up. I think about a hundred village people were working for the Japanese — a whole crowd of them. They came close to where we were camped. They set up two machine guns and opened fire but they didn't hit us. They fired at us — [noises of guns]. There were three of us — three including me. We crawled away to a big tree by our camp. We crawled towards it like crocodiles, like lizards and hid there. We hid at the base of this tree and we opened fire. I think we killed 28, 28 Japanese that night. — YAUWIGA[2]

The relationship established between the various groups in the army was warm and cordial. There was no animosity between the whites and blacks. We ate together, shared smokes, watched films, etc. We all behaved as if we were all born and brought up by one mother. At that time, I did not think I was fighting to defend Papua New Guinea. I was not paid for my services. We were only given rations and lots of it. As compensation payment, I was given K1,000 last year, 1984. Our officers did not promise us anything. Besides, at that time we were all like pigs, it did not occur to us to ask for payment. We had no education. — PETRUS TIGAVU[3]

One of the most enduring images of the Second World War from Papua New Guinea is the George Silk photograph of a wounded Australian soldier, Pvt. George C. Whittington, being escorted by a Papuan named Raphael Omibari (see illustration 11 in this volume). The photograph, taken in late 1942 during the Buna Campaign, shows the wounded Australian soldier, his eyes bandaged, clearly dependent upon his Papuan companion. The photograph portrays Papua New Guinean loyalty amid adversity and evokes genuine affection for the Papuan attendant, symbolic of all Papua New Guineans toiling for the Allied war cause.[4] Silk's photograph represents much of the mythology surrounding the Second World War in Papua New Guinea: the injured digger, the difficult trek, and the extraordinary loyalty and support of Papua New Guinean "Fuzzy Wuzzy Angels." Certainly the loyalty of many Papua New Guineans merits praise, and certainly the affection for Papuan and New Guinean laborers epitomized in Silk's photograph is genuine. Yet it is what Silk's photograph does not depict—the harsh treatment of Papua New Guinean laborers and the active participation of Papuan and New Guinean fighters and coastwatchers—that has remained on the periphery of Australia's national memory. The previous chapter explored the role of Papuan and New Guinean labor; the efforts of the "formal" soldiers of Papua and New Guinea are the subject of this chapter.

In addition to the several thousand men and women administered under ANGAU, a number of other Papuans and New Guineans had more formal employment in the military. Some of these individuals worked as coastwatchers—scouts observing enemy movements and reporting back to white officials. Others worked as police, enforcing law and order in Allied-controlled areas while engaging in limited combat operations against Japanese. Even more directly combating Japanese were the soldiers in the Pacific Islands Regiment (PIR)—a whole force of Papuan and New Guinean soldiers who directly battled Japanese throughout the war. Yet similar to both the Yolngu example and their informal Papuan and New Guinean counterparts, compensation and recognition would fall far short of adequate. The postwar era marked continuing discrimination against Papua New Guineans, albeit within a slightly improved climate. Thus, as for indigenous soldiers elsewhere, the Second World War represented Papuan and New Guinean soldiers defending the very system that had disadvantaged them and would continue to disadvantage them for decades to come.

Black Eyes: Papuan and New Guinean Coastwatchers

The first group to receive consideration here are the Pacific Islander coastwatchers. On islands across the Pacific they organized alongside white coastwatchers in the early stages of the war against Japan. In early 1942 Maj. Keith McCarthy selected Papuans and New Guineans who had taken refuge in Port Moresby and transported them to Brisbane to train as coastwatchers. Approximately 360 Papuans and New Guineans trained with the army's "M" Special Unit. The army issued them clothing (but not boots) and a full set of equipment. Training entailed formal drills, rifle instruction, and lessons on recognizing various Allied and enemy aircraft and using wireless sets. After their training the Australian Army organized the coastwatchers under white leadership and deployed them to strategic areas of Papua and New Guinea. Throughout the war additional New Guinean coastwatcher recruits were derived from among Japanese carrier deserters and former kempei-tai who now became spies.[5] Ultimately, approximately 850 to 1,040 Pacific Islanders—mostly from Papua and New Guinea—trained with "M" Special Unit. Despite training with white coastwatchers and performing similar functions, the Pacific Islanders all reported under the command of other white coastwatchers.[6] Clearly to some extent this was a logistical issue—their information needed to be filtered to Australian commanders, who were fluent in English. Nonetheless, there was no reason why the coastwatchers could not report to the commanders themselves. Instead, there was an unequal relationship: they first had to report to non-Indigenous men performing the same tasks, who then relayed the information to superiors. This unequal relationship would underscore the entire coastwatcher project throughout the Pacific, in terms of orders, compensation, and ultimately recognition.

Many of the principal coastwatchers were actually white men, but even these white men relied heavily on their Papuan and New Guinean assistants and local villagers. Both Indigenous and white coastwatchers had to convince the local populations not to help the Japanese in the wake of Australia's retreat to the southern coast. White coastwatcher Peter Figgis recalls his objective to convince villagers that "with American help the Australians were coming back, and the villagers mustn't help the Japanese. This was tremendous for morale, and it gave them a lot of confidence in us."[7] Just the presence of white coastwatchers was significant to debunk Japanese claims that all whites were dead and gone from Papua and New Guinea. White coastwatchers relied on Papuan and New Guinean villagers to protect, feed, and hide them and sometimes to provide escape from advancing Japanese.[8] Alice Wedega describes a fellow villager named Cecil who aided white coastwatchers in Milne Bay, New Guinea:

> Cecil's first job on the *Osiri* was to take Coastwatchers, or "spotters," along the coast to Suau and into Milne Bay itself, to a small station near our plantation at Kanekobe. These spotters hid themselves in the bush and gave warning by radio to Port Moresby. Cecil had to take them to their places and bring them supplies from time to time.[9]

To recruit villagers, coastwatchers offered medical treatment, cargo, and food and promised to repatriate the new coastwatchers upon completion of service. Coastwatcher veteran Malcolm Wright recalls, "Our native force grew from week to week until there were so many natives that feeding them was a problem."[10] The growing dependence certainly was, to an extent, a two-way street. Although white coastwatchers may have seen themselves as providers for local village coastwatchers, clearly they were in a vulnerable position where betrayal could dramatically alter the situation. White coastwatchers' attempts to promote goodwill also reflected, partially, an effort to foster reverse dependency so that locals would not be inclined to turn coastwatchers over to the Japanese.

One of both white and Indigenous coastwatchers' other major goals was to infiltrate local villages and assess the attitudes of Papuans and New Guineans toward both Australians and Japanese. To penetrate territory under Japanese control, Indigenous coastwatchers often posed as taro or sago traders. In enemy-occupied regions their mission was also to count enemy numbers, vessels, and munitions and to monitor the movements of kempei-tai.[11] Alice Wedega recalls the recruitment and the effective work of a coastwatcher from her village:

> Palemani was a very gentle man, but had great courage. He said he would go [scout], though Cecil made sure he wanted to, and understand what might happen to him if he was captured. Three days later Palemani came back, and was able to tell the Army how many landing craft the Japanese were putting ashore every night.[12]

Spreading propaganda also entailed encouraging villagers to loot Japanese barges and to steal bark canoes. Propaganda work was difficult in regions under Japanese control—particularly in New Guinea—because Australian forces appeared weaker than Japanese. Sometimes it was difficult to convince locals to oppose the Japanese because the villagers were so fearful of retribution. For instance, Japanese beheaded captured coastwatchers and their local allies to persuade other villagers not to assist coastwatchers. Whenever possible coastwatchers' duties also involved active support for the Allied war effort. During the campaign in the Solomon Islands coastwatchers carried food to soldiers and assisted in removing the wounded from battle zones. They traveled long hours both day and night as messengers, and they often brought news of Japanese movements and crashed airmen. Indigenous aid and secrecy protected coastwatchers throughout the Pacific; on New Britain alone coastwatchers reported sightings of over seventy submarines, over one hundred aircraft, and numerous barges. Sometimes Pacific Islander coastwatchers even infiltrated Japanese units by posing as guides, before killing stray Japanese. In other instances they used guerilla-fighting skills to attack Japanese patrols.[13]

Actual confrontation with Japanese soldiers, though, fundamentally violated the orders of coastwatchers. Yauwiga recalls: "Jack Read told me that this wasn't the job of Coastwatchers, and that I was a scout of a Coastwatcher and it was not my job to fight, because if I fought the Japanese how could I then watch and pass on the information about Japanese bombers and submarines and troop movements—that was my job."[14] The concerns that Read expressed to Yauwiga demonstrate the vital role coastwatchers played in Papua and New Guinea in providing logistical information. Similar to the Yolngu in Arnhem Land they were in a unique position to scout, which did not suit white residents or outsiders. Also like the Aboriginal adjuncts attached to the NAOU the Pacific Islander coastwatchers were auxiliaries beholden to white coastwatchers. Nonetheless, there were other white coastwatchers who violated protocol and did recruit Papuan and New Guinean locals to fight the Japanese. For instance, a number of Papuans and New Guineans traveled to New Britain in 1943; white coastwatchers armed them with bows, arrows, and spears and sent them against Japanese patrols.[15] Malcolm Wright provided muskets to a group of Nakanais on New Britain to assault Japanese in a direct battle. The armed force of at least one hundred "stalked them [Japanese] through the bush, and opened fire on them."[16] The group was highly successful in their guerilla attacks against retreating Japanese. But when the war was over, the Nakanais had to return their guns to Wright.[17] Thus like the Yolngu in Arnhem Land, Papuans and New Guineans were trusted with weapons only *during* the war. The prospect of a continuously armed Indigenous group other than police contravened colonial norms and was not acceptable to postwar Papua New Guinean life.

The Royal Papuan Constabulary

Prior to the Second World War, among the few groups of Papuans and New Guineans to receive arms training were the native constabularies of both Papua and New Guinea. One might assume that, given their existing weapons training and combat experience, they would be able to form a nucleus force of Indigenous soldiers. Indeed, in 1939 there were plans to make the Royal Papuan Constabulary liable for military action in the event of an outbreak of war. Due to legal obligations under the Defence Act these plans altered, but 1941 regulations still held members of the Royal Papuan Constabulary and the New Guinea Police Force liable for call-up as part of Citizen Forces.[18] At the outbreak of the Japanese invasion, though, police were not summoned for service. One military assessment determined, "The [Papuan] Native Constabulary have not received any military training and so far as is known, have not carried out any musketry practice, therefore their qualities as a fighting unit would be very doubtful."[19] Thus colonial officials disarmed Indigenous police and encouraged them to retreat into the bush or, in the case of New Guineans, to Papua. Sasa Goreg's oral testimony describes the actions of New Guinean police after the Japanese conquest of Rabaul:

> Our officers called us together and told us to dig a big hole in the ground. It was a big, deep, long hole. It looked somewhat like a trench. Into this hole we buried our rifles, uniforms, and any other material that belonged to the government. We followed a set procedure. When it was completed the officers stood at each end of the hole. NCOs from each squad directed their men to the edge of the hole and to hand over anything they had which belonged to the government. The officers then passed the items down to two sergeants inside the hole, who were responsible for their arrangement. When everything was buried, it was covered over with corrugated iron and timber, after which soil was used to cover the whole of the hole. When this was over, we fell into line, and our two officers instructed us on what steps we should take next — most of which consisted of how we should escape from the Japanese and make our way back home. They said, "You must not follow us." They then appointed a sergeant from

Guerillas for the White Men

Talasea who was familiar with the surrounding area to guide us to Talasea and later to assist us to travel to the Siassi Islands, after which we were to make our way to Finschhafen. The European officers were either airlifted or shipped to either Finschhafen or Lae to be evacuated to Australia. The indigenous members were given no such treatment. We had to find our own way home, even those of us who not only had to cross a group of islands but even an ocean.[20]

Goreg's testimony clearly suggests Indigenous resentment over their abandonment when the Japanese attacked Rabaul. While there may have been some altruistic motivations behind settlers making the native constabulary bury their weapons and uniforms, this was done more to protect white Australians. It was also an attempt to preclude Japanese from appropriating the extant New Guinean police force. But Goreg's testimony indicates that any concerns for Indigenous welfare certainly came across as secondary to the interests of white Australia.

The fears that prior police constables might betray white Australia for Japan, and suggestions that Papuan or New Guinean police would not be useful in modern war, led to the formal disbandment of both the Royal Papuan Constabulary and the New Guinea Police Force in April 1942. Historian James Sinclair suggests that there were some humanitarian desires to protect Papuans and New Guineans from a war not of their own making, but this clearly was not the primary motivation. At the time of disbandment the Royal Papuan Constabulary numbered 350, and the New Guinea force had 1,127 men.[21] There was no consultation with these police about the decision, and many resented and today continue to resent their disarmament. War correspondent George Johnston wrote in February 1942, "The disbanding of the native police force caused anxious bewilderment among the policemen themselves and among the men of every tribe and village."[22] Patrolman J. K. McCarthy recalls:

Among these refugees were native police, in khaki uniforms but without rifles. These were bitter, sullen men. Some I first spoke to evaded my questions. But I learned the reason for their bitterness when I met up with a policeman I had known for years. "The Australian government!" he almost spat. "Why didn't they let the police fight the Japanese? Why did they take our rifles from us just before the Japanese landed? They buried our rifles and now we are running like frightened women. We would have fought with the soldiers."[23]

The lack of consultation not only left Indigenous patrolmen to their own devices, but it also demonstrated continuing colonial control and, subtly, insecurity about the status of white Australians in Papua and New Guinea. Like in northern Australia the fear that Papuan and New Guinean persons would betray white locals underscored colonial self-awareness of their tenuous status in the region.

Despite initially disbanding the Papuan and New Guinean police forces, the Australian government reconstituted an amalgamated Indigenous police constabulary under ANGAU control. To summarize the role of this new Royal Papuan Constabulary (RPC), one lieutenant colonel wrote in 1945, "The Police Force functions to maintain law and order among the civil population and the members thereof serve to assist the Military Forces in an operational capacity."[24] RPC tasks—restricted principally to territory under ANGAU control—included maintaining law and order, disseminating propaganda, and engaging in limited paramilitary operations. Propaganda dissemination came through white leaflets and gramophone recordings in Indigenous dialects; word-of-mouth was also a common means of propaganda to promote Australian interests and opposition to the Japanese.[25] Patrols also entailed adjunct services to the military: employment as interpreters, guards, overseers, warders, guides; recruitment of labor; Indigenous "rehabilitation" in liberated areas; and sometimes even relocating villagers. Organizers hoped that police presence around the villages would maintain villagers' sense of normality and confidence in Australia.[26]

In early 1943 the RPC received an official War Establishment commission when commanders appealed that "considerable assistance has been rendered by these men in controlling the large native labour lines so essential to Military operations."[27] A year later, though, concerns over the "militaris[ation of] this Native Police Force, which is repugnant to

Guerillas for the White Men

the C-in-C's intention," led to the cancellation of the RPC's War Establishment.[28] Instead orders emphasized that "native personnel will be enlisted as police and NOT as soldiers. The Royal Papuan Constabulary will be shown on the Order of Battle NG Force as under command of ANGAU."[29] The rapid decommissioning of the RPC as a unit independent of ANGAU highlights the military's desire to maintain the RPC as a civilian force under civilian Papuan control. The RPC was performing tasks different from those of general laborers, yet the need to put RPC members under "proper" controls superseded recognition of their independent status. Indeed, the army was quite clear that white commanders of the RPC would still be recognized separately and not be under the jurisdiction of ANGAU.[30]

Thus, like the coastwatchers the RPC's members were not intended to become a regular fighting unit. Sakarias Anka recalls being told: "Your job is not to fight in the war. You are not a soldier. Your main task is to protect carriers and help transport supplies to the fighting men, rescue personnel from danger areas and look after prisoners."[31] Organizers feared that RPC members might be confused if they had dual roles, maintaining law and order, while also engaging in combat against the Japanese. There were also worries that the RPC members might not understand their new position, that bureaucracies might delay training, and that League of Nations regulations prohibited the raising of military forces in mandated territories.[32] The concerns expressed by organizers of the RPC again reflected colonial concerns of the time and did not consider Indigenous agency. Moreover, the mere assumption that Papuans and New Guineans were too ignorant to understand a dual role reflects racialized diminution of Indigenous intelligence. Certainly Papuans and New Guineans were up to the task, as the parallel formation of the Pacific Islands Regiment (discussed shortly) demonstrates. Even if maintenance of separate institutions for separate purposes — one for law and order and another for military combat — seems legitimate, the other problem was that ANGAU was responsible for recruitment of Papuans and New Guineans into all services. ANGAU arbitrarily determined the destination of recruits, without distinguishing among the recruits allocated to different organizations.

Those who signed up for the RPC signed up for three-year contracts, renewable for five-year periods.[33] Sono recalls how a white officer recruited him, stating: "'All of you policemen must not return to your villages or families. You must not be afraid. You must all join us and help us fight the Japanese. The Japanese are very bad people, they are cannibals.' When we heard our officers pleading for our help, all the men present made a solemn undertaking in front of the officers."[34] There are some indications that, as with other ANGAU labor, recruitment was not always voluntary. Historian Leo Scheps states that when villagers resisted joining RPC, its members burned villages, destroyed gardens, and placed laborers under armed guard. Scheps continues: "After June 1943 local villagers were recruited forcibly by indigenous police. In the Kerowagi area this took the form of rounding up work-gangs, loading them with supplies and walking to Goroka under armed guard."[35] Despite the potentially coercive nature of recruitment, RPC members would receive payment of ten shillings per month, but at war's end most RPC members claimed to have been underpaid.[36] Thus, as with other forms of Aboriginal, Papuan, and New Guinean labor, here the ends of Allied war victory justified dubious means to ensure an Indigenous police force, including coercion, abuse, and underpayment.

Training of the RPC involved infantry drills, elementary English education including reading and writing, marksmanship, and basic instruction in either Police Motu or Tok Pisin (Pidgin English). Unlike in the Pacific Islands Regiment, in the RPC weapons training was primarily meant for defensive purposes rather than offensive measures.[37] Jojoga Yegova recalls RPC training:

For the first three to four weeks we worked with our hands. Then we were issued with rifles. We were told that even though we would be working in the bush as policemen our training would be military in nature. We were instructed in mock battles, climbing over mounds, fences, crossed streams, swung from ropes, crawled through artificial holes, fixed bayonets, and conducted practise target shooting. I found it to be very exhausting because all these things were done at a running speed. Target shooting was done last. If a recruit was proficient he graduated and was sent away to work with the

Guerillas for the White Men

carriers, or in various other capacities. Otherwise one remained on the depot until he could prove his proficiency. Other aspects of life at the depot were much the same as those of peace times. . . . Much to my disappointment, at the need of my training I worked as a guard in Port Moresby.[38]

Yegova's recollections indicate that the level of professionalism expected of the RPC recruits was significant. Nonetheless, Yegova's point that RPC life felt "much the same as those of peace times" highlights the continuing disparities during the war. Despite holding a position of importance in maintaining order in Papua and New Guinea, the Indigenous members of the RPC experienced a subclass status in the presence of white personnel. Additionally, RPC members continued to abuse other Papuans and New Guineans when on patrol, as Native police had done before the war. Historian Neville Robinson comments that "carriers complained that the policemen always chased after them calling, 'walkabout, walkabout.' This was resented because policemen carried no loads but had weapons like shotguns and rifles."[39]

The RPC had 2,064 members in December 1943; 2,553 in December 1944; and 3,137 by war's end in September 1945. Sixty-eight RPC members perished during the war, and a handful of veterans received some awards and recognition afterward.[40] For instance, Sergeant Major Poganau was recommended for the Medal of the Order of the British Empire for helping prevent the desertion of two hundred carriers, spreading rumors to bait a Japanese attack on Port Moresby, and acting with valor in landing on Manus. Another RPC member, Constable Yarawa, was awarded a Military Medal for actions in September 1943 leading to the capture of a Japanese POW. The nomination reads:

> Learning from natives that a JAPANESE soldier was at WAMPUM (MARKHAM VALLEY), YARAWA asked the headman of a nearby village to help him. Not knowing whether the JAP was armed, YARAWA left his rifle in a safe place and, in company with other natives, approached the JAP, who had been located in a hut. He and the headman deceived the JAP with gifts of food and, having allayed his suspicions, seized him and took from him a grenade which he was carrying. YARAWA then tied him up and guarded him all night. In the morning, he brought his prisoner to WO SEARLE's HQ.[41]

Yarawa's bravery and actions demonstrate the noteworthy role RPC members played in the war effort even though they were technically civilians. The capture of the Japanese prisoner is also significant because, as a Papuan, Yarawa was in a unique position to trick the Japanese; white soldiers could not have gained the trust of the Japanese by pretending to be local villagers.

Despite RPC members having proved their worth, toward the end of the war the military began to raise concerns about the organization's postwar status. Documents show that the military and administration of Papua and New Guinea sought to return to the prewar policing situation. One such document emphasizes that "the strength of Royal Papuan Constabulary (native personnel) in Feb 42 was 350. The strength of the emergency Police Force in the Papua areas at the present time is 1,103 — a strength far in excess of that necessary for the 'effective policing' of the area."[42] In addition to recommending a reduction in numbers to prewar levels, the same report advocated once again dividing police into separate Papuan and New Guinean forces. The proposed New Guinea Force should "in the interests of ordered administration and conformity with pre-war and post-war practice, be organised on the lines of the Civil Force."[43] Such persistent references to "prewar" and "postwar" adhere to the notion that colonialism must continue. Thus the RPC example, like that provided by Yolngu soldiers, Papuan and New Guinean coastwatchers, and other Papuan and New Guinean laborers during the war, does not symbolize significantly changed colonial dynamics in Papua and New Guinea. Although the RPC offered an opportunity for advancement for some Papuans and New Guineans, its members were still in a position subservient to the interests of ANGAU, the military, and white residents. The RPC essentially replaced the prewar constabularies, in terms of both mission and application. The opportunities provided to its members were limited and ultimately would not lead to the breakdown of discrimination and racial hierarchies in Papua and New Guinea. Indigenous police continued to represent a means of colonial control over Indigenous subjects.

Guerillas for the White Men

Formal Soldiers: The Pacific Islands Regiment

Certainly both the coastwatchers and the Royal Papuan Constabulary did ultimately engage in combat with Japanese on numerous occasions. As already stated, though, this was not their *official* duty but rather a side effect of their tasks. But there was one formal military unit of Papuans and New Guineans during the war. This force—similar to the NTSRU in Arnhem Land—was formed specifically with the purpose of fighting Japanese through a combination of guerilla and conventional methods. This unit—the Pacific Islands Regiment (PIR)—was the only exclusively Papuan and New Guinean force in the Second World War.

As with the NTSRU the idea of an Indigenous defense network in Papua and New Guinea also met stiff opposition from the military and the colonial government. As early as 1939, when New Guinea commissioned the New Guinea Volunteer Rifles (NGVR), organizers deemed Indigenous participation to be impracticable because of the negative German experience with New Guinean soldiers in the First World War and because of the potentially increased cost of uniforms and equipment.[44] The colonial administrative split between New Guinea and Papua was quite pronounced at this stage, especially in records deliberating the formation of an Indigenous unit in each territory. In regards to the formation of an Indigenous unit in New Guinea, R. M. Melrose wrote in August 1941: "With regard to our conversation regarding the possibility of the native for the use as troops, I am afraid no great use could be made of him. On the other hand, however, he would be of some use after a long period of training and discipline."[45] In 1941 the New Guinea administrator also rejected the idea of Indigenous defense because New Guineans were allegedly disloyal and unpatriotic. The director of district services and Native affairs in the Mandated Territory of New Guinea would later argue, "Beneath the surface there is something of racial antagonism in this country—a contempt for the 'nigger' on the one hand and distrust of black for white on the other."[46]

Other opposition was on more practical grounds, such as the lack of sufficient English speakers or the long recruitment and training process.[47] These concerns seem trivial when one is aware of the extensive employment of non-English-speaking Pacific Islanders in other capacities. Paul Mench and Alan Powell highlight that some of the most significant opposition to the PIR and its precursor components—the Papuan Infantry Battalion (PIB) and the New Guinea Infantry Battalion (NGIB)—came from ANGAU officials; they worried that arming Papuans or New Guineans would cause problems in the postwar period. Like concerns expressed in the Northern Territory and in deliberations over ANGAU pay rates, these anxieties focused on the belief that practices that conflicted with contemporary colonial policies would disrupt the current unequal power relations, with non-Indigenous residents in control.[48] Lt. Col. J. H. Jones linked racist constructs of Papuans and New Guineans to colonial apprehensions when he wrote: "Natives were not sufficiently developed mentally to be entrusted with a knowledge of modern weapons. . . . Australia's task was not just to win the war but to ensure the future welfare and advancement of Papua New Guineans."[49] Similar to the experience in northern Australia, there was clear opposition on both racial and colonial grounds. To empower Indigenous people could wreak havoc in the postwar epoch and rupture the colonial relationship between colonizer and indigene.

In Papua officials responded more favorably than in New Guinea to proposals that a Papuan force be raised. Capt. K. M. Travis wrote in 1939: "The natives are, generally speaking an exceptionally fine type who, even with the limited training given the armed constabulary show considerable promise. . . . The fact that they are natives of the country would make them far more useful for its defense than any imported troops could be."[50] As with the NTSRU there were also economic benefits to raising an Indigenous unit. Payment, uniforms, and employment conditions would be in accordance with the local regulations governing Papuan employment. Travis continued: "The cost of maintaining a native unit would be in the nature of one twentieth of the cost of a similar white unit, and as there are so many tribes all speaking different languages there should be little fear of mutiny."[51] Thus, like their counterparts in Australia, the Indigenous residents of Papua became desirable recruits because they represented a cheap labor pool for exploitation. In fact, treasury documents determined that payment to PIR

Guerillas for the White Men

soldiers through 1 August 1945 was approximately one-fifteenth the Australian Imperial Force rate; after 1 August it increased to approximately one-tenth.[52] Moreover, even by Travis's own admission the colonial tactics of divide and conquer, which had been so prevalent in Papua prior to the war, would benefit the government. Disunity would, in effect, rally the different ethnic groups together through their only common bond—submission to Australian authority. Maj. K. D. Chalmers adopted Travis's proposal, and Papuan administrator Sir John Hubert Plunkett Murray advocated support for a Papuan force. On 19 June 1940 Maj. L. Logan raised the Papuan Infantry Battalion—the precursor incarnation of the PIR.[53]

At first Australian military officers recruited PIB members from the Papuan Constabulary to guard aerodromes and power stations, scout, and engage in jungle warfare.[54] Most of these initial recruits had attended Anglican missions and schools and thus were familiar with white customs, but they were still mostly illiterate. Training began in August 1940 with four Australian officers and 131 Papuans. Unlike the NTSRU the PIB received equipment issuances including rifles and bayonets. Volunteers enlisted for three years, and by February 1941 the strength of the PIB had grown to sixteen European commanders and 285 Papuans. Throughout 1941 the PIB continued to expand, and before Pearl Harbor its primary tasks were guarding vulnerable points of Port Moresby, road construction, wharf labor, and quarrying.[55] As with the Yolngu members of the NTSRU, the motivations to serve in the PIB varied among individuals. But one common thread was the notion of defending their own territory of Papua. PIB veteran Daera Ganiga recalls: "Then I carried out the duties of a soldier. We were all soldiers fighting for Port Moresby—native soldiers. I myself believed on that day, we are soldiers. We have to prepare as guardians for our land—Port Moresby."[56]

The PIB on 11 March 1942 engaged a flight plane, which was the first recorded battle in Papua. It first saw major action at Buna in mid-1942.[57] Daera Ganiga describes the Buna campaign as difficult, as the PIB waited in hiding for advancing Japanese. Ganiga testifies:

We saw their long track came along advance. We could see the Japanese. It's not coming one by one they came along—I couldn't say (how many) and it doesn't matter we are frightened—we look at them—Major told us to wait till he gave the firing order—Major knew the "mile"—gave us same order, safety catch forward, enemy came along—Rapid fire. Japs were surprised that we are seeing them, boys still carrying on firing exactly as the first time, some fired 9 rounds 6, 7. We killed a lot of Japs, laying on the track and we were running again for life. We came along by the bush, we looked for another station.[58]

In another battle at Gona in June 1942 the PIB used tactics such as felling trees, destroying log bridges, and firing at Japanese to slow the enemies' advance on the Kokoda Trail.[59] Alan Hooper, a white commander of the PIB, comments:

All would be expected to patrol, barefooted, hundreds of kilometers with the meager provision of groundsheet blanket, mosquito net, shared bushknife and light rations; quickly make a rainproof shelter, a fire without matches, climb trees or palms, keep an infallible sense of direction in trackless swamp and forest, see without being seen, communicate effectively with local villagers, support white patrol leaders and, if necessary, extend their operation range by living entirely off the land.[60]

By November 1942, with the Japanese advancing further through New Guinea, many refugees offered logistical support to the PIB as carriers. During the early Kokoda campaign the PIB proved ineffective at the Kumusi River, and the Australian Land Headquarters ordered the force disbanded until Maj. Gen. Basil Morris, commander of the New Guinea Force, intervened. Hooper attributes the early ineffectiveness of the PIB to insufficient training in combat techniques.[61] Somu Sigob concurs:

As for the Papua and New Guinean soldiers, they fought well, yes, but I am concerned about the fact that they were not well trained. They would just be shown how to use the trigger, align the foresight and the bullsight, and, if they did everything right, they could hit the target on the bullseye

Guerillas for the White Men

and oh! And so they could kill Japanese. That's all. I thought, well, never mind, just push out the enemy from our territory. Many won and many sold themselves as cheap food to the Japanese. Luckily they did not know me.[62]

Sigob's testimony suggests that not only was the PIB cheap, but it was also merely expedient. Rather than invest the time (in addition to the money) necessary to produce a good force, the Australian military just wanted expendable soldier-bodies to confront the Japanese. That any PIB members survived was merely an added bonus, but that was not the principal concern of military commanders.

The PIB salvaged its reputation and improved in battle, and ultimately training methods improved to incorporate guns, machetes, bows and arrows, arrows tipped with fire, marches, anti-aircraft artillery, and identification of Japanese aircraft. In December 1942, PIB patrols sank barges and axed Japanese soldiers.[63] PIB veteran William Metpi recalls firing mortars at Japanese and even setting booby traps along the mountainside. He describes the battle for Salamaua:

> I came down and planted two sticks. I held onto one with my hand while the other supported my feet. I took the grenades, picked off the pins with my teeth and threw the grenades into the [Japanese] hole. As the grenades went into the holes they exploded causing the Japanese ammunition to also explode, thus blowing out the hideout. So the holes were blown up and the Japanese died and we captured the mountain.[64]

By October 1943 unit commanders coveted the force because of its superb scouting talents. The Japanese were even aware of the PIB's existence — nicknaming them "green shadows" — and sent extra men specifically to eliminate the PIB and Pacific Islander coastwatchers. Even Gen. Thomas Blamey witnessed an impressive parade of PIB members soon after the war's conclusion.[65] Again, similar to the experience of the Yolngu, doubts about the squad's abilities diminished as they proved themselves successful through the course of the war.

Amid the success of the PIB there were calls to expand the force and to add new battalions in New Guinea. On 9 November 1943 Gen.

Thomas Blamey forwarded instructions calling for the creation of the New Guinea Infantry Battalion, akin to the PIB. Orders decreed: "The roles of the Papuan Inf[antry] B[attalio]n and the new B[attalio]n will in general be offensive reconnaissance, harassing tasks and mopping up. It will NOT be practicable to use either unit operationally as a complete B[attalio]n."[66] New regulations decreed that Papuans, New Guineans, and Australians must remain segregated rather than in mixed units. The army began to raise two New Guinea Infantry Battalions in different parts of the Markham Valley. Ultimately INGIB would be ready for deployment by May 1944 and 2NGIB by September 1944 (although not deployed until June 1945). The 3NGIB was in the training process and 4NGIB in the formative stages when the war ended in August 1945.[67] Initially, many experienced New Guinean PIB members transferred into the NGIB. The Australian decision to position all members of the "inferior" Pacific Islander races as (un)equals continues to demonstrate Australian disparagement of Indigenous cultures while their knowledge, labor, and fighting skills were sought. In the NGIB case false constructs of racial and ethnic unity among New Guineans also diminished the battalions' capacities. Unlike the PIB case the Australian military lumped people from multitudinous tribal areas and islands into the NGIB units. This enflamed interclan tensions and led to resentment and discipline problems.[68] Thus the colonial tactics of "divide and conquer" characteristic of British indirect rule, and used widely across Papua and New Guinea prior to the war, came back to haunt the colonizers when they required Indigenous unity.

Indigenous discontent within the NGIB and the PIB was not just over interethnic rivalries, though. There was also anger over working conditions, particularly when New Guineans who transferred from the PIB into the NGIB were deemed rookies. On 30 October 1944 162 New Guinean soldiers walked out of their military lines to ANGAU headquarters in Port Moresby to protest their impending transfer to INGIB and 2NGIB. Their protest was unsuccessful, and their transfer left PIB understaffed and requiring new recruits before resumption of active duty. There was even a near mutiny in 2NGIB from ex-PIB members because

Guerillas for the White Men

of their feeling that they were being disrespected.[69] NGIB veteran William Metpi points to low pay, dissatisfaction with rations, and general mistreatment as the main impetuses for the strike and ensuing skirmish. Metpi recalls the clash, which turned physical:

> The treatment we got was no different from the experience we had when we were in the Papuan Infantry Battalion so we all got cross and a big fight followed, during which two Europeans were wounded and one died. The one who died had his head smashed with rocks. As for the other two, one had his four fingers chopped off while the other was disembowelled. They were brought to the hospital and soon got better.[70]

Government documents and veteran white officer Col. Allan W. Power detail grievances over unequal dress, insignia, titles, pay, and leave as continuing points of contention in 1945 and 1946. Sometimes commanders handed Indigenous soldiers over to the RPC or ANGAU to administer punishments. This practice exacerbated resentment because Indigenous enlisted soldiers did not consider it fair that they be disciplined by civilian authorities.[71] Thus the major miscalculation the military and ANGAU made was the assumption that Papuan and New Guinean soldiers would remain ignorant of their unequal status. But this did not happen; Metpi remarks: "Many of us who had been educated at government schools and had been taught English discovered by reading newspapers, printed and given to us by Americans plus some Australians, that we were supposed to be getting good pay and good food."[72] As oral historian K. Kais perceptively notes, the entire relationship of Papuan and New Guinean soldiers to their white commanders epitomized the master-slave dynamic of colonialism.[73] The war did not change this association and only served to perpetuate it. New Guinean attempts to rectify the situation turned violent and ultimately were unsuccessful.

Despite the brewing discontent within elements of the NGIBs and the PIB, the Pacific Islands Regiment formed in October 1944 as an umbrella administrator over both the PIB and the NGIBs. After 23 July 1942 some component of the PIR—whether the PIB or one of the NGIBs—served in almost every Papua or New Guinea campaign. In all the PIR inflicted approximately 2,209 casualties; estimates of the number of PIR members range from thirty-five hundred to over five thousand.[74] By June and July 1945 the problems of discipline had reached a breaking point. Oral testimony in the Huon Gulf describes NGIB atrocities including chopping off Japanese heads; bayoneting Japanese in the chest; and even boring holes through the hands and ankles of two Japanese, tying them together and throwing them into the sea. Some PIR soldiers also alienated locals and police, which undermined the accomplishments and purpose of the battalions. There were reports of rape and pillage in regions such as Madang and the Huon Gulf. Consequently, at war's end the army disbanded the PIR, and this demobilization proceeded from January to June 1946.[75] While problems of rape, theft, and alienation of locals were quite valid concerns and should not be disregarded, it was also clear that the PIR was in part disbanded because of the continuing colonial project in Papua and New Guinea. Sinclair points out that wartime experience heightened Indigenous demands for rights, which could disrupt the prewar status quo.[76] Mench summarizes: "Because they had fought alongside Europeans[,] Papua New Guinean soldiers were less impressed by claims of European 'superiority.' They wanted a better deal from their 'masters.'"[77] Mench's point is key because it shows that the PIR was never desired, never considered equal, and was wanted solely for its members' guerilla fighting skills and knowledge of the terrain.

After the War: Continuing Disparities

Like Yolngu in Arnhem Land, Papuans and New Guineans experienced a long history of colonialism prior to the Second World War. The Australian government consistently exploited and abused Papuan and New Guinea labor to advance colonial industry and interests. When the Second World War sent Papua and New Guinea into crisis, the Australian government turned to Indigenous residents for support as coastwatchers, laborers, and even soldiers in the PIR. Certainly much of the support Papuans and New Guineans provided to Allied forces was genuine, voluntary, and in their best interests. There are oral testimonies from

Guerillas for the White Men

regions previously under Japanese occupation that demonstrate happiness and relief at the return of Australian rule. Keta Tupaing testifies: "While the Australians were looking after us, we got together pieces of sweet potato, yam, and, things like that and planted them. The Australians kept on looking after us until we had gardens. Then they left us."[78] But as for the Yolngu the Australian government and military's growing dependency on Papuans and New Guineans did not symbolize a rupture of the structures of colonialism. While certainly there was appreciation during the war from non-Indigenous soldiers who served with the RPC, PIR, or coastwatchers, the wartime experience did not place Papuans and New Guineans on an equal footing with white colonizers.

Praise for various components of the RPC and PIR came from a wide variety of sources during and after the war. For instance, one report decreed: "The Pacific Islands Regiment contributed in no small measure to the success of operations in all theatres. . . . These native soldiers employed their intimate knowledge of the jungle to surprise and outwit the Japanese, and, using modern weapons, fought with characteristic bravery and inflicted many casualties on the enemy."[79] Maj. Gen. Basil Morris wrote of the RPC: "In pre-war days there was a separate police force in each Territory. Now, however, RPC is faced with the policing for both."[80] Col. A. R. McKenzie, a U.S. commander stationed in Papua, wrote to Major Watson about the PIB: "I feel that the PIB saved us many casualties and enabled us to move and obtain information in places which would otherwise have been inaccessible to European troops. They saved us many lives and it is our sincere hope that in any future operations in jungle country we may have the privilege of operating again with this excellent Company."[81] Other comments, while intended to commend the PIR, reveal the patronizing attitudes typical of the "higher race." For instance, Brig. Ivan Dougherty wrote, "One very pleasing feature of their work is that at all times they appear to have been under excellent control no matter how difficult the situation."[82] Dougherty's statement suggests that as Papuans and New Guineans represented an inferior race, maintaining "control" was anathematic to their inner nature. Praise from C. O. S. Elliott-Smith aimed to link wartime participation of the PIR to the impending postwar order in Papua and New Guinea:

> It can be justifiably claimed that, having regard to all that has been accomplished since this unit's entry into the Pacific War, the Papuan Infantry Battalion, by its contribution, has laid the foundations for a tradition that ranks with the highest standards of loyalty, courage and devotion of duty, for which other Empire Native Units have established world wide fame in previous generations.[83]

Elliott-Smith's remarks demonstrate the key links between the PIR and other transnational examples—not just the Yolngu and the Navajo Code Talkers. Fundamentally, its purpose was always to protect the "empire," not Indigenous interests or vitality. As such, even if it did lay foundations for the future, it was a future of continuing colonialism in Papua and New Guinea.

Some reforms immediately after the war benefited Papuans and New Guineans. Gen. Thomas Blamey blamed global commercial capitalism for the past abuses in Papua and New Guinea, and he considered the Chifley Labor Government to have a unique opportunity concurrently to protect both Papuan and New Guinean rights and Australia's security through postwar reconstruction. Secretary of External Affairs, Second Section (Pacific Section), W. D. Forsyth proposed in 1943 that Australia amalgamate Papua and New Guinea and implement a Native Welfare Charter to abolish indentured labor. In 1944 the Army Directorate of Research and Civil Affairs (DORCA) was commissioned to enquire into matters of education and labor relevant for postwar reconstruction.[84] Historian and anthropologist Geoffrey Gray argues that DORCA "stood for a break with pre-war policy and practice in Papua and New Guinea, which in its view needed to be developed in keeping with the ideals expressed in the Atlantic Charter."[85]

But Papua and New Guinea had been devastated by the war. When laborers, soldiers, police, and coastwatchers returned home, they found high food prices, destroyed villages, and no sufficient resources or capital. The shortage of able-bodied labor in villages had left many women

Guerillas for the White Men

and children undernourished, and subsequent consequences included lowered resistance to diseases and lower fertility rates. The halted production of peacetime goods during the war made village reconstruction slow and difficult.[86] One journalist from the *Brisbane Courier-Mail* even wrote in April 1949, "Five years after its recapture from the Japanese, this town [Lae] looks dirtier and more dilapidated than when I saw it through a coastwatcher's field glasses in 1942."[87] A series of censuses conducted in 1945 and 1947 estimated that in some areas, one-third of village populations had been killed and at least one hundred thousand pigs had been destroyed, along with village structures, crops, and timber. Australian colonial officials also reasserted their prewar armed police patrols of some villages, much to the ire of villagers, who even used Japanese weapons and arms to resist such incursions.[88]

The Australian government did aim to address some of the grievances of Papuans and New Guineans. In October 1944 the government appointed a committee to develop a War Damages Compensation Scheme with the aim "to restore them [natives] to a condition of life which is at least equal to that which they enjoyed before the war. Finally, it should be linked to plans for the improvement of their conditions and the advancement of their welfare."[89] Some Australians opposed the development of the fund on the grounds that Australia should not have to foot the bill for Papua and New Guinea. Nonetheless, the fund passed the Australian Parliament with the purpose of compensating for death; injury; property loss; or loss of goods such as timber, trees, crops, canoes, axes, tomahawks, clothing, and household items. Even those who worked for the Japanese were eligible, so long as their employment had not been voluntary; the report outlining the compensation scheme explicitly stated "that it would be a grave injustice to exclude a community because one or more of its members gave voluntary assistance to the enemy."[90] The fund granted individuals up to eighty dollars each and villages up to four dollars per head. The administration replaced livestock, repaired infrastructure, and laid new roads. On 14 December 1946 a new Trusteeship Agreement from the United

Nations formally united Papua and New Guinea. By 1950 the government had invested almost two million dollars in compensation and reconstruction of Papua New Guinea.[91]

The goals that accompanied reconstruction of Papua New Guinea were succinctly laid out in the Australian Parliament by E. J. Ward, the minister for external territories, on 4 July 1945:

> This Government is not satisfied that sufficient interest had been taken in the Territories prior to the Japanese invasion, or that adequate funds had been provided for their development and the advancement of the native inhabitants. Apart from the debt of gratitude that the people of Australia owe to the natives of the Territory, the Government regards it as its boundless duty to further to the utmost the advancement of the natives, and considers that can be achieved only by providing facilities for better health, better education and for a greater participation by the natives in the wealth of their country and eventually in its government.[92]

Published pamphlets such as *A New Deal for Papua* and *Development and Welfare in the Western Pacific* suggest paternalistic but nonetheless humanitarian desires to improve the lot of Papua New Guineans. Anthropologists played a key role in researching the impact of the war on Papua New Guineans and contributing to subsequent policy developments. The New Deal envisaged a system of indirect rule akin to the British system over African colonies. The Australian government reformed labor laws to introduce a forty-four-hour work week, improved the ration scale, and placed a twelve-month limit on contracts. As wages increased slightly, so too child labor was abolished, a workmen's compensation scheme began, diets improved, local self-government at the village level began, and there was a gradual repeal of apartheid-like legislation. In October 1945 the government set up a Native Labour Department to send inspectors and supervisors to enforce the new labor regulations.[93] In 1952 the Sogeri school offered the first post–primary school education to Papua New Guineans, and the University of Papua New Guinea was founded in 1966. In 1962 the first white woman was allowed to marry a Papua New Guinean man, and Indigenous people earned legal permission to drink alcohol. The Papua New Guinea Act of 1949 permitted the formation of optional village councils and set up a Legislative Council, which evolved to a more powerful House of Assembly in 1964.[94]

These reforms were significant, but fundamentally the structures of colonialism in Papua New Guinea continued to operate despite pronounced aims to the contrary. Indeed, anthropologists such as David Counts, Marty Zelenietz, Hisafumi Saito, and Carl E. Thune all describe the Second World War as a brief interlude, after which Australia reimposed the previous unequal relationship between colonizers and colonized. Powell succinctly affirms, "The basic props of colonial society were not to be undermined by war."[95] To administer the compensation funds, district officers and administrators would assess compensation claims. Moreover, the money would be deposited into savings bank accounts; the guidelines stipulated: "For a period of three years no person should be allowed to make withdrawals in excess of £5 during any six months' period without the written permission of the District Officer."[96] The paternalistic reasoning behind such restrictive provisions was to protect Papua New Guineans from "evil social consequences [such as gambling that] may result from the natives possessing large sums of money which they can neither spend nor deposit safely."[97] The controls reflected wider paternalistic trends manifest in Australia's postwar planning regarding Papua New Guinea. For instance, at a press conference in San Francisco on 3 May 1945, Minister for External Affairs H. V. Evatt declared:

> Many of these [Pacific] peoples are clearly "not yet able to stand by themselves under the strenuous conditions of the modern world." This is a dangerous situation not only for them, but for all of us. It is necessary that powers capable of playing an effective part in maintaining security should be present in this region until the indigenous peoples can stand on their own feet. This goal should be approached by progressive steps, but the overriding interests of security forbid that there should meanwhile be a strategic vacuum in this vital zone.[98]

Certainly Australia had a legitimate right to maintain its security, particularly in the wake of the Second World War. Yet Evatt's statement and the ANZAC Pact of 1944, calling for Australian and New Zealand trusteeship over colonial possessions in the Pacific, justified the ongoing paternalistic status quo that was disadvantaging Papua New Guineans.[99] Historian Nicholas Gaynor even argues that security concerns led Australian and New Zealand postwar planning to seek "control of the political reins of these [Pacific] island territories thus subjugating millions of native peoples of the South Pacific and South East Asia."[100] Debate surrounding the Papua–New Guinea Provisional Administration Bill in 1945 centered on maintenance of Papua New Guinea as buffers against future Asian aggression. Although there was some concern expressed about Indigenous welfare, quite a number of parliamentarians emphasize d that the interests of white residents in Papua New Guinea must be upheld first. Paul Hasluck, minister for the territories from 1951 to 1963, later wrote, "Regarding the three elected members [to the Legislative Council in 1951], Murray's clear view was that the intention of the Act was that they should be elected by the European community to represent the Europeans."[101] Racial discourse continued to dominate debate, as a number of speakers referred to Papua New Guineans as having yet to "evolve" beyond the "mentality of a child."[102] Press coverage in the immediate postwar period also sometimes denigrated Papua New Guineans as unprepared for the responsibilities of "civilization." For example, one article in the *Age* from 1948 declared: "They [natives] had found a new freedom while the Australian troops had been in New Britain, but unfortunately they had had too much money, and had developed a desire for the privileges of European civilisation without the corresponding responsibilities. They would not work continuously, and had developed gambling habits."[103]

Despite the growing international trends of self-determination, Papua New Guinea remained an Australian colony until 1975. Only one postwar planner—Maj. Jim Taylor—recommended Papua New Guinea for Papua New Guineans. The policy directive of Papua New Guinea from 1947 technically was to aim for self-governance, but this would not happen until the implementation of self-government in 1973 and independence in 1975.[104] As historian Margriet Roe summarizes, despite improvements to labor rights and other advances in the education system, the Australian government still sought "to protect them from what they felt were undesirable features of an 'open' society."[105] Moreover, during this period Australia essentially set up a mercantilist system, whereby government officials would negotiate the purchase of Indigenous land, found and impose small plantations, and establish an export industry in Papua New Guinea before returning control of the plantations to Papua New Guinean residents. One pre-1950 agricultural policy stated:

> It is believed that the native peoples can gradually be instructed and led into the development of export industries which will supply many of Australia's tropical product requirements, such as coffee, tea, cocoa, quinine, rubber, fibres, species, etc., thereby developing a considerable mutual trade between the Commonwealth and its dependency and making possible the improvement of the living standard of the people of that dependency. It is, however, realized that a number of years will elapse before marked results can be expected since the native peoples are at present in a relatively primitive stage of development.[106]

The policy clearly set the priority of Papua New Guinean agriculture as oriented toward Australian interests, with Indigenous concerns secondary at best. Moreover, even the alleged goals of helping Papua New Guineans were tainted with assimilationist undertones and continuing constructs of primitiveness.

Regulations within Papua New Guinea also continued to disadvantage Indigenous residents, and social problems persisted. The Native Employment Ordinance of 1958 replaced "contracts" with "agreements," which essentially perpetuated a de facto indentured-labor system. The legislation extended the permitted agreement periods and authorized employers to withhold wages for "illegal absences"; one draft of the bill contained a provision (later removed) that would have required workers to carry identity cards. Laborers became classified into various categories, each carrying different levels of autonomy and requiring workers to obtain certificates from district officers. Notwithstanding increases to the minimum wage, wide disparities persisted between Papua New Guinean and non-Indigenous workers. Until 1958 the administration of Papua New Guinea racially segregated education and hospitals into separate facilities for Europeans, Asians, and mixed-race persons. Hasluck recognized the tenuous nature of racial segregation, but he justified it on the grounds that "to keep both white and black in their 'proper place' was not an unkind or intentionally repressive code. It was the maintenance of a relationship that had been found to work well in the past."[107] A United Nations Mission visit in 1950 determined that while health and education standards for Papuan New Guineans had improved over the prewar situation, their living conditions were the same as they had been prewar and that for other races the situation had actually deteriorated.[108] Despite increases to education funding, still only 50 percent of primary-school-aged children were in schools by 1975. As historian Hank Nelson remarks, "The wartime generation have had the frustration of having endured, having seen what the rewards might be, but never having been able to possess them."[109]

Problems with compensation for the war effort have also continued to plague Papua New Guineans. As mentioned in the previous chapter, under the War Gratuity Act only those Papua New Guineans enlisted in the armed forces were eligible for gratuity payments. This excluded not only laborers under ANGAU but also nonenlisted coastwatchers and the RPC. The press in Australia did not address the lack of compensation for Papua New Guinean civilian laborers but instead celebrated the rewarding of gratuities to Papua New Guinean soldiers.[110] The federal treasurer recognized the problematic nature of excluding the RPC but did not recommend amending gratuity legislation. In June 1947 J. B. Chifley wrote:

> The Department of the Army is of the opinion that any discrimination against the native policeman for equivalent war service will be interpreted by the native population as an indication that he is inferior in status and service to the native soldier, and it is felt that this would have an adverse

effect on the relationship between the native police and the native population and on the morale of the members of the police forces . . . [but] payment of gratuity under the provisions of the War Gratuity Act should not
be extended to members of the native police forces.[111]

Internal government questions over whether or not to pay gratuities to
the over three thousand members of the RPC continued as late as 1960.
The government had to grapple with the problematic fact that the RPC
was technically civilian but that for the duration of the Pacific War it
had been under army command. Moreover, after the war the members
of the RPC received war medals, and, as already indicated, their work
during the war was quite similar to that of the PIR and other Papua New
Guinean soldiers. Ultimately, though, the government maintained its
position that the RPC was ineligible for gratuities because "the native
members of the Royal Papuan Constabulary and New Guinea Police
Force were under Army control and rendered service of a military nature
but were not in either case enlisted in the Australian Military Forces."[112]

For those approximately seventy-five hundred Papua New Guineans
who did receive gratuities the amount was approximately one-tenth
that of those Australians who served in the Australian Service and one-
fifteenth the regular overseas rate of gratuity. The government deferred
many of the gratuity payments until March 1951 on the grounds that
Papua New Guineans already were financially secure or by arguing
that more goods would be available then.[113] Liz Reed notes that most
Papua New Guinean carriers still have not received adequate compensation for their work during the war.[114] The compensation fund simply was not sufficient. The two million dollars invested in Papua New
Guinea after the war averaged to an expenditure of one dollar per resident. Reconstruction money was only available for those who had lost
prewar houses; those who never possessed their own home prior to the
war were ineligible. Veterans from the PIR lobbied the Australian Returned and Servicemen's League (RSL) in 1969 to support a better deal
for Papua New Guinean veterans, but the RSL rejected their appeal.
Lobbying politicians for full repatriation benefits also had little impact, particularly after 1975, when politicians began to consider this the

government of Papua New Guinea's responsibility.[115] Even a soldier-settlement scheme in Papua New Guinea announced in 1958 by Minister for Territories Paul Hasluck proved more beneficial to white Australians than to Papua New Guineans. The scheme offered land in Papua New Guinea to Australian veterans and loans of up to twenty-five thousand dollars. The idea of incorporating Papua New Guinean veterans into the scheme never even arose until the Australian mission to the United Nations cabled to enquire as to the eligibility of Papua New Guinean veterans. Hasluck affirmed the entitlement of Papua New Guineans, but the scheme still seemed to favor white Australians. By November 1962, the government had granted 246 loans under the scheme—128 to Australians and 118 to Papua New Guineans.[116]

Veteran William Metpi summarizes the resentment at undercompensation felt by many Papua New Guineans: "We fought side by side with you, (Australians), and our labourers carried your wounded. In fact we helped in almost every way and we expect a better deal than this. We want to be recognised."[117] This is not to say that all Papua New Guineans are resentful or angry at Australia. An exchange among three Papua New Guineans—a veteran, his son, and another veteran—highlights the diverging opinions among the populace:

PAUL LAFE: I didn't get any job after the war. I just relaxed, had a rest. It had been very difficult—I nearly lost my life. When they started the army again . . .

SON: [angry] They never let anything know. He knows nothing. They haven't promised anything for him. . . . I don't want my father to say anything. We know nothing about this world war. We only supported Australians. And we get nothing from Australians.

ANOTHER MAN: Excuse me, son, that's not right to say for us.

SON: What are we getting?

ANOTHER MAN: What you mean?

SON: Are you gonna die tomorrow?[118]

Such split opinion demonstrates both how far Papua New Guinea has come since the war and also the challenges that remain to be overcome.

Guerillas for the White Men

Since independence Papua New Guinea has continued to rely on Australia both for aid and as a trading partner in the region. At the opening of the United Nations General Assembly on 10 October 1975 Papua New Guinea's first prime minister, Michael Somare, declared:

> After the Second World War Australia's role became less and less that of an overlord. As our political autonomy increased, on our own insistence, Australia took up a new role as a generous and sympathetic donor of aid. It has guaranteed that this role will continue in our new relationship as partners and neighbouring states in the Pacific. It is my sincere hope that the relationship of the past years will provide the basis for a continuing close bond of friendship and co-operation between our countries in the future.[119]

Popular memory in Australia, as well, is tenuous over the role of Papua New Guinea during the Second World War. While the Kokoda Campaign has risen to rival Gallipoli in the popular mythology of Australia, with the exception of "Fuzzy Wuzzy Angel" mythology, the Pacific Islander role is almost nonexistent in the cultural memory. Perhaps the best commentary on the position of Papua New Guinean contributions to the Second World War derives from Peter Ryan's 1959 observation: "But the terrible general suffering and devastation of the [Papua New Guinean] people's lives have faded from the active memory of almost all Australians except the soldiers who served there and who saw it."[120]

CHAPTER 5. The Navajo Code Talkers

Warriors for the Settler Nation

Magnificent specimens of "original American" manhood, they [Navajos] are already farther advanced than recruits are with so few days of training to their credit. All are of sturdy stock and "take well" to the type of discipline and military instruction offered in the Marine Corps, their instructors report. — "NAVAJO INDIANS TOTE RIFLES IN BOOT PLATFORM," *Marine Corps Chevron*, 15 May 1942[1]

Well, when they called me "Chief" I just thought that the guy doesn't know anything about Indian tribes. There's no Chiefs in the Navajo tribe but there are "Chiefs" in your comic books, and I just pass it up that way that the guy doesn't know anything about Indians. — SAM BILLISON[2]

Long ago our elderly people had many bad hardships. Accordingly, I guess we decided to go to war and protect our people from having other hardships. We have done that by the way of our thinking and teaching, just like when we approach things that are new to us. That was when we thought back about our people and our surroundings. I would think, "I'm doing this for my people." I believed what we did was right, and it was worth it. We protected the many American people, also the unborn children, which would be the generation to come. Now, I see young men and women, and I'm glad for what I did for them. — COZY STANLEY BROWN[3]

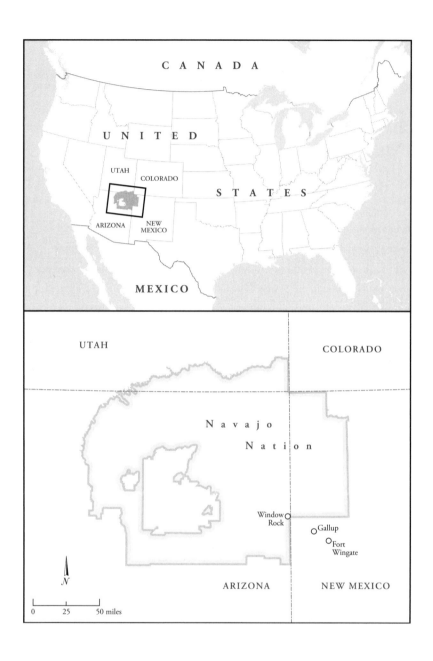

MAP 3. The Navajo Nation

At a July 2001 ceremony honoring the Navajo Code Talkers, U.S. president George W. Bush stated, "Regardless of circumstances, regardless of history, they [Navajo Code Talkers] came forward to serve America."[4] Bush's speech, through use of the word "regardless," reflects a significant aspect of the Code Talkers' history. Bush, like a number of historians, glorifies the Code Talkers' experience in celebratory stories about the Second World War rather than as part of a wider history of the Navajo Nation's relationship with the United States. Similar to Bush's standpoint most other historical studies consider the Navajo Code Talkers to signify racial harmony for Native Americans in the United States. To an extent this argument has merit—clearly the Navajo Nation supported the war effort, and undoubtedly the Navajo Code Talkers willingly partook in the Pacific campaigns. Code Talker veterans rightfully take pride in their accomplishments as vital participants in the war against Japan.

The Code Talkers story has an underside to it, though. When recontextualized within a wider framework of American Indian–U.S. relations—like the Yolngu and Papua New Guinea case studies—the Navajo Code Talkers example does not represent a fundamental break with the structures of colonialism. Rather, the U.S. government used constructions of Native Americans as a "martial race" to transform their Native skills into weapons. The next two chapters reconsider the Navajo Code Talkers from the perspective that the government and the military considered Navajos solely as tools, while their cultural and intellectual skills were otherwise derided as inconsequential or inferior to white Americans'. Therefore, although Navajo Code Talkers received significant praise during the war, the end of the war marked a stark return to discrimination and assimilationist policies. The continuity of prejudice and structural inequality crushed the hopes of many Navajos that the war would provide an opportunity for personal and collective advancement. This chapter analyzes the government's and military's mistrust and disapproval of the Code Talker project. It also considers Navajo agency through an investigation of Navajo motives to serve and questions to what extent military service fulfilled their expectations. The next chapter focuses on the contrasts between the valorous achievements of the Code Talkers in battle and the postwar neglect of the Code Talker veterans.

Precursors to the Navajo Code Talkers

The Second World War was by no means the first time the U.S. military employed Native Americans as weapons. Since the beginnings of European colonialism in the Americas, colonial powers both formally and informally employed Native Americans as scouts or fighters. After the U.S. Civil War, as the U.S. frontier pushed into the West and Southwest, American Indian scouts became critical in campaigns to "pacify" Native resistance. Racial constructs of Native American primitiveness often came into play when justifying the formal employment of such soldiers. Gen. George Crook wrote in 1886: "There are negative characters among Indians as among white men, and the nearer an Indian approaches to the savage state the more likely he will prove valuable as a soldier."[5] The idea of American Indians as valuable weapons on the frontier permeates many military stratagems of the period. Maj. E. P. Ewers grounded the use of American Indian scouts within the history of their success. He wrote in 1894: "In the past the Indians have done excellent military service. They are brave and fearless, and have been loyal and true while we have kept faith with them. In my opinion no better material can be found as an auxiliary to the army in dealing with the Indian tribes than the enlisted Indian scout or soldier."[6] Other writers in the late nineteenth century, such as H. C. Cushing, considered

Native American military service an opportunity to hasten assimilation; Cushing wrote in 1880:

> Within all the territory now occupied by our troublesome wards [Native Americans] let *military colonies* be organized, composed of the various bands of Indians. . . . Subject him to certain restraints of discipline, at first extremely light, but gradually increasing until, as he becomes accustomed to it, he learns the great lesson of obedience to, and the necessity of government.[7]

Thus, as the frontier wars continued, American Indian service was consistently positioned within the framework of fighting in service of the U.S. government against other Native Americans. This concept transcended the realities of European colonies, for even Australia similarly employed native police in all states, Papua and New Guinea.

The First World War provided an opportunity for Native Americans to serve en masse within a new framework: in opposition to other nation-states instead of against other American Indians. Instead of being employed just for their "Native" skills, American Indians served in regular (white) units as common servicemen. By the end of the First World War, approximately seventeen thousand Native Americans had served, over two-thirds of them voluntarily. Their reasons for enlistment were diverse: patriotism, the desire to achieve U.S. citizenship, to show bravery, or to seek adventure. Navajo veteran Chee Dah Spencer recalls: "Whenever we [war buddies] see each other, we ask one another, 'Are you still living?' and talked about the time we serve our country. I have seen and serve my country. I'm proud of it."[8] All Native Americans who served in the First World War received U.S. citizenship in 1919, and they received significant praise from commanders in both the United States and Europe.[9] All Native Americans subsequently received citizenship shortly after the First World War under the 1924 Indian Citizenship Act.

The First World War also represented the first international conflict exhibiting what historian Tom Holm refers to as "Indian Scout Syndrome." Holm defines Indian Scout Syndrome as such: "This conviction attributes to Indian warriors the ability to detect the presence of an enemy from a bent blade of grass or to hide themselves in an open field. Some whites credited these abilities to a kind of genetic spirituality inherent among Native peoples. Indians were scouts by nature."[10] One such form of Indian Scout Syndrome that manifested for the first time during the First World War was code talking. The most famous example from the First World War derives from a U.S. artillery unit with Choctaw soldiers who communicated in their own language to prevent German code breaking. Col. A. W. Bloor described the experiment:

> While comparatively inactive at Vaux-Champagne, it was remembered that the regiment possessed a company of Indians. They spoke twenty six different languages or dialects, only four or five of which were ever written. There was hardly one chance in a million that Fritz [Germans] would be able to translate these dialects, and the plan to have these Indians transmit telephone messages was adopted. The regiment was fortunate in having two Indian officers who spoke several of the dialects. Indians from the Choctaw tribe were chosen and one placed in each P.C.[11]

The Choctaw experiment proved successful, securing a withdrawal and an assault; there were no mishaps with or awareness from the Germans. Subsequently, Lieutenant Black trained Choctaws for more transmissions and even designed code words and expressions for military terminology. For instance, the word *tribe* represented regiment, *stone* signified grenade, and *little gun shoot fast* meant machine gun.[12] Canadians also utilized Native languages during the First World War, but the lack of military terminology made it easy for Germans to decipher their communications.

It would be in the Second World War, though, that code talking became prominent in the U.S. armed forces. Though this chapter focuses on Navajos, they certainly were not the only Native American Code Talkers. Historian William C. Meadows examines the frequently overlooked role Comanches played in Europe. Meadows even lists six Native American Nations with Code Talkers from both the United States and Canada in the First World War and thirteen in the Second World

War. Second World War Code Talkers on much smaller scales than the Navajos included Choctaws, Chippewa-Oneidas, Comanches, Hopis, Meskwakis, and Creeks, who were sought after "informal tests [were] conducted using two Creek Indians and results appear[ed] sufficiently good to warrant further exploitation use of Indian language for this purpose."[13] As Meadows argues, though, the non-Navajo Code Talker programs never grew to critical mass because of "significant amounts of skepticism, distrust and racially-biased assumptions that prohibited the full potential of using code talkers."[14] Meadows estimates that approximately six hundred Native Americans from Canada and the United States served as Code Talkers in either the First or the Second World War.[15] As the largest group the Navajo Code Talkers have become the most documented, studied, and remembered Code Talkers from the Second World War. The glorification of the Code Talkers has emerged in the secondary literature, derived mostly from journal articles but also in books and pop culture. Too often Code Talker texts isolate their experience from the wider history of Navajo-U.S. relations. Scholars such as Doris Paul — the first to publish a historical text on the Navajo Code Talkers — consider the Navajo Code Talkers' experience a sign of reconciliation that constituted a break with trends of colonialism leading up to the war:

> When the bombs fell on Pearl Harbor in 1941, the Navajos were quietly living out their lives in their own way, secluded from the pulsating life of the twentieth century. World War II jolted them into active participation in meeting the crisis that faced the nation. The effect on the Navajo and on his way of life was far-reaching.[16]

Paul's argument about Pearl Harbor jolting Navajos into the war effort certainly is accurate, though her description of Navajos being "secluded" from the twentieth century suggests a historicist interpretation of indigenous cultures. Paul's argument also overlooks how — similar to the Yolngu and Papua New Guinean cases — the Navajo Code Talkers' wartime and postwar experiences actually represented continuing government disregard for Native vitality, constitutive of colonialism.

Conceiving of and Training the Navajo Code Talkers

The idea for the Navajo Code Talkers came from Philip Johnston, the white son of a missionary who grew up on the Navajo Reservation before moving to Los Angeles. Johnston wrote in 1964: "At the age of four, in northern Arizona, I began to make the acquaintance of the Navajo Indians and to share their lives and fortunes. A strange language, which no adult has ever mastered, became as familiar to me as my native tongue. I learned their songs and ceremonials by the flickering light of many a hogan campfire."[17] In early 1942 Johnston read a newspaper story about an army division in Louisiana preparing to use a Native American language in code. Most likely this newspaper referenced the Comanche Code Talkers, who were recruited as early as December 1940 and were conducting tests in Louisiana in autumn 1941. Johnston conducted research into the feasibility of using other Native languages for military codes and concluded that Navajo, Sioux, Chippewa, and Pima-Papago were suitable. He noted these languages not only for their complexity but also because of their speakers' larger populations and their limited contact with German anthropologists during the 1930s. Johnston finally recommended Navajo to the armed forces because of his personal background with the language and the people.[18]

Johnston assured the Marine Corps "that the Navajo language was the only Indian language not thoroughly studied by Axis agents during the past two decades."[19] The Navajo language was unwritten at the time of the Second World War for numerous reasons. First, many of the sounds used in Navajo have no easy equivalent in the English alphabet. There are also different inflections within the Navajo language, and some Navajo words can have up to four inflections, each prescribing a different meaning. The language is so complicated that, with the exception of the language of the Athabascans in Alaska and northern Canada, it has no linguistic relation with another Native American language. In fact, around the Second World War it was believed that only twenty-eight non-Navajos possessed even a superficial knowledge of the language. Johnston thus wrote, "A fluency in reading Navajo can be acquired only by individuals who are first highly educated in English, and who, in turn, have made a profound study of Navajo, both in its spoken and written form."[20]

In March 1942 Johnston set up a demonstration of the Navajo language on a Los Angeles football field, impressing Gen. Clayton Vogel, commanding officer of the Marine Corps' Pacific Fleet. Vogel commissioned Johnston to enroll two hundred bilingual Navajo, but the pilot project necessitated only approximately thirty Navajo recruits.[21] Johnston's role as conceiver and founder of the Navajo Code Talkers is revealing because his role parallels that of Donald Thomson for the NTSRU. It is clear from Johnston's background and continuing respect for Navajos that he never intended to exploit Navajo culture for his own purposes. For him — as for Thomson — the Code Talkers represented a way in which the Navajos could distinguish themselves in the U.S. military. In fact, Johnston claimed that he recruited some Navajos by telling them this would be an opportunity to prove their superiority to whites.[22] Yet the fact remains that Johnston himself was non-Native, and he was placed in charge of the Code Talker project. Hence as with the NTSRU and the PIR, the actual conception of the Code Talkers was not a Native initiative, but actually a military scheme requiring indigenous labor and knowledge. The Navajo language may have been the key to the military's venture, but the power structures and power relations maintained white control over the production and manifestation of Navajo knowledge.

Recruitment of Navajo Code Talkers began at the reservation boarding schools with assistance from the Bureau of Indian Affairs. By April 1942 the pilot twenty-nine enlistees became the 382nd platoon of the U.S. Marine Corps — the first all–Native American, all-Navajo platoon in Marine Corps history.[23] Vogel's March 1942 memo calling for the formation of the Code Talkers stated that "the Navaho is the largest tribe but lowest in literacy. He [Johnston] stated, however, that 1,000 — if that were needed — could be found with the necessary qualifications."[24] Another memo declared that "about 3,000 males are between the ages of 21 and 25 of which some five or six hundred have had high school education."[25] The need for bilingual Navajos reflects problematic elements of settler colonialism. Johnston described the main qualification for recruits as "an excellent command of both the native tongue and of the English. In some cases, individuals of a tribe which has had long contact with white residents may have largely forgotten his native tongue."[26] Lt. Col. Wethered Woodworth similarly stated that "it will, of course, be necessary that the men in this group have the proper linguistic qualifications in english [*sic*] and in their Tribal dialect, so that they can transmit necessary military messages by voice over general communications system."[27] Essentially, the military was searching for Navajos who were what Meadows refers to as "bi-cultural," representing "a contradiction of being indigenous enough to retain one's language, but acculturated enough to be considered useful by the military."[28] For those Navajos previously sent to boarding schools under assimilation policies, the rules forbidding indigenous languages had eradicated their Navajo-language skills. The reverse problem existed for those Navajos never given the fair educational opportunity to learn English by their own choice. Rather than offer to teach English (without restricting the use of the Navajo language), the military merely sought to exploit bilingual Navajos without assisting the monolingual population.

Code Talkers went through boot camp and basic training, followed by eight weeks of intensive code training. Boot camp was a shocking experience for many of those Navajos who had not previously lived at boarding schools. One Code Talker remarks: "We had never been under any discipline before we entered boot camp. We had lived out in the sheep country. So this was shocking to us. The sergeant didn't make things any easier for us."[29] The same anonymous Code Talker recollects an anecdote about the learning curve Navajos experienced in boot camp through their interactions with officers:

> One of our [boot camp] sergeants was mighty quick with his fists. He didn't like the way we were boxing one day. You see we aren't aggressive in nature; we were always peaceful, but he made us box. We pretended we were hitting real hard, but he yelled, "That's no way to box!" So he lined us up, and came down the line boxing each of us . . . wham . . . wham. We

The Navajo Code Talkers

were falling all over the place. It seems that one of our guys had had some training in boxing, and when the sergeant got to him, and reared back to deliver that mean punch, this Navajo gave it to him. Well . . . that was the last of our boxing matches.[30]

Though that Code Talker had adjustment difficulties in boot camp, other Navajos who had lived in boarding schools found the experience unproblematic. Thomas Begay remarks: "My attitude towards boot camp was that this was nothing! I did this stuff in boarding school."[31] Other Navajos proved quite good trainees early on because of the skills they had acquired living on the Navajo Reservation. Harold Foster comments: "The reason we did so well [at rifle range shooting] is because on the reservation we hunt rabbit, prairie dogs, anything good to eat with our rifles. We don't waste any food like that."[32] The boot-camp experience demonstrates that in the armed forces at least Navajos were on an equal level as white servicemen. This was a sharp contrast to their previous experiences, as well as the experiences of Yolngu and Papua New Guineans. Unlike other marines, though, Navajo Code Talkers had the additional task of memorizing and implementing the secret code.

After boot camp Navajo Code Talker recruits would learn the code that the original twenty-nine Code Talkers had devised. The code entailed 413 words in addition to an alphabet based on existing Navajo words. Because military terminology did not have corresponding Navajo words, much of the code entailed symbolically denoting corresponding Navajo words. Cozy Stanley Brown describes the process of devising the code: "Then, we got together and discussed how we would do it. We decided to change the name of the airplanes, ships and English ABCs into the Navajo language. We did the changing."[33] In the end the code worked in such a way that the Navajo word for *bird carrier* signified aircraft carrier, *owl* meant observation plane, *iron fish* equaled submarine, *potato* was hand grenade, and *egg* corresponded to bomb. During training all Code Talkers learned the alphabet and then the vocabulary list—sometimes up to twenty-five words a day—with drills in classroom settings.

Much of the training entailed patience and an emphasis on the mechanics of both the code and the operation of communications equipment. After completion of training in late June 1942, two of the original twenty-nine remained in San Diego to train additional Code Talkers while the rest of the group were deployed with the Marine Corps Amphibious Corps.[34]

Based on the success of the initial twenty-nine Code Talkers, beginning in July 1942 the call went out for an additional two hundred recruits.[35] Subsequent recruitment continued on the Navajo Reservation for the duration of the war. Worries that Navajos might not understand the seriousness of the commitment drove one military commander to emphasize, "It must be clearly understood by recruits that they are enlisting as privates for general duty in the Marine Corps and for the duration of the war."[36] Recruiters turned away some Navajos for not meeting the minimum education requirements to enlist, while they also turned away a number of white men for not having any more than a basic knowledge of the Navajo language. As of February 1943 it was primarily the selective service that conducted recruitment, often through conscription. Interestingly, recruiters observed that "the Navajos, like most of the Indian tribes, are very patriotic and a large percentage of them volunteered for service in the various branches at an early date. For the most part, the numbers left are illiterate or not physically qualified."[37] Even those Navajos who signed up for other branches of the armed forces sometimes found themselves involuntarily sent to the Marine Corps. The Marine Corps eventually disregarded its policy "not to accept for enlistment applicants who are married and have more than two children . . . because of the scarcity of [Navajo] men qualified for communication duty. Allowances authorized for dependents have proved to be attractive for prospective recruits, since they represent incomes sufficient to maintain their families on the reservation."[38]

Not all recruits succeeded in becoming Code Talkers; thirty recruits failed to qualify, at least one because of alcoholism. One Navajo Code Talker instructor recalls:

I knew I didn't have any business saying that Mr. So and So *would* make it as a Navajo communicator, unless I knew in my heart he had the capability. Just because I liked the way he looked and because we got on well together was not enough. I had to know that man would qualify, that he was going to be faithful to his dying breath. Then I could say, "Yes." We weeded out and turned down some of our Navajos because they had to have a certain education—let's say tenth grade. They had to be able to spell words like *reconnaissance*.[39]

The Code Talker instructor's testimony reveals many of the complexities involved in training the recruits. The logistics of the job superseded tribal ties, and the difficult training added another significant barrier to ensuring sufficient numbers of Code Talkers. Jack Jones describes learning the code as a formidable task: "And so from there, well, it was not much time, you know, given to us to learn code talking. They give whole bunch of names like that, the names of the ships, the names of different kinds of weapons. And then there was alphabet—you got to learn how to spell this and that. And so sometimes—lots of time on the message, well, you had to use that alphabet."[40] Rising to the challenge of learning the code, 190 Code Talkers were already in action by April 1943, and over 400 would serve by the end of the Second World War, all in the Pacific theater.[41]

The role of Johnston took yet another controversial twist in the formation of the code itself. Certainly Johnston deserves credit for conceiving the *idea* of the Code Talkers, but the original twenty-nine Code Talkers themselves created the actual code. Even so, Johnston falsely took credit for devising the code and exaggerated his role in recruitment. In a 1970 interview Johnston remarked: "I was instrumental in bringing in a lot of recruits when I convinced some of the educated Navajos what the opportunity would be. Something unique. Something that had never been done before in all of history."[42] Johnston's embellished position in relation to the code and the Code Talkers has been much to the chagrin of numerous Code Talkers. Paul Blatchford remarks:

So then I knew right there and afterwards when we were in the Hawaiian islands when the new guys came over that they were saying that boy that

Johnston must have been smart! He did all this and that, everything. Then I told them that he didn't do that, it was the 29 that did that. Don't you hear him when he talks? Yeah. Yeah we notice that he don't talk real good Navajo, but how in the world could he do that? But he kept telling us that he did that. He made this all up, you have to memorize this. That's the way we heard it. But when I went in Benally and Manuelito told me they were the first ones. They were the ones that did it. They did it themselves.[43]

An even angrier recollection comes from Wilsie Bitsie:

That guy [Johnston] was sick! That's what I told them in Window Rock. I told them that in San Diego when he this group of Navajo boys. He said Wilsie who are you? I said just a recruit. How come you get so much freedom around here? I said I'm through with boot camp. I started the code and I knew somehow that we would finish it up. I made up the phonetic alphabet, that's what I did. I already had that because my dad and I worked on that because he worked on the Home Mission Board where he studied the Navajo language. He kind of gave me an idea. When I came in I had an idea of what my dad told me to do. How to make up the phonetic alphabet into a military type code. It's not hard for me. He said well what are you trying to do, take over what I'm doing? I said "you?" You go around here talking dirty language to these guys, these guys around here and you say you can talk Navajo?! That's all you do is talk dirty to them. Say dirty words then you tell the guys you're with that you talk Navajo. You're crazy! I almost busted him in the classroom. I told him to get out of there, go on get out of the classroom. He wouldn't do it. So I called the security and they finally got him out. I said I don't want this guy in here. He says he can talk Navajo but he can't I think he's a spy! So they took him out. Never came back and I never knew what happened to him after that.[44]

Blatchford's and Bitsie's testimonies indicate not only that Johnston falsely took credit for creating the code but that others believed him. While certainly Navajos may have doubted him because of his poor knowledge of the language, other military commanders may not have questioned his role. Why Johnston would falsely take credit for developing the code is unclear. Perhaps he felt that because the initial idea

The Navajo Code Talkers

was his, the entire code likewise could be considered his innovation. According to the manner in which Blatchford and Bitsie describe Johnston, it sounds like he was claiming to have created the code to sound "cool" and fit in with the Code Talkers. There is also the possibility that Johnston exaggerated his role to a small group of people, not expecting word to spread. Or, of course, there is the chance that he took credit for his own personal gain—to rise in the military hierarchy or for other career advancement. While the reason is unclear, what is certain is that a number of white officials may have believed Johnston. They had no qualms about assuming white ownership over Native knowledge and thus perpetuated colonial ideas that indigenous knowledge was meaningless unless applied properly by white men.

A significant parallel with the NTSRU's and PIR's origins is the opposition the Code Talker project faced from sectors of the military. Some concerns were pragmatic, such as the limited advantage of speedy coded messages because urgent messages were not sent in code. Col. Frank Halford wrote in March 1942:

> 2. The undersigned, at this time, wishes to express the opinion that the proposed plan has very little practicable value. Action in the field is so fast now that messages sent in the clear usually result in immediate compliance rendering them of no value to the enemy.
> 3. For combat directing officers to have to depend on an order which is being transmitted and received in a language unknown to any of the operating force renders it of very doubtful value as a scheme of communication.[45]

Other practical concerns that emerged later included limited numbers of available recruits, insufficient linguistic information about Native American languages, and the need to secure encoded confidential information over extended periods of time. When confronted with a 1943 proposal to expand code talking from the marines to the army, one colonel declared that "substitution of Indian dialects for bonafide code systems is not authorized."[46] The idea of security was a consistent theme in the military's rejection of Navajo Code Talkers. Some officials considered the code insecure and believed that the enemy could easily obtain translators.[47] In fact, this assertion was false: at one stage the Japanese did manage to find a Navajo non–Code Talker prisoner of war. Joe Lee Kieyoomia was a survivor of the Bataan Death March in the Philippines whom the Japanese tortured in Nagasaki in 1944. Under torture he managed to translate some Navajo words, but because of the code it was all nonsensical to him.[48] The theme underlining all these parallels to the other examples of indigenous service in the Pacific War is distrust in Navajo abilities to perform the task. Whereas in Australia military superiors considered white personnel more effective than Yolngu, and in Papua and New Guinea the knowledge of Pacific Islanders was not as important as their labor, in the U.S. context technological innovation was preferential to indigenous knowledge.

The other factor that deserves significant reflection is the role race played both for and against the Navajo Code Talkers. Overall, stereotypes of Navajos (and Native Americans more generally) supported indigenous participation in the war, but only under circumstances subservient to white command and control. One document opposed the formation of the Navajo Code Talkers on the grounds that "they [Native Americans of the Southwest] are not able to follow orders, since they either do not understand English, or their command of the language is limited, with very few exceptions."[49] The same document also declared that the Native American cultural norm of group leadership would make the concept of a single commanding officer difficult to comprehend. These racial constructs led military commanders to resist providing Navajos with any skilled or authoritative positions in the military. Yet racial paradigms did not lead military officials to resist Native American participation as general soldier-bodies. The Second World War was the first conflict in which Native Americans not only could enlist but were also eligible for conscription.[50] John Adair and Evon Vogt estimate that thirty-six hundred Navajos served in the military, at least eight hundred as enlistees.[51]

Notions of the "martial race" influenced public opinion and recruiters to pursue American Indians. Historian Tom Holm writes:

The equation of the American indigenous peoples with the propensity toward warriorhood led the US [through history] to actively seek Natives as military allies, auxiliaries and finally members of the regular armed forces. . . . It was only after Indian assimilation policies had been put in place, the Native population had dwindled to less than one percent of that of the United States as a whole, and Native soldiers and Marines had proven themselves in combat in World War I, that Indians were judged a politically "safe" minority group. Indian citizenship followed. By the advent of World War II, Natives had become welcome additions to all US military formations.[52]

Representations of Native Americans as a martial race came in several forms. For instance, a June 1943 *Arizona Highways* magazine article entitled "The Navajo Indian at War" stated, "The Navajo was born in the saddle, is inured to hardship, and with the will to fight, which all Navajos have, makes a good soldier."[53] Even Johnston used "martial race" ideas as propaganda to garner support for the Code Talker project. On one occasion Johnston appealed to Navajo "instinct," writing: "The Navaho are a democratic people. From time immemorial their unwritten code of conduct has fostered the same principles of justice and fair play as those incorporated into our constitution. Instinctively they loathe oppression in any form, and will go to any length to preserve their personal liberties."[54] In another document Johnston went further in his appeal to "martial race" instincts: "There is something basic in Navajo character—a ruggedness and tenacity of purpose developed by wilderness—that makes them ideal for Marine Corps service."[55] One military document declared, "On their own in jungle or wooded area, they [Navajos] are much more hardy and self supporting than the normal white man."[56] Another document praised Native Americans as great marksmen, drivers, mechanics, and foremen of civilian labor from other countries. Their tracking skills—similar to those of Yolngu and Papua New Guineans—led to the successful rescue of downed aircrews in North Africa. The same document that praised these "innate" qualities of Native Americans clarified "that those who won decorations were for the most part those who had had knowledge of the Language and 'White man's ways' prior to service."[57] A proposal for Native American units emphasized that fully commissioned Native American officers, or preferably "white officers specially (if briefly) trained in their management, would function without the difficulties encountered by some mixed units in the past."[58] Hence, as in the case of Aboriginal and Papua New Guinean involvement in the war, constructs of an inherently militaristic race necessitated white leadership to ensure its effectiveness and proper direction.

Navajo Perspectives on Code Talking

As demonstrated by the Yolngu and Papua New Guinean examples, it is essential to recognize that while the Code Talker case represents a form of white exploitation of indigenous knowledge, there was active indigenous participation in that exchange. Al Carroll rightfully affirms that to "devalue Native veteran experience or sacrifice as simply having been used by a colonial system . . . could be misinterpreted as disdaining or hostile to the sacrifices of Native veterans."[59] The principal Native American sources incorporated in this section are oral testimony, although there are some written documents as well. The oral sources derive primarily from previous secondary literature and from the Oneo Collection and the Sally McClain Collection at the Navajo Nation Museum in Window Rock, Arizona.

The Navajo Nation generally supported the United States in the Second World War and encouraged participation of its members. Many Native American nations — including the Navajo Nation — issued their own declarations of war against Germany and Japan.[60] Even before Pearl Harbor the Navajo Tribal Council on 3 June 1940 declared, "Now, Therefore, we resolve that the Navajo Indians stand ready as they did in 1918, to aid and defend our Government and its institutions against all submersive [*sic*] and armed conflict and pledge our loyalty to the system which recognizes minority rights and a way of life that has placed us among the greatest people of our race."[61]

The Navajo position on the war was a significant determinant in the ability of the armed forces both to recruit on the reservation and to enlist Navajo volunteers. Paul Blatchford recalls this being an issue when navy recruiters turned away him and his friends in January 1942:

> Then we put down that we, three of us [at the recruiting station], that we would go in the Navy, we said that we wanted to join the Navy. They told us when the United States took over your country they agreed that they would take care of you, they would build you a hospital, build schools, then they read from a government pamphlet that "no Indian should be involved in our wars." That you can not go to war, and I said well how come you took those three [other Native Americans]? Those three came to us and said they were going into the Navy. I said how come those three are accepted? He said the reason why we are taking them is because when they were in high school they joined the National Guard and their parents already signed for them that they can go. So if you had joined the National Guard and your parents had signed for you, then let us know and we will take you. But on your papers you don't show that you joined the National Guard, so you fellows still want to go you better go back to your reservation, go to your councilman and have them approve it, it's the only way.[62]

Blatchford's account shows a stark contrast between the Navajo experience and that of the Yolngu and Papua New Guineans. Because of the Navajo Nation's special status as dependent sovereign within the United States, the Tribal Council had autonomy to determine whether or not the tribe's men could go to war. This limited self-determination contrasts with the conscriptive nature of labor in Papua and New Guinea and the expectations of Yolngu support in Australia. It must be pointed out that Blatchford's account stands alone, as the only other oral testimonies about being turned away from the armed forces cite medical or education-level grounds. In regard to the Navajo Nation's official position on the war, shortly after the incident Blatchford describes, in February 1942, the Navajo Tribal Council actually voted against allowing Navajos to enlist, but they reversed their position in April 1942. In May 1942 the Tribal Council granted permission for the military to recruit men at the Navajo Nation capital of Window Rock, Arizona. Moreover, the Tribal Council permitted Secretary of the Interior Harold Ickes to purchase war bonds with tribal funds. At one point during the war the Tribal Council issued a statement affirming, "We are glad all our boys are going to the army and doing what they are told to do."[63] The Navajo Reservation eventually housed some Japanese American internees. Historian Jeré Bishop Franco notes that the Navajo Tribal Council agreed to house the internees "on the condition that all improvements left by the wartime inmates accrue to the benefit of the tribe."[64] This argument suggests that self-interest played a large role in accepting internees, rather than patriotism or racism.

Yet there were even more Navajo contributions to the war effort, both in military capacities and on the home front. Some non–Code Talker Navajos in the armed forces served alongside members of nineteen other American Indian nations in the Bushmasters. This group trained in the Panama jungle as special fighters with both rifle and knife skills. The Bushmasters proved quite successful at Arawe in New Britain in January 1944, driving back Japanese, capturing artillery, and killing 139 enemy fighters.[65] One example of Navajo contributions on the home front comes from Fred Harvey's oral testimony:

> In 1941, this is during World War II, I quit school again in order to enlist into the Armed Services. I was not accepted into the service, because of an eye defect, however, I was told that if I really wanted to do my share in the war effort, I should go to one of the Army Supply Depots and apply for a job. With this in mind I went to Barstow, California and obtained a job with the Marine Corps Supply Depot there. I worked for several years at this place.[66]

Harvey's testimony demonstrates some stark differences in the treatment of Navajos on the home front versus the treatment of Aboriginal people and Papua New Guineans. Whereas Northern Territory Aboriginal people and Papua New Guineans were conscripted into labor camps under the control of the army and the ANGAU, respectively, participation in a similar role was voluntary for Native Americans. This is one area where the different contexts of colonialism came into play. In

The Navajo Code Talkers

the United States the economy was not dependent on Native American labor, whereas the Northern Territory, Papua, and New Guinea did not have sufficient non-Indigenous labor. Furthermore, the Navajo Nation's longer contact with the U.S. government had intertwined Navajos' subsistence with the settler economy. Hence many Navajos—like Aboriginal people in more settled parts of Australia—actively sought to participate in the wartime economic boom after the Great Depression. The catch was that many of those opportunities, as Harvey indicates in his testimony, were in locations far from the Navajo Reservation. Agnes Begay recollects that it was common from 1943 to 1945 for Navajos to be encouraged to take war jobs off the reservation. The U.S. Army Air Corps even established a class in Atlantic City in February 1943 to teach English to monolingual Navajos. Navajo women participated in groups such as the U.S. Women's Army Corps, some even serving overseas. For those who did stay on the reservation support for the war effort was still omnipresent. Juan Etsicitty recalls, "Our powerful medicine men prayed hard during the second world war, and we have our V-day."[67] Thus in multiple ways the Navajo Nation proved its loyalty to the United States. Unlike the Yolngu or Papua New Guineans, who considered themselves merely to be allies in the war effort, the Navajo Nation positioned itself as an integral component of the United States. As a Navajo declaration in 1940 summarized, "There exists no purer concentration of Americanism than among the First Americans."[68]

For many of the Navajos who eventually became Code Talkers, the idea of loyalty to and membership in the United States was a major factor in their decisions to enlist. Code Talker veteran Raymond Nakai encapsulates this spirit: "Many people ask why we fight the white man's war. Our answer is that we are proud to be American. We're proud to be American Indians. We always stand ready when our country needs us."[69] David E. Patterson states, "When I was inducted into the service, one of the commitments I made was that I was willing to die for my country—the U.S., the Navajo Nation, and my family."[70] Patriotism also motivated Pahe D. Yazzie, who succinctly says, "I volunteered to serve my country."[71] Peter Yazza testifies: "I heard about a demand for Navajo Indians who knew Navajo and English to take part in the communication personnel in the United States Marine Corps as a Code Talker, so after I completed the last job for this Contractor, I volunteered in this service for my country in 1943 to 1945."[72] *Country* for some Navajos meant protection of their own homelands and families. Peter MacDonald writes:

> We were not a part of the America that had been attacked by the Japanese. . . . We were told that the Navajo needed to join in the war because the Japanese were coming to our land, our sacred mountains. We had two choices. We could fight with the army overseas, taking the battle to the Japanese wherever they had a stronghold. Or we could wait for the Japanese to come to America, then be forced to fight on our native land, near the sacred mountains, in a last-ditch struggle to save all that we held dear.[73]

MacDonald's writing aligns well with testimony from Yolngu and Papua New Guineans; the Second World War was an opportunity for indigenous peoples to defend their own homes and families from Japanese invasion.

For other Code Talkers the attack on Pearl Harbor was a key motivating factor that awakened patriotic sentiments among Navajos. One anonymous Code Talker recollects: "But during World War II, we were fighting for *our country*. Then, we were being attacked—as close as Pearl Harbor! The enemy was headed this way and we had to stop them. If someone is trying to take something from us, we fight back. If this is what you call *patriotism*, then we are very patriotic!"[74] Keith Little relates the following nationalistic anecdote explaining why he and some friends joined the military:

> Me and a bunch of guys were out hunting rabbits with a .22. We had a rabbit cooking down in the wash, and somebody went to the dorm [at boarding school], came back and said, "Hey, Pearl Harbor was bombed!" One of us asked, "Where's Pearl Harbor?"
>
> "In Hawaii."
>
> "Who did it?"

The Navajo Code Talkers

"Japan."

"Why'd they do it?"

"They hate Americans. They want to kill all Americans."

"Us, too?"

"Yeah, us too."

Then and there, we all made a promise. We were, most of us, 15 or 16, I guess. We promised each other we'd go after the Japanese instead of hunting rabbits.[75]

Little's tale hints at several Navajo perspectives on the Japanese attack on Pearl Harbor. An assault on the U.S. mainland would threaten Navajo just as much as non-Indigenous Americans. Little's anecdote also highlights that patriotism did not entail forgetting the history of inequality and discrimination. The question "Us, too?" points to the fundamental issue of whether or not Navajos counted as Americans in the Second World War. Based on the overwhelming patriotism of the Navajo Tribal Council and the aforementioned individual examples, it seems that a large portion of Navajos considered themselves both American and Navajo—the identities were not mutually exclusive in the face of a common external enemy. This adheres to assertions of Native American servicemen recognizing themselves as dual citizens of both the United States and their respective Native American nations.[76]

Patriotism was not the only reason many Navajos enlisted, and in many interviews other factors shine as more prevalent. One theme that permeates multiple firsthand accounts is the sense of excitement at the prospect of being a marine because of the associated perks and privileges. Lynn Escue argues that, for some, enlistment fulfilled a wish to travel and find adventure overseas.[77] Sam Billison describes how propaganda about the glorious marines had a profound influence on him:

I guess at that time John Wayne had already made some pictures of Marines and most of the kids were "Gung Ho" about either being a cowboy or a hero. I guess in history they always say a lot about the Marines, so I just wanted to be in the Marines. I don't know why I always wanted to be in the Marines. In the spring of 1943 I enlisted in the Marines.[78]

The glamorous image of the marines was very influential—multiple interviews specifically point to the fancy uniform as being a key component in decisions to enlist. John Kinsel explains: "I didn't even know that something was going on [about a code]. Frankly, I just like the uniform, that is why I join the Marine Corps." John Goodluck, in the same interview, adds: "And also they had this uniform too, they said they were first to fight, the Marines, Semper Fidelis and all I thought this is the way I want to go. So I joined."[79] The image of the marines was powerful enough to sway Harold Foster as well:

You register when you turn eighteen at the post office and the recruiters were taking those that were eighteen and had already registered. Then I saw a poster at the post office of a Marine in that uniform. The post office was right next door to the boys dorm and when I saw that poster I decided to become a Marine. I wanted to defend my country, my people and defend what I believed in.[80]

The promises of military recruiters were also significant in swaying Navajo attitudes. Kee Etsicitty comments:

In my senior year [at Fort Wingate], my last year [1943], the war was going on and there was a recruiter by the name of John Benal[l]y and Johnny Manuelito and they came up one day to interview some of these guys that wanted to join the Marine Corps. They said that we could get this uniform and be first to fight, you know when you are young you want to find out something for yourself. This is the idea that came to us. There were some Navy recruiters that came home on leave and told us if we joined the Navy we could see the Seven Seas and have a girlfriend in every port.[81]

Others joined the military out of desperation or joined involuntarily as conscripts. Many enrolled in the armed forces because it translated to a job and a steady income. This was an especially significant motivator after the livestock reductions of the 1930s and the Great Depression left few employment opportunities on the reservation. The Navajo Tribal Council hoped that enthusiastic contributions to the war effort would slow down the process of livestock reduction, but ultimately the petitions to end livestock reduction failed.[82] Carl Gorman remarks, "It sounded like the worst that could happen was I'd have a roof over my head and be eating regular."[83] Paul Blatchford recalls complaining to the council chairman: "We got to go [to the military] because there is no jobs, all they are doing is running to Gallup [New Mexico] and getting drunk, there is no job here on the reservation so we wanted the councilman to approve so we can go and then he said the same thing."[84] The idea of a career in the military also posed an opportunity for future generations of Navajos. Kee Etsicitty remarks, "That was the idea of fighting them [the Japanese] so that my son could go to school live a better life."[85] Some Navajos, like other American citizens, were simply drafted into the service. Joe Dedman recollects: "I enlisted to the United States Army when I was still going to school at Ft. Wingate. This was in the year 1942. I was drafted and I ha[d] no intention of going into the army."[86] Keats Begay—a Navajo non–Code Talker who survived the Bataan Death March—says: "We were told to go to war and we had to make up our minds. Some said if we wanted to join the Army we could, but otherwise, we would be drafted, even though we didn't want to join."[87]

Clearly the heterogeneity of motives to join the war effort was as diverse as in any social group. From notions of patriotism to aspirations of glory to practical concerns of employment, Navajos found many means and methods of participation in the Second World War. Fundamentally, while the government and military were using the Navajo language as a weapon, Navajo individuals were still active participants in this exchange. As historian Tom Holm summarizes:

> To the questioners, Native American service in the "white man's wars" is, at best, an irrational choice, or, at a minimum, one that would serve to legitimize them as American citizens, assimilate them into mainstream American culture, and ultimately destroy their identities as distinct peoples. . . . For the most part, Native veterans have chosen military service to maintain their identities and better serve their own distinct communities, rather than serve the cause of assimilation.[88]

Meadows similarly argues that "World War II provided opportunities for men to fulfill their traditional roles as warriors in culturally approved forms that were acceptable in both tribal and Anglo views."[89] As in any social group there were conscientious objectors; Carroll describes one Navajo who argued that Navajos should not fight unless Hitler invaded, and Peter MacDonald recalls a story of criminal Navajo activism against the Bureau of Indian Affairs in 1943.[90] Beyond these examples, though, there is no literature documenting Navajo conscientious objectors or significant opposition to the war. This may also be a symptom of the historiographical tendency to focus solely on positive Navajo contributions to the war. Franco argues that "on some reservations in other parts of the country, half the male inhabitants volunteered for army duty. Southwestern Indians, however, displayed the most enthusiasm."[91] As the next chapter will demonstrate, although some Navajo servicemen did not necessarily achieve all they hoped, they consistently remained loyal to the United States. Similar to the Yolngu in Australia and the Papua New Guineans, segments of the military would grow to appreciate indigenous assistance, while the overarching structures of colonialism continued to hinder any marked changes in Native self-determination.

17. New recruits stand at attention, Fort Wingate NM.
From left to right: John Benally, Maj. Frank Shannon,
Henry Bahe Sr., John Kinsel Sr., Benjamin Sorrel,
unidentified, Johnson Housewood, unidentified,
Roy Notah, Peter Tracy, Jimmie King, remaining four
unidentified. Photograph by Milton Snow. Courtesy of
Navajo Nation Museum, Window Rock AZ, N07-45.

18. (*Opposite top*) Maj. Frank Shannon gives instructions to
the first twenty-nine Code Talkers. *From left to right*: Eugene
R. Crawford (second man from left), John Chee, David
Curley (wearing leather jacket), Samuel H. Begay, and Carl
N. Gorman. Photograph by Milton Snow. Courtesy of Navajo
Nation Museum, Window Rock AZ, N07-46.

19. (*Opposite bottom*) Recruits eating lunch at Fort Wingate
Boarding School NM. *From left to right*: Cozy Brown, George
Dennison, Allen Dale June, Wilsie Bitsie, John Benally, and
Carl Gorman. Photograph by Milton Snow. Courtesy of
Navajo Nation Museum, Window Rock AZ, N07-112.

20. (*Above*) Navajo Code Talkers of the Third Marine Division
in Bougainville, December 1943. *Front row from left to right*:
Pvt. Early Johnny, Pvt. Kee Etsicitty, Pvt. John V. Goodluck,
and Pfc. David Jordan. *Second row*: Pvt. Jack C. Morgan, Pvt.
George H. Kirk, Pvt. Tom H. Jones, and Cpl. Henry Bahe Jr.
Courtesy of U.S. National Archives, 127-MN-069896.

21. (*Opposite top*) Three of the first twenty-nine Code Talkers
assigned to the Second Marine Division in Saipan. *From left
to right*: Cpl. Oscar B. Ilthma, Pfc. Jack Nez, and Pfc. Carl N.
Gorman. Courtesy of U.S. National Archives, 127-MN-082619.

22. (*Opposite bottom*) Pfc. Carl N. Gorman at an observation
post on Saipan, June 1944. Courtesy of U.S. National Archives,
127-MN-083734.

23. (*Above*) Code Talker Leslie Hemstreet on Okinawa, 1945.
Courtesy of U.S. National Archives, 127-MN-124944.

24. Pfc. Jimmie D. Benallie in front of a bike shop
on Okinawa. Courtesy of U.S. National Archives,
127-MN-117725.

CHAPTER 6. When the War Was Over

Forgetting and (Re)membering the Code Talkers

But our language was a weapon. We used it to kill the enemy. That's how I saw it. We have all kinds of battle scars, but I don't think we got enough recognition. We did our part, we saved lives, but hardly any of us rose above the rank of PFC. Other language specialists were Staff Sergeant, but not us. It didn't turn out to be very fair. — THOMAS BEGAY[1]

Well, in Navajo everything is in memory. . . . From the songs, prayers, everything, it's all in memory. So we didn't have no trouble. That's the way we was raised up. — WILLIAM MCCABE[2]

If I have to do it again I will. — SAMUEL J. SMITH JR.[3]

Yeah, I cried before people, many times, talking like this. 'Cause there that makes you feel that you have done something for yourself, your family, for the government, for everybody, for the youngsters, people — this is what you help with. You help one, help them. — KEE ETSICITTY[4]

The mere proposal for the Navajo Code Talkers had multiple hurdles to overcome. As the last chapter describes, the first hurdles were military approval and acceptance within the Navajo community itself. The strong war mobilization and the support of key commanders in the U.S. Marine Corps resulted in the successful implementation of a training program and in sufficient recruits to sustain it. But as for the NTSRU and the PIR there remained another key hurdle—cynical commanders. While the code in theory was a good idea, it had yet to be proven successful in battle. This test would also ultimately prove easy to overcome because the Navajo Code Talkers were, fundamentally, well trained and well prepared for the task outlined for them. One Code Talker recalls how he overcame the objections of a skeptical colonel at the Battle of Guadalcanal:

> Then the colonel had an idea. He said he would keep us on one condition: that I could out-race his "white code"—a cylinder-thing that you set a coded message on and send by radio . . . tick, tick, tick. Then the receiver signals he has received the message and gives the roger on it. We both sent messages—with the white cylinder and by voice. Both of us received answers. The race was to see who could decode his answer first. He said, "Are you ready?" I said, "I've started already." "How long will it take you?" I was asked. "Two hours?" "Two hours? I can get ready in two minutes . . . and give you a head start," I answered.
>
> I got the roger on my return message from four units in about four and a half minutes. The other guy was still decoding when I said, "Colonel, when are you going to give up that signal outfit? The Navajos are more efficient."

He didn't say anything, just started lighting up his pipe and walked away. He was still scratching his head, wondering how we had exchanged messages so fast. I called to him, "Why don't you throw the thing away?" The Colonel answered, "You people throw away your papers or whatever you learned from, and *walk around, a Code!*"[5]

The early resistance to Code Talkers dissipated after they proved their valor in battle. While the above anecdote demonstrates how Navajo Code Talkers' aptitude overcame opposition during the war, after the war their status reverted to prewar conditions. In the end, due to both the secrecy of the Navajo code but more significantly the discriminatory policies of termination and relocation, the story of the Navajo Code Talkers disappeared. Certainly recent historians have revived the story of the Navajo Code Talkers and inserted it into popular mythology about the Second World War. But as this chapter will demonstrate, like the "Fuzzy Wuzzy Angels" mythology, the (mis)appropriation of the Code Talkers' story has failed to redress the unequal conditions of Navajo veterans and, more widely, the entire Navajo community.

Navajo Code Talkers in Action

The first Code Talkers participated in the Battle of Guadalcanal in fall 1942, reducing encoding and decoding times by half and often working behind enemy lines. It took only twenty seconds on average to encode, transmit, and decode a three-line message. In addition to code talking and regular combat, Navajo skills from living off traditional land came in handy as Code Talkers hunted wild animals, scouted at night, and engaged in guerilla fighting.[6] For instance, Harold Foster recalls: "I had my knife all the time. I'm good at throwing knives, you know. I had learned it at home. So I just went like that and I got him [Japanese about to open fire] through the neck."[7] An anonymous Code Talker recounts an amusing anecdote of Navajos living off the country in Okinawa late in the war:

Some of us Indians would sneak around in the ravines and maybe see a stray goat; we'd skin it, build a fire and cook it. We'd kill a horse, butcher

When the War Was Over

it and roast it. Our commanding officer would admit that the chow was low and suggested that we might trade captured ammunition or any of the other souvenirs named, with that army unit. We actually loaded a jeep and hauled the stuff over there in broad daylight. We were caught by battalion commanders one day and they emphatically told us that we *couldn't do that!*

One day we spotted a young colt. We shot it and crawled over in the ravine, skinned it out, and we heard our white brothers say, "Hey . . . they've got some meat over there." So we invited them to join us. It was in the afternoon. We built a fire, and while the fire was going we saw spotter planes coming over; but you can be sure there was no one around that fire when the planes strafed that spot. After they had gone we put the meat on the hot coals.

Those white guys said, "Hey, Chief, where did you get this meat?" They thought we had traded souvenirs for this good beef. "Over there . . . over the hill!" I said vaguely.

Finally, after they had salted the meat and eaten it, smacked their lips over it, one of the guys who knew what it was, pointed to the kin over in the ravine and said, "Hey, Chief . . . pretty good horse!" And turning to our guests, said, "Don't you know you just got through filling up with horse meat?" Surprisingly, they didn't seem to mind, and echoed, "Sure, Chief . . . pretty good horse!"[8]

The above anecdote is rich with information about the relationships between Navajos and white soldiers. The Code Talker refers to white soldiers as "white brothers," suggesting genuine affection between the different races. Moreover, the acceptance the white soldiers show toward the Navajos — even after being duped into eating horse — reveals respect for Navajos' abilities, particularly as they were providers in this situation. Though Navajo skills may have been exploited by white powers at a structural level, on an individual level the interaction between whites and Navajos represented genuine mutual exchange and admiration.

The Navajos' traditional skills impressed white soldiers in other situations as well. One Code Talker recalls a training maneuver with some white servicemen on one of the Hawaiian Islands:

The first lieutenant (we called him Stormy) said, "We're going to see how tough you guys are. We're going to cross this desert in two days. We're going to use only one canteen of water each, and we're going to see how well you can preserve that water." We started off. It was real hot. I imagine we walked about twenty miles that first day.

He gave orders that we were not to eat the prickly pear cactus, and said, "I don't know whether they are safe to eat or not, but we'll stay on the safe side, because we don't want anybody to get sick." Well, we Indians knew about that cactus. About three o'clock that first day, when Stormy wasn't watching, we went over and cut the tops off some prickly pears, cut them down, and sucked out the liquid. We didn't touch the water in our canteens. We didn't need it.[9]

This group of Navajo Code Talkers exhibited their competitive streak because, for the first time, they were on an equal footing with white servicemen. The common military norms and experiences of training placed every individual on an equal level where, for the duration of the war at least, Navajos' particularized skills could shine through and even exceed the abilities of non-Indigenous persons.

After the Navajos' success at Guadalcanal, teams of Code Talkers were assigned to each of the Marine Corps' six Pacific divisions. The extent to which commanding officers utilized the Code Talkers was at their discretion. Transmissions of words such as *Geronimo, Hiawatha, Arizona,* or *New Mexico* indicated when a unit needed a Code Talker. Often the Code Talkers were most useful in the front lines for tasks such as spotting artillery, directing shells, or pinpointing dangerous areas.[10] Marine Corps officers found that Code Talkers were often useful beyond the realm of communications by virtue of their experience on the reservation. G. R. Lockard wrote: "Every Indian who has graduated from Government Schools has learned a trade. Many of them have learned two or more crafts. As a result, Navajo Indians may very profitably be employed in Marine Corps units requiring their particular skill."[11] While Lockard's statement is about military pragmatism, it also emphasizes how the colonial treatment of Native Americans continued

When the War Was Over

to service the colonizing governments. The learning of trades was part of the assimilationist project and, ultimately, continued to serve only the settler government rather than the interests of the Native Americans themselves. Nonetheless, as an anonymous Code Talker remarked about his service at Peleliu: "I was supposed to be a signal man—the chief of the message center, but when the call came for me to do all these things I obeyed orders. You did just what your commander told you to do, with no questions asked!"[12]

As confidence in the Code Talkers grew, the need for more trained Code Talkers became apparent, and some problems emerged. By 1943 there was a shortage of adequately trained Code Talkers available for deployment. As an interim solution, Johnston proposed that "the shortage of Navajo personnel can at least be partially offset by a plan of rationing, under which a division about to enter a combat area would be allocated a sufficient number of 'talkers' from the pool to man all voice radio circuits in the lower echelons which may be in close proximity with the enemy."[13] Later in the war, as the Code Talker program grew, along with the number of recruits, new problems occurred with standardization among the different Code Talkers who had gone through training at different times. In battle, because the complex nature of the code allowed multiple words to signify the same letter of the alphabet, improvisation was key to success. But improvisation also led to the development of new words on the battlefield, and the evolution of the code in combat needed to link back to the continuing influx of Code Talkers learning the standard code.[14] As Code Talkers became comfortable working with specific partners, commanders worried that when they were assigned elsewhere there might be "misunderstanding through difference of vocabulary or dialect that may have developed in an organization."[15] Commanders also expressed concern that if certain elements of the code were not used consistently, Code Talkers might forget them. One report from 1945 declared: "It is believed that frequent refresher courses must be instigated for all Talkers because when not used as such over a period of time they have a tendency to revert to their own vernacular in translating terms which have been standardized and in becoming mentally out of touch with communication methods and procedure."[16] Thus from 16 April to 6 May 1945 — during a period when the use of Navajo Code Talkers was becoming increasingly vital in the Pacific campaign — the Marine Corps implemented a retraining program to update and streamline the code and protocols. The retraining used five Code Talkers from each of the Third, Fourth, and Fifth Marine Corps divisions. Given that the retraining school happened near the end of the war, there is no telling to what extent it would have contributed to the ongoing success of the Navajo Code Talkers, had the war continued past August 1945.

What is certain, though, is that the retraining contributed to the successful implementation of the Navajo Code Talkers in mid-1945, as the Pacific War entered a stretch when swift communications proved vital to success. In one incident at Saipan Navajo Code Talkers saved the lives of a group of American servicemen mistaken for Japanese imitating Americans on the radio. A corporal recalls: "Then headquarters asked, 'Do you have a Navajo?' I'll never forget the message that was sent by the single Navajo in our battalion. A few minutes later we saw a cloud of smoke and dust rising from the Jap positions. We were saved from being clobbered by our own artillery!"[17] In the lead up to the Battle of Iwo Jima Navajo Code Talkers were tested with fake orders and reports. Although some code machines proved faster than the Code Talkers, their coded transmissions still conveyed perfectly, while non-Indigenous transmitters made errors. The Code Talkers earned the total support of commanders at Iwo Jima, for the first time communicating between Marine Corps headquarters and division headquarters. Code Talkers proved invaluable at Iwo Jima, with radio nets sending over eight hundred messages constantly around the clock. The intensive fighting at Iwo Jima and the extensive use of the code led to a lot of improvisation among the Code Talkers during the campaign.[18] Harold Foster recalls: "There were only two code talkers in my unit [at Iwo Jima], so it was all the people involved with communications. We were told to be as sharp and accurate as possible because everyone would be depending on us. The Morse code had been broken by the Japanese and it was going to be used as a dummy message while the real message would be sent in Navajo."[19]

Because of their racial appearance Navajos were often mistaken for Japanese. In some instances this was beneficial for the Code Talkers when engaging the enemy. At Cape Gloucester Code Talker Tom White stripped down to his waist and walked right up to a Japanese pillbox. The Japanese did not realize he was American until it was too late and he machine-gunned them all.[20] But more often than not, it was American servicemen who mistook Navajos for Japanese, and this proved dangerous. One Code Talker relates the following anecdote:

I walked over to the army supplies and started digging for orange juice when somebody put an iron in my back. I thought whoever it was was just kidding and kept on digging. He finally said, "Get out of there, you damn Jap!" The sergeant standing there said, "He has Marine Corps identification and speaks good English." The man with the gun said, "I don't care if he graduated from Ohio State. We're going to shoot him."

I finally mumbled, "I'm from right down there," but I couldn't see the direction because there was too much sweat running down into my eyes. Finally, they took me back to my outfit. I had 15 men around me, and the sergeant of the guard had a .45 cocked against my back all the way and I had my hands up all the way. When we got to the beach, they asked, "Is this your man?" and of course the answer, "Yeah . . . that's our man. Hey—are you guys serious?" "You're damn right we're serious," they said. "If you guys don't make a positive identification we're going to take him back."

Finally the lieutenant came around and said, "What's the matter?" "Well, we caught this man over there in our yard and we think he's a Jap. If you don't identify him we're going to take him back over there and shoot him."[21]

The incident above was not isolated. Chester Nez, for instance, describes a similar incident:

And that evening one guy came over and said, "You guys can gather all our equipment together and report over to that tank over there," he says. That tank was about 250 yards from where we were. So we got ready to start off. We started to walk off that place where we were. Some army guys came by and they took us for Japanese. I had a pistol, a .300 pistol to my head; and my buddies, those other guys, had a rifle on them. We didn't know what to do. We were kind of really scared. You know, these guys was going to shoot us. We told one of the guys, "Go over to that tank way up there, and get one of the lieutenants, or somebody, from over there to tell you guys that we're with the communications outfit." So one of the army guys went over there and he got a lieutenant over there. He brought him back. And he told these guys, he said, "These are my men. They're working with us. They're a bunch of Marines." So these guys didn't know what to do, and the lieutenant told these guys, "I want to see you guys in the morning." I don't know what they do to those guys.[22]

The error of misidentifying Navajos as Japanese turned tragic when Code Talker Harry Tsosie, one of the original twenty-nine, was mistakenly shot and killed while roaming during the night at Bougainville.[23] Mistaken identity became such a common problem that commanders assigned bodyguards to protect each of the Code Talkers. Bill Toledo claims he never even realized that one of his compatriots was actually his bodyguard: "I just thought that he was my partner, my foxhole buddy. . . . I didn't find out until 1987. We had our first reunion at Camp Pendleton."[24] Richard Bonham, one such guard, recalls his orders: "Very simple. Don't let him out of your sight. Neither one of us were to be captured and say no more. It's just that simple. We were not to be captured."[25] According to Kee Etsicitty, the use of bodyguards was not uniform but did demonstrate the integrality of the Code Talkers: "Bodyguards were only used when you were in relief or in traveling up to the next message center. Many of the code talkers never had guards with them, they refused the protection. That was when we realized that we were kind of important."[26]

Navajo Code Talkers recognized the significance of their position from as early as during training. One anonymous trainer recalls how he instilled the importance of the Code Talker mission into trainees:

When the War Was Over

I wanted those code talkers to guard their secrets with their lives. I thought of the idea of comparing them with the Japanese suicide pilots and the Nazi elite guards. If they were captured, they should guard the code with their lives! I would ask, "Would you refuse to give away the secret of the code if you had a samurai sword at your throat? If the enemy would ask, 'What is the word for *A*?' Would you tell them? You begin to bleed; you begin to feel your own blood trickling down . . . warm, with the cutting a little deeper. You *would* lay down your life before you would tell, wouldn't you?"

I would look them square in the eye and ask them to answer *yes* or *no*. I would say, "Are you devoted that much? Are you willing to die for this secret method?"[27]

The importance of protecting the code was so strong that Kee Etsicitty recalls a colonel handing him a pistol and stating, "You don't use this pistol on anybody. This is for *you*, when you get captured, that's when you cock that thing back, put it here [Etsicitty points to his temple], goodbye."[28] The special nature of the mission, the unique service of Navajos, and the highly classified nature of the code served as marks of pride and satisfaction for Navajo Code Talkers. Just participation on an equal level with white servicemen contributed to the self-esteem of Navajo servicemen. Harold Foster recollects: "Once I got into the Corps, they treated me like a real human being. They gave me a sense of self respect that I knew I could use later in my life."[29] He further states: "When you started sending messages and everything was correct, they started treating you like a king. . . . They'd say 'Chief, let me carry your radio for you. Let me carry your rifle for you.'"[30] Like the other bonds of war many of these friendships with white servicemen lasted lifetimes.

Code Talkers' oral testimonies point to the strenuous nature of their work, enduring "the longest hours, without being relieved, without water, without even food and medical attention, and there were so many of them that got hurt."[31] Veterans' testimonies clearly link the tough work with a sense of accomplishment. Another indicator of the special status of the Code Talkers was the extensive secrecy surrounding their work. Cozy Stanley Brown writes: "Even the colonels and the captains were not allowed to come near. We were not supposed to take orders from any officers except the high one we were assigned to."[32] As the war progressed, the increasing need for the code enhanced the esteem of Code Talkers. Sam Billison remarks: "The more I studied the more I realized the importance of this thing [code], the value of it, that it came from Navajo and that this was our weapon, so to speak. I didn't realize that it would be really significant in these island hopping campaigns throughout the Pacific War."[33] For Peter MacDonald growing self-esteem even helped to counteract the inferiority sentiments that had been instilled in his childhood: "For the first time since my initial involvement with Anglos I realized that I was not inferior, I was more than a filthy savage with no future."[34]

Code Talkers received significant praise from commanding officers during the war. Some of the tributes targeted Navajos not just for their code talking skills but for their more general capacity as servicemen. Maj. F. D. Beans, commanding officer of the Fourth Marines, wrote: "The Navajo Code Talkers have proved to be excellent Marines, intelligent, industrious, efficient . . . serving as scouts, messengers, and stretcher bearers."[35] G. R. Lockard of the First Amphibious Corps wrote:

> As individuals and as a group, these people are scrupulously clean, neat and orderly. They quickly learn to adapt themselves to the conditions of the service. They are quiet and uncomplaining; in eight months I have received only one complaint—a just one. In short, Navajos make good Marines, and I should be very proud to command a unit composed entirely of these people.[36]

The commanding general of the Fleet Marine Force commented similarly, "In addition to their value as code talkers, the Navajo Indians have shown themselves to be good Marines and are efficient in the field."[37] A May 1943 memo declared:

> (a) In their primary billets as "talkers" they have functioned very well, handling traffic rapidly and accurately.

(b) When not employed as "talkers," some of the Navajos have been used as message center men, and some as radio operators. They have functioned satisfactorily in both capacities.

(c) As general duty Marines they have, in general, been excellent, showing above average willingness to work at any job assigned them.[38]

Commendation directed specifically at code talking stated: "The full value of Navajo Talkers will not be appreciated until the Commander and Staff they are serving gains Confidence in their ability. The Navajo language is the simplest, fastest, and most reliable means we have of transmitting secret orders via radio or over telephone circuits exposed to enemy wire tapping."[39] Philip Johnston deemed the code talking project more successful than he had ever envisioned: "Through association with Navaho Marines I have had a rare opportunity to observe their sincerity and enthusiasm, which flowered into an excellence of performance that won the unstinted praise of officers and men who observed them. They marched superbly; their drills were carried out with snap and precision; their quarters were immaculate."[40] Possibly the most famous praise of the Code Talkers came from Maj. Howard M. Conner: "Were it not for the Navajos, the Marines would never have taken Iwo Jima."[41] At war's end eleven Code Talkers, including one of the original twenty-nine, had died in action.[42] Given the extent to which commanders relied on the Navajo language, the course of the war might have been different were it not for the Code Talkers.

Navajo Life after the War

The above discussion about the Navajo Code Talkers in action reveals their success and value during the Second World War. Taken in isolation, their war experience seems to provide a positive example of indigenous and non-indigenous people working together. The problem with this interpretation is that the war cannot be viewed in isolation. For years the Navajo Code Talkers received neither adequate recognition nor compensation. The Navajo Code Talkers' missions did not end with the cessation of hostilities. Paul Blatchford recalls that after the war Code Talkers were sent to Nagasaki to transmit information about the effects of the atomic bomb to San Francisco in Navajo.[43] During the Korean and Vietnam conflicts Code Talkers participated again, albeit on a much smaller scale. There were some proposals immediately after the Second World War to expand code talking within the army. One such proposal, which actually came from the Indian Association of America, stated:

> Our plan would be to organize military reserve training units now, composed of Indians. These units could make use of the WWII veterans from the tribes who do speak, both languages fluently, and who are familiar with military life. This training should specialize in communications (Radio & Telephone) so that at such times as it might be essential to put messages in code, the tribal language could be used for security, as has been done in the past, but not on a fully organized basis, or pre-trained basis.[44]

Similar proposals also existed within the armed forces, calling for Code Talkers in tactical battlefield communications. The U.S. Army rejected the proposals to expand code talking:

> With the number of Indian languages or dialects used by American Indians (approximately 1500) it would be impractical to attempt to determine, without detailed study, testing, and analysis, the particular Indian language or languages that are the most difficult to translate, which are the least known, and which could be expected to offer the greatest degree of security for communication transmissions.[45]

Ultimately, the army determined that "enciphered speech, achieved automatically through the use of specially designed radio equipment, appears to be the only practicable means of achieving security on voice circuits in the future. Present activities are proceeding in that direction, and present planning leaves no room for inclusion of 'codetalkers.'"[46] Certainly the army's rationale expressed legitimate logistical questions about the heterogeneity of American Indian languages and dialects and the efficiency of code machines. Yet the quick disregard of the proposal to expand the program overlooked — either willingly or out of ignorance — the already successful implementation of Navajos and other

Code Talkers during the Second World War. Now that the wartime sense of urgency was over, as in Australia and Papua New Guinea, the armed forces in the United States disregarded indigenous knowledge systems as immaterial to the security of the nation-state. Consequently, only those Navajos still serving in the Marine Corps would carry on the Code Talker tradition postwar.

After the war the Navajo code remained classified, so Code Talkers were not permitted to share their experiences. The code was declassified in 1968 only when byzantine computers rendered it obsolete.[47] Sam Billison recalls being told upon his return: "We finally landed at San Diego then we went through some physicals and instructions. Code Talkers they were told 'You were just in the Marine Corps like any other Marine, you don't know anything about any Navajo code. It's still top secret and you've never been in it, you don't talk about it, don't dream about it.'"[48] Many veterans accepted the dictum of silence upon their return because of the continuing need for secrecy. Code Talker Clare Thompson testifies: "If there was going to be another war, and the country needed our service, we all wanted to be ready and able to report back to duty. If we were ever again to be as effective as we were on the slopes of Mount Suribachi, we had to keep the code a secret."[49] But once they could talk about the war, many veterans found it difficult to persuade their audience to believe them or to comprehend the significance of their job. Bill Toledo declares: "Some of our own people don't understand what we did in the war. They thought we should have been on the front lines fighting. . . . We try to explain what we did but they still think that we should have been on the front line fighting. We try to tell them that we used our language to fight the Japanese, but they still don't understand."[50] One can rationalize the need to protect the secrecy of the code after the war, but the veterans' inability to share wartime experiences began a long process of forgetting, which endured until recent years.

The Navajo Nation certainly took pride in its war effort after the war, amid ongoing problems of discrimination. The Navajo Tribal Council issued a statement declaring: "We are glad all the boys went to the army and didn't come home until they turned them loose. Maybe if our boys hadn't gone and we lost the war, this country would be ruined now."[51] Yet similar to what happened in Australia and Papua New Guinea, the Navajos' postwar return to the reservation also marked a return to inequality and prejudice. Like other American Indian servicemen, some Navajos hoped that their extensive participation in the war would help develop new opportunities for collaboration with the white community as equals. The leader of the Navajos in Ramah, New Mexico, even declared in 1949: "The way I feel about these soldier boys is that most of them can already speak English and write. It looks like they should go on with the white people and learn more and more and then lead their people."[52] Raymond Nakai, former chair of the Navajo Nation, states:

> From the service, the Navajo got a glimpse of what the rest of the world is doing. The Marines particularly did a great deal for him — not only in giving him a view of the outside world, but in giving him a glimmer of hope and the necessary vision of the benefits that can be derived from certain things he has seen throughout the world. . . . The Navajo needs this type [Anglo] of education as a supplement to his strong basic, *informal* education, inherent in his rich traditional culture.[53]

Thus Navajo testimony supports Meadows's assertion: "Code talkers interacted considerably with non-Indians in the war and their experiences are perhaps better understood as maintaining their distinctiveness as Indians, while simultaneously experiencing many acculturative influences that gained them a wider and more detailed understanding of the non-Indian world."[54]

Navajo aspirations to build on the great tradition of service met stumbling blocks in the American political and legal system. Navajos still had restricted voting rights in Arizona until 1948, in New Mexico until 1953, and in Utah until 1957. In fact it was only through lawsuits, initiated by activists including Code Talker veterans, that state governments changed their voting laws to give Navajos the franchise. Navajos faced regulations against purchasing liquor until 1953, and even then Arizona and New Mexico continued to impose restrictions. Na-

When the War Was Over

vajos were also not allowed to join the American Legion or the Veterans of Foreign Wars because of their skin color.[55] Navajo veteran Albert Miguel summarizes the contrasting treatment in the armed forces and at home: "The GI's we were with in the service were much friendlier than the whites around here. The white GI's made jokes with us, and we could get along easier. . . . But I have a feeling they [local whites] don't like the Indians around here, because of the way they are treating the Indians."[56] Code Talker veteran Wilsie Bitsie describes the continuing discrimination he and other Navajo veterans faced:

> But you come back home and you get into worse, you find discrimination, you find hate and everything is mixed up here. You go someplace and you can't go in this hotel here, you can't go in this cafe here, things like that you're up against. That's how we came back. So that feeds the rest of what we went through. I know because I was told to stay away from places like that. You're still not a citizen but you still pay taxes! You gotta pay those taxes because it's your money you're spending and they want your money.[57]

A similar condemnation of prejudice is found in a 1946 letter to Philip Johnston from Code Talker Jimmie King:

> The so-called G.I. Bill of Rights is not doing a damn thing for us. Went to Hell and back for what? For the people back here in America to tell us we can't vote!! Can't do this!! Can't do that!! because you don't pay taxes and are not citizens!! We did not say we were not citizens when we volunteered for the Service against the ruthless and treacherous enemies the Japs and Germans. Why?? and what are our Buddies lieing [sic] beneath the Foreign soils for?? Is this the same America? The U.S. of America we fought and bled for? If it is let us feel it!! And make us know it!![58]

Navajos also confronted the new policies of termination and relocation that the Bureau of Indian Affairs (BIA) pursued against Native Americans across the United States until 1970. Like some of the proposals for Aboriginal enlistment discussed in the introduction, the proposals made by BIA officials during the war discussed Native American service hastening assimilation. Anthropological publications such as Evon Vogt's *Navaho Veterans: A Study of Changing Values* contributed further to such discourse about military service promoting "values change" among Native American communities.[59] *Termination* refers to the U.S. government policy of ceasing the federal trust relationship it had with Native American groups allegedly "ready" to assimilate. Relocation entailed offering moving expenses, new residences, and limited job training for Native Americans to leave their reservations and resettle in cities. The height of the termination era was from 1953 to 1958, although it continued as a possibility under the law until 1968. Relocation laws were enacted in 1956 and continued until 1980. Termination and relocation had devastating impacts on Native Americans both collectively and as individuals,[60] but fortunately for Navajos the size, conditions, and location of their community helped them resist the new colonial assimilationist policies.

As a response to threats of termination and relocation, a Navajo nationalist movement emerged in the 1950s, paralleling the wider Native American civil rights struggle. Many Native American activists in the civil rights movement were disenchanted veterans, while others were beneficiaries of the GI Bill who returned to socioeconomic problems on the reservations.[61] From 1946 to 1959 a Special Navajo Program enrolled approximately fifty thousand Navajos in vocational programs, mostly off the reservation. New legislation in 1953 provided the Navajo Reservation with capital to invest in construction and to operate public schools. In 1953 only 50 percent of Navajo children attended school, but that percentage had increased to 90 percent by 1957. In 1969 the Navajo nationalist movement culminated in the declaration of Navajo nationhood. Other Navajo initiatives included the establishment of new bicultural schools, the opening of a community college in 1970, new mining jobs after 1951, increased tourism, and even a Navajo judiciary system in 1960.[62] As the Native American civil rights movement took off in 1969, the BIA began to make arrangements for self-determination. In Senate Report 100-274 the Senate Select Committee on Indian Affairs described contemporary federal policy on Indian affairs:

When the War Was Over

The federal policy of Indian self-determination is premised upon . . . the present right of Indian tribes to govern their members and territories [which] flows from a preexisting sovereignty limited, but not abolished, by their inclusion within the territorial bounds of the United States. Tribal powers of self-government today are recognized by the Constitution, Acts of Congress, treaties between the United States and Indian tribes, judicial decisions and administrative practice.[63]

On 25 July 1972 the United States finally agreed to allow Navajos run their internal affairs rather than being administered by the BIA.[64] Thus in the continuing face of settler colonialism the Navajos responded with resistance and achieved degrees of autonomy not experienced since before the Long Walk of 1863. Code Talker veterans were involved in this movement for Navajo autonomy. Veteran Keith Little comments: "I think it's we, the veterans, of World War II are the ones that brought the meaning of education back to our people, because a lot of us became leaders, became teachers, lawyers. Some became medicine men, community leaders—influential leaders around the reservation, even off the reservation."[65]

(Mis)appropriating the Code Talkers Legend

Since the end of the Second World War many Navajo veterans, including Code Talkers, have asserted pride in their accomplishments and loyalty to the United States. Their testimonies and writings suggest that their participation in the Second World War was one event in a path to reconciliation between the Navajo Nation and the U.S. government. Howard Gorman Sr. testifies:

To this day, the white man has adopted us. They are our friends. The same way with other enemies that we fought. We are all friends nowadays. Many of you may think that the Navajos didn't have any enemies, but some of our friends were our former enemies. The United States itself was not our enemy. He was the one who saved us from being completely killed. The United States planned for us ahead of time, that some day the Navajos will be a respectable people.[66]

Native Americans — including Navajos — have continued to serve in the armed forces in large numbers, and military service has become part of the warrior tradition in many Native American nations such as the Navajo. Indeed, Al Carroll argues that "Native traditions in the military are stronger on a cultural and deeply spiritual level than those of any other ethnic group in the United States. This distinctiveness shows up in Native song, ceremony, spiritual practices, and beliefs."[67] The idea of military service as a path to reconciliation is also one that has been ongoing since the end of the Second World War. Cozy Stanley Brown writes:

> Some of our men are in the Military Services today for the same reasons. One of my nephews is in the Marine Corps today. He probably thinks the same way I thought when I was in the Service. The Anglos say "Democracy," which means they have pride in the American flag. We Navajos respect things the same way they do.[68]

The support Navajos have continued to provide to the U.S. armed forces suggests their continuing interest in defending their own nation as well as the wider United States. It also demonstrates that military service continues to provide opportunities to various sectors of the Navajo — and more widely Native American — community.

Since declassification of the code in 1968, the Code Talkers have slowly gained recognition and praise from various organizations both on and off the Navajo Reservation. In June 1969 the Fourth Marine Division honored the Code Talkers, for the first time, in Chicago.[69] President Richard Nixon sent a message to the Navajo Tribal Fair in 1971, stating: "Their resourcefulness, tenacity, integrity and courage saved the lives of countless men and women and sped the realization of peace for war-torn lands. In the finest spirit of the Marine Corps, their achievements form a proud chapter in American military history. My congratulations to them on behalf of all their fellow citizens."[70] In 1971 the surviving Code Talker veterans also founded the Navajo Code Talkers Association. In addition to raising awareness about the Code Talkers and their history, the group has organized a number of scholarships for Navajo students. In 1976 the Navajo Code Talkers led the Bicentennial Parade in Washington DC.[71] On 28 July 1982 President Ronald Reagan signed Proclamation 4954, declaring "August 14, 1982, as National Navaho Code Talkers Day, a day dedicated to all members of the Navaho Nation and to all Native Americans who gave of their special talents and their lives so that others might live."[72] Arizona senator Dennis DeConcini issued a press release in 1982, stating: "Since the Code Talkers' work required absolute secrecy, they never enjoyed the national acclaim they so much deserved. These men returned to their southwest as quietly as they had left. I do not want this illustrious yet unassuming group of Navaho Marines to fade into history without notice."[73] The Marine Corps continued its efforts to redress the forgotten legacy of the Code Talkers at an event in March 1989. Gen. A. M. Gray remarked: "The history of the Navajo Code Talkers is a history about warriors and the warrior spirit. It is this same warrior spirit which I am instilling into our Marine Corps today. We are warriors. That's what the Commandant wants and the country demands!"[74] On the thirty-ninth anniversary of the formation of the first twenty-nine Code Talkers, the U.S. Marine Corps recruited an all-Navajo platoon as a form of commemoration.[75] Additional government recognition came in December 2000 when Congress passed the Honoring Code Talkers Act, bestowing the Congressional Gold Medal on the original twenty-nine Code Talkers and the Congressional Silver Medal on the remaining Code Talkers.[76] At a commemorative ceremony on 26 July 2001 President George W. Bush declared, "Today we mark a moment of shared history and shared victory. We recall a story that all Americans can celebrate, and every American should know. It is a story of ancient people, called to serve in a modern war."[77] The long road to recognition for the Code Talkers has been part of a wider process of local, tribal, military, and government acknowledgment of Native American service, particularly in the First and Second World Wars.[78]

While these developments are important, several problematic issues emerge through closer scrutiny. It took fifty-five years after the end of the Second World War before Congress began the process of official recognition, and then only after extensive lobbying by the Navajo Code Talkers Association. Reflecting on the years of forgetfulness, Code Talker Keith Little remarked: "It finally hit home. . . . I realized we had lost our own country to foreigners and they were still getting all the recognition. Native Americans were getting nothing."[79] Little's feelings are not unique. Code Talker Carl Gorman stated, "You know, sometimes I can't help thinking these guys in Washington are waiting for us to give them a medal for helping us protect our own country."[80] On his registration form at the Navajo Code Talker Reunion in 1971, Jimmie K. King wrote: "Separation papers does not corrospond [sic] with the Honorable Discharge papers. We were never given credit for all foreign services and battle engagements, skirmishes, and expeditions."[81] Alex Williams reflected on his registration form about the continuing negative portrayal of Native Americans in pop culture: "Our grandchildren needs [sic] our remembrance by making a movie films for Navaho Tribe. And make money for our future use. No more cowboy and Indian stuff. We want real Hero's [sic]."[82] These feelings of resentment among Navajos resonate within the wider Native American community. Paul Blatchford testifies: "When we formed our [Navajo Code Talkers] Association, started marching [in parades], then the American Indian Movement said you guys are crazy! You guys weren't supposed to go into the service you guys were crazy! They yell at us when we march, even my boy when he was going to high school said we were crazy."[83] Blatchford's statement aligns with some of the comments stemming from the Papua New Guinean example (see chap. 4). While some members of the community have chosen to reflect on their recognized accomplishments during the war with pride, others have emphasized ongoing discrimination and expressed resentment over continuing disparities.

Recognition is a significant symbolic gesture, but it fails to provide what professor of politics Nancy Fraser refers to as "redistribution." Fraser outlines *redistribution* as a remedy for political and economic injustice through political or economic restructure, whereas *recognition* is merely a symbolic solution to cultural injustice. For racial groups that suffer cultural and economic injustice—like the Yolngu, Papua New

When the War Was Over

Guineans, and Navajos—Fraser delineates a need for both recognition and redistribution to redress the combination of cultural and political-economic inequalities.[84] The need for redistribution applies to Code Talker veterans most prevalently in light of the lofty legal and practical impediments to Navajos accessing veterans' benefits. Because reservation schools were reserved for youth, veterans would have to leave the reservation in order to access education under the GI Bill. Additionally, there were no on-the-job training programs for GI Bill recipients in the Southwest. This is not to say that no Navajos reaped the benefits of the GI Bill—many Code Talkers did pursue secondary and tertiary education or programs such as agricultural training.[85] However, in order to do so, they had to leave the Navajo Reservation—their spiritual and physical homeland. Housing Authority loans and Veterans' Administration hospitalization have been—and continue to be—unavailable for anyone who lives on the Navajo Reservation because the Bureau of Indian Affairs, rather than the state, administers the land.[86] Resentment over this issue emerges through testimony such as that of Wilsie Bitsie:

> So you're here and you don't have a home. The home you lived in your parents are deceased, your sister or your brother or somebody took it over so you don't have a home! So you go to the tribe, you go to the powers that be in the State, Veterans Administration, you ask for a home—can't do it. That's so and so's land, that's not Indian land, can't put a home there. Can't do this for you.[87]

Many Code Talkers have challenged the lack of adequate compensation in the court system—a drawn-out process yielding little more than appreciative rhetoric characteristic of recognition without redistribution.[88] Statistics about the socioeconomic conditions for the entire Navajo Nation also indicate continuing disparities. A report from the Navajo Nation Division of Economic Development states that in 2007, 36.8 percent of Navajos lived below the poverty line and the unemployment rate was 50.52 percent; this was actually an increase from the unemployment rate of approximately 45 percent in 1983.[89] Similar to Yolngu and Papua New Guineans, the Navajo Code Talkers may have served well, but in the end it was the United States they served rather than the Navajo Nation. This is not to say that Code Talker veterans do not or should not take pride in their achievements. Kee Etsicitty states: "Our language helped the white men, our country and our people. The radio work that I did I am proud of. I was in the right place at the right time and I did what was necessary to help end the war. Every man that went into the service helped, every parent back home helped to keep the liberty we enjoy to this day."[90] Despite such pride, though, the end of the Second World War still left Navajos under the continuing power of settler society.

National memories are important because they demonstrate the manner in which indigenous contributions to war can both disappear and be absorbed into a nationalistic (rather than an indigenous) account of history. The Navajo Code Talkers have received significant attention in recent American mythology about the Second World War. The glorification of Navajo Code Talkers has taken multiple forms, including a number of journal articles, books, newspaper features, historical fiction, children's books, and the 2002 Hollywood movie *Windtalkers*. In February 2000 a Navajo Code Talker action figure was even developed as part of the GI Joe series. Code Talker Sam Billison, who did the voice for the action figure, stated: "This will let people know about the code talkers. I think it's really going to put us on the map."[91] Certainly, as Carroll points out, the Code Talkers have been active participants in the rise of the Code Talkers mythology.[92] Yet all this material—with the notable exceptions of veterans' firsthand accounts—consistently isolates the Navajo Code Talkers in the context of the Second World War, rather than in the context of the greater history of Navajo oppression. The veneration of the Code Talkers coincides with the wider "greatest generation" mythology that emerged in the late twentieth century. Journalist Tom Brokaw's book about the war generation succinctly summarizes the "greatest generation" mythology: "They [Second World War participants] answered the call to help save the world from the two most powerful and ruthless machines ever assembled, instruments of conquest in the hands of fascist maniacs. They faced great

When the War Was Over

odds and a late start, but they did not protest."[93] Even when literature referencing the "greatest generation" acknowledges the hardships minority veterans confronted, authors tend to overlook Native Americans. Despite President Bush's statement about the Navajos serving "regardless of history," the United States has yet to reciprocate adequately in service to the Navajo Nation. As these last two chapters have shown, one cannot view the Navajo Code Talkers through a narrow lens, disregarding the wider history of their oppression.

CONCLUSION

The Soldier-Warrior in Modern War

The country would be benefited by the number of good citizens it would secure; the service would be benefited by the addition of these men to the standing army; and the [American] Indian would be inestimably benefited by the contact with the white race. —WILLIAM H. POWELL[1]

The TPNG Army [postwar Pacific Islands Regiment] is, in my book, an efficient force, being well led and trained, and recruited from excellent material which, like our own beloved Gurkhas, takes naturally to the profession of arms and appears to enjoy every moment of it. The affinity between Australian officer and Pacific Islander as he is called, is of a very high order and the dedication of the former impressed me particularly. —COL. P. H. BENSON, MBE[2]

Until indigenous Australian servicemen are included within the War Memorial, their contribution is doomed to be at best ambivalent and certainly peripheral, despite the efforts of historians. —ADAM MARRE[3]

Although a number of observers have stressed the discontinuity of the military and civilian society, for example, the "universalistic" nature of the military as against the "particularistic" nature of civilian society and so on, it seems that in the case of minority-military participation, the more prevalent pattern is one of continuity or parallelism. In addition, the parallel pattern may, in fact, be the equilibrium pattern of minority-military service. —WARREN L. YOUNG[4]

Ideas of exploiting indigenous people for colonial militaries have a long history. For instance, in a published September 1880 journal article entitled "Military Colonization of the Indians" Capt. H. C. Cushing of the U.S. Army wrote of Native Americans: "The Indian is naturally a warrior. Utilize his fighting qualities for the benefit of civilization."[5] In the article Cushing recommended that the U.S. Army should recruit Native American soldiers with a dual purpose. First, the enlisted Native Americans could use their tracking, hunting, and fighting skills to quell resistance of other Native American peoples to U.S. expansion. Second, participation in the military would hasten Native assimilation into white society because military training would entail elements of discipline, conformity, and obedience to authority.[6] The encouragement and use of indigenous people as part of the settler colonial project was nothing new to the United States circa 1880, and more widely it was nothing new to the world. Since the beginnings of European colonialism in the fifteenth century, indigenous peoples have played a significant role in the pacification or elimination of native resistance movements. Examples transcend time, colonizer, and continent—one can point to instances such as Native American scouts on North American frontiers, Aboriginal mounted police in Australia, indigenous collaboration in the Spanish conquest of Aztec Mexico and Incan Peru, and local cooperation in the European occupation of Africa.[7] Therefore, at first glance Cushing's ideas do not appear to be a break with colonial traditions, but rather the continuation of the long-established trend of colonial powers using indigenous collaborators to conquer or pacify native resistance.

By the Second World War the concept of using indigenous people for military purposes had taken a new turn. Colonial societies were not employing indigenous soldiers to quell other native peoples, but rather utilizing indigenous people in their own conflicts with other imperial powers—namely the Axis powers of Japan, Germany, and Italy. Indeed, this book has demonstrated how Australian and American militaries employed indigenous people as weapons in the Pacific War. This was not a new model per se—for instance one can point to the French and Indian War, the War of 1812, the Boer War, or the First World War as cases when indigenous people actively fought with or for one colonizing power against another. The significance of the Second World War, though, is that by that period the frontiers of colonial societies such as the United States, New Zealand, Canada, and Australia had essentially closed. The conflict among colonial powers was not over imperial control of disputed territories. Hence although colonialism persisted through policies of assimilation, child removal, and government dependency, with few notable exceptions the physical expansionism, "pacification campaigns," and subsequent frontier massacres and wars had ended.

The militaries' use of indigenous peoples against invading powers during the Second World War represents another phenomenon, which I refer to as soldier-warrior colonialism. I define soldier-warrior colonialism as the active employment of colonized indigenous people by the military of a colonial power, for the benefit of the colonial power, against a different imperial power, and with little or no consideration for the impact on indigenous societies. The trend of soldier-warrior colonialism is not restricted to the Second World War, but the temporal, technological, and strategic circumstances of that war provide some of the most concrete case studies. One can distinguish between two macrocategories of soldier-warrior colonialism. The first is the general enlistment of indigenous troops in regular units. As already mentioned, Australian regulations discouraged Aboriginal, Torres Strait Islander, and Pacific Islander enlistment because these peoples were not "of substantial European origin or descent." In the U.S. military, which segregated blacks from whites, Native Americans were classified with whites and served in the same detachments as Americans of European ancestry.

The case studies in this book from the Pacific War are unique because they also encompass the second macrocategory of soldier-warrior colonialism, under which the NTSRU, the PIR, the RPC, and Navajo Code Talkers fit—the specialized indigenous unit. All these forces utilized indigenous people not just as sources of labor or as additional soldier-bodies, but specifically for skills derived from their native cultures. Essentially, the indigenous people and their skills became the colonizers' weapons in war. The discussion of these cases has focused on the colonial governments' motives for recruiting indigenous fighters and their treatment of them, as well as on indigenous agency in and reactions to the Second World War. These three cases represent soldier-warrior colonialism because the governments exploited indigenous people and knowledge for defense while concurrently disregarding indigenous rights, vitality, and sovereignty. Indeed, the colonial governments essentially employed the various indigenous peoples as weapons to defend the very system that had disadvantaged them. This represents what historian Warren L. Young refers to as a parallel pattern of minority participation in the military. In a parallel pattern the minority group's situation in the armed forces for the most part mirrors their situation in civil society, with only some elements of discontinuity. This diverges from a discontinuous pattern, whereby participation in the armed forces can alter a minority group's societal relationship due to external factors or a military's own needs and interests.[8] Comparative analysis of the three case studies highlights some of the fundamental tenets of soldier-warrior colonialism as a parallel pattern: colonizers' disapproving attitudes, "suitable" labor tasks for native soldiers, recruitment practices, status within the military, the role of indigenous agency, prejudicial treatment, compensation (or lack thereof), and postwar civil rights claims. Certainly there were critical differences in the way these trends operated in the selected case studies, but the significance of soldier-warrior colonialism lies in the common themes.

One common theme among the three case studies is that indigenous soldiers and labor were undesirable until considered a last resort. Military superiors in Australia, Papua and New Guinea, and the United States all scoffed at the idea of native forces, believing indigenous peoples to be unintelligent, insufficiently skilled, and ineffective. Officers ultimately accepted the utilization of indigenous soldiers—under white supervision of course—only to fill gaps where white labor was insufficient. What constituted an inadequate non-indigenous workforce varied among the different countries. In Australia Aboriginal people were sought as scouts and guerilla fighters in regions devoid of significant white settlement. Essentially, they were performing a task for which there were not enough white servicemen and in places where the few servicemen available were not sufficiently familiar with the land. In Papua and New Guinea the local residents worked for both Japan and the Allies as manual laborers because, as in Australia, there were simply not enough workers. Furthermore, the development of the PIR and the RPC and the employment of Papuan and New Guinean coastwatchers came about because critical war matters necessitated any guerilla means necessary to track and confront Japanese. Papuan and New Guinean soldiers and laborers were always in subservient positions to non-indigenous authorities, though, because racial hierarchical ideas placed Papuans and New Guineans in lower positions in relation to Japanese or whites. The U.S. Marine Corps employed Navajos as Code Talkers because their unique language represented an unbreakable code. Thus in all cases the colonizers' employment of indigenous personnel was not necessarily a vote of confidence in indigenous skills or a recognition of the value of indigenous culture; instead, indigenous service represented a last resort to fill voids in the war machine.

The manner of recruitment of indigenous servicemen also varied among the different nations, but with one common theme: governments consistently ignored or negated indigenous agency and desires, as the interests of the colonizers reigned. In Australia anthropologists such as Donald Thomson and W. E. H. Stanner began planning patrols reliant on Aboriginal scouts before even consulting with locals to ascertain their interest in participating in the war effort. This is not to say that these Aboriginal people were conscripted; rather, their involvement was always assumed as a given without consideration for the desires of the local Aboriginal populations. In Papua and New Guinea recruitment was far from voluntary in many circumstances. ANGAU recruited excessive numbers of Papuan and New Guinean laborers, often having a dire impact on the viability of local villages. ANGAU also arbitrarily allocated Indigenous soldiers into services such as the RPC and the PIR, sometimes to the ire of the participants. The Japanese also disregarded the interests of New Guineans, often resorting to violence to force New Guineans' support. In the United States the recruitment of Navajos was more considerate of individual desires to join the military. Given the situation on the Navajo Reservation during the Great Depression, many Navajos actively sought employment in the U.S. military as a form of economic security. But others were drafted into the armed forces as the United States embarked on total war against the Axis powers. Certainly conscription was an experience shared by all Americans; yet Navajos did not have all the privileges of citizenship, such as voting rights in Utah, New Mexico, and Arizona. Consequently, the U.S. government expected Navajos to participate in the preservation of the nation-state, while concurrently excluding them from the most basic citizenship rights. Hence soldier-warrior colonialism operated on a premise of *presumed* indigenous allegiance and participation in the military; to what extent such participation was voluntary depended on the circumstances of each colonized people and their individual constituents.

Despite the sometimes conscriptive nature of employment, oral testimonies from Navajos, Papua New Guineans, and Yolngu suggest genuine support for the war effort. One theme that pervades testimonies from all three case studies is the notion that indigenous residents were defending their own homelands—rather than the colonizers' nation-states—from outside invasion. Other motivations for indigenous people to join the Allied war effort were hopes that the war might usher in better relations between indigenous and non-indigenous peoples, loyalty to particular individuals, or hopes for advanced citizenship rights.

Thus even in the face of ongoing discrimination native peoples hoped to use military service to their advantage and to push for a better status within the colonizers' nation-states.[9] The extent to which they succeeded in achieving a better deal varied, from secured land rights in the Northern Territory post-1976, to self-government post-1972 in the Navajo Nation, to full independence in Papua New Guinea in 1975. However, these outcomes came only after years of intense lobbying from indigenous persons and changing global conditions favoring decolonization and self-determination. In fact, colonizer governments attempted to strengthen their colonial regimes in the immediate postwar epoch and ultimately only granted self-determination on terms favorable to the colonizers.

Oral testimonies also reveal that while in some situations the living conditions of indigenous soldiers during the war were an improvement over prewar situations, they were still subject to prejudice, discrimination, and sometimes even abuse. For instance, Yolngu members of the NTSRU were almost arrested for a theft they did not commit, unjustly accused without evidence because of constructs of racial primitiveness. Navajos were often subjected to stereotypes and name-calling; because of their racial appearance they were even mistaken for Japanese and almost killed or detained by other Americans. Papuans and New Guineans withstood abuse and poor living conditions at the hands of both Japanese and ANGAU overseers. Many carriers endured physical hardship, while receiving inadequate rations or enduring substandard living quarters. Their experiences mark an extreme example of a trend common of soldier-warrior colonialism: as indigenous soldiers were considered less important than white (or Japanese) personnel, indigenous privation was not high on the militaries' agendas.

Consequently, soldier-warrior colonialism also entailed unfair compensation for indigenous soldiers. The members of NTSRU received only trade goods such as pipes, wire, and tobacco, while other Yolngu scouts and trackers received nothing. Papuans and New Guineans did receive some wages and compensation after the Second World War, but the reparation scheme was capped, benefits were distributed unevenly, and numerous Papua New Guinean veterans have angrily testified that they never received any recompense for their war services. Navajos did receive compensation at the same rate as other veterans. However, many Veterans' Administration and GI Bill benefits have been inaccessible on the Navajo Reservation. Moreover, the Navajo Code Talkers — like the members of the NTSRU — did not receive official gratitude from the U.S. government until decades after the war ended, resulting in a long, drawn-out fight for recognition. Thus soldier-warrior colonialism has entailed the erasure of indigenous service from national war memories. Intense lobbying has managed to secure recognition for some indigenous service in all three countries, but the issue of redistribution has yet to be resolved.

This links to the final major commonality among the three case studies — continuing discrimination, assimilation policies, and colonialism in the postwar period. Oral testimonies suggest some resentment transnationally among indigenous veterans because their hopes for better status after the war did not come to fruition. In the Northern Territory lack of adequate compensation and accelerated assimilation policies in the 1950s and 1960s undermined Yolngu hopes for self-determination until post-1976. In Papua New Guinea the hopes for independence were delayed for another thirty years, as Australian administrators reasserted control over the lives of Papua New Guinean residents. In the United States Navajos' and other Native Americans' excellent war service convinced the federal government that American Indians were allegedly "ready" to assimilate. The subsequent termination and relocation policies had a devastating impact on American Indian communities across the country. Thus soldier-warrior colonialism entailed continuing interracial relations on the colonizers' terms. Any advances in indigenous socioeconomic status or rights came through the benevolence of the colonizer, rather than as an automatic quid-pro-quo as gratitude for indigenous military service.

The parallel examples of the Yolngu, Navajos, and Papua New Guineans are not the only cases of soldier-warrior colonialism. Their experiences obviously contain differences that should not be trivialized, but fundamentally, individual variations do not negate the common theoretical links. It is the duty of colonial and postcolonial governments and militaries to recognize the injustice of this practice and to find ways both to recognize indigenous participation in the military and to expose the layers of inequality traditionally inherent in such experiences. The case studies in this book are significant because they demonstrate that indigenous contributions to war do not necessarily signify reconciliatory attitudes. It is easy to look back at the past and see wartime as a "shared experience" deserving tribute. Certainly the positive relations between indigenous and non-indigenous servicemen merit praise. Interpersonal relationships are often the precursors to wider structural changes to society. But one must examine the whole picture: What were the circumstances of the relations between indigenous and non-indigenous people leading up to the war? Why did the government and military seek indigenous soldiers? How did the government treat the indigenous veterans? Did the structures of colonialism change? As this book has shown, answers to these questions demonstrate that the reconciliatory interpretation of indigenous military service is incomplete.

Yet the Second World War clearly changed the world. Two new superpowers—the United States and the Soviet Union—emerged and within a few years ushered in the Cold War. The Holocaust exposed the extreme dangers of racism, and global attitudes began to shift. The prewar European colonial powers underwent a process of decolonization from the 1950s through the 1970s. Sometimes this process was fraught with conflict, and in other situations it occurred peacefully. The newly formed United Nations proclaimed in its 1948 Universal Declaration of Human Rights: "Everyone is entitled to all the rights and freedoms set forth in this Declaration, without distinction of any kind, such as race, color, sex, language, religion, political or other opinion, national or social origin, property, birth or other status."[10] New nations run by racial minorities emerged in former colonies in Africa, the Middle East, the Pacific, and Southeast Asia. In the United States a black civil rights movement took off in the mid-1950s, and in the late 1960s that movement spread to other racial minorities, such as Native Americans and Latinos. The changing global circumstances would also reverberate through Papua New Guinean nationalism and nationhood in 1975. In Australia the changing global circumstances influenced a wave of activism for Indigenous rights among Aboriginal and Torres Strait Islander people and their non-Indigenous allies. This culminated in the 1967 Referendum, in which over 90 percent of the Australian public overwhelmingly voted to remove two discriminatory clauses from the Australian Constitution. These milestone changes in civil rights for Aboriginal people and those already described for Navajos and Papua New Guineans successfully challenged legal discrimination. Although governments certainly have also made some strides in recognizing the participation of native soldiers in the Pacific War, the accompanying legacies of colonialism linger.

SOURCE ACKNOWLEDGMENTS

Portions of the introduction were originally published by the author as "Preserving a White Military: The Australian Armed Forces and Indigenous People in World War II," in *Historicising Whiteness: Transnational Perspectives on the Construction of an Identity,* ed. Leigh Boucher, Jane Carey, and Katherine Ellinghaus, 133–42 (Melbourne: RMIT Publishing in association with the School of Historical Studies, University of Melbourne, 2007).

Portions of chapter 1 were originally published by the author as "Exploited Soldiers: Navaho and Yolngu Units in the Second World War," *Journal of Northern Territory History* 19 (2008): 60–81, and "Defending Whose Country? Yolngu and the NTSRU in the Second World War," *Limina: A Journal of Historical and Cultural Studies* 13 (2007): 80–91.

Portions of chapter 2 were originally published by the author as "Contesting White Knowledge: Yolngu Stories from World War II," *Oral History Review* 37, no. 2 (2010): 170–90; "'Japan fight. Aboriginal people fight. European people fight': Yolngu Stories from World War II," *Australian Journal of Indigenous Education* 37s (2008): 65–72; and "Disrupting Assimilation: Soldiers, Missionaries, and Yolngu in Arnhem Land during World War II," *Melbourne Historical Journal* 35 (2007): 73–89, republished in *Evangelists of Empire? Missionaries in Colonial History,* ed. Amanda Barry, Joanna Cruickshank, Patricia Grimshaw, and Andrew Brown-May, 245–62 (Melbourne: Melbourne E-Scholarly Press, 2008).

Portions of chapter 3 were originally published by the author as "Australian (Mis)treatment of Indigenous Labour in World War II Papua and New Guinea," *Labor History* 98 (May 2010): 163–82, and "Black Skins, Black Work: Race and Labour in World War II Papua and New Guinea," in *Labour History in the New Century,* ed. Bobbie Oliver, 63–75 (Perth: Black Swan Press, 2009),

Portions of chapter 4 were originally published by the author as "Australian (Mis)treatment of Indigenous Labour in World War II Papua and New Guinea," *Labor History* 98 (May 2010): 163–82.

Portions of chapter 5 were originally published by the author as "'Regardless of History'? Reassessing the Navajo Codetalkers of World War II," *Australasian Journal of American Studies* 26, no. 2 (December 2007): 48–73.

Portions of chapter 6 were originally published by the author as "Forgetting and (Re)membering Indigenous Soldiers: Yolngu and Navajo Veterans of World War II," in *When the Soldiers Return: November 2007 Conference Proceedings*, ed. Martin Crotty and Craig Barrett, 41–53 (Melbourne: RMIT Publishing in association with the School of History, Philosophy, Religion, and Classics, University of Queensland, 2009); "Exploited Soldiers: Navaho and Yolngu Units in the Second World War," *Journal of Northern Territory History* 19 (2008): 60–81; and "'Regardless of History'? Reassessing the Navajo Codetalkers of World War II," *Australasian Journal of American Studies* 26, no. 2 (December 2007): 48–73.

NOTES

Abbreviations

AWM   Australian War Memorial
NAA Canberra National Archives of Australia, Canberra
NAA Darwin   National Archives of Australia, Darwin
NAA Melbourne National Archives of Australia, Melbourne
NARA   National Archives and Records Administration
NTAS   Northern Territory Archives Service

Introduction

1. Some sources that discuss other aspects of indigenous peoples in the Pacific War include White and Lindstrom, *Pacific Theater*; Falgout, Poyer, and Carucci, *Memories of War*.

2. Skocpol and Somers, "Uses of Comparative History," 176–77.

3. Berkhofer, "Political Context of a New Indian History," 364.

4. Attwood, *Making of the Aborigine*, xi. See also McGrath, "National Story," 1–4; Huggins, *Sister Girl*, 16, 23; Brock, *Outback Ghettos*, 156–67; Veracini, "Of a 'contested ground.'"

5. Jacobs, "Indian and the Frontier," 43–44.

6. Fixico, "Ethics and Responsibilities," 32–34.

7. Huggins, *Sister Girl*, 86–87, 120–25; Maynard, "Circles in the Sand"; Nakata, *Disciplining the Savages*; Tuhiwai Smith, *Decolonizing Methodologies*; Mudrooroo, *Us Mob*, 175–92.

8. A. Thomson, "Anzac Stories."

9. Cole, *From Mission to Church*, 25–27; Evans, "Arnhem Land," 1; Trudgen, *Why Warriors Lie Down and Die*, 19–27. For Indigenous accounts of the massacres see Read and Read, *Long Time, Olden Time*, 23–24; Hercus and Suggon, *This Is What Happened*, 66.

10. NAA, Canberra, ser. A1734/15, item NT1970/1409: Appointment of Professor [Professor] Baldwin Spencer.

11. Parry and Austin, "Introduction," 15.

12. Dewar, *"Black War" in Arnhem Land*, 3; Australia . . . [Fifteenth Parliament],

Report of the Board of Inquiry, 58; Austin, "Training the Yolngu"; Cole, *From Mission to Church*; Thornell, *Bridge over Time*; Harris, *One Blood*. Aboriginal accounts of missionaries, including brutality, are available in Read and Read, *Long Time, Olden Time*, 68; Lamilami, *Lamilami Speaks*, 213; Randall, *Songman*, 56–57.

13. NTAS, Gordon Sweeney, oral history interview, 1980, tape 1, side A, p. 16; NAA Canberra, ser. A1, item 1936/6237: Tribal fights—East Arnhem Land; Austin, *Never Trust a Government Man*, 142–314; NTAS, Commissioner of Police, Correspondence files, file 5/43, Roper River.

14. V. C. Hall, *Dreamtime Justice*, 80.

15. Abbott, *Australia's Frontier Province*, 147.

16. Dyer, *Unarmed Combat*, 2.

17. NAA Canberra, ser. A373, item 5903: [Japanese activities amongst aboriginals].

18. Egan, *Justice All Their Own*; *Dhakiyarr vs. the King*; V. C. Hall, *Dreamtime Justice*; Dewar, *"Black War" in Arnhem Land*; Dyer, *Unarmed Combat*; Fowler, *Guns or God*.

19. NAA Canberra, ser. A52, item 572/994 THO: "Interim General Report," 28.

20. Australia, Defence Act (as amended 1910), sections 61 (1) (h) and 138 (1) (b). Amendments removed the restrictions in section 61 in 1965 and repealed section 138 in 1951.

21. Prime Minister Robert G. Menzies to Secretary, Departments of the Army and Navy, 25 Feb. 1940, NAA Canberra, ser. A2671, item 45/1940: Enlistment in Defence Forces.

22. Lt-Colonel, name illegible, Brigadier i/c Administration for G.O.C. Southern Command, to Secretary of Military Board, 5 May 1941, NAA Melbourne, ser. MP508/1, item 275/750/1310: Aborigines Enlisted in AIF.

23. Smith, "Minorities and the Australian Army," 132.

24. R. A. Hall, *Black Diggers*, 60.

25. Colonel, Director of Organization and Recruitment, to Eastern Command, 12 Aug. 1940, NAA Melbourne, ser. MP508/1, item 275/750/618: Enlistment of Aborigines in the AIF.

26. A. P. A. Burdeu, Australian Aborigines' League, Victoria, to Minister for the Interior, 27 Feb. 1938, NAA Melbourne, ser. B1535, item 929/19/912: Military training for Aboriginal youth.

27. G. A. Street, Minister for Defence, to Senator H. S. Foll, Minister for Interior, 8 Sept. 1939, NAA Canberra, ser. A659, item 1939/1/12995: Enlistment of half-caste Aborigines; also in NAA Melbourne, ser. B1535, item 849/3/1644: [Aborigines in militia unit].

28. Australia . . . [Fifteenth Parliament], *Report of the Board of Inquiry*, 8.

29. A. Powell, *Shadow's Edge*, 3–8.

30. NAA Melbourne, ser. MP508/1, item 82/710/2: Employment of Aborigines by Defence/Army in Darwin.

31. C. Clowes, Major Staff Corps, Darwin, to Army Headquarters, Melbourne, 12 Dec. 1933, NAA Melbourne, ser. MP508/1, item 82/710/2: Employment of Aborigines by Defence/Army in Darwin.

32. Lt.-Colonel Robertson, Commandant, 7th Military District, to the Secretary, Military Board, 25 Jan. 1940, NAA Melbourne, ser. MP508/1, item 82/710/2: Employment of Aborigines by Defence/Army in Darwin.

33. Honorable Secretary, Aborigines' Friends' Association, to Senator Honorable J. S. Collins, Minister for the Interior, 18 Aug. 1942, NAA Canberra, ser. A431, item 1946/915: Employment of Natives on Work for Army.

34. Berndt and Berndt, *End of an Era*, 177; Sergeant W. Smith, "Black Australian," AWM, ser. 54, item 805/7/1: [Publications—Army Newspapers:].

35. Colonel, Director of Recruiting and Demobilization, Department of Army Minute Paper, 29 Sept. 1943, NAA Melbourne, ser. MP742/1, item 92/1/302: Employment of Native Labour in NT.

36. Colonel Sheppard, for Major General, Department of the Army Minute Paper, 31 Dec. 1943, NAA Melbourne, ser. MP742/1, item 92/1/302: Employment of Native Labour in NT. See also A. G. Cameron to Senator J. S. Collings, Minister for the Interior, 26 Jan. 1944, NAA Canberra, ser. A431, item 1946/915: Employment of Natives on Work for Army.

37. Secretary, Navy Office, to Secretary, Department of Defence Co-Ordination, 12 Feb. 1940, NAA Canberra, ser. A816, item 14/301/138: Report on Arnhem Land.

38. Extract from A. Stanfield Sampson to Mrs. Bennet, in memo to Director-General of Security, 16 July 1942, "Subject: Japanese Activities Among the Aborigines," NAA Melbourne, ser. MP729/6, item 29/401/626: Japanese Activities Among the Aborigines. See also Department of the Navy Minute Paper, NAA Melbourne, ser. MP729/6, item 29/401/618: North Australia Observer Organisation.

39. A. P. Elkin, "Voluntary War Service for Aborigines," NAA Melbourne, ser. MP508/1, item 240/701/217: [Role of Aborigines of defence of Australia]; also in NAA Canberra, ser. A659, item 1942/1/3043: Co-operation between Aboriginals and whites.

40. A. P. Elkin, "Regarding Closer Co-Operation between Our Native Peoples," 8 Apr. 1942, NAA Melbourne, ser. MP508/1, item 240/701/217: [Role of Aborigines of Defence of Australia]; also in NAA Canberra, ser. A659, item 1942/1/3043: Co-operation between Aboriginals and whites.

41. Lieutenant-Colonel, District Finance Officer, 1st M.D., to Deputy Director of Native Affairs, 15 Sept. 1941, AWM, ser. 54, item 628/1/1B: [Torres Strait Area:].

42. Milbase Brisbane to Loctown, telegram, 17 Oct. 1942, AWM, ser. 54, item 628/1/1B: [Torres Strait Area:].

43. Major, for Lieutenant-General, Comd First Aust Army, AOD, to ADV LHQ, HQ QLD L of C Area, 10 Oct. 1942, AWM, ser. 54, item 628/1/1B: [Torres Strait Area:].

44. Major, DAAG First Aust Army, "Torres Strait Islanders—Rates of Pay and

Conditions of Service," June 1944, AWM, ser. 54, item 628/1/1B: [Torres Strait Area:].

45. O'Brien, "Remaking Australia's Colonial Culture?" 97.

46. Lewis, *Plantation Dream*, 18–20; Joyce, "Australian Interests in New Guinea," 20; J. H. P. Murray, *Papua or British New Guinea*, 343; Elder, "'Inner Logic of Dispossession,'" 50.

47. Joyce, "Australian Interests in New Guinea," 19. See also Waiko, "Binandere Forced Labour," 181; Edmonds, "Dual Mandate, Double Work," 243.

48. Wolfers, *Race Relations and Colonial Rule*, 19.

49. Sir William MacGregor, introduction to J. H. P. Murray, *Papua or British New Guinea*, 24.

50. Rowley, "Occupation of German New Guinea," 57–58; Wolfers, *Race Relations and Colonial Rule*, 74; H. Nelson, *Taim Bilong Masta*, 25–26; H. Wright, "Protecting the National Interest," 65.

51. "Compensation to the Natives of Papua and New Guinea for War Injuries and War Damage," 5; NAA Canberra, ser. A463, item 1956/1096: War pensions. For a discussion of the differences between colonial policies in Papua and New Guinea, see O'Brien, "Remaking Australia's Colonial Culture?" 96–112.

52. Sinclair, *Papua New Guinea*, 73; Edmonds, "Dual Mandate, Double Work," 123; Fitzpatrick, *Law and State in Papua New Guinea*, 68; J. H. P. Murray, *Papua or British New Guinea*, 362.

53. Radi, "New Guinea under Mandate," 83.

54. Wolfers, *Race Relations and Colonial Rule*, 5.

55. Radi, "New Guinea under Mandate," 76; Edmonds, "Dual Mandate, Double Work," 130; Moore, "Workers in Colonial Papua New Guinea," 40.

56. Edmonds, "Dual Mandate, Double Work," 130, 133–34; Legge, "Murray Period," 42, 46; Wolfers, *Race Relations and Colonial Rule*, 37; Waiko, "Binandere Forced Labour," 181; Radi, "New Guinea under Mandate," 89.

57. J. H. P. Murray, *Papua or British New Guinea*, 346.

58. Lewis, *Plantation Dream*, 46–47.

59. J. H. P. Murray, *Papua or British New Guinea*, 353.

60. Lewis, *Plantation Dream*, 270; H. Nelson, *Taim Bilong Masta*, 78; Rowley, "Occupation of German New Guinea," 64–65; Wolfers, *Race Relations and Colonial Rule*, 78; Monsell-Davis, "Roro and Mekeo Labour," 187; Fitzpatrick, *Law and State in Papua New Guinea*, 61.

61. Mair, *Australia in New Guinea*, 15.

62. H. Nelson, *Taim Bilong Masta*, 79; Lewis, *Plantation Dream*, 268; Stella, *Imagining the Other*, 144–47; Fitzpatrick, *Law and State in Papua New Guinea*, 80; Wolfers, *Race Relations and Colonial Rule*, 56–59.

63. Joyce, "Australian Interests in New Guinea," 19; Wolfers, *Race Relations and Colonial Rule*, 18; Kituai, "Innovation and Intrusion," 156. See also Kituai, *My Gun, My Brother*.

64. Australia, *Royal Papuan Constabulary Ordinance* (1939), sect. 25, NAA Canberra, ser. A432, item 1939/947: Royal Papuan Constabulary Ordinance.

65. J. H. P. Murray, *Papua or British New Guinea*, 241.

66. Kituai, "Innovation and Intrusion," 157.

67. NAA Melbourne, ser. MP742/1, item 247/1/474: Rates of pay of Warrant Officers; Gammage, "Police and Power," 162–63.

68. In J. H. P. Murray, *Papua or British New Guinea*, 242.

69. Kituai, "Innovation and Intrusion," 164.

70. Kituai, "Innovation and Intrusion," 160.

71. J. H. P. Murray, *Papua or British New Guinea*, 242.

72. Wolfers, *Race Relations and Colonial Rule*, 35; Kituai, "Innovation and Intrusion," 161–63.

73. Iverson, *Diné*, 22–45.

74. Iverson, *Diné*, 46–59; Alfred Lehi, interview, recorded by Max Hanley; MacDonald, *Last Warrior*, 8–10; Mack, *It Had to Be Done*, 6.

75. Bixler, *Winds of Freedom*, 18; Iverson, *Diné*, 65.

76. Iverson, *Diné*, 95–96; Bixler, *Winds of Freedom*, 18–19.

77. Iverson, *Diné*, 83–88; Bixler, *Winds of Freedom*, 67; Paul Blatchford, interview with Sally McClain, Oct. 1991.

78. MacDonald, *Last Warrior*, 48–49. See also Paul, *Navajo Code Talkers*, 108; Mack, *It Had to Be Done*, 13–19. Most of the Navajo veterans profiled by Vogt also went to boarding school and expressed distasteful memories. See Vogt, *Navaho Veterans*.

79. Juan Etsicitty, interview, recorded 11 Jan. 1968; Blackhorse, interview, date unavailable; Franco, "Loyal and Heroic Service," 392; Townsend, *World War II and the American Indian*, 26–27; MacDonald, *Last Warrior*, 36–38; Keith Little, in Mack, *It Had to Be Done*, 6.

80. MacDonald, *Last Warrior*, 3. See also Waybenais, "Women's Army Corps—Overseas," 131; Robbins, "Self-Determination and Subordination"; Carroll, *Medicine Bags and Dog Tags*, 116.

81. Franco, "Loyal and Heroic Service," 392; Watson, "Jaysho," 2–3; Iverson, *Diné*, 145; Escue, "Coded Contributions," 14.

82. Bernstein, *American Indians and World War II*, 24; Franco, *Crossing the Pond*, 47–48; Townsend, *World War II and the American Indian*, 115–24.

83. In Franco, "Empowering the World War II Native American Veteran," 33. See also Bernstein, *American Indians and World War II*, 31–33.

84. Franco, "Empowering the World War II Native American Veteran," 33.

85. Franco, "Empowering the World War II Native American Veteran," 34; Bernstein, *American Indians and World War II*, 45–46; Townsend, *World War II and the American Indian*, 61–63; Carroll, *Medicine Bags and Dog Tags*, 115.

86. Bernstein, *American Indians and World War II*, 41; Townsend, *World War II and the American Indian*, 87–102; Stabler, *No One Ever Asked Me*, 57–58.

87. Fixico, *Termination and Relocation*, 4; Franco, "Loyal and Heroic Service," 393; Franco, *Crossing the Pond*, 62.

88. Stabler, *No One Ever Asked Me*, 49; Franco, *Crossing the Pond*, 168; Bernstein, *American Indians and World War II*, 56–57; Carroll, *Medicine Bags and Dog Tags*, 114.

89. "7th Army Indians in War Dance," *New York Times*, 25 July 1943.

90. Carroll, *Medicine Bags and Dog Tags*, 2.

91. Fanon, *Wretched of the Earth*, 232.

92. Hobson, *Imperialism*, 137.

93. Hobson, *Imperialism*, 194.

94. van den Berghe, *Ethnic Phenomenon*, 98–99.

95. Enloe, *Ethnic Soldiers*, ix.

96. Enloe, *Ethnic Soldiers*, 39.

97. Streets, *Martial Races*, 4.

98. Meadows, *Kiowa, Comanche, and Apache Military Societies*, esp. preface and chap. 6.

99. Carroll, *Medicine Bags and Dog Tags*, 2.

100. Enloe, *Ethnic Soldiers*, 25–27; Enloe, *Police, Military and Ethnicity*, 37; Streets, *Martial Races*, 173–78.

101. Holm, "Patriots and Pawns," 354. See also Holm, "Stereotypes, State Elites."

102. Young, *Minorities and the Military*, 255–56.

103. Enloe, *Ethnic Soldiers*, 25; Streets, *Martial Races*, 184.

104. Enloe, *Police, Military and Ethnicity*, 64.

1. An Exception in the Equation?

1. J. C. Jennison, "Eastern Arnhem Land: Australia's Open Door," 8 Jan. 1940, NAA Canberra, ser. A816, item 14/301/138: Report on Arnhem Land.

2. AWM, ser. 54, item 741/5/9: "Report on Northern Territory Special Reconnaissance Unit," part 1, p. 10; also in NAA Canberra, ser. AA1966/5, item 386: Northern Territory Force."

3. AWM, ser. 54, item 741/5/9: "Report on Northern Territory Special Reconnaissance Unit," part 1, p. 26.

4. NAA Canberra, ser. A52, item 572/994 THO: "Interim General Report," 43.

5. Donald Thomson to the Director, Special Operations Section, "The Place of the Natives of Arnhem Land in the Defence of the Coast of Northern Australia with a Proposal for the Organization of a Force for Scouting and Reconnaissance," June 1941, AWM, ser. 54, item 741/5/9, "Report on Northern Territory Special Reconnaissance Unit," part 1, app. 1, p. 6.

6. Oliver, *Raids on Australia*, esp. 1–22; Stanley, *Invading Australia*.

7. Jennison, "Eastern Arnhem Land."

8. Thomson to the Director, "Place of the Natives," 7.

9. Thomson to the Director, "Place of the Natives," 8.

10. Lt. Col. W. J. R. Scott, Department of Army Minute Paper, "Distant Flank

Reconnaissance and Protection of 7th Military District," 30 June 1941, NAA Melbourne, ser. MP729/6, item 38/401/138: Ketch "Aroetta" movements.

11. Lt. Col. W. J. R. Scott, Department of Army Minute Paper, "Flank Reconnaissance and Protection of 7th Military District," 1 Aug. 1941, NAA Melbourne, ser. MP742/1, item 299/4/703: A.K. "Aroetta."

12. Donald Thomson, "The Proposed Role of Arnhem Land Natives in Coastwatching and Reconnaissance and in Guerilla Warfare," June 1941, AWM, ser. 54, item 741/5/9: "Report on Northern Territory Special Reconnaissance Unit," part I, app. I, p. 12.

13. AWM, ser. 54, item 741/5/9: "Report on Northern Territory Special Reconnaissance Unit," part I, p. 25.

14. "Comments on Reconnaissance and Protection Plan in 7th Military District, 14 July 1941," NAA Melbourne, ser. MP742/1, item 299/4/703: A.K. "Aroetta."

15. "Comments on Reconnaissance . . . 7th Military District." The phrase "either themselves or from their native stockmen" was inserted by hand into the typed document.

16. Lt. Col. W. J. R. Scott, Department of Army Minute Paper, "Comments on Reconnaissance and Protection Plan in 7 M.D.," 16 July 1941, NAA Melbourne, ser. MP742/1, item 299/4/703: A.K. "Aroetta."

17. Scott, "Distant Flank Reconnaissance."

18. "Proposed Plan for Discussion with Commandant, 7 M.D." 11 Oct. 1941, AWM, ser. 54, item 741/5/9: "Report on Northern Territory Special Reconnaissance Unit," part I, app. I, p. 27.

19. "Proposed Plan for Discussion with Commandant," 9–11.

20. Thomson, "Proposed Role of Arnhem Land Natives," 13.

21. Thomson, "Proposed Role of Arnhem Land Natives," 3.

22. Scott, "Distant Flank Reconnaissance."

23. Lt. Col. W. J. R. Scott, 18 Aug. 1941, AWM, ser. 54, item 741/5/9: "Report on Northern Territory Special Reconnaissance Unit," part I, app. I, p. 17.

24. All service records are available from NAA Canberra, ser. B884, ser. accession number B884/4. Item numbers are: Q119904: TIKI; Q119906: LAKAPOLI PAPAI; Q119907: MAKAU KELAUIA; Q119908: RICHARDSON EDWIN; Q119909: GEGE.F.R. Other documents relating to Solomon Islander personnel are available in NAA Melbourne, ser. MP742/1, item 299/4/703: A.K. "Aroetta"; AWM, ser. 54, item 741/5/9: "Report on Northern Territory Special Reconnaissance Unit," part I, app. I, pp. 17, 21, 24; NAA Melbourne, ser. MP729/6, item 38/401/138: Ketch "Aroetta" movements; NAA Melbourne, ser. MP742/1, item 247/1/79: Employment of Native Crews.

25. Resident Commissioner, British Solomon Islands, Tulagi, to Secretary, Prime Minister's Department, 18 Sept. 1941, telegram, and Secretary, Department of Army, to Secretary, Prime Minister's Department, 19 Sept. 1941, telegram, both NAA Melbourne, ser. MP742/1, item 299/4/703: A.K. "Aroetta."

26. Lieutenant-Colonel, Deputy Director of Military Operations, to CFO,

"Northern Territory Special Reconnaissance Unit—Pay of Native Crew," 22 Jan. 1943, NAA Melbourne, ser. MP742/I, item 247/1/79: Employment of Native Crews." See also Donald Thomson to Director of Military Operations, LHQ, "Solomon Islands Native Crew of A.K. Aroetta," 26 Dec. 1942, NAA Melbourne, ser. MP729/6, item 38/401/138: Ketch "Aroetta" movements.

27. Colonel R. G. Booker, Deputy Director of Military Operations, 10 Feb. 1943, NAA Canberra, ser. A10857, item IV/15E: Northern Territory—Coastal Reconnaissance Unit.

28. AWM, ser. 54, item 741/5/9: "Report on Northern Territory Special Reconnaissance Unit," part 1, p. 4.

29. Col. J. A. McKenzie for Major-General, Deputy Chief of General Staff, II Sept. 1941, AWM, ser. 54, item 741/5/9: "Report on Northern Territory Special Reconnaissance Unit," part 1, app. 1, p. 21.

30. AWM, ser. 54, item 741/5/9: "Report on Northern Territory Special Reconnaissance Unit," part 1, p. 40.

31. AWM, ser. 54, item 741/5/9: "Report on Northern Territory Special Reconnaissance Unit," part 1, p. 71.

32. AWM, ser. 54, item 741/5/9: "Report on Northern Territory Special Reconnaissance Unit," part 1, p. 20.

33. AWM, ser. 54, item 741/5/9: "Report on Northern Territory Special Reconnaissance Unit," part 1, p. 24.

34. AWM, ser. 54, item 741/5/9: "Report on Northern Territory Special Reconnaissance Unit," part 1, p. 41.

35. R. A. Hall, *Black Diggers*, 92.

36. AWM, ser. 54, item 741/5/9: "Report on Northern Territory Special Reconnaissance Unit," part 1, p. 42.

37. J. C. Lovegrove, Inspector of Police, to Superintendent of Police, 25 Apr. 1939, NAA Darwin, ser. FI, item 1939/545; T. T. Webb, "Report of Aboriginal Killings at Caledon and Melville Bays," 2 Mar. 1938, NAA Canberra, ser. A1, item 1938/6715: Aboriginal Murders.

38. AWM, ser. 54, item 741/5/9: "Report on Northern Territory Special Reconnaissance Unit," part 1, p. 25.

39. Warner, *Black Civilization*, 174–76; AWM, ser. 54, item 741/5/9: "Report on Northern Territory Special Reconnaissance Unit," part 2, p. 42.

40. David Burrumura, in McIntosh, *Whale and the Cross*, 37–38 (original emphasis).

41. AWM, ser. 54, item 741/5/9: "Report on Northern Territory Special Reconnaissance Unit," part 1, p. 27.

42. AWM, ser. 54, item 741/5/9: "Report on Northern Territory Special Reconnaissance Unit," part 1, p. 48.

43. R. A. Hall, *Black Diggers*, 97.

44. Saunders, "Inequalities of Sacrifice," 136.

45. AWM, ser. 54, item 741/5/9: "Report on Northern Territory Special Reconnaissance Unit," part I, p. 48.

46. R. A. Hall, *Black Diggers*, 97.

47. AWM, ser. 54, item 741/5/9: "Report on Northern Territory Special Reconnaissance Unit," part I, pp. 30, 49. See also Hall, *Black Diggers*, 97.

48. AWM, ser. 54, item 741/5/9: "Report on Northern Territory Special Reconnaissance Unit," part I, p. 49.

49. AWM, ser. 54, item 741/5/9: "Report on Northern Territory Special Reconnaissance Unit," part I, p. 29.

50. AWM, ser. 54, item 741/5/9: "Report on Northern Territory Special Reconnaissance Unit," part I, p. 49.

51. R. A. Hall, *Black Diggers*, 97.

52. Donald Thomson, D.M.O., n.d., NAA Melbourne, ser. MP742/1, item 299/4/703: A.K. "Aroetta."

53. "7 M.D. Operation Instruction No. 13," AWM, ser. 54, item 741/5/9: "Report on Northern Territory Special Reconnaissance Unit," part I, p. 29.

54. "7 M.D. Operation Instruction No. 13," 28.

55. G. Gray, "Army Requires Anthropologists," 169. See also A. Powell, *Shadow's Edge*, 250.

56. NAA Melbourne, ser. MP729/6, item 29/401/618: North Australia Observer Organisation; AWM, F04030/01/02: Interview with Amory Vane, 14 Feb. 1991; AWM, ser. 52, item 25/1/2: 2/1 Northern Australia Observer Unit; Vane, "Surveillance of Northern Australia—Its History," 16–18.

57. Vane, "Surveillance of Northern Australia," 24–26; Walker and Walker, *Curtin's Cowboys*, 71; NTAS, Charles Curtis, oral history interview, 30 Nov. 1983, 7–8.

58. Stanner, Department of Army Minute Paper, NAA Melbourne, ser. MP729/6, item 29/401/618: North Australia Observer Organisation.

59. Department of the Navy, Minute Paper, NAA Melbourne, ser. MP729/6, item 29/401/618: North Australia Observer Organisation.

60. G. Gray, "Army Requires Anthropologists," 170.

61. Stanner, Department of Army Minute Paper.

62. NAA Canberra, ser. A705, item 68/1/700: Use of Aboriginal Labour by RAAF, quoted in Saunders, "Inequalities of Sacrifice," 135; also quoted in a letter to Amoury Vane, 5 Sept. 1981, in Walker and Walker, *Curtin's Cowboys*, 138.

63. Stanner, Department of Army Minute Paper.

64. G. Gray, *Cautious Silence*, 180; G. Gray, Chance to be of some use,'" 31.

65. Walker and Walker, *Curtin's Cowboys*, 73, 140–45; AWM, F04029/01/03: Interview with Peter Huskins, 14 Feb. 1991; NTAS, Alec Boxall, oral history interview with Alan Powell, 2 Dec. 1983, 1; "Report of Patrol By 1 Platoon, 'C' Coy., In Area Between McArthu and Limmen Rivers," Patrol 6 Oct–27 Oct 1942, AWM, ser. 52, item 25/1/2: Northern Australia Observer Unit; Stanner, Department of Army Minute Paper; NTAS, Reg Oakley, oral history interview with Alan Powell, 17 Nov. 1984,

43.

66. Evan Wenban, in Walker and Walker, *Curtin's Cowboys*, 143.

67. Des Harrison, in Walker and Walker, *Curtin's Cowboys*, 138.

68. AWM, F04030/01/02: North Australia Observer Organisation.

69. NTAS, "Tip" Carty, oral history interview with Alan Powell, 30 Nov. 1983, 29.

70. NTAS, Reg Oakley, oral history interview, 17 Nov. 1984, 43.

71. NTAS, Ron Rogers, oral history interview with Alan Powell, 3 Dec. 1983, 16.

72. Lt. C. M. Golding, "Routine Orders: By Captain W. F. Commans. Adm. Commd. North Australia Observer Unit," 11 Jan. 44, AWM, ser. 52, item 25/1/2: Northern Australia Observer Unit.

73. NAA Melbourne, ser. MP729/6, item 37/401/2145: Coast Watching and Reporting Systems; NAA Melbourne, ser. MP729/6, item 37/401/1849: Relief of NAOU; War Diary, NAOU, 1 Jan. 45–31 Jan. 45, AWM, ser. 52, item 25/1/2: Northern Australia Observer Unit; Vane, "Surveillance of Northern Australia," 29.

74. Lt. A. E. Palmer, "Deck Log," AWM, ser. 54, item 741/5/9: "Report on Northern Territory Special Reconnaissance Unit," part 1, log, p. 9.

75. Palmer, "Deck Log," part 1, p. 50.

76. Const. J. Mahony, Roper River Police Station, to Superintendent of Police, Alice Springs, 27 June 1942, "Re: Re Enlistment Guerilla Native & European Interpreters," NTAS, Commissioner of Police, NTRS F77, Correspondence files.

77. Mahony to Superintendent of Police, 27 June 1942.

78. AWM, ser. 54, item 741/5/9: "Report on Northern Territory Special Reconnaissance Unit," part 1, p. 51.

79. AWM, ser. 54, item 741/5/9: "Report on Northern Territory Special Reconnaissance Unit," part 1, pp. 51–53.

80. NTAS, Alec Boxall, oral history interview, 2 Dec. 1983, 17.

81. Thomson, "w/t Report on Work Done by Special Reconnaissance Unit," to R.A.A.F. Darwin, 25 Apr. 1942, AWM, ser. 54, item 741/5/9: "Report on Northern Territory Special Reconnaissance Unit," part 1, app. 4, p. 34. See also AWM, ser. 54, item 741/5/9: "Report on Northern Territory Special Reconnaissance Unit," part 1, app. 2, p. 5, and app. 4, p. 10; Thomson, "w/t Report on Work Done," 2.

82. Thomson, "Report on Work Done by Special Reconnaissance Unit," part 1, app. 4, p. 34.

83. Thomson, "Report on Work Done by Special Reconnaissance Unit," part 1, app. 4, p. 35.

84. Rev. Canon G. R. Harris, handwritten manuscript of autobiography, 190, NTAS, Keith Cole, Records, photographs and research material; L. E. Beavis, Maj-General, Master-General of the Ordnance, 9 Sept. 1943, AWM, ser. 54, item 963/22/12: [Transport — Sea (Allied)].

85. Albert Allen, quoted in Walker and Walker, *Curtin's Cowboys*, 77. See also Walker and Walker, *Curtin's Cowboys*, 77–79; AWM, F04029/01/03: Interview with

Peter Huskins, 14 Feb. 1991.

86. Walker and Walker, *Curtin's Cowboys*, 80–81.

87. AWM, ser. 54, item 741/5/9: "Report on Northern Territory Special Reconnaissance Unit," part 1, p. 37.

88. AWM, ser. 54, item 741/5/9: "Report on Northern Territory Special Reconnaissance Unit," part 1, p. 37.

89. AWM, ser. 54, item 741/5/9: "Report on Northern Territory Special Reconnaissance Unit," part 1, pp. 35–36.

90. AWM, ser. 54, item 741/5/9: "Report on Northern Territory Special Reconnaissance Unit," part 1, pp. 36, 53.

91. Donald Thomson, "Operation Order No. 6," to Private Kapiu, 19 Aug. 1942, AWM, ser. 54, item 741/5/9: "Report on Northern Territory Special Reconnaissance Unit," part 1, app. 2, p. 11.

92. Thomson, "Operation Order No. 6," 12.

93. Donald Thomson, "Operation Order No. 9," to Sgt. T. H. Elkington, 19 Sept. 1942, AWM, ser. 54, item 741/5/9: "Report on Northern Territory Special Reconnaissance Unit," part 1, app. 2, p. 15.

94. AWM, ser. 54, item 741/5/9: "Report on Northern Territory Special Reconnaissance Unit," part 1, p. 70.

95. Gordon Ritchie, in *No Bugles, No Drums*. Ritchie was a gunner who did not join the NTSRU until 2 Dec. 1942.

96. Northern Land Council DVD.

97. Telegram, AWM, ser. 54, item 741/5/9: "Report on Northern Territory Special Reconnaissance Unit," part 1, p. 58.

98. AWM, ser. 54, item 741/5/9: "Report on Northern Territory Special Reconnaissance Unit," part 1, p. 55.

99. Elkington, log at Caledon Bay, AWM, ser. 54, item 741/5/9: "Report on Northern Territory Special Reconnaissance Unit," part 1, p. 55.

100. Elkington, log at Caledon Bay, 56.

101. Elkington, log at Caledon Bay, 56.

102. Col. R. G. Booker, Deputy Director of Military Operations, 10 Feb. 1943, NAA Canberra, ser. A10857, item IV/15E: Northern Territory—Coastal Reconnaissance Unit; NAA Melbourne, ser. MP729/6, item 37/401/1444: Northern Territory Coastal Reconnaissance Unit; AWM, ser. 54, item 519/4/2: [Operations—General (including enemy)]; AWM, ser. 52, item 5/35/1: Northern Territory Coastal Reconnaissance Unit.

103. Palmer, "Deck Log," part 2, log, pp. 33–36; Major, A/AQMG NT Force, to Headquarters, Northern Territory Force, 11 Apr. 1943, AWM, series 54, item 519/4/2: [Operations—General (including enemy)]; Hogarth, "Donald Thomson in Irian Jaya"; NAA Canberra, ser. A9300, item THOMSON D F; AWM, ser. 54, item 577/7/32: [Owen Stanleys—Reports:].

104. Woodley, "Local Heroes," 34.

105. Christie, Fox, and Yunupiŋu, foreword, 4.

2. Allies at War

1. Const. James H. Edwards to the Enemy Alien Registration Officer, Darwin, from Roper River Police Station, 1 Feb. 1942, NTAS, Commissioner of Police, Correspondence files, NTRS F 77, item 9/42: Roper River.

2. Margaret Somerville, letter dated 11 Mar. 1942, NTAS, Margaret Somerville, Diary entries of Margaret Somerville.

3. Old Charlie, interview with Noah Riseman, 29 Sept. 2005, 13–14.

4. A. R. Driver, Administrator, to the Secretary, Department of the Interior, 15 July 1946, NAA Canberra, ser. A431, item 1946/1357: Aborigine Ex-Servicemen Restrictions.

5. Rev. Canon G. R. Harris, unpublished manuscript of autobiography, 149; NTAS, Len Harris, oral history interview with Alan Powell, 15 Sept. 1983, 7.

6. Rev. Canon G. R. Harris, unpublished manuscript of autobiography, 182.

7. NTAS, Church Missionary Society of Australia, North Australia Committee, NTRS 1098, Mission reports and station council minutes, Aug. 1942, July 1945; NTAS, Len Harris, oral history interview, 15 Sept. 1983, 14–15; Nana Bara, in McMillan, *Catalina Dreaming*, 54.

8. F. H. Moy, Director of Native Affairs, "Review Report. Milingimbi Institution. North Australia District. Methodist Overseas Missions. From Establishment to 31st December, 1949," NAA Darwin, ser. F1, item 1953/266: Methodist Overseas Mission—Milingimbi Mission.

9. Marika, *Wandjuk Marika*, 71–72 (original emphasis). See also McMillan, *Catalina Dreaming*, 136–37.

10. Gerry Blitner, in *No Bugles, No Drums*.

11. NTAS, Kevin Graham, oral history interview with H. Giese, 2 Aug. 1981, tape 2, p. 18.

12. NTAS, Church Missionary Society of Australia, North Australia Committee, NTRS 1098, Mission reports and station council minutes, Mar. 1943, June–July 1943; H. C. Evans, Acting District Superintendent, "Review Report. Yirrkala Mission. For Period Ended 30th December 1951," NAA Darwin, ser. F1, item 1949/459: Methodist Overseas Mission, Yirrkala Mission; Don Watson, former pilot, in McMillan, *Catalina Dreaming*, 54.

13. Whitlam, "Dragging the Chain 1897–1997."

14. "A Word for the Aborigines," *Argus*, 25 Mar. 1943, NAA Canberra, ser. A431, item 1946/915: Employment of Natives on Work for Army.

15. Rev. Canon G. R. Harris, unpublished manuscript of autobiography, 179.

16. "Word for the Aborigines"; *No Bugles, No Drums*.

17. Gerry Blitner, in *No Bugles, No Drums*.

18. L. J. Harris, "A Statement for the Guidance of Mr. G. R. Harris in taking over the position of C.M.S. Mission, Groote Eylandt, November 1943," NTAS, Church

Missionary Society of Australia, North Australia Committee, NTRS 868, General records, Correspondence 1933–1944.

19. NTAS, Gordon Sweeney, oral history interview with Don Dickson, 1980, tape 1, side A, p. 9.

20. "Report on Goulburn Island Mission. 1933," NAA Darwin, ser. FI, item 1949/456: Methodist Overseas Mission Goulburn Island.

21. "Missions to Australian Aborigines: Constitution and Policy," May 1944, NTAS, Church Missionary Society of Australia, North Australia Committee, NTRS 868, General records, Correspondence 1933–1944.

22. Fowler, *Guns or God*, 79.

23. Rev. T. T. Webb, "Milingimbi Mission Station. Report for Year Ending December 31st 1932," NAA Darwin, ser. FI, item 1953/266: Methodist Overseas Mission—Milingimbi Mission.

24. McKenzie, *Mission to Arnhem Land*, 141–42; Thornell, *Bridge over Time*, 138; NAA Darwin, ser. FI, item 1953/266: Methodist Overseas Mission—Milingimbi Mission; Ellemor, *Warrawi Jubilee 1916–1966*, 19.

25. NTAS, Church Missionary Society of Australia, North Australia Committee, NTRS 1098, Mission reports and station council minutes, Aug. 1942.

26. NTAS, Church Missionary Society of Australia, North Australia Committee, NTRS 1098, Mission reports and station council minutes, June 1943.

27. L. J. Harris, "Statement for the Guidance of Mr. G. R. Harris."

28. Oliver, *Empty North*, 64. See also Harris, *One Blood*, 775.

29. Rev. Canon G. R. Harris, unpublished manuscript of autobiography, 246.

30. Leonard M. Kentish, to Administrator C. L. A. Abbott, 14 Sept. 1937, NAA Darwin, ser. FI, item 1938/716: Employment of Mission Aboriginals in Darwin. See also Webb, "Milingimbi Mission Station."

31. Evans, "Review Report. Yirrkala Mission."

32. For discussions about oral societies and the uses of oral history and indigenous research see Hodge and Mishra, *Dark Side of the Dream*, 76; Wilson, "Power of the Spoken Word"; Henige, *Oral Historiography*; Vansina, *Oral Tradition as History*; Rose, *Hidden Histories*; Attwood, *Telling the Truth about Aboriginal History*, especially chap. 9; Hamilton, "Are Oral Historians Losing the Plot?"; Maddock, "Myth, History"; Neumann, "Postcolonial Writing of Aboriginal History," 282; Donaldson, "Translating Oral Literature."

33. Goodall, "Too Early Yet," 23.

34. Phyllis Batumbil, interview with Noah Riseman, 29 Sept. 2005; Batumbil, in Old Charlie, interview, 29 Sept. 2005, 4.

35. NAA Canberra, ser. A52, item 572/994 THO: "Interim General Report," 28.

36. Mowarra Gamanbarr, in *Thomson of Arnhem Land*.

37. Gerry Blitner, in *No Bugles, No Drums*.

38. George Djalming, in *No Bugles, No Drums*.

39. Old Charlie, interview, 29 Sept. 2005, 10.

40. Phyllis Batumbil, interview, 29 Sept. 2005, 17.

41. Phyllis Batumbil, interview, 29 Sept. 2005, 18.

42. Old Charlie, interview, 29 Sept. 2005, 1–2.

43. Phyllis Batumbil, interview , 29 Sept. 2005, 18.

44. Phyllis Batumbil, interview, 29 Sept. 2005, 16.

45. Phyllis Batumbil, interview, 29 Sept. 2005, 16.

46. Old Charlie and Batumbil, in Old Charlie, interview, 29 Sept. 2005, 4–5.

47. *No Bugles, No Drums*; Matthias Ulungura, as told to John Pye, 1944, in Pye, *Tiwi Islands*, 49; "Tiwi Took Our First Japanese Prisoner," 28; A. Toulson, "53 Years On, War Heroes Honoured" and "Widow Tells of War Bombs," *Northern Territory News*, 20 Feb. 1995.

48. James Gaykamangu, in Northern Land Council DVD.

49. Marika, *Wandjuk Marika*, 64.

50. Thornell, *Bridge over Time*, 129–33. See also *No Bugles, No Drums*.

51. Roy Marika, in *No Bugles, No Drums*.

52. Marika, *Wandjuk Marika*, 65–67.

53. Booth, *33 Days*, 22.

54. Booth, *33 Days*, 82–83.

55. Booth, *33 Days*, 99.

56. Booth, *33 Days*, 103. See also *No Bugles, No Drums*.

57. Lamilami, *Lamilami Speaks*, 188–89. For one more rescue story near Borroloola see *Ka-wayawayama: Aeroplane Dance*.

58. *No Bugles, No Drums*.

59. Eva Number One, Djambarrpuyngu, in Read and Read, *Long Time, Olden Time*, 131–32.

60. Old Charlie, interview, 29 Sept. 2005, 2.

61. Phyllis Batumbil, interview, 29 Sept. 2005, 20–21.

62. Willey, "Army Pay Us Nothing," 8.

63. The dance appears in *No Bugles, No Drums*.

64. Old Charlie, interview, 29 Sept. 2005, 6–7.

65. Phyllis Batumbil, interview, 29 Sept. 2005, 19.

66. Old Charlie and Batumbil, in Old Charlie, interview, 29 Sept. 2005, 10–11.

67. AWM, F04030/01/02: Interview with Amory Vane, 14 Feb. 1991.

68. Capt. N. A. Doyle, "Routine Orders. By Major M. White, C.O. North Australia Observer Unit," 25 Nov. 1944, AWM, ser. 52, item 25/1/2: Northern Australia Observer Unit.

69. Len Taylor, in Walker and Walker, *Curtin's Cowboys*, 149.

70. Anonymous from A Company to Richard Walker and Helen Walker, in Walker and Walker, *Curtin's Cowboys*, 149.

71. "Transfer of Mission Natives: Cape York Peninsula," 20 Nov. 1942, NAA Melbourne, ser. MP729/6, item 16/402/III: Transfer of Mission Natives—Cape York Peninsula. See also R. Hall, "Army and Aborigines during World War II," 64.

72. Jack Gordon, in Willey, "Army Pay Us Nothing," 9.

73. Department of Army minute paper, "Darwin Aborigine for ANZAC March," 3 Mar. 1949, NAA Melbourne, ser. MP742/1, item R/1/3617: D. 178 Raiwalla George.

74. Secretary, Department of the Interior, to Secretary, Department of Army, 25 Mar. 1949, telegram, NAA Melbourne, ser. MP742/1, item R/1/3617: D. 178 Raiwalla George.

75. "City Trip 'Death' to Bush Native," *Melbourne Herald*, 11 Mar. 1949.

76. Hasluck, *Shades of Darkness*, 86.

77. Hasluck, *Native Welfare in Australia*, 16.

78. Murphy, *Imagining the Fifties*, 169.

79. Gerry Blitner, in *No Bugles, No Drums*.

80. Both poems are by Cecil Fisher; the first is entitled "ANZAC Day Living with Granny (Cherbourg)," the second is entitled "Black ANZAC," both AWM, Private Record, PR91/163: Fisher, Cecil.

81. Australian War Memorial Museum, Second World War Gallery, Canberra, visited 31 Mar. 2005 and 30 Sept. 2010. In 2000–2001 the Australian War Memorial also produced a traveling photographic exhibit entitled *Too Dark for the Light Horse*. See http://www.awm.gov.au/events/travelling/toodark.htm. See also K. S. Inglis, *Sacred Places*, 441–51.

3. Black Skins, Black Work

1. Abraham Pap, 14 Aug. 1985, Wandokai, in Silita, "Oral Accounts of Second World War Experiences," 66.

2. Jacob Timele, interview with Hiromitsu Iwamoto, 29 July 2000, Kokopo, in Iwamoto, "Japanese and New Guinean Memories," 88.

3. Raphael Omibari, in *Angels of War*.

4. Stanner, *South Seas in Transition*, 14.

5. A. Inglis, *"Not a White Woman Safe,"* 1–4. See also Edmonds, "Dual Mandate, Double Work," 126; Stella, *Imagining the Other*, 100; Moore, "Workers in Colonial Papua New Guinea," 34.

6. Clay, *Unstable Images*, 9.

7. Clark, *Steel to Stone*, 30.

8. Stella, *Imagining the Other*, 130.

9. J. H. P. Murray, *Papua or British New Guinea*, 8.

10. A. Inglis, *"Not a White Woman Safe,"* 5.

11. Australia . . . Parliament of the Commonwealth, *Territory of Papua*, 16.

12. Woke Kilasi, Walingai, 7 Sept. 1985, in Silita, "Oral Accounts of Second World War Experiences," 64.

13. Stanner, *South Seas in Transition*, 42–44. For Australian anthropologists in Papua and New Guinea before the Second World War see G. Gray, *Cautious Silence*, 31–48.

14. Australia . . . Parliament of the Commonwealth, *Territory of Papua*, 20.

15. Hooper, *Love War and Letters*, 23. See also *Official Handbook of the Territory*

of New Guinea, 141, 328, 351.

16. *Official Handbook of the Territory of New Guinea*, 328.

17. Stella, *Imagining the Other*, 111.

18. Roe, "Papua–New Guinea and War," 139–40; Lewis, *Plantation Dream*, 298.

19. Allied Geographical Section, Southwest Pacific Area, *You and the Native: Notes for the Guidance of Members of the Forces in their Relations with New Guinea Natives*, 12 Feb. 1943, 17.

20. John Paliau, interview with Iwamoto Hiramitsu, n.d.

21. Robinson, *Villagers at War*, 169.

22. Ryan, *Fear Drive My Feet*, 95.

23. Mwahliye Mungulpe, in Allen, "Remembering the War in the Sepik," 18. See also G. Gray, *Cautious Silence*, 174–75; G. Gray, Next focus of power,'" 103.

24. Downs, *New Guinea Volunteer Rifles*, 239.

25. Hooper, *Love War and Letters*, 106.

26. R. M. Melrose, 29 Aug. 1941, NAA Melbourne, ser. MP729/6, item 16/401/455: Possibility of Raising Native Troops.

27. M. Wright, *If I Die*, 2.

28. Ryan, *Fear Drive My Feet*, 121.

29. "Notes on Approach to Port Moresby from N.E. Coast of Papua," 8 Mar. 1942, NAA Melbourne, ser. MP729/6, item 16/401/482: Formation of Native Infantry Battalion.

30. Kituai, "Involvement of Papua New Guinea Policemen," 193.

31. Joseph Tokankan, interview with Hiromitsu Iwamoto, 9 Aug. 2000. See also Ferdinand Urawai, interview with Hiromitsu Iwamoto; Sasa Goreg, interview with August Kituai, 12 Aug. 1986, Gabsongekeg Village, Markham, in Kituai, *My Gun, My Brother*, 326.

32. Iwamoto, "Japanese and New Guinean Memories," 77–78; Kituai, *My Gun, My Brother*, 169; Ham, *Kokoda*, 62–63.

33. Zelenietz and Saito, "Kilenge and the War," 171–73.

34. Iwamoto, "Japanese Occupation of Rabaul," 259.

35. Flt. Sgt. Yamaguchi Keizo, 1959, in Iwamoto, "Japanese and New Guinean Memories," 78.

36. Pvt. Yoshikazu Tamura, May 1943, in Allen and Tamura, "Food Supply and Relationships," 304.

37. Intelligence Information Memorandum 32, "The Japanese Attitude Toward Natives in New Guinea and the Solomon Islands, 1943," in Allen and Tamura, "Food Supply and Relationships," 302.

38. Japanese propaganda film, in *Angels of War*.

39. Newton, "Angels, Heroes and Traitors," 143. See also NAA Canberra, ser. MP742/1, item 85/1/671: Death and other Sentences; Robinson, *Villagers at War*, 144; Iwamoto, "Japanese Occupation of Rabaul," 268; Ham, *Kokoda*, 216.

40. Ryan, *Fear Drive My Feet*, 91. See also Thune, "Making of History," 238–39.

41. F. D. Monk, "Report on Native Affairs during enemy occupation, Madang area, 1944," in Kituai, "Involvement of Papua New Guinea Policemen," 192–93, also quoted in Kituai, *My Gun, My Brother*, 183.

42. Sinclair, *To Find a Path*, 148; Iwamoto, "Japanese Occupation of Rabaul," 265; H. Nelson, *Taim Bilong Masta*, 198.

43. Feldt, *Coast Watchers*, 207. See also Ham, *Kokoda*, 13, 62.

44. James Tumat, interview with Hiromitsu Iwamoto, in *Remembering the War in New Guinea*. See also Joseph Tokankan, interview, 9 Aug. 2000; Eliab Kaplimut, interview; Seno Samare, interview; Ferdinand Urawai, interview; Allen, "Remembering the War in the Sepik," 12; Downs, *New Guinea Volunteer Rifles*, 217; Iwamoto, "Japanese Occupation of Rabaul," 266; A. Powell, *Third Force*, 211.

45. No name to Minister for the Army, 11 Nov. 1945, NAA Melbourne, ser. MP742/1, item 85/1/816: Complaint re Treatment of Natives.

46. Ian Downs, in H. Nelson, *Taim Bilong Masta*, 198.

47. Iwamoto, "Japanese Occupation of Rabaul," 259.

48. Powell, *Third Force*, 213.

49. Iwamoto, "Japanese and New Guinean Memories," 89, 91–92; Iwamoto, "Memories and Realities," 281–84, 291; Counts, "Shadows of War," 187.

50. Somare, *Sana*, 6.

51. Joe Leleng, interview with Hiromitsu Iwamoto, in *Remembering the War in New Guinea*. See also Betuel Panu and Eliab Thomas, in *Remembering the War in New Guinea*.

52. Eliab Kaplimut, in *Remembering the War in New Guinea*.

53. ToKilala, "Valley of the Prison," 2.

54. Yanagiba Yutaka, 1986, in Iwamoto, "Japanese and New Guinean Memories," 79.

55. Mizuki Shigeru, interview with Hiromitsu Iwamoto, 5 Sept. 2000, Tokyo, in Iwamoto, "Japanese and New Guinean Memories," 80.

56. Kazuo Hoshino, *Nyūginia-sen tsuiokuki: sensōto hyūmanizumu* [Memories of the war in New Guinea] (Tokyo: Seiunsha, 1982), 142–46, in Allen and Tamura, "Food Supply and Relationships," 311.

57. Thune, "Making of History," 240–41.

58. Remi, in *Angels of War*.

59. Misiaiyai, in Allen, "Remembering the War in the Sepik," 17. See also Eliab Kaplimut, interview.

60. Brune, *Spell Broken*, 40.

61. Tutal Kaminiel, 1973, in Leadley, "Japanese on the Gazelle," 48.

62. Danks Tomila, 1971, in Tetaga, "Wartime Experience of Danks Tomila," 27–28.

63. 29 Mar. 1942, in G. H. Johnston, *New Guinea Diary*, 64.

64. Pamoi, 1946, in Kituai, *My Gun, My Brother*, 190. See also Ham, *Kokoda*, 331.

65. Sasa Goreg, interview, in Kituai, *My Gun, My Brother*, 333.

66. John Kapelis, in *Angels of War*.

67. James Tumat, interview, in *Remembering the War in New Guinea*. See also Levi Tovilivan, in *Remembering the War in New Guinea*.

68. Kesbuk, in Allen, "Remembering the War in the Sepik," 16.

69. Kituai, *My Gun, My Brother*, 191.

70. D. M. Rutledge and A. D. O. Aitape, 30 Sept. 1948, NAA Melbourne, ser. MP375/14, item WC27: War Crimes Papua/New Guinea.

71. "Statement of Longin — of Kalaba Village, Maprik sub-district, Sepik District," 13 Oct. 1948, NAA Melbourne, ser. MP375/14, item WC25: War Crimes. Papua New Guinea.

72. Byrnes, *Green Shadows*, 16; Ham, *Kokoda*, 217; Kami Kesen, interview with Hiromitsu Iwamoto, in *Remembering the War in New Guinea*.

73. 16 Oct. 1942, in G. H. Johnston, *New Guinea Diary*, 187.

74. Benggo Aikeng, interview with Patrick Silita, 14 Aug. 1985, Wandokai, in Silita, "Oral Accounts of Second World War Experiences." 65.

75. Powell, *Third Force*, 214.

76. "Native Labour Used in New Guinea," 7 June 1943, NAA Melbourne, ser. MP729/6, item 37/401/1904: Native Labour in New Guinea.

77. Sinclair, *To Find a Path*, 273. See also "Survey of Native Labour in all aspects Territories of Papua and New Guinea made by Brigadier J. E. Lloyd, CBE, DSO, MC, under direction of The Commander-In-Chief," 4, NAA Melbourne, ser. MP742/1, item 285/1/680A: Native labour survey; H. Nelson, "From Kanaka to Fuzzy Wuzzy Angel," 181–82 (journal); A. Powell, *Third Force*, 107.

78. A. Powell, *Third Force*, vii–viii.

79. A. Powell, *Third Force*, 166–77; G. Gray, *Cautious Silence*, 184; G. Gray, "'I was not consulted,'" 200–201.

80. A. Powell, *Third Force*, 56.

81. Mair, *Australia in New Guinea*, 19.

82. A. Hodges, Major-General, "Native Labour Overseers ANGAU," 19 June 1943, NAA Melbourne, ser. MP70/1, item 48/101/384: Native labour overseers. See also A. Powell, *Third Force*, 140–66.

83. Stanner, *South Seas in Transition*, 80; Major General, GOC, ANGAU, 27 Mar. 1943, in NAA Melbourne, ser. MP729/6, item 37/401/1904: Native Labour in New Guinea.

84. ANGAU, 23 Apr. 1943, NAA Melbourne, ser. MP742/1, item 247/1/1290: Conditions of Service; "Report on the Activities of ANGAU in Respect of Native Relief and Rehabilitation in the Territory of Papua and the Mandated Territory of New Guinea. February 1942–September 1944," app. B, pp. 17–18, NAA Melbourne, ser. MP742/1, item 5/3/147: Australia—New Guinea Administrative Unit; Finance Authority for Expenditure, 10 Sept. 1945, NAA Melbourne, ser. MP742/1, item 131/1/82: ANGAU Reward to Natives.

85. F. R. Sinclair, Secretary, to E. C. Harris, 11 Jan. 1943, NAA Melbourne, ser.

MP508/1, item 247/701/953: Pay of Native Workers.

86. "Rarua Tau's account of his evacuation," in Robinson, *Villagers at War*, 196.

87. Ham, *Kokoda*, 213; A. Powell, *Third Force*, 36.

88. "Compensation to the Natives of Papua and New Guinea for War Injuries and War Damage," 10; Pilger, "Courage, Endurance and Initiative," 15; Jackman, "Brothers in Arms," 71.

89. Mair, *Australia in New Guinea*, 202; Downs, *Australian Trusteeship: Papua New Guinea 1945–75*, 38–39; A. Powell, *Third Force*, 52–53; Ham, *Kokoda*, 399.

90. Report cited in Stanner, *South Seas in Transition*, 81.

91. "Survey of Native Labour in all aspects Territories of Papua and New Guinea made by Brigadier J. E. Lloyd . . . ," 2–3, NAA Melbourne, ser. MP742/1, item 285/1/680A: Native labour survey.

92. Sinclair, *To Find a Path*, 182–83; Major-General, GOC ANGAU, 2 Jan. 1946, to Headquarters, ANGAU Lae, AWM, ser. 54, item 506/5/19: [Natives—Labour] Statistics and Employment; A. Powell, *Third Force*, 195.

93. First Army to Landforces, 7 Aug. 1945, NAA Melbourne, ser. MP742/1, item 247/1/1152: Conditions of Service; also in NAA Melbourne, ser. MP742/1, item 247/1/1172: Pay of Native Troops.

94. "Native Labour Australian New Guinea. An Appreciation," n.d., AWM, ser. 54, item 506/5/1: [Natives—Labour] Utilisation.

95. Captain Gloucester, July 1944, in Stanner, *South Seas in Transition*, 82.

96. Song composed by Fava Heovake, trans. Rex Marere, in Robinson, *Villagers at War*, 195.

97. "Survey of Native Labour in all aspects Territories of Papua and New Guinea made by Brigadier J. E. Lloyd . . . ," 4–5, NAA Melbourne, ser. MP742/1, item 285/1/680A: Native labour survey; "Compensation to the Natives of Papua and New Guinea for War Injuries and War Damage," 10. Footage of Papuan and New Guinean laborers performing such tasks is available from AWM, F01213: War Supply Route; F01872: Finisterre Ranges; F07174: Malahang compound Lae area; F07096: Visit to New Guinea of the Minister for External Territories. See also Jackman, "Brothers in Arms," 71–72; H. Nelson, "From Kanaka to Fuzzy Wuzzy Angel," 183; H. Nelson, *Taim Bilong Masta*, 198; "Report on the Activities of ANGAU," app. B, p. 21.

98. F. H. Moy, Captain, District Officer, to District of Mambare, Headquarters, 6 May 1943, AWM, ser. 54, item 506/5/1: [Natives—Labour] Utilisation. See also "HQ New Guinea Force ADM Instruction No 106."

99. Notes of Interview, Lieutenant-Colonel Sharpe, HQ Q LD L of C Area, Lt. Col. B. J. O'Loughlin, AAG First Aust Army, n.d., AWM, ser. 54, item 628/1/1B: [Torres Strait Area:].

100. Iven Mackay, Lt-Gen, GOC New Guinea Force, 29 Mar. 1943, NAA Melbourne, ser. MP729/6, item 37/401/1904: Native Labour in New Guinea.

101. *You and the Native*, 15.

102. *You and the Native*, 4.

103. "Native Labour Australian New Guinea. An Appreciation."

104. Mr. Mea, in Modjeska, "Wartime Experience of Mr Asi Arere," 20. See also A. Powell, *Third Force*, 192

105. H. Nelson, "More Than a Change of Uniform," 242–43; A. Powell, *Third Force*, 134–39; Robinson, *Villagers at War*, 38.

106. Mair, *Australia in New Guinea*, 236; Stanner, *South Seas in Transition*, 82. Footage of medical treatment and hygiene lessons available from AWM, F07174: Malahang compound Lae area.

107. Ham, *Kokoda*, 213.

108. "Report on the Activities of ANGAU," app. B, p. 19. See also J. A. Bennett, "Malaria, Medicine, and Melanesians."

109. "Compensation to the Natives of Papua and New Guinea for War Injuries and War Damage," 11; Mair, *Australia in New Guinea*, 203; Stanner, *South Seas in Transition*, 80.

110. Nora Vagi Brash, in *Angels of War*.

111. Capt. G. H. Vernon, in A. Powell, *Third Force*, 46.

112. Ham, *Kokoda*, 51. See also A. Powell, *Third Force*, 220–23.

113. "Report on the Activities of ANGAU," app. A, p. 6. See also "Reasons for Proposed Amendments and Additions to ANGAU WE," 11 Oct. 1943, NAA Melbourne, ser. MP729/6, item 19/401/388: ANGAU Proposed New War Establishment; NAA Melbourne, ser. MP729/6, item 47/402/2514: Native Rations — New Guinea. Alamo Task Force; "HQ New Guinea Force ADM Instruction No 106."

114. Ham, *Kokoda*, 211–12.

115. Col. M. A. Bishop, in Downs, *New Guinea Volunteer Rifles*, 287.

116. 3 Sept. 1942, in G. H. Johnston, *New Guinea Diary*, 149.

117. Sigob, "Story of My Life," 32.

118. William Metpi, in Kais, "Discontent among Indigenous Soldiers," 30.

119. "Report on the Activities of ANGAU," app. B, p. 23.

120. *You and the Native*, 15.

121. Robinson, *Villagers at War*, 60; A. Powell, *Third Force*, 113; Scheps, "Chimbu Participation in the Pacific War," 81–82.

122. Asi Arere, in Modjeska, "Wartime Experience of Mr Asi Arere," 16.

123. Ovivi Arai, in *Angels of War*.

124. A. Powell, *Third Force*, 196–97.

125. Sigob, "Story of My Life," 32.

126. Jackman, "Brothers in Arms," 72; H. Nelson, "More Than a Change of Uniform," 242; Robinson, *Villagers at War*, 78–79; Ham, *Kokoda*, 214.

127. "Native Labour Australian New Guinea. An Appreciation."

128. *You and the Native*, 17.

129. Asi Arere, in Modjeska, "Wartime Experience of Mr Asi Arere," 16.

130. *You and the Native*, 16.

131. Mair, *Australia in New Guinea*, 200.

132. Auwepo of Kegebwai hamlet, Loboda, in Thune, "Making of History," 246.

133. Zelenietz and Saito, "Kilenge and the War," 177.

134. Anonymous to Minister for the Army, 11 Nov. 1945, NAA Melbourne, ser. MP742/1, item 85/1/816: Complaint re Treatment of Natives (original emphasis).

135. Maj. John Stewart Milligan, 6 Dec. 1945, NAA Melbourne, ser. MP742/1, item 85/1/816: Complaint re Treatment of Natives.

136. 9 Aug. 1942, in H. Nelson, *War Diaries of Eddie Allan Stanton*, 57.

137. 8 Jan. 1944, in H. Nelson, *War Diaries of Eddie Allan Stanton*, 206.

138. *You and the Native*, 91.

139. Robinson, *Villagers at War*, 103–4.

140. 11 Oct. 1942, in H. Nelson, *War Diaries of Eddie Allan Stanton*, 84.

141. 12 May 1945, in H. Nelson, *War Diaries of Eddie Allan Stanton*, 283.

142. 3 Feb. 1944, in H. Nelson, *War Diaries of Eddie Allan Stanton*, 212.

143. Arthur Dunas, in *Angels of War*.

144. H. Nelson, "From Kanaka to Fuzzy Wuzzy Angel," 183–84; Major-General, GOC ANGAU, to Headquarters, ANGAU Lae, 2 Jan. 1946, AWM, ser. 54, item 506/5/19: [Natives—Labour] Statistics and Employment; H. Nelson, "More Than a Change of Uniform," 243; Stanner, *South Seas in Transition*, 79; Jackman, "Brothers in Arms," 72.

145. Report cited in Stanner, *South Seas in Transition*, 89.

146. T. R. Fenner, Assistant Director of Naval Intelligence, to Supervising Intelligence Officer, North Eastern Area, 15 Nov. 1946, NAA Melbourne, ser. MP151/1, item 487/202/2626: War Gratuity.

147. Reed, "'Part of Our Own Story,'" 163.

148. Wamanari, in *Angels of War*.

149. Asina Papau, in *Angels of War*.

150. Stella, *Imagining the Other*, 111.

151. Ham, *Kokoda*, 533.

152. Maj-General, GOC ANGAU, 6 Feb. 1943, NAA Melbourne, ser. MP742/1, item 5/1/34: Future Native Welfare.

153. Gen. Thomas Blamey, 14 Sept. 1942, in G. H. Johnston, *New Guinea Diary*, 156. See also A. Powell, *Third Force*, 54

154. Newton, "Angels, Heroes and Traitors," 144.

155. Luke Romero, in Vogt, *Navaho Veterans*, 130.

156. Beros, "Fuzzy Wuzzy Angels," in *Fuzzy Wuzzy Angels*, 11–12.

157. Morea Mea, in *Angels of War*.

158. Reed, "'Part of Our Own Story,'" 161.

159. Feldt, *Coast Watchers*, 5.

160. Feldt, *Coast Watchers*, 182.

161. Feldt, *Coast Watchers*, 317.

162. M. Murray, *Hunted*, 85.

163. Benson, "Waltzing Matilda and the Powerful Owls," 66.

164. Feldt, *Coast Watchers*, 293.

4. Guerillas for the White Men

1. Palili, interview with Richard Curtain, in Curtain, "Labour Migration from the Sepik," 61.

2. Yauwiga, in *Angels of War*.

3. Petrus Tigavu, interview with August Kituai, 16 Apr. 1985, Madang, in Kituai, *My Gun, My Brother*, 318–19.

4. George Silk photograph, AWM, ID 014028, http://cas.awm.gov.au/PROD/cst. acct_master?surl=1068514052ZZZUNORNRYNC46294&stype=3&simple search=&v_umo=&v_product_id=&screen_name=&screen_parms=&screen _type=RIGHT&bvers=4&bplatform=Microsoft%20Internet%20Explorer& bos=Win32 (see illustration 11 in this volume).

5. M. Murray, *Hunted*, 28–41; M. Wright, *If I Die*, 21, 60–61.

6. James Sinclair cites the number at 1,040, but some military documents cite 877. See Major-General, GOC ANGAU, to Headquarters, ANGAU Lae, 2 Jan. 1946, AWM, ser. 54, item 506/5/19: [Natives — Labour] Statistics and Employment; Sinclair, *To Find a Path*, 131; Kituai, *My Gun, My Brother*, 172; M. Murray, *Hunted*, 65.

7. Peter Figgis, in H. Nelson, *Taim Bilong Masta*, 197.

8. M. Wright, *If I Die*, 3–9; Kituai, *My Gun, My Brother*, 172.

9. Wedega, *Listen, My Country*, 68.

10. M. Wright, *If I Die*, 59. See also unknown author, 14 Sept. 1945, NAA Melbourne, ser. MP151/1, item 487/202/2626: War Gratuity.

11. M. Murray, *Hunted*, 65; Hooper, *Love War and Letters*, 169; M. Wright, *If I Die*, 122.

12. Wedega, *Listen, My Country*, 70.

13. Ryan, *Fear Drive My Feet*, 46; M. Wright, *If I Die*, 78, 132; Feldt, *Coast Watchers*, 242, 253, 271, 291, 297, 306, 322–23, 351–52.

14. Yauwiga, in Sinclair, *To Find a Path*, 285.

15. J. Brown, "Coastwatchers on New Britain," 4 (electronic document).

16. M. Wright, *If I Die*, 168–69.

17. M. Wright, *If I Die*, 142–47.

18. J. T. Fitzgerald, Secretary, to the Secretary, Department of Defence Co-Ordination, 26 Mar. 1941, NAA Canberra, ser. A472, series accession number A472/6, item W3119: National Security . . . Regulations; NAA Canberra, ser. A432, item 1939/947: Royal Papuan Constabulary Ordinance.

19. Colonel, M.O. 2, 16 July 1941, NAA Melbourne, ser. MP729/6, item 16/401/482: Formation of Native Infantry Battalion.

20. Sasa Goreg, interview with August Kituai, Gabsongkeg Village, Markham, 12 Aug. 1986, in Kituai, *My Gun, My Brother*, 327–28; excerpt also appears in Kituai, "Involvement of Papua New Guinea Policemen," 188.

21. Kituai, "Involvement of Papua New Guinea Policemen," 175; Sinclair, *To Find*

a Path, 124; Kituai, *My Gun, My Brother*, 173; A. Powell, *Third Force*, 23–24; Mair, *Australia in New Guinea*, 42.

22. 26 Feb. 1942, in G. H. Johnston, *New Guinea Diary*, 31.

23. J. K. McCarthy, *Patrol into Yesterday: My New Guinea Years* (Melbourne: Cheshire, 1963), 196, quoted in Kituai, "Involvement of Papua New Guinea Policemen," 196–97. See also A. Powell, *Third Force*, 24.

24. Lt-Col, DDCA, 10 Mar. 1945, AWM, ser. 54, item 506/8/3: [Natives—General:] Police and prisons.

25. Kituai, "Involvement of Papua New Guinea Policemen," 190–92, 201; Kituai, *My Gun, My Brother*, 172, 178–80, 200; Robinson, *Villagers at War*, 24.

26. Kituai, *My Gun, My Brother*, 181, 189; A. Powell, *Third Force*, 231.

27. Herring, Lieutenant-General, G.O.C. New Guinea Force, "Proposed War Establishment—Royal Papuan Constabulary," 15 Jan. 1943, NAA Melbourne, ser. MP742/1, item 96/1/45: W. E. Royal Papuan Constabulary.

28. Major-General, Adjutant-General, 2 Dec. 1943, NAA Melbourne, ser. MP742/1, item 96/1/982: Organ.—Royal Papuan Constabulary.

29. E. J. Milford, Major-General, General Staff, "Organisation—Royal Papuan Constabulary," 24 Jan. 1944, NAA Melbourne, ser. MP742/1, item 96/1/982: Organ.—Royal Papuan Constabulary (original emphasis).

30. Milford, "Organisation—Royal Papuan Constabulary." See also Lt-Col, DDCA, 10 Mar. 1945, AWM, ser. 54, item 506/8/3: [Natives—General:] Police and prisons.

31. Sakarias Anka, interview with August Kituai, Okiufa village, Goroka, Eastern Highlands Province, 19 Aug. 1986, in Kituai, "Involvement of Papua New Guinea Policemen," 198.

32. Kituai, "Involvement of Papua New Guinea Policemen," 195–96; Kituai, *My Gun, My Brother*, 189.

33. A. Powell, *Third Force*, 230.

34. Sono, interview, 1985, in Kituai, *My Gun, My Brother*, 174.

35. Scheps, "Chimbu Participation in the Pacific War," 80.

36. Kituai, "Involvement of Papua New Guinea Policemen," 201.

37. A. Powell, *Third Force*, 230; Kituai, *My Gun, My Brother*, 179–80.

38. Jojoga Yegova, interview with August Kituai, 21 June 1985, in Kituai, "Involvement of Papua New Guinea Policemen," 179. Footage of RPC training is available in AWM, F01685: Royal Papuan Constabulary, Feb. 1944.

39. Robinson, *Villagers at War*, 64–65.

40. D. M. Cleland, Administrator, "Casualties Suffered by the Royal Papuan Constabulary During the 1939–45 War," 12 Mar. 1956, AWM, ser. 54, item 171/2/39: [Casualties—Reporting:]. See also Mair, *Australia in New Guinea*, 22; A. Powell, *Third Force*, 228–29.

41. Recommendation for Military Medal, submitted 18 Oct. 1943, passed 17 Nov. 1943, AWM, ser. 54, item 391/11/85: [Honours and Rewards—Infantry:].

42. Lt Col, DDCA, 10 Mar. 1945, AWM, ser. 54, item 506/8/3: [Natives—General:] Police and prisons.

43. Lt Col, DDCA, 10 Mar. 1945, AWM, ser. 54, item 506/8/3: [Natives—General:] Police and prisons.

44. Downs, *New Guinea Volunteer Rifles*, 34.

45. R. M. Melrose, 29 Aug. 1941, NAA Melbourne, ser. MP729/6, item 16/401/455: Possibility of Raising Native Troops.

46. Director of District Services and Native Affairs, Mandated Territory of New Guinea, to Brigadier-General Sir Walter McNicoll, in Sinclair, *To Find a Path*, 212–13.

47. Robert E. Jackson, Major-General, Northern Command, to Secretary, Military Board, Melbourne, "Formation of Native Infantry Battalion in Territory of New Guinea," 29 Mar. 1941, NAA Melbourne, ser. MP729/6, item 16/401/482: Formation of Native Infantry Battalion; Adjutant of 2NGIB, Don Barrett, in Sinclair, *To Find a Path*, 249.

48. Mench, *Role of the Papua New Guinea Defence Force*; A. Powell, *Third Force*, 236–37.

49. Lt. Col. J. H. Jones, Mar. 1945, AWM, ser. 54, item 419/5/6: [Infantry—Papuan and New Guinea Infantry Battalions:].

50. Capt. K. M. Travis, Australian Staff Corps, 27 Feb. 1939, NAA Melbourne, ser. MP729/6, item 16/401/482: Formation of Native Infantry Battalion.

51. Capt. K. M. Travis, Australian Staff Corps, 27 Feb. 1939, NAA Melbourne, ser. MP729/6, item 16/401/482: Formation of Native Infantry Battalion.

52. J. B. Chifley, Treasurer, "War Gratuity for Natives of New Guinea and Papua. Report by Department of the Treasury," June 1947, NAA Melbourne, ser. MP151/1, item 487/202/2626: War Gratuity; also in NAA Melbourne, ser. MP927/1, item A131/2/43: War Gratuity Natives.

53. H. Nelson, "As Bilong Soldia," 23; Barrett, "Pacific Islands Regiment," 493; Sinclair, *To Find a Path*, 132.

54. Lynch, "Coming Army," 22. See also Coady, "P.I.R.," 29. Coady's article also appears, verbatim, as W. Nelson, "P.I.R.," 9, 33. Whether or not Nelson plagiarized Coady's article is unclear, but the exactness of the two articles is suspicious.

55. Hooper, *Love War and Letters*, 47; Sinclair, *To Find a Path*, 132; Coady, "P.I.R.," 29; Granter, *Yesterday and Today*, 9; Byrnes, *Green Shadows*, 6.

56. Daera Ganiga, in Robinson, *Villagers at War*, 201.

57. Sinclair, *To Find a Path*, 135; Lynch, "Coming Army," 22.

58. Ganiga, in Robinson, *Villagers at War*, 202–3.

59. Coady, "P.I.R.," 30–31.

60. Hooper, *Love War and Letters*, 48.

61. Sinclair, *To Find a Path*, 151–52; Mench, *Role of the Papua New Guinea Defence Force*, 13; Hooper, *Love War and Letters*, 132.

62. Sigob, "Story of My Life," 33.

63. AWM, F07097: 1 Papuan Infantry Battalion training; AWM, F01872: Finisterre Ranges; AWM, F07239: Mount Shiburangu action; 26–27 Dec. 1942, in Hooper, *Love War and Letters*, 169.

64. William Metpi, in Kais, "Discontent among Indigenous Soldiers," 26.

65. Sinclair, *To Find a Path*, 187; Hooper, *Love War and Letters*, 173; Byrnes, *Green Shadows*, 1; AWM, F07397: Parade and march.

66. In Sinclair, *To Find a Path*, 212.

67. Lynch, "Coming Army," 22; Sinclair, *To Find a Path*, 248–49, 273.

68. Sinclair, *To Find a Path*, 274; Barrett, "Pacific Islands Regiment," 497; "Report of Court of Inquiry," 29 July 1945, NAA Melbourne, ser. MP742/1, item 247/1/1172: Pay of Native Troops.

69. Byrnes, *Green Shadows*, 71–73; Barrett, "Pacific Islands Regiment," 495–96.

70. William Metpi, in Kais, "Discontent among Indigenous Soldiers," 29.

71. "Report of Court of Inquiry," 29 July 1945; Power, "Review of the Post-War Years," 192. See also A. Powell, *Third Force*, 238.

72. William Metpi, in Kais, "Discontent among Indigenous Soldiers," 29.

73. Kais, "Discontent among Indigenous Soldiers," 28.

74. Lynch, "Coming Army," 22; Barrett, "Pacific Islands Regiment," 498; Granter, *Yesterday and Today*, 13; Sinclair, *To Find a Path*, 122, 131; B. Hall, "Murray System and the War," 64. Kituai firmly poses the number of PIR members at 3,582 by war's end. See Kituai, *My Gun, My Brother*, 172.

75. Silita, "Oral Accounts of Second World War Experiences," 72; Granter, *Yesterday and Today*, 19; Mench, *Role of the Papua New Guinea Defence Force*, 17, 20; Byrnes, *Green Shadows*, 121–22; A. Powell, *Third Force*, 238–40.

76. Sinclair, *To Find a Path*, 284.

77. Mench, *Role of the Papua New Guinea Defence Force*, 19.

78. Keta Tupaing, interview with Patrick Silita, Ago, Huon Peninsula, 30 Aug. 1985, in Silita, "Oral Accounts of Second World War Experiences," 68.

79. "Commander Allied Forces Report on Operations in Australian Mandated Territory of New Guinea," in Sinclair, *To Find a Path*, 247.

80. Maj. Gen. Basil Morris, GOC ANGAU, "Proposed War Establishment of Royal Papuan Constabulary (PROV)," 19 Oct. 1943, NAA Melbourne, ser. MP742/1, item 96/1/982: Organ. — Royal Papuan Constabulary.

81. Col. A. R. McKenzie, Commander U.S. 162 Infantry Regiment, to Major Watson of PIB, in Sinclair, *To Find a Path*, 171.

82. Brig. Ivan Dougherty, Commanding 21st Australian Infantry Brigade, in Sinclair, *To Find a Path*, 180.

83. Lt. Col. S. Elliott-Smith, Commanding Officer of PIB, 1 Sept. 1945, in Sinclair, *To Find a Path*, 272; also in Byrnes, *Green Shadows*, 120.

84. H. Wright, "Protecting the National Interest," 74–75; Mair, *Australia in New Guinea*, 19.

85. G. Gray, *Cautious Silence*, 185. See also G. Gray, "Stanner's War," 152–54.

86. "Compensation to the Natives of Papua and New Guinea for War Injuries and War Damage," 11; Robinson, *Villagers at War*, 121–23; Downs, *Australian Trusteeship: Papua New Guinea 1945–75*, 55.

87. Osmar White, "Jungle Creeps In while Town Plans Gather Dust," *Brisbane Courier-Mail*, 13 Apr. 1949.

88. "Compensation to the Natives of Papua and New Guinea for War Injuries and War Damage," 17; H. Nelson, "Payback," 336; Allen, "Remembering the War in the Sepik," 27.

89. "Compensation to the Natives of Papua and New Guinea for War Injuries and War Damage," 18–19.

90. "Compensation to the Natives of Papua and New Guinea for War Injuries and War Damage," 25–26.

91. NAA Melbourne, ser. MP742/1, item 247/1/1290: Conditions of Service; H. Nelson, "Payback," 342; Downs, *Australian Trusteeship*, 40; Stanner, *South Seas in Transition*, 118–19, 159; A. Powell, *Third Force*, 199; 254; Mair, *Australia in New Guinea*, 22–23; Roe, "Papua–New Guinea and War," 148; G. Gray, "Passing," 37.

92. E. J. Ward, Minister for External Territories, 4 July 1945, in Downs, *Australian Trusteeship*, 14; Stanner, *South Seas in Transition*, 100; Mair, *Australia in New Guinea*, 21–22; A. Powell, *Third Force*, 242; G. Gray, "Passing," 37. See also E. J. Ward, Minister for the Territories, "Papua–New Guinea: Native Labour," 27 June 1945, approved by Full Cabinet, 2 July 1945, NAA Melbourne, ser. MP742/1, item 247/1/1172: Pay of Native Troops.

93. Mair, *Australia in New Guinea*, 207; Stanner, *South Seas in Transition*, 134; Ward, "Papua–New Guinea: Native Labour." For anthropology's role see G. Gray, *Cautious Silence*, 189–202; G. Gray, "'I was not consulted,'" 201–8; G. Gray, "'Next focus of power,'" 110–17; G. Gray, "'Chance to be of some use,'" 33–41.

94. Downs, *Australian Trusteeship*, 101–6, 200–201, 408–9; Wolfers, *Race Relations and Colonial Rule*, 119–21; H. Nelson, "Enemy at the Door," 137–38; Mair, *Australia in New Guinea*, 81–82; 205–7; Stanner, *South Seas in Transition*, 132–34; Roe, "Papua–New Guinea and War," 148; Kadiba, "Papua New Guinea and the War," 8–11.

95. A. Powell, *Third Force*, 192; Counts, "Shadows of War," 188; Zelenietz and Saito, "Kilenge and the War," 177–79; Thune, "Making of History," 249–51; White and Lindstrom, *Pacific Theater*.

96. "Compensation to the Natives of Papua and New Guinea for War Injuries and War Damage," 35, 42.

97. "Compensation to the Natives of Papua and New Guinea for War Injuries and War Damage," 48.

98. Minister for External Affairs, H. V. Evatt, San Francisco press conference, 3 May 1945, 52, NAA Canberra, ser. A463, item 1956/1096: War Pensions.

99. Stanner, *South Seas in Transition*, 96; Downs, *Australian Trusteeship*, 5.

100. Gaynor, "To Be Colonised or a Coloniser?" 9.

101. Hasluck, *Time for Building*, 41.

102. G. Gray, "Passing," 37–42.

103. "Bet Their Wives on Turn of a Card," *Melbourne Age*, 7 Jan. 1948, NAA Melbourne, ser. MP927/1, item A131/2/43: War Gratuity Natives. See also "Natives Gambling Wives in NG," *Melbourne Herald*, 1 June 1948, NAA Melbourne, ser. MP927/1, item A131/2/43: War Gratuity Natives.

104. A. Powell, *Third Force*, 253–55; Ryan, "Some Unfinished Business," 13; Downs, *Australian Trusteeship*, 480–81.

105. Roe, "Papua–New Guinea and War," 149.

106. Cited in Stanner, *South Seas in Transition*, 145.

107. Hasluck, *Time for Building*, 43.

108. E. J. Ward, Minister for External Territories, 27 June 1945, NAA Melbourne, MP742/1, item 247/1/1172: Pay of Native Troops; Mair, *Australia in New Guinea*, 69, 210–16, 227, 239; Downs, *Australian Trusteeship*, 76–77, 314–17; Stanner, *South Seas in Transition*, 129.

109. Nelson, "Enemy at the Door," 138.

110. "Gratuity Granted to Papuan Natives," *Canberra Times*, 3 July 1947; "Early War Gratuity: Board's Wider Powers," *Sydney Morning Herald*, 6 May 1948.

111. Chifley, Treasurer, "War Gratuity for Natives."

112. B. White to the Secretary, Department of the Territories, 21 Mar, 1960, NAA Melbourne, ser. MT1131/1, item A253/1/2: Eligibility of members.

113. Chifley, "War Gratuity for Natives"; R. H. Doherty, Department of the Army, "Report on Payment of War Gratuity for Natives of New Guinea and Papua," 26 Feb. 1948, NAA Melbourne, ser. MP927/1, item A131/2/43: War Gratuity Natives.

114. Reed, "'Part of Our Own Story,'" 163.

115. Ryan, "Some Unfinished Business," 11; Robinson, *Villagers at War*, 125, 182–83; R. A. Waters to Don Cameron, MP, 13 Sept. 1981, AWM, private record, PR87/078: Cameron, Donald M, part 1.

116. Downs, *Australian Trusteeship*, 134–35.

117. William Metpi, in Kais, "Discontent among Indigenous Soldiers," 30.

118. Conversation in *Angels of War*.

119. Prime Minister Michael Somare, 10 Oct. 1975, in Downs, *Australian Trusteeship*, 565.

120. Ryan, *Fear Drive My Feet*, 10.

5. The Navajo Code Talkers

1. "Navajo Indians Tote Rifles in Boot Platoon," *Marine Corps Chevron*, 15 May 1942, in *Our Fathers, Our Grandfathers, Our Heroes*, 20.

2. Sam Billison, interview with Sally McClain, 31 May 1993.

3. C. B. Brown, "Code Talker — Pacific Theater," 56.

4. Bush, "Remarks by the President."

5. Crook, "Apache Problem," 263.

6. Ewers, "Military Service of Indians," 1188.

7. Cushing, "Military Colonization of the Indians," 373. See also Holm, "Strong Hearts," 134–37.

8. Chee Dah Spencer, interview, recorded 31 Oct. 1967.

9. Krouse, *North American Indians in the Great War*; Britten, *American Indians in World War I*; Carroll, *Medicine Bags and Dog Tags*, 101–13; Holm, "Fighting a White Man's War," 69–71; Hale, "Forgotten Heroes," 39–41; Keene, *World War I*.

10. Holm, "Strong Hearts," 138.

11. A. W. Bloor, Colonel 142nd Infantry, to the Commanding General, 36th Division, 23 Jan. 1919, NARA, Records of the National Security Agency (Record Group 457), SRH-120: Utilization of American Indians, box 34, 018–019.

12. Bloor to the Commanding General, 23 Jan. 1919; Tate, "From Scout to Doughboy," 432.

13. COMGENSOPAC to AGWAR, 6 Sept. 1943, telegram, re: Solomon Islands, NARA, Records of the National Security Agency (Record Group 457), SRH-120, box 34, 0020; M. Bennett, "Meskwaki Code Talkers"; Meadows, *Comanche Code Talkers*, 241–42; Meadows, "North American Indian Code Talkers."

14. Meadows, "North American Indian Code Talkers," 164.

15. Meadows, "North American Indian Code Talkers," 201.

16. Paul, *Navajo Code Talkers*, 107.

17. P. Johnston, "Indian Jargon Won Our Battles," 131.

18. Philip Johnston, interview with John Sylvester, 7 Nov. 1970, Flagstaff AZ, 42–43, NARA, Records of the U.S. Marine Corps (Record Group 127), USMC Reserve and Historical Studies, 1942–88; Gen. Clayton B. Vogel to the Commandant, U.S. Marine Corps, 6 Mar. 1942, memo, NARA, Records of the United States Marine Corps, Record Group 127, http://www.archives.gov/education/lessons/code-talkers/images/letter-01.jpg.

19. F. Whitehead to the Personnel Department, 11 Aug. 1943, memo, NARA, Records of the U.S. Marine Corps (Record Group 127), box 33.

20. Philip Johnston, "Proposed Plan for Recruiting Indian Signal Corps Personnel," in Paul, *Navajo Code Talkers*, 154.

21. Bernstein, *American Indians and World War II*, 48; P. Johnston, "Indian Jargon Won Our Battles," 133; McCoy, "Navajo Code Talkers of World War II," 68.

22. Philip Johnston, interview, 7 Nov. 1970.

23. *Our Fathers, Our Grandfathers, Our Heroes*, 23; Commandant, U.S. Marine Corps, to Western Recruiting Division, 6 Apr. 1942, NARA, Records of the U.S. Marine Corps (Record Group 127), box 600.

24. Gen. Clayton B. Vogel to the Commandant, U.S. Marine Corps, 6 Mar. 1942, memo, NARA, Records of the United States Marine Corps, Record Group 127, http://www.archives.gov/education/lessons/code-talkers/images/letter-01.jpg.

25. Lt. Col. Wethered Woodworth to the Director, Division of Recruiting, 26 Mar. 1942, NARA, Records of the U.S. Marine Corps (Record Group 127), box 600.

26. P. Johnston, "Proposed Plan for Recruiting Indian Signal Corps Personnel," 154.

27. Lt. Col. Wethered Woodworth, U.S. Marine Corps Reserve, to Mr. Daiker, 6 Apr. 1942, in *Our Fathers, Our Grandfathers, Our Heroes*.

28. Meadows, "North American Indian Code Talkers," 171.

29. Anonymous Code Talker, in Paul, *Navajo Code Talkers*, 15.

30. Paul, *Navajo Code Talkers*, 16.

31. Thomas Begay, interview with Sally McClain, Aug. 1992. See also MacDonald, *Last Warrior*, 59.

32. Harold Foster, interview with Sally McClain, Oct. 1991. For other boot-camp stories see Alfred Newman, Bill Toledo, Jack Jones, Samuel Tso, and Kee Etsicitty, all in Mack, *It Had to Be Done*, 29–33.

33. C. S. Brown, "Code Talker—Pacific Theater," 54. See also Chester Nez, in Mack, *It Had to Be Done*, 25–26.

34. D. M. Randall, Officer in Charge, to Commandant, U.S. Marine Corps, 25 Apr. 1942, and Geo T. Hall, Commanding Officer, Recruit Depot, Marine Corps Base, San Diego, to Commandant, U.S. Marine Corps, 16 June 1942, both NARA, Records of the U.S. Marine Corps (Record Group 127), box 600; "Navajo Talkers Course: Methods of Instruction"; NARA, Records of the U.S. Marine Corps (Record Group 127), box 33; Durrett, *Unsung Heroes of World War II*, 50. For a complete code dictionary see *Our Fathers, Our Grandfathers, Our Heroes*.

35. A. F. Howard, by direction of The Commanding General, Camp Elliott, San Diego, to Commandant, U.S. Marine Corps, 20 July 1942, NARA, Records of the U.S. Marine Corps (Record Group 127), box 600.

36. Commandant, U.S. Marine Corps, to Western Recruiting Division, 26 Aug. 1942, NARA, Records of the U.S. Marine Corps (Record Group 127), box 600.

37. F. H. Shannon to Colonel Woodworth, 25 May 1943, NARA, Records of the U.S. Marine Corps (Record Group 127), box 598.

38. "Procurement of Navajo Personnel for Communication Duty," n.d., in Paul, *Navajo Code Talkers*, 162.

39. Anonymous Navajo instructor, in Paul, *Navajo Code Talkers*, 45–46.

40. Jack Jones, in Mack, *It Had to Be Done*, 33.

41. Escue, "Coded Contributions," 17; Paul, *Navajo Code Talkers*, 46, 75, 108; Paul Blatchford, interview, Oct. 1991; Bixler, *Winds of Freedom*, 68; Bernstein, *American Indians and World War II*, 49.

42. Philip Johnston, interview, 7 Nov. 1970.

43. Paul Blatchford, interview, Oct. 1991.

44. Wilsie Bitsie, interview with Sally McClain, 2 June 1993.

45. Col. Frank Halford, U.S. Marine Corps (Ret.), Director of Recruiting, 26 Mar. 1942, NARA, Records of the U.S. Marine Corps (Record Group 127), box 600.

46. Col. Carter W. Clarke, General Staff, to Assistant Chief of Staff, G-2, 8 Oct. 1943, NARA, Records of the National Security Agency (Record Group 457), SRH-120, box 34, 036.

47. First Lt. Chas E. Henshall to Director of Communications Research, 17 June 1944, NARA, Records of the National Security Agency (Record Group 457), SRH-120, box 34, 105.

48. Escue, "Coded Contributions," 18; McCoy, "Navajo Code Talkers of World War II," 70–71; Gilbert, *Native American Code Talker in World War II*, 47–48.

49. "Background Material Regarding the American Indians who Have Lived Much or all of their Lives Upon the Reservations and not in Direct Contact With White People," n.d., NARA, Records of the National Security Agency (Record Group 457), SRH-120, box 34, 042.

50. Holm, "Fighting a White Man's War," 69.

51. Adair and Vogt, "Navaho and Zuni Veterans," 551; Vogt, *Navaho Veterans*, 3.

52. Holm, "Strong Hearts," 130.

53. Stewart, "Navajo Indian at War," 20.

54. P. Johnston, "Marine Corps Hymn in Navaho," 153.

55. Philip Johnston to Mr. Dover Trent, Assistant Superintendent, Navajo Reservation, 11 July 1943, NARA, Records of the U.S. Marine Corps (Record Group 127), USMC Reserve and Historical Studies, 1942–88.

56. "The Use of Navajo Indians for Radio Transmission Security Purposes," NARA, Records of the National Security Agency (Record Group 457), SRH-120, box 34, 102.

57. "Background Material Regarding the American Indians," n.d., 043.

58. "Background Material Regarding the American Indians," n.d., 043.

59. Carroll, *Medicine Bags and Dog Tags*, 10.

60. Franco, *Crossing the Pond*, 65; Bixler, *Winds of Freedom*, 60.

61. Navajo Tribal Council declaration, signed by chairman J. C. Morgan and vice-chairman Howard Gorman, in Paul, *Navajo Code Talkers*, 3.

62. Paul Blatchford, interview, Oct. 1991.

63. Statement of Navajo Tribal Council, n.d., in Paul, *Navajo Code Talkers*, 552. See also Paul Blatchford, interview, Oct. 1991; Frank, introduction, 6; Holm, "Fighting a White Man's War," 73; Stewart, "Navajo Indian at War," 20–22.

64. Franco, "Loyal and Heroic Service," 399.

65. Franco, "Loyal and Heroic Service," 396.

66. Fred Harvey, interview, date unavailable.

67. Juan Etsicitty, interview, 11 Jan. 1968. See also Franco, "Loyal and Heroic Service," 399; A. R. Begay, "Interview with Agnes R. Begay," 48; Chee, "Women's Army Corps"; Emma H. Sandoval, interview.

68. In Watson, "Jaysho," 2.

69. Raymond Nakai, in Franco, *Crossing the Pond*, 65.

70. David E. Patterson, in Kawano, *Warriors*, 75.

71. Pahe D. Yazzie, in Kawano, *Warriors*, 98.

72. Peter Yazza, "My Personal History," NARA, Records of the U.S. Marine Corps (Record Group 127), USMC Reserve and Historical Studies, 1942–88.

73. MacDonald, *Last Warrior*, 60. See also Mack, *It Had to Be Done*, 71.

74. Anonymous Code Talker, in Paul, *Navajo Code Talkers*, 111.

75. Keith Little, in Watson, "Jaysho," 2. Little also recollects his reaction to Pearl Harbor in Mack, *It Had to Be Done*, 21–22.

76. Meadows, "North American Indian Code Talkers," 166; Meadows, *Kiowa, Apache, and Comanche Military Societies*, 399; Carroll, *Medicine Bags and Dog Tags*, 3.

77. Escue, "Coded Contributions," 15.

78. Billison, interview, 31 May 1993.

79. John Kinsel and John Goodluck, interview with Sally McClain, 26 July 1991.

80. Harold Foster, interview, Oct. 1991.

81. Kee Etsicitty, interview, 16 Apr. 1992. See also Bill Toledo and Alfred Newman, in Mack, *It Had to Be Done*, 26–27.

82. Bixler, *Winds of Freedom*, 62; Franco, "Loyal and Heroic Service," 399.

83. Carl Gorman, in McCoy, "Navajo Code Talkers of World War II," 68.

84. Paul Blatchford, interview, Oct. 1991.

85. Kee Etsicitty, interview, 16 Apr. 1992. See also MacDonald, *Last Warrior*, 57–58.

86. Joe Dedman, interview, date unavailable. Most of the veterans profiled in Vogt, *Navaho Veterans*, were also drafted.

87. K. Begay, "Ex-Prisoner of War—Pacific Theater," 13.

88. Holm, "Strong Hearts," 127.

89. Meadows, *Kiowa, Apache, and Comanche Military Societies*, 390.

90. Carroll, *Medicine Bags and Dog Tags*, 117; MacDonald, *Last Warrior*, 41–42.

91. Franco, "Loyal and Heroic Service," 392.

6. When the War Was Over

1. Thomas Begay, interview, Aug. 1992.

2. William McCabe, in Watson, "Jaysho," 4.

3. Samuel J. Smith Jr., registration form, Navajo Code Talker Reunion, 9–10 July 1971, NARA, Records of the U.S. Marine Corps (Record Group 127), USMC Reserve and Historical Studies, 1942–88.

4. Kee Etsicitty, in Mack, *It Had to Be Done*, 70.

5. Anonymous Code Talker, in Paul, *Navajo Code Talkers*, 32–33 (original emphasis). See also Bill Toledo, in Mack, *It Had to Be Done*, 38–39.

6. "Use of Navajo Indians for Radio Transmission Security Purposes"; Bernstein, *American Indians and World War II*, 49; McCoy, "Navajo Code Talkers of World War II," 68; Jevec and Potter, "Navajo Code Talkers," 262.

7. Harold Foster, Doris Duke Oral History Collection, ms. 417, University of

Utah Marriott Library, 6, in Durrett, *Unsung Heroes*, 67.

8. Anonymous Code Talker, in Paul, *Navajo Code Talkers*, 92 (original emphasis).

9. Anonymous Code Talker, in Paul, *Navajo Code Talkers*, 62.

10. Paul Blatchford, interview, Oct. 1991; Bernstein, *American Indians and World War II*, 49; Durrett, *Unsung Heroes of World War II*, 64; Paul, *Navajo Code Talkers*, 54–56.

11. G. R. Lockard to the Commanding General, First Marine Amphibious Corps, 7 May 1943, NARA, Records of the U.S. Marine Corps (Record Group 127), box 598.

12. Anonymous Code Talker, in Paul, *Navajo Code Talkers*, 69.

13. Philip Johnston to the Commandant, U.S. Marine Corps, 30 Aug. 1943, in Paul, *Navajo Code Talkers*, 167.

14. Bixler, *Winds of Freedom*, 80.

15. Nels H. Nelson, "Communications during the PALAU Operation," 23 Oct. 1944, 4, NARA, Records of the U.S. Marine Corps (Record Group 127), box 298.

16. "Report on Navajo Training Program Conducted 16 April to 6 May 1945, Inclusive," NARA, Records of the U.S. Marine Corps (Record Group 127), Records of Amphibious Corps, 1940–46.

17. In P. Johnston, "Indian Jargon Won Our Battles," 137.

18. "Annex OBOE (Signal Communications) to 5th Marine Division Action Report of Iwo Jima Operation," 2 Apr. 1945, 12, NARA, Records of the U.S. Marine Corps (Record Group 127), box 90; Col. H. G. Newhart, "Iwo Jima Operation, Observer's report on Communication Phases," 18, NARA, Records of the U.S. Marine Corps (Record Group 127), box 83; P. Johnston, "Indian Jargon Won Our Battles," 135; "Report on Navajo Training Program Conducted 16 April to 6 May 1945."

19. Harold Foster, interview, Oct. 1991. For other recollections of Iwo Jima, see Mack, *It Had to Be Done*, 51–57.

20. Bixler, *Winds of Freedom*, 88.

21. Anonymous Code Talker, in Paul, *Navajo Code Talkers*, 87.

22. Chester Nez, in Mack, *It Had to Be Done*, 44–45. For other similar stories see Bill Toledo, in Mack, *It Had to Be Done*, 45; Bixler, *Winds of Freedom*, 85; Paul, *Navajo Code Talkers*, 85–91; Escue, "Coded Contributions," 19–20; Durrett, *Unsung Heroes of World War II*, 77.

23. Gilbert, *Native American Code Talker in World War II*, 38.

24. Bill Toledo, interview with Sally McClain, Aug. 1992. See also Bill Toledo, in Mack, *It Had to Be Done*, 43–44.

25. Richard Bonham, interview with Sally McClain, 20 July 1993.

26. Kee Etsicitty, interview, 16 Apr. 1992.

27. Anonymous Code Talker, in Paul, *Navajo Code Talkers*, 83 (original emphasis).

28. Kee Etsicitty, in Mack, *It Had to Be Done*, 45 (original emphasis).

29. Foster, interview, Oct. 1991.

30. Harold Foster, in Watson, "Jaysho," 5.

31. Jimmie King, Marine Corps Navajo Code Talkers Collection, ms. 504, 67, in Durrett, *Unsung Heroes of World War II*, 81.

32. C. S. Brown, "Code Talker—Pacific Theater," 55.

33. Sam Billison, interview, 31 May 1993.

34. MacDonald, *Last Warrior*, 63.

35. F. D. Beans, Commanding Officer, Fourth Marines, to Commanding General, Sixth Marine Division, 16 Nov. 1944, file on "Code Talkers," Marine Corps Archives, in Bernstein, *American Indians and World War II*, 49.

36. G. R. Lockard, commanding officer of the Special and Service Battalion of First Amphibious Corps at Camp Goettge, 7 May 1943, in Paul, *Navajo Code Talkers*, 20.

37. Lemuel C. Shepherd Jr., Commanding General, Sixth Marine Division, to Commanding General, Fleet Marine Force, 1 Dec. 1944, NARA, Records of the U.S. Marine Corps (Record Group 127), Correspondence of Marine Divisions, 1941–46, box 59.

38. Julian C. Smith, Office of the Commanding General, to Commanding General, FMAC, 15 May 1943, in Paul, *Navajo Code Talkers*, 164.

39. "Annex OBOE (Signal Communications) to 5th Marine Division Action Report of Iwo Jima Operation," 2 Apr. 1945, 26.

40. P. Johnson, "Marine Corps Hymn in Navaho," 153.

41. Maj. Howard Conner, quoted in P. Johnston, "Indian Jargon Won Our Battles," 130. See also Paul, *Navajo Code Talkers*, 73.

42. Durrett, *Unsung Heroes of World War II*, 79.

43. Paul Blatchford, interview, Oct. 1991.

44. Dr. Frank Becker, National Secretary, Indian Association of America, Inc., to President Harry Truman, 15 Sept. 1950, NARA, Records of the National Security Agency (Record Group 457), Special Research Histories, SRH-120: Utilization of American Indians as Communication Linguist, box 34, 073.

45. ACofs, G-2-ASA, to ACofs, G-3, 26 Oct. 1950, memo, NARA, Records of the National Security Agency (Record Group 457), Special Research Histories, SRH-120: Utilization of American Indians as Communication Linguist, box 34, 005A.

46. Director of Intelligence to Chief Signal Officer, 23 Nov. 1948, NARA, Records of the National Security Agency (Record Group 457), SRH-120, box 34, 057A. See also ACofs, G-2-ASA, to ACofs, G-3, 26 Oct. 1950, memo, NARA, Records of the National Security Agency (Record Group 457), SRH-120, box 34, 005A and 005B; extract from "Action Report of 5th Marine Division on Iwo Jima 19 February 1945 to 26 March 1945," NARA, Records of the National Security Agency (Record Group 457), SRH-120, box 34, 033.

47. McCoy, "Navajo Code Talkers of World War II," 71; Escue, "Coded Contri-

butions," 20.

48. Sam Billison, interview, 31 May 1993. See also Bill Toledo, in Mack, *It Had to Be Done*, 62.

49. Clare Thompson, in Belleranti, "Code Talkers," 42.

50. Bill Toledo, interview, Aug. 1992.

51. Statement of Navajo Tribal Council, n.d., in Paul, *Navajo Code Talkers*, 552.

52. In Escue, "Coded Contributions," 20.

53. Raymond Nakai, in Paul, *Navajo Code Talkers*, 108–9 (original emphasis).

54. Meadows, "North American Indian Code Talkers," 172. See also Vogt, *Navaho Veterans*.

55. Yazza, "My Personal History"; Watson, "Jaysho," 3; Adkins, "Secret War," 343; Franco, "Empowering the World War II Native American Veteran," 33–34; Franco, "Loyal and Heroic Service," 403; MacDonald, *Last Warrior*, 74; Samuel Tso, in Mack, *It Had to Be Done*, 63; Stabler, *No One Ever Asked Me*, 122.

56. Albert Miguel, in Vogt, *Navaho Veterans*, 144.

57. Wilsie Bitsie, interview, 2 June 1993. Technically Navajos had been U.S. citizens since the Snyder Act in 1924 bestowed citizenship on all Native Americans, but citizenship, as for other racial groups, did not signify equality.

58. Jimmie K. King to Philip Johnston, 6 June 1946, NARA, Records of the U.S. Marine Corps (Record Group 127), USMC Reserve and Historical Studies, 1942–88.

59. Holm, "Fighting a White Man's War," 76; Vogt, *Navaho Veterans*.

60. Fixico, *Termination and Relocation*; La Farge, "Termination of Federal Supervision"; Robbins, "Self-Determination and Subordination"; Philp, "Termination"; Philp, "From New Deal to Termination"; Philp, "Stride toward Freedom"; Burt, "Roots of the Native American Urban Experience"; Meadows, *Kiowa, Comanche, and Apache Military Societies*, 392–93.

61. Bernstein, *American Indians and World War II*, 171–75

62. Iverson, *Diné*, 193–98, 219–23, 245; Fixico, *Termination and Relocation*, 165; Paul, *Navajo Code Talkers*, 109–10; Bixler, *Winds of Freedom*, 114.

63. See http://www.navajonationcouncil.org/NNprofile.htm. For more information about the Native American civil rights movement see Josephy, Nagel, and Johnson, *Red Power*; P. C. Smith and Warrior, *Like a Hurricane*; T. R. Johnson, Nagel, and Champagne, *American Indian Activism*; T. R. Johnson, *Occupation of Alcatraz Island*; Nagel, *American Indian Ethnic Renewal*.

64. Paul, *Navajo Code Talkers*, 150.

65. Keith Little, in Mack, *It Had to Be Done*, 71. See also MacDonald, *Last Warrior*.

66. Howard Gorman Sr., interview, date unavailable.

67. Carroll, *Medicine Bags and Dog Tags*, 9. See also Holm, "Strong Hearts," 143–46; Holm, *Strong Hearts Wounded Souls*; Morningstorm, *American Indian Warrior Today*; *20th Century Warriors*.

68. C. S. Brown, "Code Talker—Pacific Theater," 61.

69. Belleranti, "Code Talkers," 76; Paul, *Navajo Code Talkers*, 127.

70. White House to Peter MacDonald, 8 Sept. 1971, telegram, in Paul, *Navajo Code Talkers*, 150; also in *Our Fathers, Our Grandfathers, Our Heroes*, 79.

71. Belleranti, "Code Talkers," 42, 76.

72. Reagan, "Proclamation 4954."

73. Senator Dennis DeConcini, in Belleranti, "Code Talkers," 76.

74. Gen. A. M. Gray, "CMC's Address."

75. Durrett, *Unsung Heroes of World War II*, 106; Meadows, *Comanche Code Talkers of World War II*, 202; Meadows, "North American Indian Code Talkers," 175.

76. The act was incorporated as section 1102 of an appropriations bill. See United States, Congress, House, 106th Cong., 3rd sess., H.R. 4577.

77. Bush, "Remarks by the President."

78. Meadows, "North American Indian Code Talkers," 175–83.

79. Keith Little, in Watson, "Jaysho," 6.

80. Carl Gorman, in McCoy, "Navajo Code Talkers of World War II," 75.

81. Jimmie King, registration form, Navajo Code Talker Reunion, 9–10 July 1971, NARA, Records of the U.S. Marine Corps (Record Group 127), USMC Reserve and Historical Studies, 1942–88.

82. Alex Williams, registration form, Navajo Code Talker Reunion, 9–10 July 1971, NARA, Records of the U.S. Marine Corps (Record Group 127), USMC Reserve and Historical Studies, 1942–88.

83. Paul Blatchford, interview, Oct. 1991.

84. Fraser, "From Redistribution to Recognition?" 73, 81.

85. Franco, "Loyal and Heroic Service," 402; Bixler, *Winds of Freedom*, 108–9; Adkins, "Secret War," 343; MacDonald, *Last Warrior*, 81, 89; Bill Toledo and Samuel Tso, in Mack, *It Had to Be Done*, 67–68. Several of the veterans profiled in Vogt, *Navaho Veterans,* attended agricultural training classes.

86. McCoy, "Navajo Code Talkers of World War II," 75; Stabler, *No One Ever Asked Me*, 129.

87. Wilsie Bitsie, interview, 2 June 1993. See also Vogt, *Navaho Veterans*, 54, 56.

88. McAree, "Navajo Code Talker's Long Fight for Recognition."

89. *2009–2010 Comprehensive Economic Development Strategy, The Navajo Nation*, 119–20, 128. For the 1983 unemployment rate see MacDonald, *Last Warrior*, 273.

90. Kee Etsicitty, interview.

91. Sam Billison, in Meadows, *Comanche Code Talkers of World War II*, 204.

92. Carroll, *Medicine Bags and Dog Tags*, 132.

93. Brokaw, *Greatest Generation*, xix.

Conclusion

1. W. H. Powell, "Indian as a Soldier," 235.

2. Benson, "Waltzing Matilda and the Powerful Owls," 67.

3. Marre, "Historian's Lot," 6.

4. Young, *Minorities and the Military*, 283.

5. Cushing, "Military Colonization of the Indians," 375.

6. Cushing, "Military Colonization of the Indians," 373–74.

7. For other examples see Young, *Minorities and the Military*, 5–19; Streets, *Martial Races*, esp. chaps. 1-3.

8. Young, *Minorities and the Military*, 248–52.

9. See Krebs, *Fighting for Rights*.

10. United Nations, "Universal Declaration of Human Rights," Article 2.

BIBLIOGRAPHY

Archival Sources

National Archives of Australia, Canberra (NAA Canberra)

Series A1, item 1936/6237: Tribal fights — East Arnhem Land, Northern Territory. Contents date range 1936–1936.

Series A1, item 1938/6715: Aboriginal Murders Arnhem Land NT. Contents date range 1938–1938.

Series A52, item 572/994 THO: Interim General Report of preliminary expedition to Arnhem Land, Northern Territory of Australia, 1935–36, by Dr Donald Thomson. Contents date range 1936–1937.

Series A373, item 5903: [Japanese activities amongst aboriginals]. Contents date range 1943–1943.

Series A431, item 1946/915: Employment of Natives on Work for Army (NT). Contents date range 1942–1946.

Series A431, item 1946/1357: Aborigine Ex-Servicemen Restrictions in Civil Life. Easing of. Contents date range 1946–1946.

Series A432, item 1939/947: Royal Papuan Constabulary Ordinance: Papua. Contents date range 1939–1940.

Series A463, item 1956/1096: War pensions — Torres Strait Islanders — [Contains report on compensation to natives of Papua and New Guinea for war injuries and war damage]. Contents date range 1945–11 Nov 1955.

Series A472, series accession number A472/6, item W3119: National Security (New Guinea Police Force) Regulations — National Security (Royal Papuan Constabulary) Regulations. Contents date range 1941–1941.

Series A659, series accession number A659/1, item 1939/1/12995: Enlistment of half-caste Aborigines in the Militia Forces at Darwin. Contents date range 1939–1939.

Series A659, series accession number A659/1, item 1942/1/3043: Co-operation between Aboriginals and whites in event of enemy invasion. Contents date range 1942–1942.

Series A816, item 14/301/138: Report on Arnhem Land. Elcho Is. Contents date range 1940–1940.

Series A1734/15, item NT1970/1409: Appointment of Professer [*sic*] Baldwin Spencer as Special Commissioner for the Aborigines in the Northern Territory. Contents date range 1970–1970.

Series A2671, item 45/1940: Enlistment in Defence Forces of aliens and persons of non European descent. Contents date range 18 January 1940–27 June 1940.

Series A9300, item THOMSON D F: THOMSON DONALD FERGUSON: Service Number—250194: Date of birth—26 Jun 1901: Place of birth—Unknown: Place of enlistment—Unknown: Next of Kin—THOMSON G. Contents date range 1939–1948.

Series A10857, item IV/15E: Northern Territory—Coastal Reconnaissance Unit —RAE—War Establishment—provisional. Contents date range 1943–1943.

Series AA1966/5, item 386: Northern Territory Force—Report on organisation of the Northern Territory Coastal Patrol and the Special Reconnaissance Unit. Contents date range 1941–1943.

Series B884, series accession number B884/4, item Q119904: TIKI: Service Number—Q119904: Date of birth—01 Jan 1926: Place of birth—BRITISH SOLOMON ISLANDS: Place of enlistment—BRISBANE QLD: Next of Kin—TENASAN. Contents date range 1940–1947.

Series B884, series accession number B884/4, item Q119906: LAKAPOLI PAPAI: Service Number—Q119906: Date of birth—01 Jan 1917: Place of birth—SOLOMON ISLANDS: Place of enlistment—BRISBANE QLD: Next of Kin—TEAIKI. Contents date range 1940–1947.

Series B884, series accession number B884/4, item Q119907: MAKAU KELAUIA: Service Number—Q119907: Date of birth—01 Jan 1916: Place of birth—BRIT SOLOMON ISLANDS: Place of enlistment—BRISBANE QLD: Next of Kin—MOENAKI. Contents date range 1940–1947.

Series B884, series accession number B884/4, item Q119908: RICHARDSON EDWIN: Service Number—Q119908: Date of birth—15 Aug 1910: Place of birth—SOLOMON IS ʻBRITʼ: Place of enlistment—BRISBANE QLD: Next of Kin—KAPUNAGANA. Contents date range 1940–1947.

Series B884, series accession number B884/4, item Q119909: GEGE: Service Number—Q119909: Date of birth—01 Jan 1916: Place of birth—BRIT SOLOMON ISLANDS: Place of enlistment—BRISBANE QLD: Next of Kin—VONA. Contents date range 1940–1947.

Series MP742/1, item 85/1/671: Death and other Sentences Imposed on Natives in New Guinea. Contents date range 1945–1945.

National Archives of Australia, Darwin (NAA Darwin)

Series F1, item 1938/716: Employment of Mission Aboriginals in Darwin. Contents date range 1937–1937.

Series F1, item 1939/545: Information supplied to Dr Donald Thomson re Rainfall

Records, Geological Expeditions and Police Expeditions, Arnhem Land. Contents date range 1939–1939.

Series FI, item 1949/456: Methodist Overseas Mission Goulburn Island. Contents date range 1932–1952.

Series FI, item 1949/459: Methodist Overseas Mission, Yirrkala Mission. Contents date range 1933–1952.

Series FI, item 1953/266: Methodist Overseas Mission — Milingimbi Mission. Contents date range 1932–1953.

National Archives of Australia, Melbourne (NAA Melbourne)

Series B1535, item 849/3/1644: [Aborigines in Militia Unit]. Contents date range 1939–1939.

Series B1535, item 929/19/912: Military training for Aboriginal youth in Australia. Contents date range 1938–1939.

Series MP70/1, item 48/101/384: Native labour overseers ANGAU [recruitment]. Contents date range 1943–1943.

Series MP151/1, item 487/202/2626: War Gratuity for Natives of New Guinea and Papua. Contents date range 1946–1947.

Series MP375/14, item WC25: War Crimes. Papua New Guinea. Kalabu Execution of Natives at. Contents date range 1947–1948.

Series MP375/14, item WC27: War Crimes Papua/New Guinea. Execution of unknown Native. Contents date range 1948–1948.

Series MP508/1, item 82/710/2: Employment of Aborigines by Defence/Army in Darwin [Contains information re conditions, rates of pay, finance authorities, etc] [Box 126]. Contents date range 1933–1940.

Series MP508/1, item 240/701/217: [Role of Aborigines of defence of Australia — suggestion of Prof Elkin.] Contents date range 1941–1942.

Series MP508/1, item 247/701/953: Pay of Native Workers in New Guinea. Contents date range 1942–1943.

Series MP508/1, item 275/750/618: Enlistment of Aborigines in the AIF. Contents date range 1940–1940.

Series MP508/1, item 275/750/1310: Aborigines Enlisted in AIF. Contents date range 1940–1942.

Series MP729/6, item 2/401/154: HQ New Guinea Force Admin Instruction No 106 Native Labour. Contents date range 1943–1943.

Series MP729/6, item 16/401/455: Possibility of Raising Native Troops in Territory of New Guinea. Contents date range 1941–1941.

Series MP729/6, item 16/401/482: Formation of Native Infantry Battalion in Territory of New Guinea. Contents date range 1939–1941.

Series MP729/6, item 16/402/111: Transfer of Mission Natives — Cape York Peninsula. Contents date range 1942–1943.

Series MP729/6, item 19/401/388: ANGAU Proposed New War Establishment. Contents date range 1943–1943.

Series MP729/6, item 29/401/618: North Australia Observer Organisation—Provision of Funds [North Australia Observer Unit, NAOU]. Contents date range 1942–1942.

Series MP729/6, item 29/401/626: Japanese Activities Among the Aborigines. Contents date range 1942–1942.

Series MP729/6, item 37/401/1444: Northern Territory Coastal Reconnaissance Unit—RAE Raising of. Contents date range 1943–1943.

Series MP729/6, item 37/401/1849: Relief of NAOU [North Australia Observer Unit]. Contents date range 1943–1943.

Series MP729/6, item 37/401/1904: Native Labour in New Guinea. Contents date range 1943–1944.

Series MP729/6, item 37/401/2145: Coast Watching and Reporting Systems. Contents date range 1943–1945.

Series MP729/6, item 38/401/138: Ketch "Aroetta" movements. Contents date range 1941–1943.

Series MP742/1, item R/1/3617: D. 178 Raiwalla George—Anzac Day March. Contents date range 1949–1949.

Series MP742/1, item 5/1/34: Future Native Welfare in Territories of Papua and New Guinea. Contents date range 1943–1943.

Series MP742/1, item 5/3/147: Australia—New Guinea Administrative Unit ANGAU. Contents date range 1942–1944.

Series MP742/1, item 85/1/816: Complaint re Treatment of Natives by ANGAU Officials E J Ward MP. Contents date range 1945–1946.

Series MP742/1, item 92/1/302: Employment of Native Labour in NT (Northern Territory). [Re disbandment of No. 10 Employment Company and proposed formulation of NT Employment Company of Aborigines]. Contents date range 1943–1945.

Series MP742/1, item 96/1/45: W. E. Royal Papuan Constabulary. Contents date range 1943–1943.

Series MP742/1, item 96/1/982: Organ.—Royal Papuan Constabulary. Contents date range 1943–1944.

Series MP742/1, item 131/1/82: ANGAU Reward to Natives. Contents date range 1944–1945.

Series MP742/1, item 247/1/79: Employment of Native Crews for Coastal Reconnaissance Ketch—"Aroetta." Contents date range 1941–1943.

Series MP742/1, item 247/1/474: Rates of pay of Warrant Officers in Royal Papuan Constabulary. Contents date range 1943–1943.

Series MP742/1, item 247/1/1152: Conditions of Service: Natives of Papua and New Guinea Enlisted in or Employed by the Forces. Contents date range 1945–1945.

Series MP742/1, item 247/1/1172: Pay of Native Troops & Native Labour in Papua and New Guinea. Contents date range 1945–1945.

Series MP742/1, item 247/1/1290: Conditions of Service: Natives of Papua New Guinea [and Torres Strait Islanders]. Contents date range 1942–1946.

Series MP742/1, item 285/1/680A: Native labour survey—Papua & New Guinea—December 1944–March 1945. Contents date range 1944–1945.

Series MP742/1, item 299/4/703: a.k. "Aroetta" [Special NT Recce. Unit]—General File. Contents date range 1941–1943.

Series MP927/1, item A131/2/43: War Gratuity Natives of New Guinea and Papua who are members of the Forces. Contents date range 1946–1957.

Series MT1131/1, item A253/1/2: Eligibility of members of Royal Papuan Constabulary and New Guinea police force for Ex-Servicemen's Credit Schemes. Contents date range 1960–1960.

Australian War Memorial (AWM)

F00519: Aborigines are True Soldiers of the King (Cinesound news No. 488). 1 min 44 sec. 7 March 1941.

F01213: War Supply Route. 2–15 July 1942.

F01685: Royal Papuan Constabulary. February 1944.

F01872: Finisterre Ranges. 1943.

F04029: Interview with Peter Huskins (When the war came to Australia). 14 February 1991.

F04030: Interview with Amory Vane (When the war came to Australia). 14 February 1991.

F07096: Visit to New Guinea of the Minister for External Territories. 19–21 April 1944.

F07097: 1 Papuan Infantry Battalion training. 1 July 1943.

F07174: Malahang compound Lae area. 6 December 1944.

F07239: Mount Shiburangu action, Wewak area. 26 June 1945.

F07397: Parade and march past of Pacific Infantry Battalion & review of 3 Division by the Commander in Chief General Sir Thomas Blamey, Torokina. 29 October 1945.

Private Record, PR87/087: Cameron, Donald M (MHR for Fadden (Qld)); not defined. 1981–1987.

Private Record, PR91/163: Fisher, Cecil 1933–. Date made 1991; 1993.

Series 52, item 5/35/1: Northern Territory Coastal Reconnaissance Unit (NT Coastal Recce Unit) [Whole diary—1 item] (January 1946). Contents date range 1946–1946.

Series 52, item 25/1/2: 2/1 Northern Australia Observer Unit [North Australia Observer Unit, NAOU]. Contents date range 1942–1945.

Series 54, item 171/2/39: [Casualties—Reporting:] Casualties Suffered by the Royal Papuan Constabulary during the 1939–1945 War. Contents date range 1956–1956.

Series 54, item 391/11/85: [Honours and Rewards—Infantry:] Recommendations for Honours and Rewards, Royal Papuan Constabulary. Contents date range 1943–1945.

Series 54, item 419/5/6: [Infantry—Papuan and New Guinea Infantry Battalions:] Reports submitted by Major General Morris, General Officer Commanding, Australian New Guinea Administration Unit (ANGAU) and Officers of his unit, on the unsuitability and impracticability of recruiting natives for Infantry Battalions, under existing system of training and requirements, including criticism of European Officers of such units. Reply by Lieutenant-General Sturdee refuting the charges and stressing necessity of such units, 1944–1945. Contents date range 1943–1945.

Series 54, item 506/5/1: [Natives—Labour] Utilisation of Future Possibilities, particularly regarding the Mandated Territory of New Guinea, 1943. Contents date range 1943–1944.

Series 54, item 506/5/19: [Natives—Labour] Statistics and Employment of New Guinea Natives 1942–1945 including Casualties, Honours and Awards etc including names of recipients (February 1970). Contents date range 1970–1970.

Series 54, item 506/8/3: [Natives—General:] Police and prisons—policy Royal Papuan Constabulary—General, 1945. Contents date range 1945–1945.

Series 54, item 519/4/2: [Operations—General (including enemy)—Instructions:] Northern Territory Operation Instruction No 65-1943, To OC Northern Territory Coastal Unit RAE (Recce), Advice regarding auxiliary ketch AROETTA—inventory of stores and equipment. Contents date range 1943–1943.

Series 54, item 577/7/32: [Owen Stanleys—Reports:] Documents and notes used in writing Volume 5 (Army) South West Pacific Area First Year [Official History]. Includes appraisal of U.S. and Australian officers and troops; and the arrival of U.S. troops in Australia, 1941–1944 [9 Feb 1942–1948]. Contents date range 1942–1948.

Series 54, item 628/1/1B: [Torres Strait Area:] Torres Strait Islanders, 1944. File dealing with enlistment, rates of pay, conditions of service, and employment of natives in the Army [1st copy]. Contents date range 1942–1944.

Series 54, item 741/5/9: Report on Northern Territory Special Reconnaissance Unit, by Squadron Leader D F Thomson, R.A.A.F. Contents date range 1941–1943.

Series 54, item 805/7/1: [Publications—Army Newspapers:] Articles submitted for publication in "Salt." Contents date range 1940–1944.

Series 54, item 963/22/12: [Transport—Sea (Allied)—Small Ship Coys and Small Ship Log Books:] File dealing with Water Transport (small craft)—4 Australian Water Transport Coy (small craft) (Type C) Reorganization of Acquisition power dinghy—NAOU [North Australia Observation Unit], War Establishment, Northern Territory Force Water Transport Group, Extract from report of Major J C Boyle, covering tour of inspection—Sydney—Brisbane—NT Force, WA—List of vessels NT Force, 19-42/44. [North Australia Observer Unit]. Contents date range 1942–1944.

Northern Territory Archives Service (NTAS)

Boxall, Alec. NTRS 226. Oral History Interview. TS 21. Location 173/1/1. Interviewer: Alan Powell, 2 December 1983.

Carty, "Tip." NTRS 226. Oral History Interview. TS 24. Location 173/1/1. Interviewer: Alan Powell, Sydney, 30 November 1983.

Church Missionary Society of Australia, North Australia Committee. NTRS 868. General records of the Angurugu Community. Location 128/3/1. Contents date range 1921–1985.

———. NTRS 1098. Mission reports and station council minutes of the Angurugu Community. Location 52/1/2. Contents date range 1939–1979.

Cole, Keith. NTRS 694. Records, photographs and research material about mission life in Northern Australia. Location 139/5/1. Contents date range 1915–1985.

Commissioner of Police. NTRS F 77. Correspondence files, annual single number series. Location 101/1/4. Contents date range 1935–1959.

Curtis, Charles. NTRS 226. Oral History Interview. TS 35. Location 173/1/1. Interviewer: Alan Powell, Sydney, 30 November 1983.

Graham, Kevin. NTRS 226. Oral History Interview. TS 221. Location 173/1/1. Interviewer: H. Giese, Buderim, QLD, 2 August 1981.

Harris, Len. NTRS 226. Oral History Interview. TS 64. Location 173/1/1. Interviewer: Alan Powell, 15 September 1983.

Oakley, Reg. NTRS 226. Oral History Interview. TS 412. Location 173/1/1. Interviewer: Alan Powell, 17 November 1984.

Rogers, Ron. NTRS 226. Oral History Interview. TS 390. Location 173/1/1. Interviewer: Alan Powell, 3 December 1983.

Somerville, Margaret. NTRS 1432/PI. Diary entries of Margaret Somerville. Contents date range 1941–1942.

Sweeney, Gordon. NTRS 226. Oral History Interview. TS 337. Location 173/1/1. Interviewer: Don Dickson, 1980.

National Archives and Records Administration of the United States of America (NARA)

Records of the National Security Agency (Record Group 457). Special Research Histories. SRH-120: Utilization of American Indians as Communication Linguist. Box 34.

Records of the Office of the Chief of Naval Operations (Record Group 38). Records Relating to Naval Activity During World War II. WW II Action and Operational Reports. (Guam). USMC, Fleet MARPHICORPS 21 Mar 1944 to Third MARPHICORPS 3 Sep 1944. Folder: COMGEN III Amphibious Corps, vol. 1, box 1587.

Records of the Office of the Chief of Naval Operations (Record Group 38). Records Relating to Naval Activity During World War II. WW II Action and Operational Reports. (Okinawa). USMC, First Marine Division, Cape Gloucester Operation to 10 July 1945. Folder: COMGEN First Marine Division, vol. 2, 10 July 1945 Report, box 1603.

Records of the U.S. Marine Corps (Record Group 127). History and Museums Division. Correspondence of Marine Divisions, 1941–46. Sixth Marine Division. From 2295 (G-2 Periodic Reports) through 2295 (S-3 Reports). Folder 3, Intelligence, box 59.

Records of the U.S. Marine Corps (Record Group 127). History and Museums Division. Records of Amphibious Corps, 1940–1946. Third Amphibious Corps. CKT Logs, 29 Jul 44 to Navajo Indian Talker Training. Box 77.

Records of the U.S. Marine Corps (Record Group 127). History and Museums Division. Records Relating to Public Affairs. The USMC Reserve and Historical Studies, 1942–88. "C" Course Wash Daily News. 4 folders: Misc/1942, 1943, 1946, 1967, 1969–1971 (Navajo Indians).

Records of the U.S. Marine Corps (Record Group 127). History and Museums Division. Subject File Relating to World War II. Mountain Warfare to Naval Gunfire — Doctrine. Folder 3: Navajo Code Talker, box 33.

Records of the U.S. Marine Corps (Record Group 127). Office of the Commandant General Correspondence, 1939–1950 (Entry 18A). File 1535-75, folders 13–14, 17–20, boxes 597, 598, 600.

Records of the U.S. Marine Corps (Record Group 127). Office of the Commandant General Correspondence, 1939–1950 (Entry 18A). File 2185-20, folder 4, box 1427.

Records of the U.S. Marine Corps (Record Group 127). Records Relating to United States Marine Corps Operations in World War II ("Geographic Files"). (Iwo Jima). Folder A8.5-1: Signal Questionnaire, box 77.

Records of the U.S. Marine Corps (Record Group 127). Records Relating to United States Marine Corps Operations in World War II ("Geographic Files"). (Iwo Jima). Folder A9-30: Office of Signal Officer, Communication. "Observer's Report on Communication at Iwo Jima. 4 Apr 45." Box 83.

Records of the U.S. Marine Corps (Record Group 127). Records Relating to United States Marine Corps Operations in World War II ("Geographic Files"). (Iwo Jima). Folder A16-10: 5th Marine Division "M" to "R." "Annex OBOE to 5th Marine Division Action Report of Iwo Jima." Box 90.

Records of the U.S. Marine Corps (Record Group 127). Records Relating to United States Marine Corps Operations in World War II ("Geographic Files"). (Peleliu). Folder A4-10: III MAC Operational Report, Signal. "Communications during the PALAU Operation." Box 298.

Interviews

Batumbil, Phyllis. Interview with Noah Riseman. Recorded at Mata Mata, Northern Territory, 29 September 2005. Tapes and transcripts available from author or from Australian Institute for Aboriginal and Torres Strait Islander Studies (AIATSIS).

Begay, Thomas, John Kinsel, and Bill Toledo (Navajo Code Talkers). Interview with Sally McClain. August 1992. Available from the Navajo Nation Museum, Window Rock AZ.

Billison, Sam (Navajo Code Talker). Interview with Sally McClain. 31 May 1993.
Available from the Navajo Nation Museum, Window Rock AZ.

Bitsie, Wilsie (Navajo Code Talker). Interview with Sally McClain. 2 June 1993.
Available from the Navajo Nation Museum, Window Rock AZ.

Blackhorse. Date unavailable. Tuba City Agency, number 16. Oneo Collection.
Available from the Navajo Nation Museum, Window Rock AZ.

Blatchford, Paul (Navajo Code Talker). Interview with Sally McClain. October
1991. Available from the Navajo Nation Museum, Window Rock AZ.

Bonham, Richard (Navajo Code Talker). Interview with Sally McClain. 20 July
1993. Available from the Navajo Nation Museum, Window Rock AZ.

Dedman, Joe. Date unavailable. Chinle Agency, number 36. Oneo Collection.
Available from the Navajo Nation Museum, Window Rock AZ.

Etsicitty, Juan. Recorded 11 January 1968. Shiprock Agency, number 62. Oneo Collection. Available from the Navajo Nation Museum, Window Rock AZ.

Etsicitty, Kee (Navajo Code Talker). Interview with Sally McClain. 16 April 1992.
Available from the Navajo Nation Museum, Window Rock AZ.

Foster, Harold. Interview with Sally McClain. October 1991. Available from the Navajo Nation Museum, Window Rock AZ.

Gorman, Howard, Sr. Date unavailable. Chinle Agency, number 54. Oneo Collection. Available from the Navajo Nation Museum, Window Rock AZ.

Harvey, Fred. Date unavailable. Chinle Agency, number 49. Oneo Collection.
Available from the Navajo Nation Museum, Window Rock AZ.

Kaplimut, Eliab (Papua New Guinean). Interview with Iwamoto Hiromitsu.
Trans. and transcribed by Pastor Jacob Aramans. Available from *Remember-
ing the War in New Guinea*, http://ajrp.awm.gov.au/ajrp/remember.nsf/pages/
NT000020F6.

Kesen, Kami (Papua New Guinean). Interview with Iwamoto Hiromitsu. Trans.
and transcribed by Pastor Jacob Aramans. Available from *Remembering the
War in New Guinea*, http://ajrp.awm.gov.au/ajrp/remember.nsf/pages/
NT000020F6.

Kinsel, John, and John Goodluck (Navajo Code Talkers). Interview with Sally Mc-
Clain. 20 July 1991. Available from the Navajo Nation Museum, Window Rock AZ.

Lehi, Alfred. Recorded by Max Hanley. Tuba City Agency, number 24. Oneo Collection. Available from the Navajo Nation Museum, Window Rock AZ.

Leleng, Joe (Papua New Guinean). Interview with Iwamoto Hiromitsu. Trans. and
transcribed by Pastor Jacob Aramans. Available from *Remembering the War in
New Guinea*, http://ajrp.awm.gov.au/ajrp/remember.nsf/pages/NT000020F6.

Old Charlie. Interview with Noah Riseman. Trans. Phyllis Batumbil. Recorded
at Mata Mata, Northern Territory. 29 September 2005. Tapes and transcripts
available from author or from Australian Institute for Aboriginal and Torres
Strait Islander Studies (AIATSIS).

Paliau, John. Interview with Iwamoto Hiromitsu. Trans. and transcribed by Pastor

Jacob Aramans. Available from *Remembering the War in New Guinea*, http://ajrp.awm.gov.au/ajrp/remember.nsf/pages/NT000020F6.

Panu, Betuel (Papua New Guinean). Interview with Iwamoto Hiromitsu. Trans. and transcribed by Pastor Jacob Aramans. Available from *Remembering the War in New Guinea*, http://ajrp.awm.gov.au/ajrp/remember.nsf/pages/NT000020F6.

Samare, Seno (Papua New Guinean). Interview with Iwamoto Hiromitsu. Trans. and transcribed by Pastor Jacob Aramans. Available from *Remembering the War in New Guinea*, http://ajrp.awm.gov.au/ajrp/remember.nsf/pages/NT000020F6.

Sandoval, Emma H. Chinle Agency, tape number 90. Oneo Collection. Available from the Navajo Nation Museum, Window Rock AZ.

Spencer, Chee Dah. Recorded 31 October 1967. Crownpoint Agency, number 22. Oneo Collection. Available from the Navajo Nation Museum, Window Rock AZ.

Thomas, Eliab (Papua New Guinean). Interview with Iwamoto Hiromitsu. Trans. and transcribed by Pastor Jacob Aramans. Available from *Remembering the War in New Guinea*, http://ajrp.awm.gov.au/ajrp/remember.nsf/pages/NT000020F6.

Tokankan, Joseph (Papua New Guinean). Interview with Iwamoto Hiromitsu. 9 August 2000. Trans. and transcribed by Pastor Jacob Aramans. Available from *Remembering the War in New Guinea*, http://ajrp.awm.gov.au/ajrp/remember.nsf/pages/NT000020F6.

Toledo, Bill (Navajo Code Talker). Interview with Sally McClain. 19 August 1993. Available from the Navajo Nation Museum, Window Rock AZ.

Tovilivan, Levi (Papua New Guinean). Interview with Iwamoto Hiromitsu. Trans. and transcribed by Pastor Jacob Aramans. Available from *Remembering the War in New Guinea*, http://ajrp.awm.gov.au/ajrp/remember.nsf/pages/NT000020F6.

Tumat, James (Papua New Guinean). Interview with Iwamoto Hiromitsu. Trans. and transcribed by Pastor Jacob Aramans. Available from *Remembering the War in New Guinea*, http://ajrp.awm.gov.au/ajrp/remember.nsf/pages/NT000020F6.

Urawai, Ferdinand (Papua New Guinean). Interview with Iwamoto Hiromitsu. Trans. and transcribed by Pastor Jacob Aramans. Available from *Remembering the War in New Guinea*, http://ajrp.awm.gov.au/ajrp/remember.nsf/pages/NT000020F6.

Published Sources

Abbott, C. L. A. *Australia's Frontier Province*. Sydney: Angus and Robertson, 1950.

Adair, John, and Evon Vogt. "Navaho and Zuni Veterans: A Study of Contrasting Modes of Culture Change." *American Anthropologist* 51, no. 4, part 1 (1949): 547–61.

Adkins, Adam. "Secret War: The Navajo Code Talkers in World War II." *New Mexico Historical Review* 72, no. 4 (1997): 319–47.

Allen, Bryant. "Remembering the War in the Sepik." In Toyoda and Nelson, *Pacific War in Papua New Guinea*, 11–34.

Allen, Bryant, and Keiko Tamura. "Food Supply and Relationships between Japanese Troops and Villagers in the Inland Aitape-Wewak Campaign, Papua New Guinea, 1942–45." In Toyoda end Nelson, *Pacific War in Papua New Guinea*, 297–319.

Angels of War. Produced and directed by Gavan Daws, Hank Nelson, and Andrew Pike. 54 minutes. Australian National University, Research School of Pacific Studies, 1981. Videocassette.

Attwood, Bain. *The Making of the Aborigines*. Sydney: Allen and Unwin, 1989.

———. *Telling the Truth about Aboriginal History*. Crows Nest NSW: Allen and Unwin, 2005.

Austin, Tony. *Never Trust a Government Man: Northern Territory Aboriginal Policy 1911–1939*. Darwin: Northern Territory University Press, 1997.

———. "Taming the Yolngu: Methodists, Race, and Schooling in Arnhem Land 1916–1939." In Austin and Parry, *Connection and Disconnection*, 223–51.

Austin, Tony, and Suzanne Parry, eds. *Connection and Disconnection: Encounters between Settlers and Indigenous People in the Northern Territory*. Darwin: Northern Territory University Press, 1998.

Australia. The Parliament of the Commonwealth of Australia, 1937 [Fifteenth Parliament]. *Report of the Board of Inquiry Appointed to Inquire into the Land and Land Industries of the Northern Territory of Australia*. 10 October 1937.

———. The Parliament of the Commonwealth of Australia, 1939. *Territory of Papua. Report for Year 1937–38*. Presented by command, 5 May 1939.

Australian War Memorial Museum. *Too Dark for the Light Horse*. Available at http://www.awm.gov.au/events/travelling/toodark.htm.

Barrett, Maj. Don. "The Pacific Islands Regiment." In *History of Melanesia*, 493–502.

Begay, Agnes R. "Interview with Agnes R. Begay." In Johnson, *Navajos and World War II*, 48–50.

Begay, Keats. "Ex-Prisoner of War—Pacific Theater." In Johnson, *Navajos and World War II*, 11–46.

Belleranti, Shirley W. "Code Talkers." *Westways* 75, no. 5 (1983): 40–42, 76.

Bennett, Judith A. "Malaria, Medicine, and Melanesians: Contested Hybrid Spaces in World War II." *Health and History* 8, no. 1 (2006): 27–55.

Bennett, Mary. "Meskwaki Code Talkers." *Iowa Heritage Illustrated* 84, no. 4 (2003): 154–56.

Benson, Col. P. H.. "Waltzing Matilda and the Powerful Owls." *British Army Review* 38 (August 1971): 62–69.

Berkhofer, Robert F., Jr. "The Political Context of a New Indian History." *Pacific Historical Review* 40, no. 3 (1971): 357–82.

Berndt, Ronald M., and Catherine H. Berndt. *End of an Era: Aboriginal Labour in the Northern Territory*. Canberra: Australian Institute of Aboriginal Studies, 1987.

Bernstein, Alison R. *American Indians and World War II: Toward a New Era in Indian Affairs*. Norman: University of Oklahoma Press, 1991.

Beros, Sapper Bert. *The Fuzzy Wuzzy Angels and Other Verses . . .* Sydney: F. H. Johnston Publishing Company, 1943.

Bixler, Margaret T. *Winds of Freedom: The Story of the Navajo Code Talkers of World War II*. Darien CT: Two Bytes Publishing Company, 1992.

Booth, George. *33 Days*. Elwood VIC: Greenhouse Publications, 1988.

Britten, Thomas A. *American Indians in World War I: At Home and at War*. Albuquerque: University of New Mexico Press, 1997.

Brock, Peggy. *Outback Ghettos: A History of Aboriginal Institutionalisation and Survival*. Cambridge: Cambridge University Press, 1993.

Brokaw, Tom. *The Greatest Generation*. New York: Random House, 1998.

Brown, Cozy Stanley. "Code Talker—Pacific Theater." In Johnson, *Navajos and World War II*, 51–63.

Brown, John. "Coastwatchers on New Britain Provided Intelligence and Helped to Keep the Japanese Bottled up at Rabaul." *World War II* 18, no. 1 (1998): 8–9. Available as electronic document from Academic Search Premier.

Brune, Peter. *The Spell Broken: Exploding the Myth of Japanese Invincibility*. St. Leonards NSW: Allen and Unwin, 1997.

Burt, Larry W. "Roots of the Native American Urban Experience: Relocation Policy in the 1950s." *American Indian Quarterly* 10, no. 2 (1986): 85–99.

Bush, George W. "Remarks by the President in a Ceremony Honoring the Navajo Code Talkers." 26 July 2001. White House. Available at http://www.white house.gov/news/releases/2001/07/20010726-5.html.

Byrnes, G. M. *Green Shadows: A War History of the Papuan Infantry Battalion, 1 New Guinea Infantry Battalion, 2 New Guinea Infantry Battalion, 3 New Guinea Infantry Battalion*. Newmarket QLD: G. M. Byrnes, 1989.

Carroll, Al. *Medicine Bags and Dog Tags: American Indian Veterans from Colonial Times to the Second Iraq War*. Lincoln: University of Nebraska Press, 2008.

Chee, Peggy Jane. "Women's Army Corps—in United States." In Johnson, *Navajos and World War II*, 51–63.

Christie, Michael, Steve Fox, and Ṉawuŋgurr Yunupiŋu. Foreword to *N.T.S.R.U. 1941–1943: Northern Territory Special Reconnaissance Unit*, by Donald Thomson. Yirrkala NT: Yirrkala Literature Production Centre, 1992.

Clark, Jeffrey. *Steel to Stone: A Chronicle of Colonialism in the Southern Highlands of Papua New Guinea*. Oxford: Oxford University Press, 2000.

Clay, Brenda Johnson. *Unstable Images: Colonial Discourse on New Ireland, Papua New Guinea, 1875–1935*. Honolulu: University of Hawai'i Press, 2005.

Coady, C. F. "The P.I.R.—A Proud Tradition." *Australian External Territories* 6 (October 1966): 29–34.

Cole, Keith. *From Mission to Church: The CMS Mission to the Aborigines of Arnhem Land 1908–1985*. Bendigo VIC: Keith Cole Publications, 1985.

Counts, David. "Shadows of War: Changing Remembrance through Twenty Years in New Britain." In White and Lindstrom, *Pacific Theater*, 187–203.

Crofton, D. C. *Fire over the Islands: The Coast Watchers of the Solomons*. Sydney: Reed, 1970.

Crook, Brig. Gen. George H. "The Apache Problem." *Journal of the Military Service Institution of the United States* 8 (1886): 257–69.

Curtain, Richard. "Labour Migration from the Sepik." *Oral History* 6, no. 9 (1978): 60–63.

Cushing, H. C. "Military Colonization of the Indians." *United Service* 3 (September 1880): 370–75.

Dewar, Mickey. *The "Black War" in Arnhem Land: Missionaries and the Yolngu 1908–1940*. Darwin: Australia National University, North Australia Research Unit, 1992.

Dhakiyarr vs. the King. Produced by Graeme Isaac. Directed by Tom Murray and Allan Collins. 53 minutes. Film Australia, 2003. Videocassette.

"Discover Navajo." The Official Tourist Website of the Navajo Nation. Available at http://discovernavajo.com/.

Donaldson, Tamsin. "Translating Oral Literature: Aboriginal Song Texts." *Aboriginal History* 3, part 1 (1979): 62–83.

Downs, Ian. *The Australian Trusteeship: Papua New Guinea 1945–75*. Canberra: Australian Government Publishing Service, 1980.

———. *The New Guinea Volunteer Rifles NGVR 1939–1943 A History*. Broadbeach Waters QLD: Pacific Press, 1999.

Durrett, Deanne. *Unsung Heroes of World War II: The Story of the Navajo Code Talkers*. New York: Facts on File, 1998.

Dyer, Alfred J. *Unarmed Combat: An Australian Missionary Adventure*. Sydney: Edgar Bragg and Sons Pty. Ltd. Printers, 1954.

Edmonds, Penelope. "Dual Mandate, Double Work: Land, Labour and the Transformation of Native Subjectivity in Papua, 1908–1940." In *Collisions of Cultures and Identities: Settlers and Indigenous Peoples*, ed. Patricia Grimshaw and Russell McGregor, 123–41. Carlton VIC: University of Melbourne, Department of History, 2006.

Egan, Ted. *Justice All Their Own: The Caledon Bay and Woodah Island Killings 1932–1933*. Melbourne: Melbourne University Press, 1996.

Elder, Peter. "'The Inner Logic of Dispossession': Land Acquisition in the Northern Territory and Papua." *Journal of Northern Territory History* 11 (2000): 37–56.

Ellemor, Rev. A. F. *Warrawi Jubilee 1916–1966: An Account of the Establishment and Development of the Methodist Missions in Arnhem Land, Especially GOULBURN ISLAND.* Darwin: North Australia District of Overseas Missions, 1966.

Enloe, Cynthia H. *Ethnic Soldiers: State Security in Divided Societies.* Athens: University of Georgia Press, 1980.

———. *Police, Military and Ethnicity: Foundations of State Power.* New Brunswick NJ: Transaction Books, 1980.

Escue, Lynn. "Coded Contributions: Navajo Talkers and the Pacific War." *History Today* 41 (July 1991): 13–20.

Evans, Ted. "Arnhem Land: A Personal History." Talk delivered at the State Reference Library of the Northern Territory, Darwin, 29 April 1987. Darwin: Northern Territory Library Service, 1990.

Ewers, Maj. E. P. "The Military Service of Indians." *Journal of the Military Service Institution of the United States* 15 (November 1894): 1188–92.

Falgout, Suzanne, Lin Poyer, and Laurence M. Carucci. *Memories of War: Micronesians in the Pacific War.* Honolulu: University of Hawai'i Press, 2008.

Fanon, Frantz. *The Wretched of the Earth.* Trans. Constance Farrington. New York: Grove Press, 1963.

Feldt, Eric. *The Coast Watchers.* Oxford: Oxford University Press, 1946. Reprint, Ringwood VIC: Penguin Books, 1991.

Fitzpatrick, Peter. *Law and State in Papua New Guinea.* London: Academic Press, 1980.

Fixico, Donald L. "Ethics and Responsibilities in Writing American Indian History." *American Indian Quarterly* 20, no. 1, special issue, *Writing about (Writing about) American Indians* (1996): 29–39.

———. *Termination and Relocation: Federal Indian Policy, 1945–1960.* Albuquerque: University of New Mexico Press, 1986.

Fowler, Donald H. *Guns or God: The Story of the Caledon Bay Peace Expedition 1933–34.* Brighton VIC: Donald Fowler, 1985.

Franco, Jeré Bishop. *Crossing the Pond: The Native American Effort in World War II.* Denton: University of North Texas Press, 1999.

———. "Empowering the World War II Native American Veteran: Postwar Civil Rights." *Wicazo Sa Review* 9, no. 1 (1993): 32–37.

———. "Loyal and Heroic Service: The Navajos and World War II." *Journal of Arizona History* 27, no. 1 (1986): 391–406.

Frank, Benis M. Introduction to *Warriors: Navajo Code Talkers,* by Kenji Kawano. Flagstaff AZ: Northland Publishing Company, 1990.

Fraser, Nancy. "From Redistribution to Recognition? Dilemmas of Justice in a 'Post-Socialist' Age." *New Left Review* 212 (July–August 1995): 68–93.

Gammage, Bill. "Police and Power in the Pre-War Papua New Guinea Highlands." *Journal of Pacific History* 31, no. 2 (1996): 163–77.

Gaynor, Nicholas. "To Be Colonised or a Coloniser? Dilemmas of Security and Race in Australia's Post World War Two Planning, 1943–1947." Thesis for Master of Arts in History, University of Melbourne, 2006.

Gilbert, Ed. *Native American Code Talker in World War II*. Oxford and New York: Osprey Publishing, 2008.

Goodall, Heather. "Too Early Yet or Not Soon Enough? Reflections on Sharing Histories as Process." *Australian Historical Studies* 118 (2002): 7–24.

Granter, Maj. N. E. W. Granter, comp. and ed. *Yesterday and Today: An Illustrated History of the Pacific Islands Regiment from Its Formation on 19th June, 1940 until the Present Day*. Port Moresby: South Pacific Post Pty., 1970.

Gray, Gen. A. M., Commandant of the United States Marine Corps. "CMC's Address at the Opening of the Phoenix Plaza Honoring the Marine Corps' Navajo Code Talkers in Phoenix, Arizona, 02 March 1989." Available from United States Marine Corps Collection on Navajo Code Talkers. Available from the Navajo Nation Museum.

Gray, Geoffrey. "The Army Requires Anthropologists: Australian Anthropologists at War, 1939–1946." *Australian Historical Studies* no. 127 (April 2006): 156–80.

———. *A Cautious Silence: The Politics of Australian Anthropology*. Canberra: Aboriginal Studies Press, 2007.

———. "'A chance to be of some use to my country': Stanner during World War II." In *An Appreciation of Difference: W. E. H. Stanner and Aboriginal Australia*, ed. Melinda Hinkson and Jeremy Beckett, 27–43. Canberra: Aboriginal Studies Press, 2008.

———. "'I was not consulted': A. P. Elkin, Papua New Guinea and the Politics of Anthropology, 1942–1950." *Australian Journal of Politics and History* 40, no. 2 (1994): 195–213.

———. "'The next focus of power to fall under the spell of this little gang': Anthropology and Australia's Postwar Policy in Papua New Guinea." *War and Society* 14, no. 2 (1996): 101–17.

———. "The Passing of the Papua–New Guinea Provisional Administration Bill 1945." In Nelson, Lutton, and Robertson, *Select Topics*, 37–42.

———. "Stanner's War: W. E. H. Stanner, the Pacific War, and Its Aftermath." *Journal of Pacific History* 41, no. 2 (2006): 145–63.

Hale, Duane K. "Forgotten Heroes: American Indians in World War I." *Four Winds* 3, no. 2, issue 10 (1982): 39–41.

Hall, Basil. "The Murray System and the War." *Australian Quarterly* 18, no. 2 (1946): 63–71.

Hall, Robert. "The Army and Aborigines during World War II." Thesis for Master of Arts in History, Australian National University, 1978.

Hall, Robert A. *The Black Diggers: Aborigines and Torres Strait Islanders in the Second World War*. 2nd ed. Canberra: Aboriginal Studies Press, 1997.

Hall, Victor C. *Dreamtime Justice*. Adelaide: Rigby Limited, 1962.

Ham, Paul. *Kokoda*. Sydney: HarperCollins, 2004.

Hamilton, Paula. "Are Oral Historians Losing the Plot?" *Journal of the Oral History Association of Australia* 18 (1996): 44–46.

Harris, John. *One Blood: 200 Years of Aboriginal Encounter with Christianity: A Story of Hope*. Sutherland NSW: Albatross Books Pty., 1990.

Hasluck, Paul. *Native Welfare in Australia: Speeches and Addresses by the Hon. Paul Hasluck, M.P., Minister for Territories*. Perth: Paterson Brokensha Pty., 1953.

———. *Shades of Darkness: Aboriginal Affairs, 1925–1965*. Carlton VIC: Melbourne University Press, 1988.

———. *A Time for Building: Australian Administration in Papua and New Guinea 1951–1963*. Melbourne: Melbourne University Press, 1976.

Henige, David. *Oral Historiography*. London: Longman, 1982.

Hercus, Luise, and Peter Suggon, eds. *This Is What Happened: Historical Narratives by Aborigines*. Canberra: Australian Institute of Aboriginal Studies, 1986.

The History of Melanesia: Papers Delivered Jointly by the University of Papua and New Guinea, the Australian National University, the Administrative College of Papua and New Guinea, and the Council of New Guinea Affairs, and Held at Port Moresby from 30 May to 5 June 1968. Canberra and Port Moresby: The Australia National University and The University of Papua and New Guinea, 1969.

Hobson, J. A. *Imperialism: A Study*. 1902. 2nd ed., 1905. 3rd ed., entirely revised and reset, 1938. Reprint, London: Unwin Hyman, 1988.

Hodge, Bob, and Vijay Mishra. *Dark Side of the Dream: Australian Literature and the Postcolonial Mind*. Sydney: Allen and Unwin, 1991.

Hogarth, Christine. "Donald Thomson in Irian Jaya." Thesis for Graduate Diploma in Material Culture, James Cook University, 1984.

Holm, Tom. "Fighting a White Man's War: The Extent and Legacy of American Indian Participation in World War II." *Journal of Ethnic Studies* 9, no. 2 (1981): 69–81. Reprinted in *The Plains Indians of the Twentieth Century*, ed. Peter Iverson, 149–68. Norman: University of Oklahoma Press, 1985.

———. "Patriots and Pawns: State Use of American Indians in the Military and the Process of Nativization in the United States." In Jaimes, *State of Native America*, 345–70.

———. "Stereotypes, State Elites, and the Military Use of American Indian Troops." *Plural Societies* 15, no. 3 (1984): 265–282.

———. "Strong Hearts: Native Service in the U.S. Armed Forces." In Lackenbauer, Sheffield, and Mantle, *Aboriginal Peoples and Military Participation*, 127–51.

———. *Strong Hearts Wounded Souls: Native American Veterans of the Vietnam War*. Austin: University of Texas Press, 1996.

Hooper, Alan E. *Love War and Letters: PNG 1940–45*. Coorparoo DC, QLD: Robert Brown and Associates, 1994.

Hudson, W. J., ed. *Australia and Papua New Guinea*. Sydney: Sydney University Press, 1971.

Huggins, Jackie. *Sister Girl: The Writings of an Aboriginal Activist and Historian*. St. Lucia: University of Queensland Press, 1998.

Inglis, Amirah. *"Not a White Woman Safe": Sexual Anxiety and Politics in Port Moresby 1920–1934*. Canberra: Australian National University Press, 1974.

Inglis, K. S. *Sacred Places: War Memorials in the Australian Landscape*. Melbourne: The Miegunyah Press, 1998.

Iverson, Peter. *Diné: A History of the Navajos*. Albuquerque: University of New Mexico Press, 2002.

Iwamoto, Hiromitsu. "Japanese and New Guinean Memories of Wartime Rabaul 1942–1946." In Toyoda and Nelson, *Pacific War in Papua New Guinea*, 77–98.

———. "The Japanese Occupation of Rabaul, 1942–1945." In Toyoda and Nelson, *Pacific War in Papua New Guinea*, 252–77.

———. "Memories and Realities of Japanese Occupation of Mainland New Guinea." In Toyoda and Nelson, *Pacific War in Papua New Guinea*, 278–96.

Jackman, Harry H. "Brothers in Arms." *Quadrant* 24 (August 1980): 71–73.

———. "Papua New Guinea in the Defence of Australia." *Journal of the Royal United Services Institute of Australia* 6, no. 1 (1983): 32–36.

Jacobs, Wilbur R. "The Indian and the Frontier in American History: A Need for Revision." *Western Historical Quarterly* 4, no. 1 (1973): 43–56.

Jaimes, M. Annette, ed. *The State of Native America: Genocide, Colonization, and Resistance*. Boston: South End Press, 1992.

Jevec, Adam. "Semper Fidelis, Code Talkers." *Prologue: Quarterly of the National Archives and Records Administration* 33, no. 4 (2001): 270–77.

Jevec, Adam, and Lee Ann Potter. "The Navajo Code Talkers." *Social Education* 65, no. 5 (2001): 262. Available from Expanded Academic ASAP Plus as electronic document.

Johnson, Broderick H., ed. *Navajos and World War II*. Tsaile, Navajo Nation, AZ: Navajo Community College Press, 1977.

Johnson, Troy R. *The Occupation of Alcatraz Island: Indian Self-Determination and the Rise of Indian Activism*. Urbana: University of Illinois Press, 1996.

Johnson, Troy, Joane Nagel, and Duane Champagne, eds. *American Indian Activism: Alcatraz to the Longest Walk*. Urbana: University of Illinois Press, 1997.

Johnston, George H. *New Guinea Diary*. Sydney: Angus and Robertson, 1943.

Johnston, Philip. "Indian Jargon Won Our Battles." *Masterkey for Indian Lore and History* 38, no. 4 (1964): 130–37.

———. "Marine Corps Hymn in Navaho." *Masterkey for Indian Lore and History* 19, no. 5 (1945): 153–55.

Jones, Renee. "Comanche Codetalking on D-Day." Available at http://www.signal .army.mil/ocos/ac/WWII/CODETALK.asp.

Josephy, Alvin M., Jr., Joane Nagel, and Troy Johnson, eds. *Red Power: The American Indians' Fight for Freedom*. 2nd ed. Lincoln: University of Nebraska Press, 1999.

Joyce, R. B. "Australian Interests in New Guinea Before 1906." In Hudson, *Australia and Papua New Guinea*, 8–31.

Kadiba, John. "Papua New Guinea and the War: A Catalyst for Change." *Journal of Northern Territory History* 6 (1995): 1–14.

Kais, K. "Discontent among Indigenous Soldiers." *Oral History* 1, no. 6 (1974): 24–31.

Ka-wayawayama: Aeroplane Dance. Produced and directed by Trevor Graham. 58 minutes. Film Australia, 1994. DVD.

Kawano, Kenji. *Warriors: Navajo Code Talkers*. Flagstaff AZ: Northland Publishing Company, 1990.

Keene, Jennifer. *World War I: The American Soldier Experience*. Lincoln: University of Nebraska Press, 2011.

Kituai, August. "Innovation and Intrusion: Villagers and Policemen in Papua New Guinea." *Journal of Pacific History* 23, no. 2 (1988): 156–66.

———. "The Involvement of Papua New Guinea Policemen in the Pacific War." In Toyoda and Nelson, *Pacific War in Papua New Guinea*, 186–208.

———. *My Gun, My Brother: The World of the Papua New Guinea Colonial Police, 1920–1960*. Honolulu: University of Hawai'i Press, 1998.

Krebs, Ronald R. *Fighting for Rights: Military Service and the Politics of Citizenship*. Ithaca NY: Cornell University Press, 2006.

Krouse, Susan Applegate. *North American Indians in the Great War*. Lincoln: University of Nebraska Press, 2007.

Lackenbauer, P. Whitney, R. Scott Sheffield, and Craig Leslie Mantle, eds. *Aboriginal Peoples and Military Participation: Canadian & International Perspectives*. Kingston ON: Canadian Defence Academy Press, 2007.

La Farge, Oliver. "Termination of Federal Supervision: Disintegration and the American Indians." *Annals of the American Academy of Political and Social Science* 311, *American Indians and American Life* (May 1957): 41–46.

Lamilami, Rev. Lazarus. *Lamilami Speaks: The Cry Went Up: A Story of the People of Goulburn Islands, North Australia*. Sydney: Ure Smith, 1974.

Leadley, Allan. "The Japanese on the Gazelle." *Oral History* 3, no. 3 (1975): 48.

Legge, J. D. "The Murray Period: Papua 1906–40." In Hudson, *Australia and Papua New Guinea*, 32–56.

Lewis, D. C. *The Plantation Dream: Developing British New Guinea and Papua 1884–1942*. Canberra: Journal of Pacific History, 1996.

Lynch, P. R. "The Coming Army; 'Loyalty, Stability, Discipline.'" *New Guinea and Australia, the Pacific and South-east Asia* 4 (March–April 1969): 21–25.

MacDonald, Peter, with Ted Schwarz. *The Last Warrior: Peter MacDonald and the Navajo Nation*. New York: Orion Books, 1993.

MacGregor, Sir William. Introduction to *Papua or British New Guinea*, by John Hubert Plunkett Murray, 21–28. London: T. Fisher Unwin, 1912.

Mack, Stephen, ed. *It Had to Be Done: The Navajo Code Talkers Remember World War II*. Cortaro AZ: Whispering Dove Design, 2008.

Maddock, Kenneth. "Myth, History and a Sense of Oneself." In *Past and Present: The Construction of Aboriginality*, ed. Jeremy R. Beckett, 11–30. Canberra: Aboriginal Studies Press, 1988.

Mair, L. P. *Australia in New Guinea*. 2nd ed. Melbourne: Melbourne University Press, 1970.

Marika, Wandjuk, as told to Jennifer Isaacs. *Wandjuk Marika: Life Story*. St. Lucia: University of Queensland Press, 1995.

Marre, Adam. "A Historian's Lot — The Difficulty of Giving WWI New Guinean Servicemen a Voice?" In *Proceedings Social Change in the 21st Century Conference 2006*, ed. C. Hopkinson and C. Hall, 1–9. Carseldine: Queensland University of Technology, 2006.

Maynard, John. "Circles in the Sand: An Indigenous Framework of Historical Practice." *Australian Journal of Indigenous Education* 36s (2007): 117–20.

McAree, Dee. "Navajo Code Talker's Long Fight for Recognition." *National Law Journal* 26, no. 26 (2004). Available as an electronic document from Expanded Academic ASAP Plus.

McCoy, Ron. "Navajo Code Talkers of World War II: Indian Marines Befuddled the Enemy." *American West: The Land and Its People* 18, no. 6 (1981): 67–75.

McGrath, Ann. "A National Story." In *Contested Ground: Australian Aborigines under the British Crown*, ed. Ann McGrath, 1–54. St. Leonards NSW: Allen and Unwin, 1995.

McIntosh, Ian. *The Whale and the Cross: Conversations with David Burrumurra M.B.E.* Darwin: Historical Society of the Northern Territory, 1994.

McKenzie, Maisie. *Mission to Arnhem Land*. Adelaide: Rigby Limited, 1976.

McMillan, Andrew. *Catalina Dreaming*. Sydney: Duffy and Snellgrove, 2002.

Meadows, William C. *The Comanche Code Talkers of World War II*. Austin: University of Texas Press, 2002.

———. *Kiowa, Apache, and Comanche Military Societies: Enduring Veterans, 1800 to the Present*. Austin: University of Texas Press, 1999.

———. "North American Indian Code Talkers: Current Developments and Research." In Lackenbauer, Sheffield, and Mantle, *Aboriginal Peoples and Military Participation*, 161–213.

Mench, Paul. *The Role of the Papua New Guinea Defence Force*. Development Studies Centre Monograph, no. 2. Canberra: The Australian National University, 1975.

Modjeska, Drusilla. "The Wartime Experience of Mr Asi Arere, A Papuan from Porebada Village." In Nelson, Lutton, and Robertson, *Select Topics*, 14–23.

Monsell-Davis, Michael. "Roro and Mekeo Labour for Government Work: Papua New Guinea." In Moore, Leckie, and Munro, *Labour in the South Pacific*, 186–88.

Moore, Clive. "Workers in Colonial Papua New Guinea: 1884–1975." In Moore, Leckie, and Munro, *Labour in the South Pacific*, 30–46.

Moore, Clive, Jacqueline Leckie, and Doug Munro, eds. *Labour in the South Pacific*. Townsville: James Cook University of North Queensland, 1990.

Morningstorm, J. Boyd. *The American Indian Warrior Today: Native Americans in Modern U.S. Warfare*. Manhattan KS: Sunflower University Press, 2004.

Mudrooroo. *Us Mob: History, Culture, Struggle: An Introduction to Indigenous Australia*. Sydney: Angus and Robertson, 1995.

Murphy, John. *Imagining the Fifties: Private Sentiment and Public Culture in Menzies' Australia*. Sydney: University of New South Wales Press, 2000.

Murray, John Hubert Plunkett. *Papua or British New Guinea*. London: T. Fisher Unwin, 1912.

Murray, M. *Hunted: A Coastwatcher's Story*. Adelaide: Rigby Limited, 1967.

Nagel, Joane. *American Indian Ethnic Renewal: Red Power and the Resurgence of Identity and Culture*. New York: Oxford University Press, 1996.

Nakata, Martin. *Disciplining the Savages, Savaging the Disciplines*. Canberra: Aboriginal Studies Press, 2007.

Nelson, Hank. "As Bilong Soldia: The Raising of the Papuan Infantry Battalion in 1940." *Yagl-Ambu* 7, no. 1 (1980): 19–27.

———. "The Enemy at the Door: Australia and New Guinea in World War II." In Toyoda and Nelson, *Pacific War in Papua New Guinea*, 124–43.

———. "From Kanaka to Fuzzy Wuzzy Angel: Race and Labour Relations in Australian New Guinea." *Labour History* 35 (1978): 172–88. Journal also published as *Who Are Our Enemies? Racism and the Australian Working Class*, ed. Ann Curthoys and Andrew Markus. Neutral Bay NSW: Hale and Iremonger, 1978.

———. "Looking Black: Australian Images of Melanesians." In Toyoda and Nelson, *Pacific War in Papua New Guinea*, 144–58.

———. "More Than a Change of Uniform: Australian Military Rule in Papua New Guinea, 1942–1946." In Toyoda and Nelson, *Pacific War in Papua New Guinea*, 232–51.

———. "Payback: Australian Compensation to Wartime Papua New Guinea." In Toyoda and Nelson, *Pacific War in Papua New Guinea*, 320–48.

———. *Taim Bilong Masta: The Australian Involvement with Papua New Guinea*. Sydney: Australian Broadcasting Commission, 1982.

———, ed. *The War Diaries of Eddie Allan Stanton: Papua 1942–45; New Guinea 1945–46*. St. Leonards NSW: Allen and Unwin, 1996.

Nelson, Hank [H. N.], N. Lutton, and S. Robertson, eds. *Select Topics in the History of Papua and New Guinea*. Port Moresby: University of Papua and New Guinea, 1973.

Nelson, W. "The P.I.R.—A Proud Tradition: Papua and New Guinea Soldiers." *Reveille* 42, no. 7 (1969): 9, 33.

Neumann, Klaus. "A Postcolonial Writing of Aboriginal History." *Meanjin* 51, no. 2 (1992): 277–99.

Newton, Janice. "Angels, Heroes and Traitors: Images of Some Papuans in the Second World War." *Research in Melanesia* 20 (1996): 141–56.

No Bugles, No Drums. Produced by Debra Beattie-Burnett. Directed by John Burnett. 49 minutes. Seven Emus Productions, in association with Australian Television Network, 1990. Videocassette.

Northern Land Council. DVD provided courtesy of filmmaker Nick Brenner. Date unknown, late 1990s.

O'Brien, Patricia. "Remaking Australia's Colonial Culture? White Australia and its Papuan Frontier 1901–1940." *Australian Historical Studies* 40, no. 1 (2009): 96–112.

Official Handbook of the Territory of New Guinea Administered by the Commonwealth of Australia under Mandate from the Council of the League of Nations. Compiled under the authority of the Prime Minister of the Commonwealth. Canberra: L. F. Johnston, Commonwealth Government Printer, 1937, 1943.

Official Website of the Twenty-second Navajo Nation Council. Available at http://www.navajonationcouncil.org.

Oliver, Pam. *Empty North: The Japanese Presence and Australian Reactions 1860s to 1942.* Darwin: Charles Darwin University Press, 2006.

———. *Raids on Australia: 1942 and Japan's Plans for Australia.* Melbourne: Australian Scholarly Publishing, 2010.

Our Fathers, Our Grandfathers, Our Heroes . . . : The Navajo Code Talkers of World War II: A Photographic Exhibit. Gallup NM: Circle of Light Navajo Educational Project, 2004.

Parry, Suzanne, and Tony Austin. "Introduction: Making Connections or Causing Disconnections." In Austin and Parry, *Connection and Disconnection* 1–26.

Paul, Doris A. *The Navajo Code Talkers.* Philadelphia: Dorrance and Company, 1973.

Philp, Kenneth R. "From New Deal to Termination: Liberalism and Indian Policy, 1933–1953." *Pacific Historical Review* 46, no. 4 (1977): 543–66.

———. "Stride toward Freedom: The Relocation of Indians to Cities, 1952–1960." *Western Historical Quarterly* 16, no. 2 (1985): 175–90.

———. "Termination: A Legacy of the Indian New Deal." *Western Historical Quarterly* 14, no. 2 (1983): 165–80.

Pilger, Alison. "Courage, Endurance and Initiative: Medical Evacuation from the Kokoda Track, August–October 1942." *War and Society* 11, no. 1 (1993): 53–72.

Powell, Alan. *The Shadow's Edge: Australia's Northern War.* 2nd ed. Melbourne: Melbourne University Press, 1992.

———. *The Third Force: ANGAU's New Guinea War, 1942–46.* Oxford: Oxford University Press, 2003.

Powell, William H. "The Indian as a Soldier." *United Service* (March 1890): 229–38.

Power, Col. Allan W. "A Review of the Post-War Years 1945–1947." In *Green Shadows: A War History of the Papuan Infantry Battalion, 1 New Guinea Infantry Battalion, 2 New Guinea Infantry Battalion, 3 New Guinea Infantry Battalion,* by G. M. Byrnes, 187–98. Newmarket QLD: G. M. Byrnes, 1989.

Pye, John. *The Tiwi Islands.* Darwin: J. R. Coleman Pty., 1977.

Radi, Heather. "New Guinea under Mandate 1921–41." In Hudson, *Australia and Papua New Guinea*, 74–137.

Raines, Rebecca C. "Book Review: *The Comanche Code Talkers of World War II*. By William C. Meadows." *Journal of Military History* 68, no. 1 (2004): 289–91.

Randall, Bob. *Songman: The Story of an Aboriginal Elder of Uluru*. Sydney: ABC Books, 2003.

Read, Peter, and Jay Read, eds. and comps. *Long Time, Olden Time: Aboriginal Accounts of Northern Territory History*. Alice Springs: Institute for Aboriginal Development Publications, 1991.

Reagan, Ronald. "Proclamation 4954." 28 July 1982. Ronald Reagan Presidential Library Archives. Available at http://www.reagan.utexas.edu/archives/speeches/1982/72882c.htm.

Reed, Liz. "'Part of Our Own Story': Representations of Indigenous Australians and Papua New Guineans within *Australia Remembers 1945–1995*—the Continuing Desire for a Homogeneous National Identity." *Oceania* 69, no. 3 (1999): 157–70.

Remembering the War in New Guinea. Available at http://ajrp.awm.gov.au/ajrp/remember.nsf/pages/NT000020F6.

Riseman, Noah. "Australian (Mis)treatment of Indigenous Labour in World War II Papua and New Guinea." *Labour History* 98 (May 2010): 163–82.

———. "Black Skins, Black Work: Race and Labour in World War II Papua and New Guinea." In *Labour History in the New Century*, ed. Bobbie Oliver, 63–75. Perth: Black Swan Press, 2009.

———. "Contesting White Knowledge: Yolngu Stories from World War II." *Oral History Review* 37, no. 2 (2010): 170–90.

———. "Defending Whose Country? Yolngu and the NTSRU in the Second World War." *Limina: A Journal of Historical and Cultural Studies* 13 (2007): 80–91.

———. "Disrupting Assimilation: Soldiers, Missionaries, and Yolngu in Arnhem Land during World War II." *Melbourne Historical Journal* 35 (2007): 73–89. Republished in *Evangelists of Empire? Missionaries in Colonial History*, ed. Amanda Barry, Joanna Cruickshank, Patricia Grimshaw, and Andrew Brown-May, 245–62. Melbourne: Melbourne E-Scholarly Press, 2008.

———. "Exploited Soldiers: Navajo and Yolngu Units in the Second World War." *Journal of Northern Territory History* 19 (2008): 60–81.

———. "Forgetting and (Re)membering Indigenous Soldiers: Yolngu and Navajo Veterans of World War II." In *When the Soldiers Return: November 2007 Conference Proceedings*, ed. Martin Crotty and Craig Barrett, 41–53. Melbourne: RMIT Publishing in association with the School of History, Philosophy, Religion and Classics, University of Queensland, 2009.

———. "'Japan fight. Aboriginal people fight. European people fight': Yolngu Stories from World War II." *Australian Journal of Indigenous Education* 37S (2008): 65–72.

———. "Preserving a White Military: The Australian Armed Forces and Indigenous People in World War II." In *Historicising Whiteness: Transnational Per-spectives on the Construction of an Identity*, ed. Leigh Boucher, Jane Carey, and Katherine Ellinghaus, 133–42. Melbourne: RMIT Publishing in association with the School of Historical Studies, University of Melbourne, 2007.

———. "'Regardless of History'? Reassessing the Navajo Codetalkers of World War II." *Australasian Journal of American Studies* 26, no. 2 (2007): 48–73.

Robbins, Rebecca L. "Self-Determination and Subordination: The Past, Present, and Future of American Indian Governance." In Jaimes, *State of Native Amer-ica*, 87–121.

Robinson, Neville K. *Villagers at War: Some Papua New Guinean Experiences in World War II*. Canberra: The Australian National University, 1979.

Roe, Margriet. "Papua-New Guinea and War 1941–5." In Hudson, *Australia and Papua New Guinea*, 138–50.

Rose, Deborah Bird. *Hidden Histories: Black Stories from Victoria River Downs, Humbert River and Wave Hill Stations*. Canberra: Aboriginal Studies Press, 1991.

Rowley, C. D. "The Occupation of German New Guinea 1914–21." In Hudson, *Aus-tralia and Papua New Guinea*, 57–73.

Ryan, Peter. "The Australian New Guinea Administrative Unit (ANGAU)." In *His-tory of Melanesia*, 531–48.

———. *Fear Drive My Feet*. Sydney: Angus and Robertson, 1959.

———. "Some Unfinished Business from the Second World War." *Quadrant* 39, no. 9 (1995): 9–18.

Saunders, Kay. "Inequalities of Sacrifice: Aboriginal and Torres Strait Islander La-bour in Northern Australia during the Second World War." *Labour History*, no. 69 (November 1995): 131–48. Republished in *Aboriginal Workers*, ed. Ann McGrath and Kay Saunders, with Jackie Huggins. Sydney: Australian Society for the Study of Labour History, 1995.

Scheps, Leo. "Chimbu Participation in the Pacific War." *Journal of Pacific History* 30, no. 1 (1995): 76–86.

Sigob, Somu. "The Story of My Life." *Gigibori* 2, no. 1 (1974): 32–36.

Silita, Walingai Patrick B. "Oral Accounts of Second World War Experiences of the People of the Huon Peninsula, Morobe Province, Papua New Guinea." *O'O: A Journal of Solomon Islands Studies* 4 (1988): 63–74.

Sinclair, James. *Papua New Guinea: The First 100 Years*. Bathurst NSW: Robert Brown and Associates, 1985.

———. *To Find a Path: The Life and Times of the Royal Pacific Islands Regiment*. Volume 1, *Yesterday's Heroes 1885–1950*. Comp. and ed. for the Trustees RPIR by Lt. Col. M. B. Pears. Brisbane: Boolarong Publications, 1990.

Skocpol, Theda, and Margaret Somers. "The Uses of Comparative History in Mac-rosocial Inquiry." *Comparative Studies in Society and History* 22, no. 2 (1980): 174–97.

Smith, Hugh. "Minorities and the Australian Army: Overlooked and Underrepresented?" In *A Century of Service: 100 Years of the Australian Army. The 2001 Chief of Army's Military History Conference*, ed. Peter Dennis and Jeffrey Grey, 129–49. Canberra: Army History Unit, Department of Defence, 2001.

Smith, Paul Chaat, and Robert Allen Warrior. *Like a Hurricane: The Indian Movement from Alcatraz to Wounded Knee*. New York: New Press, 1996.

Somare, Michael. *Sana: An Autobiography of Michael Somare*. Port Moresby: Niugini Press Pty., 1975.

Stabler, Hollis. *No One Ever Asked Me: The World War II Memoirs of an Omaha Indian Soldier*. Ed. Victoria Smith. Lincoln: University of Nebraska Press, 2005.

Stanley, Peter. *Invading Australia: Japan and the Battle for Australia, 1942*. Camberwell VIC: Viking, 2008.

Stanner, W. E. H. *The South Seas in Transition: A Study of Post-War Rehabilitation and Reconstruction in Three British Pacific Dependencies*. Sydney: Australasian Publishing Company, 1953.

Stella, Regis Tove. *Imagining the Other: The Representation of the Papua New Guinean Subject*. Honolulu: University of Hawai'i Press, 2007.

Stewart, James H. "The Navajo Indian at War." *Arizona Highways* (June 1943): 20.

Streets, Heather. *Martial Races: The Military, Race and Masculinity in British Imperial Culture, 1857–1914*. Manchester: Manchester University Press, 2004.

Tate, Michael L. "From Scout to Doughboy: The National Debate over Integrating American Indians into the Military, 1891–1918." *Western Historical Quarterly* 17, no. 4 (1986): 417–37.

Tetaga, Jeremiah. "The Wartime Experience of Danks Tomila." *Oral History* no. 4 (1973): 27–28.

They Talked Navajo— "dine hi-zaad choz-iid": The United States Marine Corps Navajo Code Talkers of World War II: A Record of their Reunion, July 9–10, 1971. Window Rock AZ.

Thomson, Alistair. "Anzac Stories: Using Personal Testimony in War History." *War and Society* 25, no. 2 (2006): 1–21.

Thomson, Donald. *Donald Thomson in Arnhem Land*. Comp. and introduced by Nicolas Peterson. 2nd ed. Carlton VIC: Miegunyah Press, 2003.

———. *N.T.S.R.U.: Northern Territory Special Reconnaissance Unit*. Yirrkala NT: Yirrkala Literature Production Centre, 1992.

Thomson of Arnhem Land. Produced by Michael Cummins and John Moore. Directed by John Moore. 56 minutes. Film Australia, in association with John Moore Productions, 2000. Videocassette.

Thornell, Harold, as told to Estelle Thompson. *A Bridge over Time: Living in Arnhemland with the Aborigines 1938–1944*. Melbourne: J. M. Dent Pty,, 1986.

Thune, Carl E. "The Making of History: The Representation of World War II on Normanby Island, Papua New Guinea." In *The Pacific Theater: Island Representations of World War II*, ed. Geoffrey M. White and Lamont Lindstrom, 231–56. Honolulu: University of Hawai'i Press, 1989.

"Tiwi Took Our First Japanese Prisoner." *Land Rights News* 2, no. 7 (1988): 28.

ToKilala, W. "The Valley of the Prison." *Oral History*, no. 5 (May 1974): 1–4

Townsend, Kenneth W. *World War II and the American Indian*. Albuquerque: University of New Mexico Press, 2000.

Toyoda, Yukio, and Hand Nelson, eds. *The Pacific War in Papua New Guinea: Memories and Realities*. Tokyo: Rikkyo University Center for Asian Area Studies, 2006.

Tuhiwai Smith, Linda. *Decolonizing Methodologies: Research and Indigenous Peoples*. Dunedin: University of Otago Press, 1999.

Trudgen, Richard. *Why Warriors Lie Down and Die: Towards an Understanding of Why the Aboriginal People of Arnhem Land Face the Greatest Crisis in Health and Education since European Contact*. Darwin: Aboriginal Resource and Development Services, 2000.

20th Century Warriors: Native American Participation in the United States Military. Washington DC: United States Department of Defense, 1996.

2009–2010 Comprehensive Economic Development Strategy, The Navajo Nation. Window Rock AZ: Division of Economic Development, The Navajo Nation, 2010. Available at http://www.navajobusiness.com/pdf/CEDS/CED_NN_Final _09_10.pdf.

United Nations. "Universal Declaration of Human Rights." 10 December 1948. Available at http://www.un.org/Overview/rights.html.

United States. Congress, House, Departments of Labor, Health and Human Services, and Education, and Related Agencies Appropriations Act, 2001. 106th Cong., 3rd sess., HR 4577. *Congressional Record*, daily ed. (15 December 2000): H12296.

———. 109th Cong., 1st sess., HR 4299, SR 1035.

van den Berghe, Pierre L. *The Ethnic Phenomenon*. New York: Elsevier, 1981.

Vane, Amoury. *North Australia Observer Unit: The History of a Surveillance Regime*. Lotus NSW: Australian Military History Publications, 2000.

———. "The Surveillance of Northern Australia—Its History. The Story of Stanner's Bush Commando 1942." *Defence Force Journal*, no. 14 (January–February 1979): 15–30.

Vansina, Jan. *Oral Tradition as History*. Madison: University of Wisconsin Press, 1985.

Veracini, Lorenzo. "Of a 'contested ground' and an 'indelible stain': A Difficult Reconciliation between Australia and Its Aboriginal History during the 1990s and 2000s." *Aboriginal History* 27 (2003): 224–39.

Vogt, Evon. *Navaho Veterans: A Study of Changing Values*. Cambridge MA: Peabody Museum of Harvard University, 1951.

Waiko, John. "Binandere Forced Labour: Papua New Guinea." In Moore, Leckie, and Munro, *Labour in the South Pacific*, 181–85.

Walker, Richard, and Helen Walker. *Curtin's Cowboys: Australia's Secret Bush Commandos*. Sydney: Allen and Unwin, 1986.

Warner, W. Lloyd. *A Black Civilization: A Social Study of an Australian Tribe*. New

York: Harper and Brothers Publishers, 1937.

Watson, Bruce. "Jaysho, moasi, dibeh, ayeshi, hasclishnih, beshlo, shush, gini. (World War II voice code)." *Smithsonian* 24, no. 5 (1993): 34–43. Available as an electronic document from Expanded Academic ASAP Plus.

Waybenais, Myrtle. "Women's Army Corps—Overseas." In Johnson, *Navajos and World War II,* 129–33.

Wedega, Alice. *Listen, My Country.* Sydney and New York: Pacific Publications, 1981.

White, Geoffrey M., and Lamont Lindstrom, eds. *The Pacific Theater: Island Representations of World War II.* Honolulu: University of Hawai'i Press, 1989.

Whitlam, Gough. "Dragging the Chain 1897–1997." The Second Vincent Lingiari Memorial Lecture. Northern Territory University. 29 August 1997. Available at http://www.austlii.edu.au/cgi-bin/disp.pl/au/other/IndigLRes/car/1997/2908. html?query=%5e+vincent+lingiari+memorial+lecture+gough+whitlam.

Willey, Keith. "The Army Pay Us Nothing." *Bulletin: An Australian Journal of Comment and Opinion,* 24 November 1962, 8–9.

Wilson, Angela Cavender. "Power of the Spoken Word: Native Oral Traditions in American Indian History." In *Rethinking American Indian History,* ed. Donald L. Fixico, 101–16. Albuquerque: University of New Mexico Press, 1997.

Wolfers, Edward P. *Race Relations and Colonial Rule in Papua New Guinea.* Sydney: Australia and New Zealand Book Company, 1975.

Woodley, Brian. "Local Heroes." *Australian Magazine,* 8–9 June 1996, 34–39.

Wright, Huntley. "Protecting the National Interest: The Labor Government and the Reform of Australia's Colonial Policy, 1942–45." *Labour History,* no. 82 (May 2002): 65–79.

Wright, Malcolm. *If I Die: Coastwatching and Guerrilla Warfare behind Japanese Lines.* Melbourne: Lansdowne Press Pty., 1965.

Young, Warren L. *Minorities and the Military: A Cross-National Study in World Perspective.* Westport CT: Greenwood Press, 1982.

Zelenietz, Marty, and Hisafumi Saito. "The Kilenge and the War: An Observer Effect on Stories from the Past." In White and Lindstrom, *Pacific Theater: Island Representations of World War II,* 167–84.

INDEX

Owen Stanley Range, 102, 132

Ryan, Peter, 107, 108, 111, 167

Saipan, 202
Salamaua, 115, 153
Salate, 116
Sanford, Clarence, 84–85
Scott, W. J. R., 39–41, 42–43
segregation: American military, 25; Papua and
    New Guinea, 104, 164, 225; of white troops and
    Aboriginal people, 12; of white troops in Papua
    and New Guinea, 123–24
selective service. *See* conscription
self-determination, 228; and John Collier, 24;
    Native American, 212–13
Sepik, 107, 112
sexual relations: in Australia, 94–95; in Papua and
    New Guinea, 129–30
Shigeru, Mizuki, 113–14
Siassi Islands, 143
Sigob, Somu, 126, 127, 152–53
Silk, George, 137
Singapore, 45
Sioux, 176
Smith, Samuel J., Jr., 195
soldier settlement, 166
soldier-warrior colonialism. *See* colonialism
Solomon Islanders: as crew for *Aroetta*, 42–44
Solomon Islands, 39, 140
Somare, Michael, 113, 167
Somerville, Margaret, 67
Sono, 146
sovereignty: conflicting Yolngu-Australian
    perspectives on, 9–10
Spencer, Chee Dah, 173
Spencer, W. Baldwin, 8
Stanner, W. E. H.: and Aboriginal wartime
    employment, 53–54, 226; as commander of NAOU,
    52–54; and Papua and New Guinea, 124
Stanton, Eddie Allan, 129–30
stereotypes, 30; Native American, 25–26, 169, 174,
    184–86, 216, 223, 228; Yolngu, 85, 87. *See also* chiefs;
    constructs of indigeneity; "martial race"
Sweeney, Gordon, 74

Takankan, Joseph, 109
Talasea, 143
Tamura, Yoshizaku, 111
Tau, Rarua, 120
Taylor, Jim, 162
Taylor, Len, 94
termination, 198, 211–12, 229. *See also* relocation

Thompson, Clare, 209
Thomson, Donald, 9, 108, 226; Arnhem Land
    expeditions of, 9, 37, 79; contradictions to
    narrative of, 81–83, 92–93; leadership of, 50–51;
    and preservation of Yolngu culture, 38, 42, 49–50,
    64, 119; and pride in NTSRU, 51; proposal for NTSRU
    by, 35, 39–41; and support for Yolngu, 37–38, 48,
    61, 65, 79, 80, 177
Thornell, Harold, 84
Tigavu, Petrus, 135
Timele, Jacob, 99
Tiwi Islanders, 83
ToKilala, W., 113
Toledo, Bill, 204, 209
Tomila, Danks, 115
Torres Strait Light Infantry Battalion, 15
Townsville, 42
trackers: in NAOU, 55; proposals for wartime, 13–14
Travis, K. M., 150–51
treaty. *See* Navajo(s): treaty
trepangers, 1
Trial Bay, 46
Tsosie, Harry, 204
Tulagi, 101
Tumat, James, 112
Tupaing, Keta, 157

United Nations, 159–60, 164, 166, 167, 230
Universal Declaration of Human Rights, 230
University of Papua New Guinea, 160
Urapunga Station, 8, 57, 58–59, 60, 69
U.S. Army, 208
U.S. Navy, 187, 192
U.S. Senate, 212–13

Vane, Maurie, 55, 94
Vernon, Geoffrey, 125
veterans: challenging status of, 30, 210–11;
    community leadership by, 30, 210, 212–13;
    discrimination against, 209–12; Papua New
    Guinean conditions on, 131–32
Veterans' Administration, 217, 229
Veterans of Foreign Wars, 211
Vietnam War, 208
Vogel, Clayton, 177
vote, Native Americans, 24, 25, 210, 211

wages. *See* compensation; pay
Walingai, 104
Wamanari, 131
war crimes, 116–17